FERNAND BRAUDEL

THE IDENTITY
OF FRANCE

Volume I

History and Environment

Translated from the French
by Siân Reynolds

COLLINS
8 Grafton Street, London W1
1988

William Collins Sons and Co. Ltd
London · Glasgow · Sydney · Auckland
Toronto · Johannesburg

BRITISH LIBRARY CATALOGUING IN PUBLICATION DATA

Braudel, Fernand, *1902–1985*
The identity of France.
Vol. 1: History and environment
1. France, to 1985
I. Title   II. L'identité de la France.
English
944

ISBN 0–00–217773–0

First published in France under the title *L'Identité de la France*, 1986
copyright © Les Editions Athaud, Paris, 1986

English translation copyright © Siân Reynolds 1988

Diagrams and maps in the translation by
RDL Artset Ltd, Cheam, Surrey
Photoset in Itek Bembo by Ace Filmsetting Ltd, Frome, Somerset
Printed and bound in Great Britain by
T.J. Press (Padstow) Ltd, Padstow, Cornwall

To my grandmother
EMILIE CORNOT,
light of my childhood

CONTENTS

CONTENTS

LIST OF FIGURES

TRANSLATOR'S NOTE

The Identity of France contains many words and phrases, mostly referring to institutions, which have been left in French, since to translate them might be long-winded or misleading. The reader is asked to consult the glossary at the end of the book.

I would particularly like to thank Madame Paule Braudel, who saw the French edition through the press, and who has been generous with her time and expert knowledge in checking the English version for mistakes or ambiguities. Any that remain are my own fault.

S.R.

Introduction

'History is made without knowing of its making.'
Jean-Paul Sartre[1]

Let me start by saying once and for all that I love France with the same demanding and complicated passion as did Jules Michelet; without distinguishing between its good points and its bad, between what I like and what I find harder to accept. But that passion will rarely intrude upon the pages of this book. I shall keep it carefully to one side. It is possible that it will play tricks on me and catch me out, so I shall keep it under close watch. And I shall warn the reader as I go along of potential moments of weakness. For I am determined to talk about France as if it were another country, another fatherland, another nation: 'to observe France' as Charles Péguy said, 'as if one were no part of it'.[2] The historian's craft, as it has developed, is in any case driving us towards ever greater restraint, towards the exclusion of feeling. Were it otherwise, history, which is only too fond of contact with the social sciences, would not have found itself becoming, like them, a very imperfect science perhaps, but a science all the same.

As detached an 'observer' as possible, the historian must take what might be termed a personal vow of silence. Perhaps this will be made easier for me by the work I have done in the past. In my books on the Mediterranean or on capitalism,[3] I was viewing France from a distance, sometimes a great distance: as a reality yes, but as one among others and like any other. So I have come rather late in the day to my home ground, though with a pleasure I will not deny: for the historian can really be on an equal footing only with the history of his own country; he understands almost instinctively its twists and turns, its complexities, its originalities and its weaknesses. Never can he enjoy the same advantages, however great his learning, when he pitches camp elsewhere. So I have saved my white bread until last; there is some left for my old age.

15

Our aim then should be to rid ourselves of our passions, whether they are dictated by our nature, our social position, our personal experience, our fits of rage or enthusiasm, our individual 'equations', the course our life happens to take, or the many pervasive influences of our age – something Hippolyte Taine certainly did not succeed in doing (whatever he believed) in his book *Les Origines de la France contemporaine.* He wanted, he said, to observe France as if it were an insect in metamorphosis.[4] Alexis de Tocqueville was more successful in his admirable work *L'Ancien Régime et la Révolution française.*[5] For my part, I hope to manage at least a respectable attempt.

All the same, was it reasonable of me to add yet another to the endless series of histories of France – to the *Thrésor des histoires de France* as G. Corrozet (d. 1583) entitled his book (a disappointing one as it happens) published posthumously in 1615? Even earlier, at the end of the fifteenth century, Robert Gaguin had described his collection as a 'Sea of chronicles and historical Mirror of France'! Today one would have to call it an ocean. And all these histories, ready to hand, are good, often very good. There is Michelet's[6] – unrivalled; Lavisse's[7] (now partly re-issued)[8] – indispensable; Robert Philippe's – an excellent work of reference.[9] Even the briefest essays, to my mind, have much to offer. I shall often be referring to them to advantage. There is for instance Jacques Madaule's *Histoire de France,*[10] whose balanced approach appeals to me; and the essays by Lucien Romier,[11] Neculai Iorga,[12] Ernst Curtius,[13] and Eugène Cavaignac;[14] or Julien Benda's *Esquisse d'une histoire des Français dans leur volonté de former une nation* (1932) as well as Lucien Febvre's lost book, *Honneur et Patrie* (Honour and Fatherland), the revised version of the lectures he gave at the Collège de France in 1946 and 1947, and of which I actually held the finished manuscript in my hands in August 1956. Fortunately I know what it intended to say. And that is not to mention the simply fantastic mass of books, theses, studies and articles which have appeared over the last ten years to swell our already considerable knowledge of our country's past.

I have also found time to read many other books, more doubtful from the point of view of scholarship, mostly essays with the virtue of opening up longer perspectives and freeing us from the endless recital of events. And I have also indulged a preference (or perhaps it is a weakness) for a certain number of polemics and maverick books whose advantage is that they shake us out of received ideas and habits of mind and propel us towards fruitful doubt and controversy, transforming or modifying our perspectives, if not turning them completely upside down.

But, to return to the question: was it right to add one more title to this lengthy bibliography? To tell the truth, the project, despite all its difficulties, appealed to me I think for the same reasons that led Lucien Febvre thirty years ago to undertake his projected *Histoire de France*, on which unfortunately he never had the time to work seriously: the profession of historian has changed so utterly over the last half-century that the images and problems of the past have taken on a completely new complexion. They still unavoidably confront us, but in different terms. So it is worth taking stock of where we stand, all the more so since the past is both instructive and a solid component of our own lives – so to define France's past is to place the French people within their own existence. 'What we need', says a letter to me from a fellow historian, 'is for someone to bring our history out from behind the walls, or rather ramparts, in which so many other people have enclosed it'.[15]

Such a revolutionary breach in the walls, usually signifying a sharp challenge to previous approaches, is primarily the consequence of encroachment, on the rather poorly fenced territory of the historian, by the various social sciences – geography, political economy, demography, politics, anthropology, ethnology, social psychology, cultural studies, sociology. History has allowed light to be shed on to it from all sides, and has accepted a multitude of newly-formulated questions. The problem (as historians do not always realize) is that none of these sources of light must be overlooked. Even if in practice none of us is capable of the necessary tour de force, we are all under an obligation to speak in terms of the global, of 'historical totalization',[16] to reaffirm that 'total history [is] the only true history',[17] or as Michelet long ago put it, 'everything stands and falls together, everything is connected'.[18]

But if France's past is to be examined from the perspective of every single social science, the poor historian will find himself obliged to embark on routes he does not well know. Theoretical approaches he has never or only inexpertly handled before may lead him who knows where, and the results may surprise, dismay or shock the proponents of received wisdom. When today's historians argue that the unity of France (which is not of course the same thing as its history) was not really attained either with Joan of Arc nor even entirely with the French Revolution, but more probably with the later extension of the railway network (a miracle in its own day), and the spread of primary school education – such a pedestrian thesis may irritate more people than it convinces. And yet the *modern* notion of *la patrie*, the fatherland, had scarcely appeared in the sixteenth century; the nation took on its first explosive form with the Revolution: and the word *nationalism* first appears only from the pen of Balzac[19] – when everything was still to be played for.

It is clear that a nation in the process of creating or recreating itself is not a simple character, 'a personality' as Michelet rhapsodically put it.[20] It is a multitude of realities and living beings to which justice can but imperfectly be done by a chronological narrative day by day, week by week, year by year. Inability to go beyond short-term reality is the besetting sin of narrative history, of that 'serial-story history of France' as Jacques Bloch-Morhange calls it,[21] which as children we all learnt by heart, with a certain thrill, from the unforgettable pages of the Malet-Isaac school reader.[22] But for those of us beyond childhood, another kind of history, one that is attentive to longer time-scales, enables us to distinguish the extraordinary accumulations and amalgams, the surprising repetitions of the human past, to perceive the huge responsibilities of a multisecular history, that prodigious mass that bears within it a living but often unconscious heritage, discoverable only by that deeper-probing history, much as psychoanalysis in the early twentieth century revealed the depths of the subconscious. Arnold Toynbee may have been exaggerating slightly when he wrote that 'the four or five centuries [since Columbus and Vasco da Gama] are a twinkling of an eye on the time-scale that our geologists . . . have now revealed to us',[23] but his words suggest a salutary escape from other absurdly narrow scales of measurement. So I note with unmixed delight that certain historians are today boldly extending their chronological range and pursuing the 'unofficial and unrecognized aspects of human life' (as Malinowski put it)[24] or that they have, like Pierre Bonnaud, been fired with enthusiasm for 'the weightiness of [our] origins'. But to attempt such things, one needs the raw materials: a plentiful record of lived time. We have no choice but to work with *la longue durée*.

I mentioned a moment ago Taine's *Origins of Contemporary France*, and Tocqueville's *The Ancien Régime and the French Revolution*. Their congenital fault, if I dare speak this way of works I admire, is that they accept without question that France 'began' in the eighteenth century with the age of Enlightenment, that France was born of the dramatic ordeal to which it was subjected during the violence of the Revolution – that Revolution with a capital R which not so long ago, (though we young historians did not always realize it) was a sort of sacred text, an index of commitment, an obligatory ideological reference. I now of course dislike such piety as I would any other retrospective piety or idealization. But what irks me even more is the drastic curtailing of chronology it implies: the *ancien régime* and the French Revolution are near to us in time, almost contemporary. Stretching out our hands, we can all but touch them. We ought rather to be reckoning with the entire span of France's past as a whole, from before the Roman conquest of Gaul to the present day. The France of Louis XVI was already unquestionably a very old 'person'. So it is a pity for instance that Theodore Zeldin's monumental and very fine book about France (the French title of which is *Histoire des passions françaises*) begins only in 1848.[25] Are we such a young people? Have we (and our passions) only just come into the world? I must also protest when a sociologist and economist as intelligent as Robert Fossaert compresses the history of France as if he were squeezing an accordion: 'Gaul', he writes, 'as mystical as a newborn lamb, has almost nothing to do with *our country*, which does not date back to the mists of time but came into being in the historical era'.[26]

As if history did not reach back into the mists of time! As if prehistory and history were not one and the same process, as if our villages were not already taking root in our soil in the third millennium before Christ, as if Gaul had not already traced the outline within which France would grow up, as if the expansion beyond the Rhine in the fifth century by the Germanic tribes – small groups of men but well able to keep themselves aloof from Gaul and its magic and who therefore preserved their own language – did not constitute, across hundreds and hundreds of years, a living feature of the present-day world! (One has only to see how Belgium is linguistically split in two.) As if, what is more, the retrospective analysis of blood groups[27] had not revealed in our own blood and our own lives, indelible traces of those far-off 'barbarian invasions', as if our beliefs and our languages did not equally come down to us from the dark ages of the most distant past. It is precisely this kind of history – an obscure history, running along under the surface, refusing to die – which this book proposes, if possible, to bring to light.

Similarly, the present-day territory of France, the 'hexagon' as we call it, is not the only standard of measurement we need refer to. Within it are sub-measurements: regions, provinces, *pays*, which long maintained and still do maintain a significant degree of autonomy; while beyond it there is Europe and beyond Europe the world. Marc Bloch used to say, 'There is no such thing as French history, there is European history',[28] but taking up another of his remarks, 'universal history is the only real history',[29] one might go on to say, 'there is no such thing as European history, there is world history'. 'I can only conceive of the hexagon', Paul Morand wrote, 'as inscribed within the sphere'.[30]

Europe and the world are indeed participants in our past, crowding in on us and sometimes crushing us. But are we ourselves so innocent towards them? Since Edgar Quinet first wrote in 1827 that 'one of the great glories of modern peoples is to have conceived of universal history',[31] his words have had time to collect plenty of ambiguities. But it should be understood that for no nation does the obligatory and increasingly burdensome dialogue with the outside world mean an expropriation or obliteration of its own history. There may be some intermingling but there is no fusion. Is 'the most radical change to have come about in France, the loss of control by the French of their own destiny?', asks Theodore Zeldin.[32] Definitely not. The ambiguity posed by a history of France absorbed, at one level and in some measure, into the destiny of Europe and the rest of the world, greatly troubled my original plans for this book. But I need not have worried. For I realized as I went along that a history of France can, in itself, and beyond its own vicissitudes, be an excellent means of sampling, or of focusing on the onward march of Europe and the world.

The *longue durée* then (first and indeed foremost), the hexagon, Europe, the world – these are the dimensions of space and time with which I shall be working. Taking these dimensions from the start makes it possible, across time and space, to draw the essential comparisons, to carry out *experiments* as we may term them, but experiments conducted according to a preconceived purpose, experiments I can alter as I please, by varying the constituent elements. Thus France, viewed retrospectively, takes the form of an experimental laboratory for 'interspatial and intertemporal' comparisons,[33] by which we are once more put in a position to observe the continuities, the trends (I will not say *laws*), the repetitions which turn this history-in-depth into a retrospective sociology, one that is indeed indispensable to the social sciences as a whole. Jean-Paul Sartre was after all ready to say that it is through history that the dialectic and human praxis reach their apogee. 'Even sociology is but a provisional moment in historical totalization'.[34] And did not Emile Durkheim himself predict that 'the day will come when the historical spirit and the sociological spirit will differ only in shades of meaning'?[35] That day has not yet come. But there is only one way to try to bring about such a meeting: by writing *comparative* history, a history that seeks to compare *like with like* – the condition of all social science if the truth be told.

So in successive chapters I have tried to look at the entire history of France in the light of the various social sciences in turn. Let me list them once more in order: geography, anthropology, demography, political economy, politics or political science, the study of cultures and mentalities (can we call it culturology?), sociology, international relations (France's external presence).

This is certainly not an approach that can be taken for granted; rather it is something of a gamble. Every social science has its own territory, its own set of explanations. And yet each of them implies the whole constellation of social realities, in other words the subject matter of all the other social sciences. Each of them is both self-determined and over-determined from outside; the zone it illuminates abuts on other zones. If we look down on Paris from the top of Notre-Dame or from the Montparnasse tower, we do not see exactly the same city-scape, but we see the entire city each time. In the end, any example, any attempt to find the 'real thing' is a global endeavour as Robert Fossaert says: it implies the whole social fabric.[36] So there can be no science of humanity which does not in the end lead to generalization. How then can history in particular avoid doing so, since history, tackling the past, must raise alone as many questions as are raised by *all* the social sciences put together when they tackle the present?

Here lie both the danger and the advantage of this particular gamble. At every step, we shall be faced with the entire history of France, something far too large to be contained within any previously determined category. So it will be impossible from chapter to chapter to avoid some repetition, some revisiting of the same ground – even if the already-said is never quite the same thing when repeated; even if looking at the same processes from a different vantage-point actually takes the observation forward. In the end, I felt myself compelled simply to say what I could see and what, once seen, I thought I understood. How then could I, when speaking of say, geography, avoid speaking of economics and society, of politics, anthropology and so on? What we are about to observe forms a single mass, which one must seek to illuminate patiently, lighting and relighting one's lamp. So without hesitating overmuch, I have allowed myself to be drawn into observation and direct commentary, without being unduly concerned whether or not I was sticking strictly to the boundaries of our scientific categories – categories which are after all man-made.

Another difficulty – but this time mostly for the reader – is that my approach will always be mixing the distant past with the recent past, and past with present. For if the past is cut off from the present by a series of obstacles – hills, mountains, chasms, contrasts – it also has ways and means of restoring contact – roads, paths and streams. The past is all about us, unrecognized and insinuating, and we are caught in its toils without always realizing it. The past 'brings the tide right up to our feet' as one sociologist has written, 'and no phenomenon can be regarded as outside it'.[37] It is precisely that tide and the deep-flowing currents of France's past that I am seeking to detect, to trace, the better to judge how they flow into the present, as rivers flow into the sea.

The title of a book is never entirely neutral. So was I right to call this book *The Identity of France*? The word 'identity' appealed to me, but has not ceased to torment me over the years. The title alone raises once more, from an oblique angle, all the problems I have just described and a few more besides. Its ambiguity is manifest: it stands for a string of questions – no sooner do you answer one than the next arises and so on *ad infinitum*.

What then, do we mean by the identity of France – if not a kind of superlative, if not a central problematic, if not the shaping of France by its own hand, if not the living result of what the interminable past has patiently deposited, layer by layer, just as the imperceptible sedimentation of the seabed in the end created the firm foundations of the earth's crust? It is in sum a residue, an amalgam, a thing of additions and mixtures. It is a process, a self-inflicted conflict, destined to go on indefinitely. If it were to stop, everything would fall apart. A nation can have its *being* only at the price of being forever in search of itself, forever transforming itself in the direction of its logical development, always measuring itself against others and identifying itself with the best, the most essential part of its being; a nation will consequently recognize itself in certain stock images, in certain passwords known to the initiated (whether the latter are an elite or the mass of people, which is not always the case); it will recognize itself in a thousand touchstones, beliefs, ways of speech, excuses, in an unbounded subconscious, in the flowing together of many obscure currents, in a shared ideology, shared myths, shared fantasies. And any national identity necessarily implies a degree of national unity, of which it is in some sense the reflection, the transposition and the condition.

These considerations warn us to distrust from the start any language that is too simple. It is certainly futile to try to reduce France to *one* discourse, *one* equation, *one* formula, *one* image or *one* myth (as suggested by Raymond Rudorff's disappointing book which although long on harsh words about our country, is short on home truths).[38]

Is there any Frenchman after all who has not asked himself questions about his country, whether at the present time or in particular during the tragic hours through which our destiny has repeatedly taken us as it has run its course? Such catastrophes are like great rents in the canvas of history, or like those gaping holes in the clouds glimpsed from an aeroplane, plunging shafts of light at the bottom of which we see the earth below. Yawning disasters, gaping chasms, plunging tunnels of gloomy light – there is no shortage of these in our history. To go no further back than the nineteenth century, we have had the fateful dates 1815, 1871, 1914. And then there was 1940, when the knell tolled for us a second time at Sedan: when the drama of Dunkirk was played out in the indescribable disorder of defeat. It is true that in time even these monstrous wounds heal, fade, are forgotten – according to the iron law of all collective life: a nation is not an individual or a 'person'.

I have lived through some of these disasters. Like many other people, I was brought face to face with these questions in that summer of 1940 – which by an irony of fate was gloriously hot, radiant with sunshine, flowers and joie de vivre. We the defeated, trudging the unjust road towards a suddenly-imposed captivity, represented the lost France, dust blown by the wind from a heap of sand. The real France, the France held in reserve, *la France profonde*, remained behind us. It would survive, it did survive. And as long as mankind does not in some future use the diabolical new weapons of destruction, France will continue to survive our anxieties, our lifetimes, will continue to survive a history shot through with eventful happenings, a dangerous history that dances every day before our eyes like a flame, a gaudy and distressing history but one that passes. Ever since those days, already so long ago, I have never ceased to think of a France buried deep inside itself, within its own heart, a France flowing along the contours of its own age-long history, destined to continue, come what may. Out of this fascination grew the present book's ambiguous title, to which I have gradually become accustomed.

Another example kept me company on the way. Spain (the reader may know that Spain has meant a great deal in my life) has also lived through many tragedies and terrible moments of truth. In 1898, the unequal war with the United States dealt Spain an exceedingly hard blow, taking away at a stroke what remained of its old imperial heart, and stripping it of any notion of grandeur, of any pretence, any excuse. It is in this context that one must see the passionate reaction of the intellectuals known as the '1898 generation' who had been brought abruptly face to face with their country's destiny. The response of Miguel Unamuno was his book on *The Essence of Spain*;[39] Angel Ganivet went in search of the Spanish ivory tower in his *Idearium*;[40] later again, Ortega y Gasset would see Spain as an 'invertebrate' body, a pessimistic and unbearable image.[41]

I have found pleasure in the companionship of this illustrious group of men, and in sharing their reactions. But I shall remain far from their conclusions. I do not, let me repeat, believe that there is a *single* 'essence' of France (or of Spain either for that matter). I do not believe in any single formula. Nor do I attach any value to the word or the concept of 'decadence'. I propose simply to carry out a reasonable investigation, exempt from any *a priori* judgements, by climbing in turn to several familiar vantage points and trying from there to understand how the long history of France has been constructed in its depths, how it has followed its own currents and those of the rest of the world. I shall try to keep my feelings out of it.

The Identity of France is divided into four main sections: I. *History and Environment* (inspired by geography); II. *People and Products* (demography and political economy);* III. *State, Culture and Society* (politics, cultural studies, sociology); IV. *France outside France* (which will go beyond the usual remit of international relations and provide a conclusion for the whole work).

---

* Only the first two were completed before the author's death.

Within this sequence, the reader should not imagine too logical a pattern of development. But the plan of a book can no more be truly *neutral* than the title is. Would it really be possible to shuffle its elements with impunity, like a set of interchangeable geometrical permutations? Georges Gurvitch used to think that all research moved, or ought to move, from what is easy and can be grasped without too much trouble towards what is revealed only gradually and with increasing difficulty.[42] In other words from the simple to the complex, from the superficial to the profound.

In my search for the identity of France, have I unconsciously proceeded in something of this manner? Geography after all is as concerned with concrete realities as anything can be: open your eyes, start from what you see, from what is visible to everyone. In theory at any rate, there is nothing very difficult about that. Demography is a new science, rather preoccupied with itself, but still easily accessible. Economics, the most scientific of the social sciences, is a set of rules which lend themselves to recycling by any determined historian. When we get to the state, matters become more complicated. With civilization, which is filtered and diffused in every direction, it gets worse. And with society, which we in the social sciences have not yet managed to define, in other words to master, our problems increase. But with the last section, *France outside France*, surely we shall be back on more solid ground. Has the subject not been tackled exhaustively by traditional history? Well yes it has, but today we do not see things the same way as in the past. I have even gradually succeeded in convincing myself that the destiny of France has above all been a sector of the destiny of the world – not merely in our own time when the forces of the outside world are setting solid about us and freezing us in, imprisoning us whether we like it or not, but in the past too. Think of Gaul being subjugated by Rome, 'the greatest catastrophe of our history', according to Ferdinand Lot;[43] of France being dragged, along with the rest of Europe, into the Crusades; of France being caught up, reshaped and relegated to an inferior status by the capitalist economy which became established in Europe well before the sixteenth century; or of France afloat on the troubled and uncertain waters of present-day world history.

Past and present then – a diabolical and inseparable couple to whom we must add the future. 'History', wrote Julien Gracq, 'has *essentially* become a warning addressed by the Future to the Present' (my italics).[44] Jean-Paul Sartre said the same thing in his own way: 'The dialectic, as the movement of reality, collapses if time is not dialectical, that is if one refuses to allow a certain degree of action to the future as such'.[45] In short, the present has no substance unless it is prolonged into tomorrow, when we pass through the 'gates of today'.[46]

So history is invited to forsake the calm pleasures of retrospection for the risky business of prediction. But is this not the natural bent of historical reflection, to pass as Joseph Chappey put it, 'from the historical truth which is apparent to the historical truth which is hidden',[47] or to the historical truth that is yet to come? When I ask myself questions about the identity of our country, as observed primarily through the dense layers of its past, am I not at the same time tormenting and questioning myself about the France of tomorrow? The contradictory forces of past and present, locked together, are forever reproducing, and becoming, that deep history on which France drifts into the future. They will still be there tomorrow, forces on which everything is founded and by which everything is sometimes destroyed, without our being able always to guess the true reasons for it, still less the exact moment.

Fortunately the planned later volumes will require no further explanation or justification. In them I shall tackle chronologically the problems that all previous historians have discussed before me, although the answers I suggest may not be quite the same as theirs. But that is after all the rule of the game. For me in any case, it will be a chance to draw on the accumulated 'treasury' of histories of France, to pay my debts, to carry the challenge of this book through to the end. For if the identity of France with which our search begins can, at least in some degree, explain the destiny of France, if it constitutes its true foundations, then my gamble will have paid off, in very large measure, and the direction of my undertaking will at least have been justified.

Les Ponthieux (Haute-Savoie)
2 October 1981

27

It seems there is no end to the business of introducing a book to the reader. Is it so as to keep him at one's side a little longer? Pressed by the friendly but insistent questions of Jean-Claude Bringuier for the purposes of a long television programme (August 1984), I had to admit that I undertook this *History of France* not only for the reasons already mentioned, but also to satisfy myself that the kind of history I am arguing for could prove itself in an example accessible to a wide audience. It is not enough to have a correct (or at least reasonable) theoretical perspective: it must be put to the test of the facts. As a young historian has expressed it, and his meaning is I think clear, 'the systematic must bow to the empirical'.[48] Perhaps I shall thus be able to light my way on two levels: that of general and theoretical history on the one hand, and that of a history of France on the other. Both of them are close to my heart.

Taillet, 11 July 1985

VOLUME I

HISTORY AND
ENVIRONMENT

Foreword

At the outset of the three chapters making up this first volume (and all in reality part of one and the same debate), I should put the reader on guard and alert him or her to the guiding spirit behind them. My aim here is to discuss the relations – multiple, intertwined, elusive – between the history of France and the physical territory by which it is confined, sustained and in a way (though not of course completely) explained.

There are, to be sure, a number of ways of turning geography to account. It can be practised for its own sake, concentrating on its own problems and on its points of convergence with the other social sciences or the natural sciences. Geographers themselves, being concerned primarily with the present day, do precisely this. But for us, geography will be above all a way of re-reading, re-estimating and re-interpreting France's past, in accordance naturally with our present concerns. As it happens, geography readily lends itself to such an approach. Landscapes and panoramas are not simply realities of the present but also, in large measure, survivals from the past. Long-lost horizons are redrawn and recreated for us through what we see; the earth is, like our own skin, fated to carry the scars of ancient wounds.

A moment's thought or imagination, after all, is enough to make our environment take on once more the colours of the past – in the old centres of carefully preserved towns like Vézelay and Autun for instance, or more naturally still in the many country districts not yet entirely transformed by the modern world: the Forez,[1] the *pays* of Bigorre,[2] the Rouergue,[3] the Gâtine of Poitou,[4] Bar-sur-Seine,[5] and hundreds of other *pays* where the stored-up past obstinately survives. Forget for a moment that the Rhône and the Rhine are the tame and domesticated rivers of today, and see instead tempestuous waters, barely navigable yet tackled whatever

31

the cost by indefatigable flotillas of boats. In spirit, you have already left the present day.

But the pages that follow will not only be dictated by a journey into the past: there will be a series of return trips between yesterday and today. The value of geographical observation lies in the depth, the duration and the abundance of densely-packed realities, which must first be distinguished then related to each other once more. At once immediate and retrospective, geography has a particular light to shed, helping to explain links between past and present. *Earth, milieu, environment, eco-system* are all words indicating the concepts it can offer us, the connections it urges us to make and which have as much to tell us as the richest documents in the archives.

The three sections of the present volume will enable us to explore these problems.

First comes a series of evidence showing France as diverse and 'plural', as an assemblage of autonomous *pays*, the many-shaped and multicoloured fragments of the mosaic that is France. It is this plurality that I have tried to 'visualize' in Part I: *The diversity of France*.[6]

But the fragments of mosaic are bound together by solid cement – by constraints, by complementary differences, by the trade and communications that have tirelessly woven links between *pays* and regions, villages and bourgs,* bourgs and towns, provinces and nation. This will be what Part II: *Patterns of settlement: village, bourg and town*, sets out to explain. Its aim will be to discover the connecting tissues which created, within the rural or urban landscape, identifiable units of varying size and cohesion.

Such units could be large, and soon approached the scale of what would one day be the nation. For France as a unitary whole, an overall design, did in the end manage to construct itself, to prevail and to endure. Physical geography and the nature of that geography even worked to this end. For this was a France built on home ground, in a certain location within Europe and the world – hence the title of Part III: *Was France invented by its geography?*

* See glossary for both *pays* and bourg.

Such is what my teachers of long ago would have called the 'connecting thread' of these first chapters, as they confront physical space, human beings and history. The reader will forgive me if I do not always keep to the straight and narrow, but indulge in the pleasure of a few detours on the way, if I wander off in search of examples, of symphonies whose every note I should like to be heard at once.

But who could resist such temptations?

PART I

The Diversity of France

To begin with, it is simplest to present things just as one sees them, as they seem on first acquaintance – I almost said at first glance. From this initial overview, one quickly becomes aware that the unity of France is hard to keep in sight. Having assumed it would be obvious from the start, we find it escaping us: we are faced with a hundred, a thousand different Frances of long ago, yesterday or today. Let us then accept this truth, this wealth of material, this pressing invitation to which it is neither unpleasant nor even very dangerous to succumb.

CHAPTER ONE

Describing,
seeing, making others see

It is of course a commonplace to say that France is diverse to the point of absurdity, or, which comes to the same thing, that its geography, 'varied to a degree met in few countries in the world',[1] obstinately betrays an extraordinarily 'local character',[2] a 'mosaic of landscapes of a variety encountered nowhere else'.[3] 'Even for the traveller on foot . . . the landscape is always changing'.[4] Every village, every valley, *a fortiori* every *pays* (a word derived from the Gallo-Roman *pagus* and meaning an area with its own identity, as in the *pays de Bray, pays de Caux*), every town, every region, every province has its own distinct character – visible not only in the particular features displayed in the landscape and in the many imprints man has left upon it, but also in a lived culture, 'a way of life and a way of death, a set of rules governing basic human relations between parents and children, men and women, friends and neighbours'.[5] All these differences were more marked in the past than they are now: not so long ago there still survived intact local privileges (by the dozen), local dialects, folklore, traditional houses (built of stone or lava, brick, cob or wood), and local costumes. Then there were the weights and measures, of extravagant diversity to modern eyes, so varied that according to Lavoisier in 1787, the *élection* of Péronne alone 'boasted 17 sorts of *arpens*, all differing both in the number of *perches* and in the size of the *perche*'.[6]

This extraordinary range of measurements was an administrator's nightmare. 'Is it possible to lay down a single standard capacity for the cask of wine?' the *intendant* of Poitou was asked in 1684. Out of the question, he replied, reeling off a bewildering list of different kinds of 'casks', whose names and capacities varied

37

from one place to the next and which were all used concurrently, not to mention casks from Berry, Limousin, Bordeaux and elsewhere, which also turned up in market places in Poitou. Imposing a single measure would be like trying to square the circle.[7]

We must imagine the complexities of a system which, simply in order to record grain prices in the markets of a given region, required its officials to report the measures in which wheat, rye or oats were sold in every town or village and then to 'convert them into *poids de marc*' (the only possible unit of comparison). The archives still contain some of these 'grain price registers', drawn up fortnightly on ready printed forms.

Costume too could vary over short distances. The Bretons for example wore red in Cornouaille, blue in Léon, purple in Trégor.[8] A hundred years ago, in 1878, the 'age-old' costume of the Morvan was as follows: 'all women young or old, dress in woollen cloth with broad stripes; they all wear white wool stockings and on their feet clogs . . . with sheepskin uppers; on their heads they all have a broad and heavy quilted calico bonnet, with their hair pinned up in a chignon behind'.[9]

Houses also used to conform to different local traditions, varying from place to place: in the Jura, 'every mountain had its own *immeuble*', as they used to say and do so still, meaning its own shape of house.[10]

True, all these things have changed or are changing today, differences are blurred – but are by no means wiped out. The present archbishop of Paris, and former bishop of Orleans, Mgr Lustiger, has recalled that 'when I used to speak of the diocese of "Orleans" (that is the whole *département* of the Loiret) the people in the Gâtinais used to say to me "but we're not from Orleans!" '[11]

Lucien Febvre used to say, and we can say after him, that 'France's name is diversity'.[12] I would almost prefer to say (though it sounds duller) 'France *is* diversity', since this is no mere appearance or label, but corresponds to concrete reality: it is the dazzling triumph of the plural, of the heterogeneous, of the never-quite-the-same, of the never-quite-what-you-find-elsewhere. No doubt England, Germany, Italy or Spain, examined in detail have a perfect claim to be named diversity too, but not perhaps with quite the same exuberance or obstinacy. When the American historian Eugen Weber looked at the France of 1900, he found it slipping through his fingers into a multitude of particular Frances, all inclined to draw apart from one another, and to remain unrepentantly ignorant of each other.[13]

One might have thought that all these contrasts, which flourish still, would have been smoothed out or at least attenuated by the France 'one and indivisible'[14] of the Jacobins, which now has almost two centuries of existence behind it (and what centuries!), not to speak of the paternalist, prudent, but equally centralizing monarchy that preceded it. *A fortiori*, with the speeding up of communications, the triumphant spread of the French language (the language of the Ile-de-France, all-conquering since the year 1000), with the industrial growth of the nineteenth century and finally the extraordinary and unprecedented prosperity of 'the thirty glorious years' 1945–75,[15] it would be logical to suppose that such mighty forces would have, if not quite flattened everything, at least spread a thick coat of monochrome paint over the mosaic with its hundreds and thousands of coloured fragments. But not at all. 'Industrial society', as Hervé Le Bras and Emmanuel Todd rightly remarked in 1981, 'has not annihilated the diversity of France, as can be demonstrated by cartographical analysis [which they brilliantly provide] of several hundred indicators, ranging from family structure to suicide rates, from illegitimacy to divorce, from age at marriage to incidence of alcoholism'[16] or indeed to the ravages wrought by mental illness. Other indicators – or simple everyday observation – lead to the same conclusion: the plural submerges and swallows up the singular. France, as Yves Florenne jokingly concludes, is 'one and *divisible*'.[17] It is easy to believe Giono when he says that he can only write about his peasant characters when they are 'set in their own landscape', that familiar and unique background with which they are at one. Whether in the high Provençal Alps, or in the plains of the Camargue, all his people 'arrange their lives (and loves) around the trees, the sandhills, the wild bees, the oxen, sheep and horses'.[18] We must conclude then that those who predict, not implausibly, that French society will soon be completely uniform, are as mistaken as Stendhal was in 1838 when he said: 'All shades of difference are fast vanishing now in France. In fifty years time perhaps, there will be no Provençals left, and no Provençal language'.[19] Stendhal for once was wrong.

But while geographers, historians, economists, sociologists, essayists, anthropologists and political scientists all agree about the diversity of France, even taking a sort of gourmet pleasure in doing so, it is only to turn away immediately, once the ritual reference has been made, and thereafter entirely to concern themselves with France as a unit. As if what really mattered was to move the focus from the peripheral and elementary to the essential; to look not at diversity but at unity; not at the real but at the desirable; not at the forces alien or hostile to Paris, but at the mainstream national history of France. Two young historians have written jokingly: 'our country has built something of a reputation on its diversity: everyone knows that in France there is a fabulous range of landscapes, ways of thought, racial groups, roof-tops and cheeses'[20] – a good start though the list is not quite complete. But as a rule, after a glimpse of the fabulous range, the blinkers are put back on and we are given a history of France that rolls down the familiar old track. One essayist has even saluted France as 'the fatherland one and indivisible *because* diverse and ever-changing. [France] has for centuries attracted contrasting elements and – for such is its miraculous power – has been able to weld them into a whole in which they retain their originality'.[21] I do not deny the would-be-united fatherland, which has succeeded in becoming so. But the elements and agents resistant to such unification are not simply the foreign immigrants drawn, as in any other country, into a sort of melting-pot: resistance has come if anything even more from the various 'Frances', as old as history, which have had to be held together. To say that they have been 'welded into a whole' is surely going too far.

It is at any rate impossible, in this dialogue between plural and singular, to brush aside the first term. Unless it is restored to pride of place, we shall never grasp the problem of problems in our national past, the fragmentation underlying it, the contrasts, tensions, misunderstandings or complementary compromises – they do exist – but also the quarrels, bitter antagonisms and mutual taunts. The house is always ready to go up in flames: and the historian Marc Ferro has even calmly remarked that France's *real* talent is for civil war.

The provinces: jigsaw puzzles of regions and 'pays'

Yet what Frenchman could fail to take pleasure in the sight of a France that is many-coloured, full of the unexpected, one in which the landscape, way of life, flora and fauna, colours and types of settlement change every thirty or forty kilometres? Each of us moreover is personally attached to some little piece of the jigsaw: we come not merely from one particular province (dear to our heart above all others) but from some precise locality in our province. It is at least a part of our own identity. Should we feel sorry then for those who have no provincial roots and are attached only to the anonymity of Paris? Not necessarily. For not only was Paris in the past, with its *quartiers* and its *faubourgs*, an amalgam of villages and towns of which something still survives. But Paris also had within its class divisions its own traditions, whether working-class, intellectual or bourgeois. When Daniel Roche writes, in a book called *Le Peuple de Paris*, 'I am a Parisian going back five generations', that is certainly equal to any provincial pedigree.[22]

Such particularities go deep into the mass of the French population, and as I have said, they cling to life today. The vital thing for every community is to avoid being confused with the next tiny 'patrie', to remain *other*. This is the surprising thing, which present-day geography can still reveal: for progress, marching with giant strides throughout the land, turns out to have changed one *pays* more than its neighbour, or perhaps to have changed it in a particular way, creating a new difference which becomes a new cleavage. The basic fragmentation has thus been maintained in recognizable form (or very nearly so) since earliest times. And when I visit, or revisit, certain *pays* that I know better than others – the Ornois on the banks of the Meuse, the Faucigny in Savoie, the Vallespir in Roussillon, northern Alsace between Wissembourg and the holy forest of Haguenau, the *Heiliger Forst*, with its rivers flowing silently over sand, and the magnificent Rhine valley to the east – I have the feeling that before my eyes lies unique evidence about the past. For the scene in front of me reveals to the naked eye the presence, here and now, of a life necessarily *all-inclusive*, one where all activities are inter-connected, where the horizon is near enough for me to be able to encompass it with ease; to see everything or almost everything; to understand everything or almost everything. At the same time the sight before me bears witness to what it does not show, it betrays information about long-past situations, helps to reconstitute the balance of former times, gives meaning to the remarks of travellers, famous or otherwise, who have been there before us and seen almost the same things – ah, but it is that 'almost', the often tiny differences that plunge us back into the life of the past.

So this patchwork France, rich in colour, is where any 'sincere' history of France should begin. Throughout its history, this underlying 'plural' France has been contradicting the 'one' France which has dominated it, controlled it, sought to blur its individualities while unfairly monopolizing the limelight and the attention of traditional history. Whereas France is not *one*, but many: indeed there is not 'one' Brittany even, but many Brittanies; not 'one' Provence, but as Giono insisted, many Provences – and many Burgundies, Lorraines, Franche-Comtés, Alsaces and so on.

I think I can claim to know the Franche-Comté quite well. It was in 1926 that I travelled through it for the first time, on foot and by bicycle, with three army friends, one of them a geographer, now dead.[23] We had set out from the Valdahon camp above Besançon, and the main part of our journey took us up the astonishing valley of the Loue, from Ornans, home of the Granvelle family; then along the long *cluse* of Nantua to the Valserine and Bellegarde, where in those days you could see the extraordinary 'swallow' of the Rhône; next came a long hike across the breathtaking pays of Gex, which we decided (highest of compliments) was as beautiful as Alsace; and finally a slow climb up to the Col de la Faucille, where we were rewarded by the sight of Geneva in the distance.

Since then, every year or almost, I have crossed the Jura by

FIGURE 1

A province and its 'pays': Savoie (Savoy) in the eighteenth century

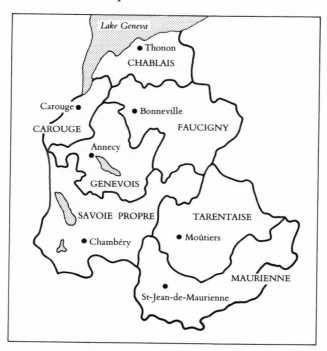

Any French province divides into units of which some are more coherent than others; but most have survived to the present day.

After Paul Guichonnet, *Histoire de la Savoie.* Map from F. Braudel, *The Perspective of the World.*

every imaginable route, rediscovering it each time with the same enthusiasm and emotion, whether at Arbois or Château-Chalon; at Pontarlier, Saint-Claude, Saint-Amour or Les Rousses; at the lake of Saint-Point or the tiny pool of Sylans. I think I could even recognize the Jura simply by the colour of its grass: a subtle blue insistently mingles with a deep and dazzling acid green, whereas in the neighbouring Alps the green of the hayfields is softened by a

43

wide palette of yellows. And of course, the textbook distinction – between the flat Saône valley and the tableland Jura to the west, and the folded Jura to the east with its wooded slopes and long narrow meadows (think of the splendid Ain valley) – merely provides us with broad categories: within them, given the extreme variety of soil, climate, crops and human settlement, we must fit, one by one, all the different pieces of the jigsaw, the *pays* they contain. Take the Haut-Doubs and the upper Ain valley, for instance: here are the Val Romey, and the Mijoux and Mièges valleys – all small *pays*, each different but complementary and at times obliged to live together as best they can.[24]

Nor by the same token can Provence be described as 'one and indivisible'. 'One' perhaps if we think of the Provençal climate, the blue skies, the trees and plants accustomed to drought, and the vast *herms* empty of human habitation – yes of course, as anyone could tell you. But Provence is pulled this way and that, between the Mediterranean, the Rhône valley and the lowering mass of the Alps stretching away to the north, and accounting for over half its territory.

Inland Provence is everywhere composed of the same unvarying elements: limestone spurs and plateaux (a very hard and massive limestone); platforms of ancient rock, only partly eroded; plains and valleys generally rather narrow; and depressions like the one surrounding the ancient twin massifs of the Maures and the Esterel. But these elements are shuffled by the caprice of the relief which combines them to form new landscapes at every turn. Roughly (very roughly) the province is split between on one hand the high country lacking in resources, and on the other the plains, fragments of plain, hollows and river banks where human cultures have instinctively taken refuge.

The high country consists of the original oak and pine forests and the rocky landscape dotted with scrub known as the *maquis*, or *garrigue*, sometimes a *garrigue* despoiled by men's past or present attempts at farming, and which 'itself now devastated, is giving way to a stunted heathland where plumes of spurge and spears of asphodel hide the last traces of cereal crops'.[25] Yet this high country, as such repeated depredations themselves prove, once played a not insignificant role in the Provençal economy of former times. As late as 1938, a geographer could still write that

> north of the Montagne Sainte-Victoire, the thick copses of oak and holm-oak of the Sambuc are busy every spring: teams of workers paid by contractors take possession of these lonely heights. Each has a fixed task: lumberjacks cut down the trees; lime-burners collect green wood for bake-ovens and lime-kilns; women armed with mallets beat the branches to strip them of bark, charcoal-burners saw up the peeled branches, carters carry off the end-product, taking the bark to the tanning-mills of Jonques or Peyrolles.[26]

This age-old activity, now on the verge of extinction, tends to bear out Pierre Gourou's unusual explanation of the hill villages of Provence. Far from retreating to the hilltops, as it has always been thought, did they not rather choose a site midway between the crops in the valley and the forests of the mountain-sides?[27] As the latter cease to be worked, today's villagers build houses further down the slope – the village 'slides downhill'. Elsewhere a village might be perched between the vines (which do well on the upper slopes) and the cereals down in the valley.[28]

In the past, the economy of Provence, like that of the entire Mediterranean littoral, was founded on the trinity of wheat, tree-crops (olives, almonds, vines) and small livestock, especially sheep. The trees and shrubs acclimatized to the light, dry, stony soil; the spring rains were good for the wheat and the autumn rains brought fresh grass to *garrigues* and heaths where 'the animals could find grazing'.[29] All in all, each region managed to be almost self-sufficient, as the past compartmentalization of Provence required.

But once the old barriers began to crumble in the eighteenth century, the various *pays* of Provence were one after another driven to choose a single major activity – whether cereal-growing as in the Arc basin, livestock as in the Arles region, or winegrowing, which spread from Cassis to Toulon.

Take for instance the high valleys of the Provençal Alps around Laragne, that strange region between the Mont Ventoux, the Lure and Sisteron, which Jean Giono held in such affection, wrote about

45

FIGURE 2
Gascony: a complex province

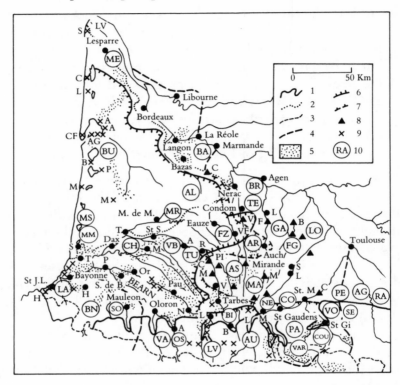

An explanation of the origins of *pays* in geographical, historical, ethnic and toponymic terms. From Pierre Bonnaud, *Terres et Langages*, II, p. 364.

1. Foothills of the Pyrenees.
2. Limit of pine forests of the Landes.
3. French State frontier.
4. Limit of area where Gascon was spoken, where this does not coincide either with the frontier or with the Garonne river.
5. Main areas of distribution of place names ending in *-os* and *-ein*.
6. Limit of dense occurrence of place names ending in *-ac* and *-an*.

7. Limit of area with many *bastides*, *castelnaus* and other feudal settlements dating from the early Middle Ages.
8. *Bastides*, *castelnaus*, etc., integrated into the network of villages and small towns.
9. Towns, bourgs, other centres (industry, tourist centres) developed within the French national system.
10. Abbreviations for the names of the Gascon 'pays':

AG:	Aganaguès	FG:	Fézensaguet	OS:	Vallée d'Ossau
AL:	Albret	FZ:	Fézensac	PA:	Pays d'Aspe
AR:	Armagnac	GA:	Gaure	PE:	Pédaguès
AS:	Astarac	LA:	Labourd	RA:	Razès
AU:	Aure (vallée d')	LO:	Lomagne	SE:	Sérounès
BA:	Bazadais	LV:	Lavedan	SO:	Soule
BI:	Bigorre	MA:	Magnoac	TE:	Tenarèze
BN:	Basse Navarre	ME:	Médoc	TU:	Tursan
BR:	Bruilhois	MM:	Marenne	VA:	Vallée d'Aspe
BU:	Pays de Buch	MR:	Marsan	VAR:	Val d'Aran
CH:	Chalosse	MS:	Marensin	VB:	Vicq Bilh
CO:	Comminges	NE:	Nébouzan	VO:	Volvestre
COU:	Couserans				

The interest of this complicated map, showing 37 Gascon *pays* (for a full reading in detail, see Pierre Bonnaud's book), lies in its very complexity, since it is intended to indicate not only geographical divisions (mountains, deep valleys with poor communications; *landes* cutting the region off from useful contact with the coast; the plains of Aquitaine) but also ethnic and linguistic divisions imprinted on the region by history. What Pierre Bonnaud calls the 'particularly individualized ethnic substratum of Aquitaine' has been subject to a series of 'northern and eastern pressures', from the infiltrations of the Gauls, the bridgeheads of the Romans and the waves of Iberian refugees, to the 'acculturating effort of feudal society' in the Middle Ages, emanating from Toulouse, and in most recent times, 'economic investment by the French system'. The pays of Gascony are thus still linked to their distant prehistory, to 'an inextricable mixture of internal causes of fragmentation and the fragmentation brought by outside intervention'.

---

and explored in every direction. It is a sign of the times that specialization has come to play a role here too.

It may be thought surprising, [he writes] that these peasants

FIGURE 3
The 'pays' of Burgundy

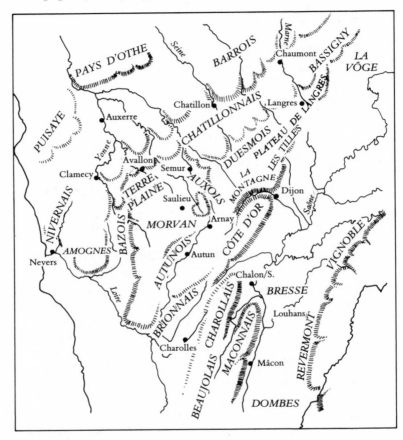

Map by Jacques Bertin.

do not more often set their hands to the plough, but these peasants are sheep farmers. That is what keeps them outside (or above) mechanical progress. No one has yet invented a machine to guard sheep . . . They cultivate only enough land to grow the wheat, barley, potatoes and vegetables needed to keep the family or the individual alive, and that is why so many of these peasants remain bachelors and live on their own: their needs are so few that they barely scratch the earth's surface for one month of the year.[30]

Sheep farming is the typical window a backward region has on to the outside world.

Neither can it be said that there is a single Normandy – there are at least two: Haute-Normandie looking towards Rouen and the sea, and Basse-Normandie looking towards Caen and its lush countryside. And there are plenty of contrasts between the 'rich meadows of the pays d'Auge, the forests in the bends of the Seine, the fields and hedges of the Orne and the Virois, the heathland of the Cotentin and the wheatfields of the Caux and the Vexin',[31] as Frédéric Gaussen said in his review of Armand Frémont's very fine book *Paysans de Normandie* (1981). The list is only indicative: a dozen other names spring to mind; the Petit Caux, the pays de Bray, the Beauvaisis, Madrie, Neubourg, the Roumois, the Ouche, Bessin and Houlme, the Séois, the Alençon country, the Falaise country, the Hiemois, Passais, the plains of Caen, Avranchin, Bauptois and Corlois. As Frédéric Gaussen rightly remarks, 'Every "pays" [in Normandy] engenders a type of inhabitant and a way of life. Every *pays* imposes its own history'.[32] One could, it is true, turn this observation back to front – for every history also creates a kind of inhabitant, a type of landscape, and ensures the survival of a *pays*. The galloping urbanization of today may be blurring some of these ancient differences, but it often provides no more than a superficial veneer.

If one were to count all the *pays* that make up each province of France, Champagne would no doubt come near the top of the list (after Gascony, cf. Figure 2). It is a regular coral reef of *pays* set at greater or lesser intervals – at least thirty altogether. As Hervé Fillipetti writes, 'While some [of them] still retain generally recognized names and boundaries (the Porcien, the Perthois, the Rémois, the Senonais or the Bassigny), others are no longer perceived as original and living entities: who, these days, talks about the Arcesais, the Briennois or the Atenois'[33] – or one might add the Provinais or the Vallage? Are there perhaps deserted *pays*, as there are deserted villages, whose outline and traces we should be looking for on the ground – something requiring careful fieldwork before it is too late?

But do not the smallest regional units also divide automatically into even smaller ones? The mountain basin of the Gave de Pau – the Lavedan – is actually a collection of seven different *pays* of the Pyrenees and their foothills: the Barèges valley, the Cauterets valley, the Val d'Azun, the Estrème de Salles, the Batsurguère, the Davantaygue and the Castelloubon.[34]

So let us not be too eager to follow those hasty writers who take the cohesion of the old French provinces for granted. Henri Focillon for instance, thinking of the age of Romanesque architecture, speaks of Burgundy as 'threefold and one over a century and a half of history'.[35] Threefold perhaps if one is thinking only of the Romanesque churches, but the analogy will not work for geography and history. Burgundy is an explosion of individual *pays*, as the sketchmap based on Henri Vincenot's work demonstrates (Figure 3).[36] One cannot speak of the unity of Burgundy except in the sense that one speaks of the unity of France as a whole. Both Burgundy and France exist at a number of levels – singular at the top, plural at the base. So I believe it is salutary, indeed essential, to keep repeating 'Don't forget that France is diversity', just as André Siegfried was forever telling his students, 'Don't forget that Britain is an island'.

Diversity observed: taking to the road

But there is no point in talking theoretically about the diversity of France: you must see it with your own eyes, take in the colours and smells, touch it with your own hands, eat and drink it, to get its authentic favour. It was not only the history of France that Michelet liked to 'get his teeth into' as Roland Barthes might put it,[37] but France itself. Michelet was always travelling through France and feasting on it. Lucien Febvre had the same boundless passion. I too share it in my way.

In our time, travel by car – I dare no longer say by aeroplane since they fly so high these days – makes it possible to indulge this passion, on condition one does not drive on too many faceless motorways (although some of them are admittedly magnificent, like the road from Geneva to Annemasse, then to Bonneville by way of the Faucigny, which finally takes you snaking over the void, perched on huge pillars, up to Chamonix and the Mont-Blanc tunnel). But as a general rule it is better to take the minor roads, marked yellow on the map, for they are the most beautiful in the world: splendidly laid out, they follow the lie of the land and speak the very language of the contours. One should stop often. And if you share my personal taste, watch out especially for the breaks in continuity, the frontier zones. Be alert to the moment when the shape or the materials of the roofs change, or when the wells have a different structure (a revealing but rarely-noticed piece of evidence). Look out for the magic signs which protect (or fail to protect) the house from bad luck: in Alsace you will find them everywhere. Ask yourself why in Champagne there are so many extravagant weathervanes on the roofs, whereas in Lorraine a weathervane indicates the dwelling of the squire or a rich family – there was only one in my native village. Were they perhaps in Champagne a belated form of revenge by the humble class of peasants and artisans, a way of proclaiming social equality while at the same time advertising one's trade? But then why in Champagne and so little elsewhere?

My advice then is to be on the lookout for divergences, contrasts, breaks, frontiers. For

if the notion of frontiers between little *pays* has by now [become] alien to us and seems totally artificial . . . it is still very much alive and has a clear meaning in the minds of country people. It is precisely within the landscape of their everyday activities that farmers can draw such boundaries: across the stream, past the wood, at the foot of the hill, another *pays* begins.[38]

These lines are from Hervé Fillipetti's book on the peasant dwelling: the finest book – both for text and pictures – that one can read on the France of long ago, in that it retraces those frontiers, or rather enclosures, inside which rural France can still be glimpsed in today's landscape. It is a book that shows the links between the peasant dwelling and the local context, the soil, the climate, the nearest building materials, the social order of the village and the types of production – in short it resurrects a whole way of life.

Let us say then that you have left the dark pine trees, steep meadows and high-banked roads of the Jura: driving west, you come out suddenly on to the low flatlands of the Bresse, where grassy fields are interspersed with sheets of standing water and lines of trees. At the same time, the great square, massive houses of the Jura, with their high stone walls and broad arched barn doors, give way to the brick and half-timbering of the farms of the Bresse; under tiled roofs with upturned eaves, hang long rows of rust-coloured corncobs. You have suddenly entered a quite different world.

Or you are travelling from Paris to Orleans: after Etampes, you leave the leafy valley of the Juine (once upon a time navigable and lined with mills) and presently the Beauce appears with its vast horizons, its huge wheatfields planted as if by geometers, and its expanses of red clover. Is this the most beautiful plateau in the world? Perhaps, but the Beauce villages 'walled, surly and (today) deserted',[39] huddled round their church towers, are certainly not the loveliest villages in France.

Sometimes a mere quarter of a hour in the car can bring a change of scene as quickly as the interval does at the theatre. Any French-man who has been a soldier will know only too well the huge army camp at Mailly in what is known as 'la Champagne pouilleuse'. He will have marched and tramped round it on rainy days when the chalk, unprotected by vegetation, turns into whitish mud and every step leaves its trace. I can still see the dirty white marks left by the hobnails of our old army boots. In this Haute-Champagne, as it was once known, travellers were already remarking in the eighteenth century,[40] that 'the countryside stretched as far as the eye could see', with no trees, and very few springs. Even today, when you approach it from the west, from the wine-growing part of Cham-pagne (the slopes of the Ile-de-France) this 'chalk desert' is still a 'disconcerting' sight.[41] But this part of Champagne does have a few valleys, in which the villages – on sites dictated by running water or wells, by rich alluvial soil, or by grazing land on the lonely plateaux known as the *savarts* – are a monotonous succession of gloomy half-timbered houses. It was a hard life here in the past, but then where was life not hard in the France of the old days? There was no wood: the peasants

> heated their bread-ovens with straw gathered from the fields of wheat and rye (harvested by sickle in those days); they would parsimoniously buy twenty-five or thirty bundles of wood in the Brie [*champenoise*] or in the *bocage*; while the poorest of all were reduced to warming themselves by burning 'dry leaves', lucerne roots, thistles, buckwheat straw, rape-seed stalks . . . Older people can [still] recall the days when they spent the evenings in the cellars or cowsheds to keep warm from the cold.[42]

Today, the *savarts*, which were not so long ago being sold off *à la hollée*, 'by earshot',[43] have been stripped of the stunted pines planted in the nineteenth and twentieth centuries, ploughed and reploughed to reconstitute an arable soil, and have become, thanks to tractors and fertilizers, remarkable cereal-growing areas.

But since Champagne is par excellence a land of contrasts, a short walk to the east will take you out of the monotonous chalk country and into the soggy clay Champagne, *la Champagne humide*, a name borne out by its green pastures and woods, its many river banks, its stretches of marshland that never seem to dry up. Here the houses are protected from the rain by wide overhanging eaves, or sometimes have every wall clad against the weather with curious wooden laths and shingles. And if you go a very little further, you will find the Argonne, dense, compact and dark, with its hamlets in forest clearings, apparently a protective zone against the outside world. (Only apparently: there are no Thermopylae there now to guard France.) But if you still hanker after sudden contrasts, there are always the Ardennes to the north, the forest of Othe to the south; and looking towards Paris, at the edge of the Brie, on the heights of the Ile-de-France already mentioned, there are the famous vineyards in their rolling landscape, dotted with clusters of stone-built villages.

53

FIGURE 4
Distribution of roofing materials in France

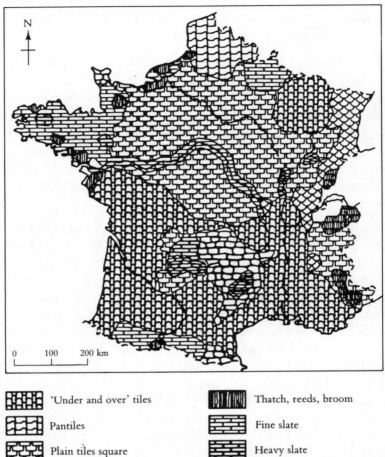

'Under and over' tiles		Thatch, reeds, broom	
Pantiles		Fine slate	
Plain tiles square		Heavy slate	
Plain tiles bevelled		Roofing stones, schist	
Shingles		Roofing stones, limestone	

Map from Jean-Robert Pitte, *Histoire du paysage français*, I, based on *A la découverte des villages de France*.

54

For as striking a surprise as any, try starting from the chalky plateaux of Picardy (as bare a landscape as you will find – only an occasional tree from time to time) and go down towards the river valleys, the sites chosen by the earliest prehistoric settlements: long swathes of green, tree-lined river banks, where still waters sleep. The frontier of France long depended on the marshy stretches of the Somme. What a fragile frontier it was though, and how easily pierced in places! The Spanish in 1557 took Saint-Quentin, inside which Coligny had barricaded himself; and in 1596 they surprised Amiens, which Henri IV reoccupied not without difficulty, the following year. In 1636 (the year after another war had broken out) they entered Corbie and the alarm ran like a trail of gunpowder to Paris.[44] True these were poor fortresses: a cannonade, a breach or a determined assault could quickly overwhelm their defences, and cannonballs would rain down in the main square. But they were really only warning posts, capable of holding out for a few days at most. Their chief function was to sound the alarm.

I recently made the journey from Beaune to Vézelay by Autun, then took a leisurely route across the national park of the Morvan. The hillsides around Beaune are the most beautiful series of vine-yards I know in the world – the pleasure of the eye can be combined with certain other pleasures. Before you reach Nolay (with its old market-hall, church and sixteenth-century houses) you are in the Massif Central, and it is like entering another world: here vines are few and in the broad meadows divided by hedges or lines of trees, herds of creamy white Charollais cattle are grazing. It feels as if one is going back into the past, an impression even stronger in Autun, in the quiet and lovely streets of the old town. But the countryside round Autun still has an air of openness and easy living, which one leaves behind as one approaches the Settons reservoir, built by damming the bed of the Cure. Not so long ago this was a way-station for logs floating down river to Paris. Even on a sunny day in October, entering the Morvan national park means travelling through a dense and dark forest of deciduous trees, punctuated here and there by compact regiments of conifers. Can it be that these silent woods, with roads already empty and edged with golden bracken in autumn, are no longer being forested? Alongside some impressively high piles of logs by the roadside, I saw no workmen and only one logging machine, which was not working. From time to time there are clearings, valley beds with a few acres of cultivable soil, the *ouches*. In each of these one finds a hamlet of three or four houses. The further north one goes, slates gradually begin to replace tiles on their roofs. There are a few sparse villages too, and some fields of wheat, rye or potatoes, but mostly there are meadows and yet more meadows, with hedgerows or lines of trees – really a *bocage* landscape, like the many *bocages* of western France under the Atlantic rains. There are no towns of any size here to bring animation to the region. Those that might have done so – Autun, Avallon – in fact look outwards to the world rather than inward to the Morvan. Is it really a 'godforsaken country'? asks Jacqueline Bonnamour in her excellent thesis on a region which is certainly far from privileged.[45] Since another thesis, also excellent,[46] was written on the area over fifty years ago, we have two separate accounts of the Morvan and an opportunity to measure the *recent* human decline of the region. It has lost over half its population and today only the wildlife seems really at home there. Vidal de la Blache used to say that the Morvan could only be properly understood by looking down on it from the Vézelay spur, one of the limestone outcrops that dominate the approaches to the Morvan. Seen from this viewpoint, it looks almost like a mountain range – which in reality it is not: the highest point is only 902 metres. But if you cross the Morvan at the end of winter, snow and frost will still be lingering there, whereas the fruit trees will already be in flower in Vézelay and Autun.

Of course, the 'surprise' which I have been urging on the reader as a guiding principle, does not replace geographical observation. But it is a way of being alert to change, of being conscious, to the point of obsession, of the quasi-biological diversity of our country. Even Renan – certainly no geographer – did not escape this feeling. Leaving Sète on the arid Mediterranean coast in September 1852, he came to Toulouse on the Garonne: 'The countryside grows green again', he writes, 'and here the streams which in Provence are merely torrents that dry up in summer, water the fields in every direction: the olive tree vanishes; the vine which in Provence is only a stock laden with grapes, here looks more like the vine of our northern regions'.[47]

I will just mention my two last examples of surprises. The first was when last year I was going up the valley of the Têt in the Conflent area of Roussillon. After kilometres of Mediterranean drought, relieved only by patches of vines hacked out of the rocky *garrigues*, I suddenly found myself, rounding a bend in the road, face to face with a landscape from the Savoy Alps: grassy meadows and dense stands of tall pine-trees. The second surprise came simply from reading, in this case a book by Jean Giono, who has written some surprising pages on the southern wilderness of the Camargue – the part which if you are in a car and always obliged to go by Arles, you see only in glimpses, too quickly, or not at all. It is a world teeming with insects, with reptiles, with birds from every part of the earth; a world with water in every direction, a world of oppressive sands, of wild animals, bulls and horses, of men who even seem to have remained wild, and of white cabins 'like sugar-cubes'.[48] My curiosity is more aroused by this Camargue than by the recently introduced melon-beds, or the blue-green rice-fields (now rather in decline and under threat from flocks of flamingoes).

Let us stop here though, even if I have not mentioned every part of France – or anything like it: not Brittany or the Loire valley, neither Poitou nor Guyenne. Do not fear, we shall reach them. And the reader will certainly have his or her own store of images and surprises, memories which probably do not coincide with mine, but complement them. I meant only to suggest a general outline of the problem. Will this do for now?

CHAPTER TWO

Explaining France's diversity –
if it can be explained

It remains for us to explain this diversity – the breaks and contrasts, extreme and not so extreme, and the chronic fragmentation of the whole. The task is a difficult one, since explanations can be attempted only if enlightenment is sought from many quarters: from geography (itself the sum of several sciences), from economics, retrospective politics, cultural analysis. The social sciences speak in a number of registers at once, yet none of them can grasp at most more than a segment of reality. In any case we are here engaged in no more than a first attempt, seeking at best to identify the basic problems and to outline the most obvious explanations, the ones that suggest themselves. The true answers will emerge (if they emerge at all) only later and out of the present work as a whole.

The diversity of Europe, the diversity of France

The territory occupied by France is but a section of the geography of Europe. Europe encloses it, occupies it and is prolonged into it in such a way that here, at this western end where the continent narrows, there are forced together into heightened opposition those contrasts which in the vaster expanses of Central and Eastern Europe have more room to move apart and to lose their force in the distances between the northern seas on one hand and the Mediterranean and the Black Sea on the other.

The European massifs for example are extended into France by the Ardennes, the Vosges, the Massif Central and the lower

Armorican plateaux – a whole series of geological platforms, ridges and vast tablelands. Originally very high, then worn away by millennia of active erosion, the old massifs were 'peneplained', reduced to peneplains, land theoretically exhausted, infertile and desolate. Subsequently, they were raised and 'rejuvenated' by the powerful upward thrust of the foldings in the tertiary period, the source of the many faults, collapses and upraisings, of the deep valleys, the fertile alluvial plains and volcanic eruptions in the Auvergne and the Velay. 'The Massif Central could be described as almost entirely the product of fire'.[49] The Velay was probably still volcanically active as late as AD 580. Rich soils now lie where large surfaces collapsed and thick deposits of sedimentary material accumulated: the Paris basin is the classic example (140,000 square kilometres, or over a quarter of the national territory).

Of the ancient massifs, the largest is the Massif Central (85,000 square kilometres in all) a 'fortress almost exactly in the middle of the country'[50] dispatching rivers, roads and people in every direction. Perhaps it should be accorded more importance than it usually receives from historians for its role in the creation and preservation of France. Its bulk forms a barrier between the different Frances, keeping them apart it is true, yet at the same time linking them together, nourishing them with its waves of emigration, the most abundant in all France. 'Yes, it is a reservoir of men', writes Jean Anglade, '[men] who have left home by every possible way, by mule or donkey, by cart, by log-train on the Allier [or the Loire] by *gabarre* on the Lot . . . But above all on their own two feet, taking Shanks's pony'.[51] In the end, and more than one might suppose, France is to be explained by these central highlands, by the way they have divided, blocked and even protected it.[52] To take only one example, how vital the Massif Central was in the desperate days of the last phase of the Hundred Years' War, in the reign of Charles VII, 'the king of Bourges', who found timely defenders there.

At the same time as they remodelled the architecture of our massifs, the more recent foldings of the tertiary period (occurring simultaneously throughout Europe) also threw up along our frontiers the Jura, the Alps and the Pyrenees, like so many enormous fortifications, but ones which human life instinctively sought out, and which trade was soon crossing with alacrity. For these mountains were not barren wastes, hostile to human settlement – the exception perhaps (but it takes us well outside France) being the harsh and desolate Apennines stretching down into Italy. Our tertiary mountains are without question the most populated of the globe. The Alps especially, with their sledges and pack animals, their strings of villages linked by haulage, did not hinder but rather accelerated exchange across them. Having once by train and three times by plane crossed the Andes at the latitude of Santiago, where the mountain tops are covered with eternal snow, and having seen at close quarters the joys of winter sports at Farellones, I nevertheless retain a desolate memory of those black and white South American deserts, where there are no trees, no villages, no people; the memory of the well-peopled Alps pursues one in these gigantic wastes.

France then has three kinds of relief: ancient massifs, raised up or eroded, in varying degrees; sedimentary plains; and mountain ranges of the Alpine type. But this initial division is only a crude classification. Three categories will certainly not be enough.

Climate combines with these primary forms of divergence. Continental to the east, as in Germany, Atlantic to the west, as in England, Mediterranean in the sheltered south-east, climate brings more complications and differences. Think how much depends on the triangle soil-climate-relief – nothing less than agriculture, settlement patterns, diet, way of life, communications and sources of energy. France, as Pierre Deffontaines nicely puts it, is the result of 'a battle between different climates and types of vegetation'.[53] Less concisely, we might say that the battle is also between types of relief, types of soil, and, what is more, between different histories and lived experiences in the past.

Mention climate, and there immediately comes to mind the image of that stark contrast familiar to all French people, between the north and the Midi, marked simply and most strikingly by the northern limits of the plants of the south – vines, olives, chestnuts, mulberries, and that more recent arrival from America, maize. (I will not count wheat which was established in France in prehistoric

FIGURE 5
The northern limits of some southern plants

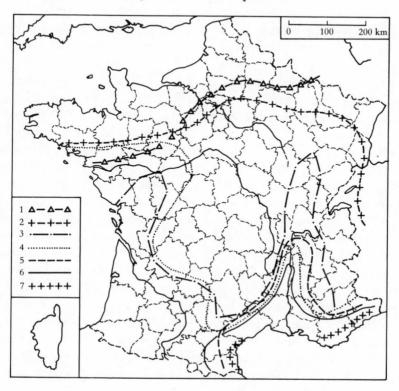

1. Vine
2. Chestnut
3. Maize (before introduction of hybrids)
4. Evergreen oak
5. Mulberry
6. Olive
7. Citrus fruit

After P. Pinchemel, *La France, Milieux naturels, populaires, politiques.*

times and had plenty of time to acclimatize itself throughout the country.)

Starting from the Narbonne region conquered by the Romans in 120 to 100 BC, the vine made giant strides to reach the northern half of the country: ordinary people's thirst, the luxurious tastes of the rich, encouragement from the high clergy and not least the need for communion wine, all assisted this successful advance which reached its furthest point on the banks of the Somme.[54] Did not the Roman traders encourage the Gauls' taste for wine from the start, in the days when an amphora of wine could be exchanged for a slave? So one historian has remarked, only half in jest, that wine opened up the road to Gaul for the conquering Roman legions, just as later on spirits and rum were used by the English and the French to manipulate the poor American Indians.[55]

Other southern plants were less successful in the naturally inhospitable north. None of them (apart from hybrid maize in our own time) has managed to spread throughout French soil. But that is perhaps just as well. Which northerner, travelling to the Mediterranean, has not had the pleasure of spotting that sign of welcome, the first olive tree, glimpsed on the banks of the Rhône,[56] south of Valence, or perhaps on the leisurely descent of some Alpine valley, telling him he will soon be among the terraced fields and fragrant plants, the flat-roofed houses built of honey-coloured stone, under the luminous southern sky? The first signs of the south have always cheered my heart.

But it is still rare even today for a man of the north to let himself be won over at once by the south, so different is it from everything he knows. At Montélimar, wrote the English traveller Arthur Young, in 1787,

you meet not only the olive tree, but for the first time the pomgranate (sic), the arbor judae, the paliurus, figs and the evergreen oak; and with these plants I may add also that detestable animal the mosquito. In crossing the mountains of Auvergne, Velay and Vivarais, I met between Pradelles and Thuytz mulberries and flies at the same time. By the term flies I mean those myriads of them which form the most disagreeable circumstance of the southern climates. They are the first of torments in Spain, Italy and the olive district of France: it is not that they bite, sting or hurt, but they buz, teize and worry; your mouth, eyes, ears and nose are full of them: they swarm on any eatable, fruit, sugar, milk, everything is attacked by them in such myriads that if they are not driven away incessantly by a person who has nothing else to do, to eat a meal is impossible.[57]

A century earlier, in 1662, Jean Racine was no happier when he found himself in Uzès, far from his native Valois, hoping for a clerical living which in the end he failed to get. The girls of the Languedoc were pretty enough, but would he not spoil his style and even his manner of speaking by listening to their 'foreign' tongue, as far from 'French' as any Breton? And the heat in summer! If you were here, he wrote to a friend,

> you would see a gang of harvest-workers, roasted by the sun, working like demons and when they are out of breath, they fling themselves to the ground, still out in the sun, sleep the length of a *miserere*, then jump up again. For my part, I can only watch this from our windows, for I could not spend a moment outdoors without collapsing: the air is almost as hot as a bake-oven.[58]

Racine was amazed; he could not get used to the heat, nor to the cicadas, nor even 'the politeness of these sunburnt peasants in their sabots, threshing the grain on the barn floor and saluting [me] with a dancing step'.[59]

Micro-climates, micro-environments

These great climatic divisions are too general to account for everything. Living in 'the Alps' or 'the Massif Central' does not mean much unless you specify exactly where you live. Since at least the time of Maximilien Sorre, who frequently emphasized the point, French geographers have tended to speak of our micro-climates, 'one of the most useful and realistic of notions'. The climate, explains Sorre, presents in each locality its own individual character, which may be irreducible to that even of its nearest neighbour. A slight change in altitude, the difference between two sides of the same hill, a shift from slope to plateau – and daily hours of sunshine, wind speeds, temperature and rainfall all change. So too do the vegetation and the reactions of the organism . . . The local nature of climate is the essential reality, the only first-hand datum of all climatology.[60]

Everyone will have his or her own experience of such things. So to speak only of what I know, the Haut-Faucigny in the Alps, that is the Montjoie valley, through which the Bonnant flows, facing the Miage and the Mont d'Arbois, is a sort of high hollow, almost entirely ringed round by mountains. The result is a certain dryness in the air, a sign that we are near the high Alps, by contrast with the well-watered pre-Alps to the west. In fact this enclosed region has an exceptional capacity for allowing rainwater to drain off, enabling the earth to 'settle' and the roads to dry quickly after a storm. Another micro-climate, also a favoured one, is the corner of the Vallespir, in the Aspre, where my house is built, looking down on Céret and the Pyrenees. On the map, it lies directly in the flight-path of the *tramontane*, and when that blows, as we all know, it howls and whistles round the roof tops, hurls itself threateningly against the walls, buffeting the oak trees that shudder in their vain effort to hold on to the last brown leaves of autumn, and breaking the flexible branches of the evergreen oaks. So it does, but not round my house, which it only reaches in milder mood, as if it had blown itself out; and not in Céret either, the little town nearby which enjoys the same favour. Indeed the people there even say that the *tramontane* is a sign that good weather is on the way.

In Provence too, the lee of a hill, the hollow of a valley can be enough to protect a lucky village or beach from the *mistral* which may be blowing as fiercely as the *tramontane* if not more so, only a short distance away. And why, in northern Alsace, does spring rush in so suddenly – a moment of sheer delight – and so early that it astonished Goethe, a Rhinelander from Frankfurt hardly any distance away?[61]

So let us regret that the reality of the micro-climate has been but 'rarely accepted with its full consequences', by geographers. Let us even regret that no one has explored the notion further, to see whether there are not corresponding micro-environments, creating a micro-biology of the earth on which we live.

For the earth is alive too. The earth is rarely composed of the same soil and sub-soil throughout any given area. If the sub-soil is chalky – as so often in the Paris basin – the topsoil, repeatedly turned over by plough or pick, will regularly be drained by the sub-soil, rainwater will soak deep underground, and ploughing will not be hindered by surface water which has quickly filtered off. In times of drought, moisture is drawn up by capillarities to rescue the plants. What a contrast with clayey soil: heavy under the spade, resistant to effort, it bogs down cartwheels and allows pools of water to collect and become barriers and obstacles. If you stand on the chalk downs of the pays de Caux, a few steps to the north will bring you within sight of the pays de Bray – known to geographers as *la boutonnière* (the buttonhole) of Bray, a land of clayey soil, of ponds and streams, but a land too of lush grass and foliage, of apple and pear trees covered with white blossom in spring.[62]

So the mosaic of soils, sub-soils and micro-climates is translated into the patchwork of the French landscape. Man has unquestionably been the architect and labourer of these gardens and fields, orchards and villages, no two of which are ever exactly alike. Man has been the agent and the designer, but his handwork has also been prompted, helped or even in part dictated from outside.

I cannot help thinking by contrast of the monotony of so many landscapes in northern Europe, where the glacial deposits have overlaid everything, adhering to the soil like a coat of indelible paint. I think too of the laterite zones, that red, dusty earth of tropical countries like Madagascar and Brazil: the landscape looks as if it has been sprayed with minium, trees and all. Travelling through it, your clothes, face and hair are quickly covered in red dust. In the Argentine Pampas, an unbroken train-ride without a single bend to relieve the monotony will carry you for hours through the same scenery. Do not tell me that geography has nothing to answer for where France is concerned.

Local economies, or how France's diversity was safeguarded

Before the industrial revolution, every portion of France's territory tended to look inward, sufficient to itself, closed to the outside world. Economic diversity thus echoed regional diversity, shedding light on it, adapting to it, to some extent explaining it.

The area we call France was of course subject as a whole to historical movements and conjunctural trends, which washed over it like sudden or persistent flood-tides. But such things took place on a higher plane, on the grand stage of general history with its landmarks and favoured terrains. Whereas I want, at this point in our exploration, to concentrate on the elementary local economies, operating over a narrow radius, with their tendency to self-sufficiency. Each of them, for better or for worse, harboured a given population group, whose numbers might rise or fall depending on the resources available, which in turn varied with the rhythm of harvests and prices.

For there was a vital minimum – in terms of food, shelter and clothing – below which no individual could survive. And it was this minimal standard of living, naturally, that had to be preserved, come what might. In the France of the past, it was a standard that varied little, apart from a few striking exceptions, by definition very rare. If this perilous balance could be maintained, or restored reasonably soon when threatened, a small *pays* would manage to hold on to its population, its customs and its way of life. But if a serious crisis arose, requiring a sustained response, a number of solutions were possible, indeed in many cases unavoidable. For instance, if the population increased, land would have to be cleared and concerted efforts made to extend the area under cultivation; or new crops might be introduced (buckwheat, maize, potatoes), thus making possible higher yields and perhaps further population increase. We may also imagine the spread of cash crops such as vines, which were always poised to invade new areas, despite official prohibitions; or dye-plants; or even some profitable line in livestock – all of these being broadly speaking *natural* solutions.

But there were also *artificial* remedies to hand: trade, haulage, industry. Some kinds of trade were necessary, others developed for profit and created surpluses; haulage turned the peasant-carrier into a travelling merchant; industry was a more likely choice since it served the interests of neighbouring towns. It was poverty that inspired and promoted so-called 'rural industry', whether this took the form of proto-industry or grassroots artisanal manufacture, whether it appeared in the north, as in Villedieu-les-Poêles in the Normandy *bocage*, which became an early centre for the manufacture of cooking pots;[63] or in the south, in the Gévaudan for example, where the thick cheap fabrics known as *cadis* were woven in villages deep in the Massif Central, along perilous or impassable roads.[64] Thousands of similar examples could be cited: thousands of little *pays* after all saved themselves by the rattle of the loom. Sometimes too the population adapted spontaneously to hardship, postponing the age of marriage so as to limit births and preserve its chances of survival.

All these solutions rescued and preserved the micro-economies of the past and along with them the tenacious diversities of our *pays*. For they never wholeheartedly opened up to the outside world; they took from outside only what was indispensable, preserving their self-contained character.

This closure is all the more revealing since it runs directly counter to what was the recourse of almost all local economies in times of prolonged or recurrent crisis, or of serious overpopulation – namely emigration, whether permanent, temporary, or merely seasonal and therefore recurrent. At first a trickle, then a stream, eventually a flood-tide of humanity – a 'hydrographic system' covering all of France and going back centuries – the system only becomes really visible to us towards the end of the Middle Ages, but it must surely have been in operation long before. As time passed at any rate, it became established, increased, and came to affect the entire country. The nineteenth century was its high water mark, that 'restless' period both before and after the coming of the railways. It is only in our own time, since the 1970s, that this human flow has slowed down, with the dwindling of the rhythms, routes and reasons that prompted it in the past.

FIGURE 6
FIGURE 6
The territory of the Cinq Grosses Fermes (tax farms)
see pp. 72–6

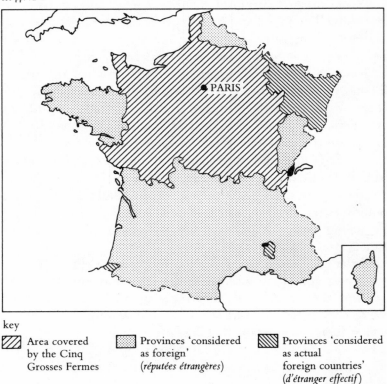

key

▨ Area covered by the Cinq Grosses Fermes	▦ Provinces 'considered as foreign' (*réputées étrangères*)	▨ Provinces 'considered as actual foreign countries' (*d'étranger effectif*)

Until the Revolution, France was divided by internal customs barriers, except inside the area known as the Cinq Grosses Fermes, in which Colbert had instituted a customs union in 1664.

In the old days, want and misery called the tune. Waves of emigration came (in descending order of size) from the Massif Central, the Alps, the Pyrenees, the Jura and certain regions on the edge of Paris basin – in short from areas which, taken together with others nearby, could still today be called 'the poorer France'.

Nothing is easier than to reconstruct these patterns of emigration, whether they led to building sites in the towns which were always being built and rebuilt, or to the rich farming plains where itinerant workers were badly needed at times of harvest, grape-picking, carting and threshing. But what interests us more than their destinations or their journeys is how such movements affected the equilibrium of the little districts people had left behind and to which they unfailingly returned, in the apt words of the proverb: *Noël avec les vieux, Pâques où tu veux* (Christmas at home, Easter we'll roam). Departures and returns brought desperately needed relief to the community of origin: departures because they reduced the number of mouths to feed, returns because they brought home cash savings, necessary for taxes, for unavoidable purchases and for the refloating of many Lilliputian smallholdings.

The system did not always work ideally. There were half-successes and sometimes emigration was a last resort. I believe that the high region of Auvergne round Aurillac, which from very early times sent migrants to Spain, really did make a success of it. The case has been closely studied: the mountain villages were better-off, and more open to the outside world even than those of the lower Auvergne, although the latter had more natural advantages.[65] One could also rate as a success, or a partial success, the example of the Montjoie valley, high up in the Faucigny in Haute-Savoie. The populations of the three villages of Saint-Gervais, Saint-Nicolas-de-Véroce and Les Contamines, were already sending emigrants in the fourteenth century to Alsace and southern Germany. They continued, in later times, to find their way to these Catholic areas, where several Savoyards made spectacular fortunes. Later again, under the Regency (1715–23) they flocked to Paris, but now as porters, removal men, ostlers, chimney sweeps and domestic servants, all used to hard work, living together in groups and saving every penny. This emigration by the poor brought back to the villages substantial sums of money (15,250 francs in 1758).[66]

Such was not always the case. In Ussel, on the borders of the Limousin and the Auvergne, a land 'carved up by [river] gorges and great stretches of heath', life was hard. Only in 1830 did it get 'a coach road, from Lyon to Bordeaux, bringing money'.[67] The emigration, permanent or temporary (between midsummer and Michaelmas), 'of young men leaving for the sawmills or building sites', did not automatically bring prosperity.[68] According to the grievance registers of 1789, those who were left behind 'have nothing to eat but soup and bread'.[69] It was the same sad story in the Limousin highlands, according to a report addressed to Turgot (their *intendant* in 1762) by the villagers of Saint-Pardoux-la-Croisille:

> Monseigneur, every year a prodigious number of people leave most of our parishes, abandoning their native soil, from which they are driven by poverty and where they lack for bread, in order to become mercenaries in wealthier places. Spain takes many from us, for example; others go as masons, tilers, or sawyers to the various provinces of the kingdom. You may say that they bring back money with them; but out of ten of these travellers or workmen who return, there are not two who have made good; sickness, journeys and debauchery have eaten all they had; and in any case, how can the coin they do bring back to our province make up for the harm these people have done to the progress of agriculture?[70]

The problem of migration certainly never occurs in the same shape twice. What is more, many forms of migration tended to become habitual, almost a profession, rather than an episodic response to poverty. A Savoyard from Magland might be selling watches in southern Germany, travelling long distances to do so, because his father and grandfather had plied the same trade all their lives.[71] But in the end, whatever their character, their motivation or their itinerary, such migrations restored the balance of the diversity of France, enabling it to survive.

If this was so, it was of course because the economy as a whole, calling the tune from above, allowed it to happen, willingly or otherwise. *Mutatis mutandis*, is the same not true today? Large numbers of immigrants, from abroad this time, have flowed in to fill the gaping holes in the French economy. The North African, Portuguese, Spanish and black African workers whom we now meet everywhere, are only working in France to the extent that our economy and society tolerates and indeed invites them. So too in the past: migration was an index of the general conditions which caused it. When those conditions disappeared at the beginning of this century, the flow was bound to dry up and so it did.

But population shifts did not come to a halt, far from it. Other imperatives arose and had to be obeyed: above all the great urban expansion already long under way but accelerating vertiginously after 1950, and literally depopulating the French countryside. By the 1970s, people were used to talking about 'Paris and the French desert', or indeed of 'Tours and the Touraine desert', 'Clermont-Ferrand and the Auvergne desert' and so on.[72] Many astonishing examples could be cited of the devastating effect on the country-side, from very early on, caused by the random force of attraction of the towns. This happened to the villages 'of Burgundy, around Le Creusot; to the villages of Lorraine, near the steelworks; to those of Champagne, near Troyes . . . No city was as powerful and far-reaching a magnet as Paris. The population of Paris comes from every French province: since mid-nineteenth century, two-thirds of the people living in Paris have not been Parisians born and bred'.[73] Since those words were written, the balance has shifted even more decisively towards the towns: they exert even more attraction than in the past and rarely let their captives go.

But this flood-tide did not, as one might perhaps have expected, wash away the country's underlying variety – on the contrary. Those who remained behind in the villages – or new incomers – divided existing resources among their now reduced ranks and were sometimes even able to develop them rapidly, thanks to their newfound means. In Espelette, a village in the Basque country, in 1981, 'whereas the farming population was in steep decline, the area under cultivation increased not only in size but in quality, so that productivity . . . rose considerably'; over 300 hectares of heathland were reclaimed, and the arable land increased by 40 per cent – thanks to the purchase of tractors.[74] On the other hand, crops have been abandoned around the cities where suburbs have grown up, and in regions where mechanization has proved difficult or impossible. Grazing in high mountain districts has often been

71

abandoned too. Although deeply altered by the modern economy, the old mosaic of the French countryside has by and large been preserved and with it that undeniable, even defiant diversity.

State and society combine to allow diversity and confusion to persist

Nor shall we find unity where we might have expected in theory to find it – at the level of political power. No structuring force from the political centre ever succeeded in imposing unity on a diversity which seemed to have ineradicable vitality. No sooner was it disciplined than it broke out again: neither political, social nor cultural order ever contrived to foist more than surface unity on the whole.

During the last centuries of the *ancien régime*, the monarchical state tended, in its efforts to discipline and unite the kingdom, to build an ever-heavier political and administrative machine. But what difficulties, obstacles, forces of inertia and counter-powers it had to face! The *ancien régime* reaped what it had sown. From its long past, it inherited a farrago of disorganization, confusion, institutional diversity, administrative incoherence, or downright impotence. French society was by no means under the firm hand of the state, far from it. Nobody could say of it in those days, as Alain Touraine has said of our own time (whether he is right is another matter) that it simply echoed 'its master's voice'.[75] Even now we are not yet confronted with a 'global' society, to use Georges Gurvitch's expression,[76] that is a single unified society, ruled by patterns, customs and institutions tending to uniformity, if not entirely uniform. There could be no such thing as an even halfway unified society in France until the French nation had been forged – something which is still so recent that we almost think of it as accomplished within living memory.

France is not one society then but many societies, whether one analyses them 'vertically' in the usual way, or 'horizontally', in such a way as to bring out their basic heterogeneity. Exaggerating a little, one might suggest that every territorial division in the past was also a social division, insofar as each one housed a society of variable but restricted dimensions, providing it both with its limits and its raison d'être, a society that depended primarily on its internal communications. The divisions in question were the villages, the bourgs, the towns and the provinces. And in every case, the telltale indicator of each society was its hierarchy. For no society is built on equality: the only way any of them can be presented schematically is as a pyramid and whenever the top of the pyramid is visible, there will be a dominant local class, linked to a particular underlying society that supports it, explains it, and is in turn explained by it.

Of all these societies, the village is the most basic, the smallest in size, and the oldest – pre-dating by far either the church or the feudal system. As a unit, the village had its own territory, its own collective property (the jealously-watched and defended *communaux*). Economically, it was virtually self-sufficient. It had its own customs, festivals, songs, its own way of speech which was not necessarily the same as that of the next village. It had its own assembly, its elected officers with titles that varied (mayors, syndics, consuls), its own legal identity. Rétif de la Bretonne said of his little parish, Sacy in Burgundy, that 'it governs itself, like a big family'.[77] Each village would also be subject to the authority of the local squire and the ever-present authority of the parish priest. 'For every square league and every thousand inhabitants' in France under the *ancien régime*, writes Taine, 'we should imagine a noble family in its big house with a weathercock; in every village, a priest and parish church; and every six or seven leagues, a religious community of men or women'.[78]

As well as the often oppressive presence of the authorities, there was also the hierarchy internal to the village, governing daily life season by season: on one hand the better-off peasants, with perhaps a local 'cock of the walk',[79] and on the other, the poor peasants. In the Paris basin and eastern France, in about 1789, the wealthier villagers were still known as *laboureurs*. The same people would be called *ménagers* in Provence and in some places, by an irony of language, *bourgeois*. Such a privileged person – never a share-cropper, sometimes a tenant-farmer, but if so, in the service of 'some rich family or powerful religious institution', would usually possess 'several teams of horses or oxen, at least ten cows and about 50 sheep; some large wheeled ploughs, harrows, rollers, scythes and carts with iron axles'; he would also employ farmhands and servant girls and might, according to one possibly over-generous estimate, own as much as 10 hectares of land or even 20 or more.[80] By contrast, smallholders had only paltry plots of land, and since they owned neither team, plough, nor cart, would borrow these from a *laboureur* when they needed to. In exchange, they would work for him at hay-making, harvest and grape-picking. Such arrangements between rich and poor peasants were still to be found in eastern France in 1914, and I remember (with a certain retrospective irritation) one such in my native village. Their significance is obvious: the numerical ratio between the farmhands or day-labourers and the *laboureurs* is an infallible index of the tensions or equilibrium of village society. Where there was one day-labourer for each well-off peasant, it was as if the latter had only one subordinate associate obliged to work for him, as in the *département* of the Meuse in 1790.[81] But where there were two day-labourers to each farmer, as in the Metz countryside[82] in 1768, one must conclude that in this region – visibly richer than the area south of the Meuse – there was greater concentration of property and probably therefore some increase in social tensions.[83]

But we should not oversimplify: there were thousands and thousands of villages in France, no two ever exactly alike. Depending on time and place, village society could be fully-developed or repressed, more or less prosperous or more or less in decline. A village could often be crushed under a seigneurial regime which in certain poor regions survived in all its oppressive weight. Such was the Gévaudan, where the bishop of Mende was the sovereign seigneur – 'all but king'.[84] Yet other village communities in the same region had the power to deliberate and decide. By contrast, there were some regions too wealthy, too well-developed, or too near a large town, such as the Beauce or the Brie, where the grip of capitalism made itself felt very early. Think too of the differences in the legal system (a written code in the south, customary law in the north) which varied from province to province; and lastly, differences arising from the range of economic activities.

If we turn to towns, matters are no more simple, but our conclusions will be the same. The towns – over a thousand of them, 1099 to be precise and of all sizes according to an official register of 1787 – had by then all more or less completely shaken off the seigneurial regime which had spread throughout the country in the eleventh and twelfth centuries. This emancipation must be seen in the context of the vast 'communal movement' which affected the whole of Europe in complex and irregular fashion depending on time and place. Even in towns which accomplished the change effectively, like Caen or Arras, it is easier to see the result than to trace the process. Nor can it be assumed that these towns were delivered once and for all from the seigneurial bonds in which they had, in their original weakness, long been entangled.

It would be easy enough, though not perhaps very interesting, to point out the traces of the seigneurial era still surviving in the towns into the 'communal' period. For traces were left everywhere, sometimes in the shape of hindrances, as in Roanne, which had to cope with the demands made by the duc de la Feuillade who was also duke of the Roannais; or in Laval, where the municipal administration, with its perpetual mayor and ex officio members, as we would call them, long remained bound by the regulations laid down by the local seigneur, the duc de La Tremoille. When in 1722, the town demanded that its council have the right to elect its own mayor (a privilege which custom or charter allowed many other towns) it was defeated by a decree of the king's council in 1729. Whereupon the seigneur magnanimously granted by his goodwill and favour what he had refused the people of Laval as of right.[85] He nevertheless continued to exercise his feudal rights over various districts of the town – collecting dues in money or kind, claiming *droits de mutation* (transfer dues), or insisting that dough kneaded at home be baked in one of the feudal bakehouses leased to town bakers, and so on.[86]

Escaping the clutches of one's seigneur was comparatively easy in the long run. But royal power was a different kettle of fish. The king's tax authorities were always harassing the towns, putting pressure on them and calling them to order. Perennially short of money, the government was perennially attracted by the wealth and financial possibilities of the towns. Let two examples stand for thousands: the declaration of 21 December 1647 by which the government doubled the *octroi* (duties on goods entering towns) and pocketed the increase itself; or in 1771, the restoration of venality of municipal offices, which obliged the towns to buy them up themselves, in order to retain their freedom to elect their own aldermen.

Royal authority nevertheless sometimes had to give way to seigneurial privilege. The monarchy always struggled in vain for instance against the proliferation of tolls. As early as 1437, Charles VII had suppressed all unauthorized tolls, that is ones set up by local landowners without permission. But in 1669, 1677 and 1789, the problem was still the same: trying to get toll-owners to produce their deeds of entitlement. If the battle was so hard-fought, it was, as a memorandum of 1789 explains, because 'toll dues annexed to feudal fiefs increase the latters' value'. What was at stake was the income and 'property of the leading seigneurs'.[87] Another fruitless struggle occurred in the spring of 1683: the *intendant* of Poitou, Lamoignon de Basville, was preparing to introduce 'a tax on houses' in the town of Poitiers. Having drawn up the roll, he was congratulating himself on the revenue this would fetch: over 7000 *livres* a year, 'a fairly considerable sum, which would be even greater if almost half the town' alas, had not been part of 'the fiefs of Saint-Hilaire, Monstierneuf and Anguitard and other small fiefs, with well-defined limits, which have always been recognized by the king's officers'. There was no question of taxing these.[88] In Angoulême in 1695, there is an even more amusing example: here the dispute was not about who should receive the money but who should pay it out. The town's château was in very poor shape, needing 'urgent repairs', but 'we do not know who should carry them out, the king or Madame de Guise'.[89]

Every town a different social equation

These examples give some idea of the situation of the towns. Under constant scrutiny from the *intendants*, from owners of fiefs, from tax officers and the royal judiciary which paralleled seigneurial justice, they were the site of a struggle among several powers: the power of the seigneur, on the wane but still preserved in numerous privileges; the power of the crown, on the increase, but having to compromise with ancient traditions, customs and immunities; and the power of the commune, sometimes thwarted, sometimes victorious, and exerted by a newly-enriched and almost all-powerful bourgeoisie. For town government, which is often presented as originally having the backing of a democratic movement (an over-simplification in itself) was in any case very soon appropriated by a handful of powerful families. There were elections, true, but these were merely a front. A few dynastic clans, united among themselves, presided without interruption over the destinies of Marseille or Lyon, and practically all other French cities. The ceremonial of elections in Paris (whose detail it is impossible to study and keep a straight face) was a very well organized scenario, since the same privileged individuals remained imperturbably *in situ*. Everywhere, over and above the mass of general labourers, over and above the organized craft guilds, a hierarchy was firmly installed, with the local élite – whatever form that took – at its summit.

So it would be wrong to think that this élite was without power, or that it had no control over the day-to-day running of the town. In Laval, from the reign of Louis XV onwards, the merchants and rich landowners began modernizing their houses at great expense, which usually meant rebuilding the facade and piercing windows. For even such elementary building work, they had to obtain permission from the local authorities. So if you have ever complained about delays in getting planning permission, remember that the French have been familiar with such annoyances since time immemorial.[90] I am not exaggerating. On 1 November 1689 – in a letter which is probably the most telling indictment in existence of the ruling aristocracy of the city of Lyon – the *intendant* de Bérulle recounts the following anecdote:

> Yesterday, a householder came to complain that after having
> mended the jamb of his door, which had collapsed when the

door was slammed, workmen were sent to prop up the house while the door-jamb was demolished, because he had not asked permission from the town officers.

(The *intendant*'s intervention, incidentally, did no good!)[91]

Towns might seem to resemble each other, but as a rule there were as many patterns, as many 'social equations' as there were towns. In the wool town of Montauban, the clothiers (of Protestant origin) provided the local high society: luxurious houses, glittering literary salons, hunting parties and picnics, patronage of local painters – everything spoke of their wealth. Rennes was above all an administrative and legal town, a provincial capital. In Toulouse, an administrative centre too, but one in the heart of a rich agricultural region, or in Caen the centre of a prosperous countryside, wealth mostly went with land. The gigantic ports of Rouen, Nantes, Bordeaux and Marseille, rapidly expanding business centres, looked seawards and could thus be unusually independent of central authority. Dunkerque was ensconced in its immense privilege of being a free port – no one paid *taille*, *gabelle* or stamp tax here: a dozen families ruled the local roost.[92] And what of Paris, or that other capital city, Lyon, whose fortunes were blocked and hindered from a distance by Paris? Depending on the town under scrutiny, a social order can be discerned with its own originality and character, its own particular destiny.

Provincial particularism

The particularities of the towns were complicated by the fact that they were embedded within the vigorous particularisms of the provinces. During the long history of the building of the unified kingdom of France, achieved through a series of conquests, marriages, inheritances and adjudications, the monarchy was led to negotiate, willingly or unwillingly, formally or informally, a series of 'historic compromises' with its new subjects in the annexed territories. The addition of these provinces to the French crown did not therefore create identical situations or regimes within

them. Far from it. Each province managed to obtain the maintenance of its particular privileges, traditions and 'freedoms' (in
other words its means of defence), as well as the survival of
inconsistencies inherited from its own past.

The logical outcome was that the crown failed to smoothe out
differences between provinces. Rather it adapted itself to them,
taking pains to insinuate itself between them in order to attain its
vital ends: public order, respect for royal justice, the supply of
grain, the establishment of an insidious yet constantly thwarted
fiscal system, and the repeated creation (and sale) of public office.
With a few exceptions to prove the rule, the crown learnt to
respect as far as possible the prerogatives, delays and imperatives
of tradition and of provincial institutions, although from at least
the days of Colbert, it was often well aware of the flagrant harm
they did both to the crown itself and to the 'peoples' who were
their victims. But seeking to lance the boil was risky and not always
helpful. The easier way out prevailed: allowing local institutions to
survive, sometimes letting them die, but only of old age (like the
estates of Normandy in 1655 or of Auvergne in 1651). A large array
of sometimes subtle defence mechanisms was moreover brought to
bear, in unison or in succession, against central authority. I confess
to being quite captivated by the legal cunning and inventiveness of
some of the manoeuvres of the *cour des comptes* of Dole or the
parlement of Besançon.

The provinces then fairly bristled with counter-powers: some
of them preserved their estates (*états*) (with delegates from the
three orders) which had financial powers and the responsibility of
apportioning and collecting taxes: this was a position of
strength, between king and taxpayer, so negotiation was always
possible. The *parlements* were more aggressive and everywhere acted as defenders of the provinces. To these one should
add, since the crown left all ancient institutions alone, a sort of
undergrowth of institutions, half asleep but capable of being
roused to action or to challenge each other: *élections*, *prévôtés*,
bailliages, *sénéchaussées*, *présidiaux*, plus dozens of groups of minor
office-holders. Royal authority could make no headway in this
maze of circles, virtually independent of it since the offices had

been bought and their holders heeded only their own interests and vanities.

The reaction of the crown, in the course of the crises of the seventeenth century, was to create the *intendants*, its direct representatives with theoretically almost unlimited powers: their official title was indeed '*intendants* [that is overseers] of justice, police and finance'. John Law even claimed that the thirty *intendants* of his day really governed the country:

> You have neither parliaments nor estates nor governors, I am even tempted to say no king or ministers: it is on thirty *maîtres de requêtes*, delegated to the provinces that the good or bad fortune of the provinces, their prosperity or sterility, depend.[93]

In fact they were generally loyal servants of the state and more efficient administrators than is sometimes allowed. So it is all the more striking to see that, especially after 1750, when economic prosperity was leading to large-scale modernizing policies and major public works programmes throughout France, the *intendants* increasingly identified with 'their' provinces, becoming defenders of the latter against Versailles. But could it really have been otherwise? In 1703, the *intendant* of Brittany, Béchameil de Nointel, was already saying: beware, 'the minds in this province are not to be ruled as others are'.[94] And he criticized the maréchal d'Estrées as tactless when the latter fiercely condemned two gentlemen who had spoken out strongly in the estates of Brittany against the demands of the government. Similarly, the *intendant* of Metz thought it worth explaining to Versailles that the city of Metz 'still remembers that it lost its sovereignty only by the Peace of Münster',[95] that is in 1648, whereas Henri II had first occupied the city in 1552.

Nevertheless in the eighteenth century, in a France now developing rapidly, formal respect for countless established rights, which had probably lost all rationale with the passage of time, led to some visibly absurd consequences. If the centralism of the revolutionaries eventually abolished this plethora of administrations, it was undoubtedly in response to a general disquiet already felt before the Revolution. A curious memorandum of 1782 explains at length the extravagant privileges attached to the 'Petit Franc Lyonnais', a strip of land along the banks of the Saône on either side of the little town of Trévoux, north of Lyon. The anonymous author concludes his reflections as follows:

> If . . . one considers only the general principles of governments, and the order and uniformity which ought to be the basis of all good administration, one would be justified in thinking that the subjects of the same state should be ruled by the same laws, should enjoy the same prerogatives and bear the same charges, and that it seems extraordinary that a territory consisting at most of 2½ leagues' surface area, lying more or less at the centre of the kingdom, should obtain privileges which can only excite the jealousy of neighbouring parishes and . . . an animosity which has already led more than once to scenes which could only be stopped, and which will only be forestalled in future, by deploying all the rigour of the authorities.[96]

Extraordinary indeed. And we may ask ourselves why the provinces turned their faces against what would often quite clearly have meant progress all round. One must allow for a certain local patriotism, for if there was not yet a French 'nation', the local *patrie* did service for it and nourished what would nowadays be called 'autonomist' sentiments. Such sentiments were extremely strong on the eve of the Revolution, which was to put a speedy end to this curious upsurge. But is there any way of drawing up an exact balance sheet of the action of the government vis-à-vis the provinces in the last years of the *ancien régime*? Can we agree with Tocqueville and several well-informed historians that centralism notched up a few victories during this period?

The province had to be sure long ceased by then to be an official territorial division; it was 'falling into disuse, as a political unit, in favour of the *généralité*',[97] the seat of the *intendant*. A new division was thus being superimposed on old boundaries, a process not without similarity to the subsequent division of France into *départements*, under the Constituent Assembly, which was definitely intended to be a clean break with the past. But perhaps it is going too far to compare the two cases? I would willingly concede that with France's economic take-off after 1750 there was some increase in royal authority, yet at the same time, the specificity of the provinces was also being reinforced. For in every provincial capital, the provinces continued to produce a concentrated, tough and dominant elite, well endowed with privileges – privileges it defended in the name of the public good. Was this not the dominant pattern? Territorial organization is impossible without some form of social organization as its cornerstone and necessary accompaniment.

Take for example the particularly dazzling example of Burgundy. Could it have existed, imperious and aloof, without the exclusive caste that dominated the province, the social circle of the Dijon *parlement*? The latter hardly stirred itself, and then only out of habit, to defend its leading position against the *cour des comptes* and the surviving estates of the province, whose pretensions it found irritating on occasion. On the other hand, this social group got on better than is usually thought with the military governor, a person of some prestige especially when, as from 1754 to 1789, the incumbent was a prince de Condé. A little consideration was enough to persuade it to follow the lead of the *commandant*, the local representative of the governor. And there were no serious or insoluble conflicts with the *intendant*. In order to monopolize the *parlement*, this social group had only to rely on its own standing, prestige, wealth and property – its land, woods, vineyards, houses, foundries and rents – scattered throughout Burgundy. A closed society, it maintained by means of partnerships and marriages a closely-knit network of dynasties, careful to fend off any intrusion by newly enriched merchants or bourgeois. Once bourgeois itself, it had long since crossed with ease the boundary into the *noblesse de robe* and could even boast a few nobles of ancient lineage, like the family of the famous président de Brosses (1709–77), descended from a nobleman killed at Fornovo in 1495.

What we have here then is a caste: 'the men of the *parlement* are not content to pass on their office to their children but bring into the company their brothers, brothers-in-law, sons-in-law and nephews'. This was the clan triumphant. An endogamous society, it lived peacefully undisturbed for many long years, organizing plentiful occasions for meeting, corresponding by letter and exchanging views on everything. 'Balls, concerts, plays, gambling, ceremonials, banquets for a hundred guests' were all occasions for the clan to meet, to conspire and to assert itself. On 30 March 1785, the bells in Dijon cathedral rang out to announce the birth of the duke of Normandy, the future Louis XVII: the président Joly de Bévy gave a supper for 110 guests and in front of his illuminated town house, 'he installed two fountains of wine for the people'.[98]

We might equally well have gone to Rennes, Toulouse, Grenoble or Bordeaux, to get the measure of these dominant groups who, by defending their own privileges in the first instance, acted as vigilant watchdogs for provincial liberties. One could linger long over Grenoble for example. Was it perhaps because the 'province' was tucked away in a corner of the kingdom, enmeshed in its privileges and customs, that the *parlement* of Grenoble was a very bastion of watchfulness, of particular interests, keeping the city hall of Grenoble and the local town and village communities firmly under its thumb?

> I realize every day [wrote the *intendant* d'Herbigny in 1679] the need to put a police magistrate [in Grenoble] and to remove from the *parlement* all knowledge of what happens in the city hall. Of all the companies in the kingdom, this is the most determined to attract and keep for itself all authority in the province, and when one of its members takes an interest in any affair, his protégé is unlikely to lose.[99]

The *intendant* was not exaggerating the authoritarian ways of the members of the Grenoble *parlement*, to judge by the experiences of the maréchal de Tessé in 1707 during the War of the Spanish Succession. The French troops defeated before Turin were painfully making their way back to France, and the marshal had been appointed to the command of the armies in the south-east, by letters patent from the king, which, he was told at Versailles, had to be registered on the spot by the *parlement* of Grenoble. Arriving straight from court, no doubt he presented himself with less than the requisite humility. At all events, he was immediately subjected to all manner of hindrances and discourtesies by the président de Gramont, who accused him of seeking to assume in the assembly a position to which he was not entitled. The marshal reported all this in his letters with exasperated astonishment, but when, after an absence of three days to inspect the troops in Savoy, he learnt on his return that the *parlement*, judging his powers too extensive, had reduced them on its own authority, he simply exploded. His powers had been laid down by the king and that was that. No one else had the right to limit them, and it was from the king that he 'demanded justice'. He got it too, and the président de Gramont was obliged to apologize. But this absurd quarrel over precedence is revealing.[100]

In Bordeaux, the proud and powerful *parlement* was the centre of a fabulously rich and high-living society controlling a very ancient source of revenue: the Bordeaux vineyards. As early as 1608, Henri IV, whose plain speaking is irresistibly appealing, gave a piece of his mind to this immensely privileged clique:

> You say my people are trampled underfoot. And who pray is doing the trampling if not you and your Company? . . . Who wins lawsuits in Bordeaux if not the man with the biggest purse? . . . Where is the peasant whose vineyard does not belong to the President or a councillor [of the *parlement*]? Where is the impoverished gentleman whose land is not pledged to one of these? One has only to be a councillor to be rich without lifting a finger.[101]

In Lyon in 1558, it was a group consisting of about thirty people 'almost all merchants', whom the clergy accused of ruling the town. In Montpellier, we move a rung up the ladder of success, since the financier-merchants of the Languedoc in the reign of Louis XV went to Paris, where they more or less took over the *Ferme générale* (the government tax farm),[102] in other words a large slice of France's wealth. Quite an achievement.

Langue d'oc, langue d'oïl

Failing physical, economic and social unity, did France perhaps enjoy cultural unity? Possibly. But we already know beyond the shadow of a doubt that while there has at the highest level been a single French 'civilization' – élitist, dazzling, seeing itself as spectacle and all-enveloping environment, structure or rather superstructure, domination and constraint – there have at the same time been for centuries, within France, at least two great underlying civilizations at loggerheads, each with a linguistic realm: the northern civilization of *oïl*, eventually victorious, and the southern civilization of *oc*, fated to become on the whole a near-colony, crushed by the north and its material prosperity.

Since I am equally fond of both, doing my best to understand them and not to favour one over the other, I shall no doubt be taken for a unifying nationalist – something I try to avoid when looking retrospectively at their history.

We have a split then, a yawning divide between the north and the south of France, which lie either side of the long linguistic frontier running from La Réole on the banks of the Garonne to the Var basin, taking in a large slice of the Massif Central and the Alps. Possibly the crucial cultural frontier goes even further north than this linguistic divide, reaching roughly as far as the Loire itself, if we are prepared to lend an ear to the evidence, criteria and hypotheses suggested by certain historical geographers who have recently turned to interpreting data from place-names and dialects. Pierre Bonnaud for example, does not regard the frontier between *oïl* and *oc* as a line fixed for all time, but as a 'median' zone of Romance civilization, with shifting limits and many traces of the past, whether northward or southward – the most obvious consequence of which is to remove from the France of *oc* a large slice usually attributed to it, consisting of the Limousin, Auvergne and Dauphiné (see Figure 8).

But let us leave that question open for the moment. What can be said with confidence is that France's history took a different course north and south of this median zone. As a rule, what happened in the north did not happen in the same way in the south and vice versa. What we think of as civilization (the way people are born, live, love, marry, think, believe, laugh, eat, dress, build houses, lay out fields or behave towards each other) was practically never the same in the south (where the word for yes was *oc*) as in the north, (where it was *oïl* later *oui*).[103] There always has been and always will be 'another' France in the south.

Another France, another country, as northerners have never stopped discovering and loudly remarking, pertinently or impertinently, for their astonishment has more than once turned to bad temper (though that is entirely their loss).

We find Racine for instance – whose complaints about Uzès have already been mentioned – cursing because he cannot understand a word anyone says south of Valence. And yet goodness knows *patois* was common enough in the whole of France in his time. But we must assume that a northerner could more or less understand the dialects until he crossed the frontier to the land of *oc*. 'I swear to you', he wrote to La Fontaine,

> that I need an interpreter here as much as a Muscovite would in Paris. Yesterday, happening to need some little nails (*clous à broquette*) . . . I sent my uncle's valet to town, telling him to buy me two or three hundred *broquettes*; what did he bring me but three bundles of matches (*bottes d'allumettes*); you may imagine how one can be driven mad by such misunderstandings.

To another correspondent he wrote, 'I can't understand their French in this country and they can't understand mine'.[104]

These were two foreign worlds in the full sense of the word, as an admirer of the Camisards put it when he published in London in 1707 an 'account of divers marvels newly worked by God in the Cévennes'. He had seen the 'inspired' – simple folk and 'all without guile' – 'give fine speeches' in French 'during their revelation'. A miracle indeed, since 'it is no less difficult for a peasant from these parts to make a speech in French than it would be for a newly-landed Frenchman to speak English in England'.[105] It is a miracle we can explain though, for the Camisards read the Bible in French and sang psalms composed in French by Marot.

And what do we hear from Prosper Mérimée – a Parisian of Norman extraction, and a lucid and intelligent observer whom one is inclined to trust – when he landed in Avignon from the steam-boat bringing him down the Rhône in 1836? That he felt he was in a foreign country.[106] Not that this prevented him from returning to die at Cannes in 1870. His excuse, if one can be allowed, is that he firmly annexed Corsica, daughter of the Mediterranean, to main-stream French literature: *Colomba* was published in 1840.

Lucien Febvre, born in Nancy in 1878, but of Franche-Comté origin and affections, received a real shock – the shock of a differ-ent civilization – on taking a journey through south-west France. 'I arrived here' (in Cauterets where he was going for treatment) he wrote to me on 20 July 1938,

> taking the long way round: Limoges–Périgueux–Agen–Moissac–Auch–Lourdes. A beautiful cross-section of France. But should one call it France? How exotic and remote these places are to us northern and eastern folk! The basilica as it might be of Saint Sophia, that rears up in front of one in Périgueux; a recreation of Courbet's Jura near Eyzies; the desperate banality of Moissac which has sold its soul for a basket of grapes, and whose Eglise Saint-Pierre, with its sculptures and bell tower, looks totally deserted and disaf-fected; the extraordinary soul one guesses a town like Auch must have – a stony and warlike acropolis, obviously con-sumed by deep sectarian passions, now silent – all this is so strangely disturbing and makes you feel far, far from home.

Marshal Lyautey, a 'prince of Lorraine',[107] remarked more laconi-cally: 'I don't feel at home in Béziers'.[108]

In every generation, the surprise is renewed and lives again. In 1872 it was the turn of Ernest Renan to pull a long face. 'I may be mistaken', he dares to write with false diffidence,

> but there is a view derived from historical ethnography which seems more and more convincing to my mind. The similarity between England and northern France appears

increasingly clear to me every day. Our foolishness comes from the south, and if France had not drawn Languedoc and Provence into her sphere of activity, we should be a serious, active, Protestant and parliamentary people.[109]

What a list of lost virtues – and of shaky hypotheses too when one recollects that it was Paris (which is not in the south) and Brittany (ditto) that saved the Catholic cause in the sixteenth century. Whereas Nîmes and the Cévennes . . . For all Renan's intelligence, indeed because of his intelligence, this is a distasteful not to say distressing text.

But then northerners are often quite shameless in claiming the better part, attributing to themselves merits they may or may not possess, and which in any case they owe less to their own virtue than to the political and economic superiority that history, and history more or less unaided, has conferred on northern France.

By way of compensation, can we summon some more generous witnesses for the defence? One thinks of Stendhal claiming joyfully: 'I have turned myself into a man of the Midi and it was not so difficult after all'.[110] But, you may object, Stendhal was born (in 1783) in Grenoble so he was already at least halfway there by birth. Grenoble is not really the north. And then Stendhal was after all Stendhal, desperately in love with that other dazzling southern horizon, Italy: does the south of France not have 'striking connections with Italy'?[111] May we perhaps call Van Gogh then as a witness? Yes and no. In February 1888, after two difficult and unhappy years in Paris, this authentic northerner arrived in Arles. He was at once dazzled by the nature and colours of the south: 'immense rocks; a green park with pink pathways, a sky of sheer cobalt'. 'I don't doubt that I shall always love nature here', he wrote to his brother. 'So far, loneliness has not greatly troubled me, so fascinating do I find the stronger sunlight here and its effect on nature . . . Ah, those who do not believe in the southern sun are unbelievers indeed'. Even 'the accursed *mistral*' though unbearable, is fine 'to see'. But as for the people, the local inhabitants,

It is an enormous disadvantage not to speak the southern patois. So far I have not made a centimetre's progress into the hearts of the people . . . A great many days go by therefore without my speaking a word to a soul, except to order my dinner or a coffee. And it has been like this from the start.

We should not read this simply as a warning sign of the madness that was to overtake him, but as evidence of genuine disorientation:

Shall I tell the truth? [he wrote in March 1888, shortly after his arrival] and add that the zouaves, the brothels, the adorable little Arlésiennes making their first communion, the priest in his cassock who looks like a dangerous rhinoceros, the absinthe drinkers, all seem to me like . . . beings from another world.[112]

One would like in fairness, to be able to counter the disillusions, diatribes, and unjust reproaches of the 'northerners' with some criticisms, witticisms or irony from the south. But in this respect it must be admitted that, although I have consulted several connoisseurs of the Occitanian languages, the harvest is rather meagre: the odd joke in an Occitan play, an occasional proverb or jeer. Nothing very biting. I could find no equivalent of the colourful reports by those sixteenth-century Spaniards, miserably enduring exile in England or the Netherlands, but confident of their own superiority, roundly cursing the northern food fried in butter, emptying their bladders of northern beer with horror and ill temper[113] and sometimes boycotting the local residents, like one ambassador of the Spanish king in London whose disgust was such that he never set foot out of doors. 'Non si accomoda niente alli costumi della nacione', the Genoese representative reported of him in 1673, 'vive sempre retirato, non ama conversazione'.[114] (He has not adapted to any of the English customs, lives like a recluse and does not like conversation). But then Spain is a special kind of south, and London a north more confirmed in its originality than any other north.

Did the French Midi simply become accustomed to all this

extravagant language, resigned and indifferent? That would be going rather far, since Occitanian culture has been reviving in recent years and putting out new shoots. Or have southerners perhaps stopped bothering to argue, secure in the fortunes (of more than recent date) which they have made in the north, in careers in academic life, politics, administration and business – secure that is in their success and social promotion? More likely, the prestige of the north, essentially identified with that of Paris, has been felt in the south and tends to influence the dialogue. When in 1842, Mary-Lafon, a forerunner of the defenders of Occitania, published his *Histoire politique, religieuse et littéraire du Midi de la France* he did not mock 'the French', that is the men from the north of the Loire, but he did contrast the southerners of the Middle Ages, refined and freedom-loving, with the 'brute barbarism' of the 'knights from across the Loire'[115] – violent, fanatical and pillaging – but victorious, much as the Terror of the Montagnards later triumphed over the Girondins, 'the true revolutionaries' who were in many ways men of the Midi. Mary-Lafon condemns and accuses. But it is not so easy to laugh at one's conqueror. Did the Midi perhaps not rather feel towards the 'French', the 'Franciaux', as they were called in Toulon, the resentment one feels towards an occupying foreign power?

It takes a Stendhal to be ironic about the gloomy France of the north – pompous, ceremonious and stuck up. 'Happiness seems to disappear when one loses the southern accent', he remarked, cheering up again as he travelled down the Rhône:

Good nature, unaffectedness . . . break out in Valence. Now we are really in the Midi . . . I have never been able to resist this joyful impression. It is the very opposite of the politeness of Paris whose function is above all to remind you of the respect for himself felt by the person speaking to you and which he expects from you in return.

Here on the contrary, every man when he speaks, 'thinks only of satisfying the feeling which moves him', and not at all 'of building up a noble picture of himself in the mind of the person listening, still less of paying the requisite respects to the social position of that person. Monsieur de Talleyrand if he were here would certainly say "Nothing is respected in France any more"!'

Continuing his travels, Stendhal spent three days at the Beaucaire fair, amusing himself by mingling with the festive crowds. 'What is rarely found in Beaucaire', he notes 'is the *haughty manner* that is de rigueur in Paris . . . I find here very few of those sour, gloomy and suspicious countenances [so frequent] . . . in the streets of Lyon or Geneva. One reason for this short supply of *sourness and gloom* is that in Beaucaire the huge crowds mainly consist of people from the Midi.'[116]

And the old differences have not been wiped out even today. Only a few years ago, the mayor of Armissan, a little town in the Languedoc, said to a historian friend of mine: 'Monsieur Laugénie, you must remember that the day you came through the Naurouze gap, you left France, you are now in the land of *oc*, not in France any more'. Of course today everyone speaks French, from the north of the country to the south. But I have just heard a rather striking remark on television (31 July 1985). Michel Audiard, the scriptwriter, was protesting that he had never used *argot* (slang) in his film scripts, simply the ordinary everyday language of Paris, 'le parigot'. His interviewer reminded him that someone had once said of his films that 'they needed subtitles for audiences south of the Loire!' Is there still such a distance between the popular language of the north and that of the south?

Local dialects: the thousand and one patois of the eighteenth century

The north–south divide is not everything of course; for large cultural units only imperfectly conceal their many internal differences. If one looks at all closely, the superabundance of local particularities is obvious, indeed breathtaking. For all our awareness that customs, folklore, costume, proverbs and even patterns of inheritance (despite the letter of the law) can indeed ring all the changes over a quite short distance, it still takes one's breath away to read the replies collected in 1790 by the Abbé Grégoire to his survey on the many provincial patois or dialects – rightly considered, by Barrère in particular, to be an obstacle to the spread of revolutionary propaganda and 'public spirit'. The survey proves, with a wealth of concrete examples, that France did not only have the languages of *oc* and *oïl* (not to mention the more or less foreign languages on the outer periphery of the kingdom: Basque, Breton, Flemish dialects in the north, German in the east) but that there were also, north and south of the Loire, whole families of provincial patois, themselves subdivided almost to infinity. When he summarized the information he had collected in his report to the Convention, Grégoire listed 30 different patois in France.[117] And within each of these, from one town or village to another, the patois could vary more or less according to locality. In the face of such variety, the *directoire* of the *département* of Corrèze on 1 December 1792 expressed doubts of the usefulness of translating political texts into patois: 'The translator, who happened to come from the canton of Juillac, did not speak with the same accent as the other cantons which all vary slightly; the difference becomes marked at a distance of seven or eight leagues'.[118] More readily understandable therefore is the self-satisfied letter that Pierre Bernadau, a former counsel at the *parlement* of Bordeaux, wrote to Grégoire; 'The knowledge I have of the country districts nearby has inspired me with the idea of translating into a language *midway between* all the different jargons of the people who live there, the revered Declaration of the Rights of Man'. He had come up with an early version of Esperanto.[119]

To take a few precise examples, Gascon (spoken in Gascony and Guyenne) was quite distinct from Languedocien and Provençal. But Gascon was itself divided by the Garonne river: on either side of it, 'two completely different patois' were spoken.[120] Every little district too had its own version: a traveller from Auch to Toulouse or Montauban would find difficulty in communicating. Within the district of Bordeaux, reported someone who knew it well, 'there are [broadly] only two kinds of dialect'. And that is not to mention differences 'of detail'! In the Landes, these were such that 'people often find it hard to understand what someone from the next parish is saying'.[121]

Were things different in the north? The Burgundy patois, a particular family of dialects, changes as one goes from Dijon to Beaune, to Chalon, to the Bresse or the Morvan. In the Mâconnais, 'the patois varies from village to village, in accent, pronunciation and final consonants'.[122] Around Salins, the language spoken in each village 'varies to the point of being unrecognizable', and 'what is more extraordinary', the town itself, 'being almost half a league in length, is divided by language and even customs, into two distinct halves'.[123] Nor should we imagine that Breton, which reigned both in town and country, was a kind of uniform national language. There was the Breton spoken in Tréguier and the Breton spoken in Léon – and the existing written grammars refer to the former rather than to the latter. Above all, there were such differences in pronunciation 'over twenty leagues, that [a native has to] do a little studying if he wants to understand the Breton spoken at this distance from his own *pays*'.[124]

To pursue further this linguistic voyage across the France of the past would be pointless and repetitive. Of one thing we can be sure: the French language did not carry all before it. As the eighteenth-century *Encyclopédie* definition has it, 'Patois: corrupt language as it is spoken in almost all the provinces. The language is spoken only in the capital'.[125] Secondly, local variants were legion. Did La Chétardie[126] not say in 1708, a propos of religious education: 'We need almost as many catechisms as there are parishes and schools'?[127] There was, nevertheless, one very important difference north and south of the Loire: in the north, apart from Brittany, Flanders and the east, everyone at least *understood* French, without necessarily being able to speak it: public notices, sermons by local priests, schools (however rudimentary they might be) all used the French language. Patois was certainly the everyday language of the countryside, and of the ordinary people in the towns as well. But it was in northern France that the patois died out quickest (see Figure 6). Virtually everywhere in the south by contrast, the local dialect was uppermost. It was spoken in the countryside but also in the towns, by people of all social conditions – 'even the learned and the rich', as a correspondent in the Aveyron put it.[128] And while the *grands bourgeois* and cultivated people could also

speak French, the great mass of the people could not even understand it. In Gascony, 'customary law is almost all in dog-Latin, as
are public notices', wrote an anonymous correspondent from
Auch.[129]

Was this not the logical thing to do, if French could not serve as
a *lingua franca* and if according to the same correspondent, on leaving Auch for Montauban, 'it is easy neither to understand nor to be
understood'?[130] The language barrier could be comically impenetrable. Abbé Albert, a native of the southern Alps, describes an
encounter:

> Journeying a few years ago in the Limagne of Auvergne, I
> was never able to make myself understood by the peasants I
> met on the road. I spoke to them in French, I spoke to them in
> my native patois, I even tried to speak to them in Latin, but
> all to no avail. When at last I was tired of talking to them
> without their understanding a word, they in their turn spoke
> to me in a language of which I could make no more sense.[131]

So we should not be surprised at the indignant protests that came
from parishioners in Arles or Tarascon when, in the fifteenth century, they found a priest from Brittany or Châlons-sur-Marne
wished upon them. They could not understand a word of his
Sunday sermons![132]

All the same, population shifts more than once encouraged the
spread of French-speaking. To stay with the fifteenth century,
northern immigrants were by then becoming more and more
numerous in Arles, where of course they could not understand the
local way of speech. It was thanks to them that French-speaking
spread among both the elite and the lower classes of the town. 'So it
is no accident that Arles was already, in 1503, well before the edict
of Villers-Cotterets (1539), the first place in Provence where the
minutes of the town council were kept in French'.[133]

Such intermingling of populations certainly explains why by the
end of the eighteenth century so many French expressions had
entered and transformed the various patois. On this point, all Abbé
Grégoire's correspondents report the same thing from every corner of France. Indeed in the towns, encouraged by trade, it was

becoming fashionable to speak French. In Bordeaux, where once the wealthy merchants had spoken Gascon, 'now [patois] is found only in the mouths of fishwives, market porters and chambermaids'. Even artisans spoke French.[134]

Most of Grégoire's correspondents thought that this slowly-accomplished transformation had begun about fifty years earlier, others dated it from barely thirty years before. All of them related it to the spread of trade and to the major road-building which completely transformed communications, at least between towns and cities. But what were even these road works, the pride and joy of eighteenth-century engineers of the *Ponts et Chaussées*, alongside the enterprises of the following century? And more important than the roads or even the railways, primary schooling, as it became widespread, ensured the progress of the French language. The 'Frenchification' of country districts was not achieved overnight even then. 'Our peasants of the *langue d'oc*', writes Pierre Bonnaud, 'had only a modest smattering of French until about 1850'.[135] And if in 1878, Robert Louis Stevenson on his *Travels with a Donkey in the Cévennes*, had no difficulty talking with the people he met, it does not mean that patois had died out. In August that year, he found himself at Monastier, a large bourg about 40 kilometres from Le Puy. Some lacemakers whom he met asked the foreign visitor about his own country:

'Do they speak patois in England?' I was once asked, and when I told them not, 'Ah then French?', said they. ['No no,' I said, 'not French'.] 'Then', they concluded, 'they speak patois'.[136]

In some regions, French took even longer to be adopted. In 1902, in spite of instructions from Paris, many Breton parish priests refused to preach in the national language. Catalan is still alive and well in the Roussillon: all native inhabitants understand it if they do not all speak it. And in 1983, in an interview with Jean Laugénie, André Castera the former leader of the winegrowers' action committee, dated the disappearance of the language of the Languedoc from the late 1950s. It was not the influence of the primary school, now long established, that he blamed for this break

FIGURE 7
The slow decline of local dialects

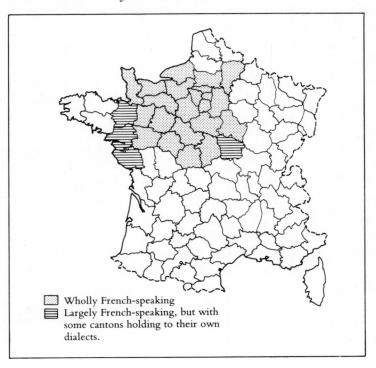

Wholly French-speaking
Largely French-speaking, but with
some cantons holding to their own
dialects.

with the past: television and the media were certainly responsible, but there was also a newfound popular desire to acquire what had once been a distinctive sign of town-dwellers and the bourgeoisie, a form of social promotion.

Dialectology and toponymy: aids to prehistoric geography

Patois, or as one ought perhaps to say local dialects and ways of speech, do not tell us only about eighteenth- or nineteenth-century France. Dialectology and toponymy (the study of place-names),

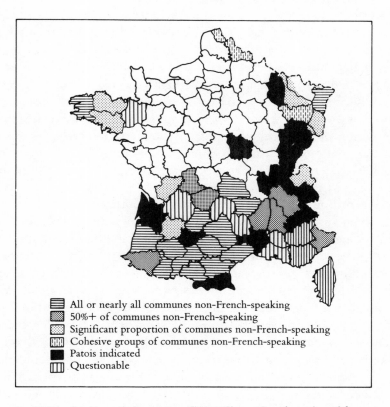

All or nearly all communes non-French-speaking
50%+ of communes non-French-speaking
Significant proportion of communes non-French-speaking
Cohesive groups of communes non-French-speaking
Patois indicated
Questionable

In 1835, the French language was still confined to the old
'France of *oïl*.' In 1863, according to an official survey by the
Ministère de l'Instruction publique, local dialects still
predominated in much of the country.
Left: French-speaking *départements* in 1835. Source: Abel
Hugo, *La France pittoresque* (1835), I, p. 16.
Right: Patois-speaking communes, 1863. Source: Archives
Nationales F[17] 3160, Ministère de l'Instruction publique,
'Statistique: Etats divers'.

Maps from Eugen Weber, *Peasants into Frenchmen* (1976),
p. 68.

nowadays active branches of linguistics, offer a prodigious fund of information about the distant past of our country, which neither traditional geography nor the 'new history' have yet explored. The young geographer Pierre Bonnaud deserves attention for making the first serious attempt to incorporate this wealth of evidence into the explanatory framework of history and geography.

For dialects (or what is left of them) and place-names (altered perhaps, but their alterations can be detected and used as evidence too) are so many chronological landmarks: difficult to interpret certainly, and to fit together properly, but able nevertheless to illuminate many other things besides the spread of French-speaking, which is after all a recent reality. They can send beams of light into the darkest corners of our past.

Pierre Bonnaud's method is really something of a tour de force, a patient interweaving of other contributory disciplines. It starts from clues scattered over time, distinguishing one from another: this place-name is older than that, the limits of this dialect are located in such and such an area on the edge of a particular region. But these numerous pieces of evidence do not fit neatly and automatically into any single scale. Specialists in dendrochronology – the science of reading tree-trunk rings – proceed in much the same manner, since they too have precise data about locality, but a sequence of dates which are *relative* not absolute. Their problem is to fit them into the chronology of history, and in particular into prehistory. After this, in the light of the results achieved, the researcher is inevitably led to modify in some degree the previously accepted image of the past. Similarly, Pierre Bonnaud's painstaking research seeks to discover, by means of many linguistic clues, the ethnic groups, those very ancient 'basic cells' which, from the very earliest inhabitation of the earth, each placed an indelible mark on a 'territorial unit' of greater or smaller dimensions, both as regards its landscape and its deepest cultural realities. Whatever upheavals they may afterwards have experienced, 'their nucleus emerges after every storm'. Here lies the key to the enduring diversities of our country, diversities still recognizable even if eroded or smoothed over by the arch-enemy – the French state, which from its commanding stronghold in the Paris basin, and by means of a national language, has pursued its work of gradual absorption and imposition of uniformity.[137]

Pierre Bonnaud's research thus throws all our assumptions into question, subjecting human geography to a sort of X-ray. First and foremost, it reveals a rural past, inscribed into the very earth itself. We are centuries and centuries, millennia even, removed from the present day, and listening fascinated to the age-old dialogue between man and his environment. We are obliged, in order to make good use of it, to weigh up the dialectic between habitat and landscape. For there is a whole sequence of repeated determinisms at work here, since the existing social and economic structures vary constantly as they meet either the recalcitrance or the cooperation of the environment. It is now possible to trace to previously unsounded depths that first 'occupation of space' accomplished by the efforts of human groups, by their determination, their settlement and acquisition of roots, after centuries of nomadic life.

But it would be wrong to talk as if this occupation of space by humans was accomplished once for all time, however long ago. Even when attached to the soil, *homo stabilis* does not automatically turn into *homo immobilis*. He is constantly pitted against the physical environment, either adapting or failing to adapt to its natural demands and the necessities of production.

It seems probable then that until the Carolingian period, and the last 'great invasions', a large proportion of the peoples living in what is now France, were still at least partly nomadic; that the cereal field, something brought to us by the prehistoric peoples of central Europe, was only just becoming established in those places where it would later triumph; that whole areas were still given over entirely to more or less nomadic flocks, with transhumance between plains and mountains the dominant pattern.

In other words, the diversity of France, the 'mosaic' of landscapes changed and re-shaped itself, over a period marked by little mobility, it is true, but enough to alter the picture. 'The present pattern of settlement', our guide informs us, 'is nowhere original'.[138] And the distant past forces upon us a series of different Frances. This is as true of those basic cells we call *pays* as it is of the regions, agglomerations of *pays* variously reassembled, and tending

FIGURE 8
The 'southern medio-romanesque zone'

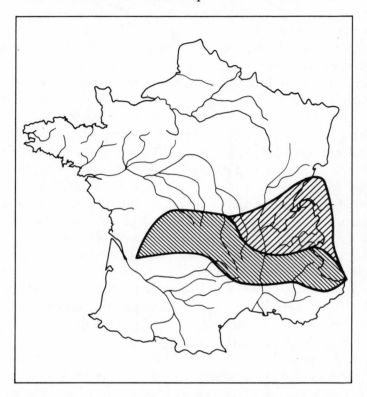

The dark grey zone is what P. Bonnaud distinguishes from the 'land of *oc* proper', as a 'southern medio-romanesque zone' Limousin, Auvergne and Dauphiné. Its northern limit coincides with the usual dividing line between *oc* and the *oïl*; the light grey zone is that of 'Provençal' French.

---

to fragment at the edges of more or less solid units. In the heart of central France, the Limousin and particularly the Auvergne dear to the author's heart, emerge from Pierre Bonnaud's book with rather changed faces. Together they now appear to form a new 'median' France, running as I have already suggested, from west to east –

FIGURE 9
The 'limes' running through central Gaul in about 400

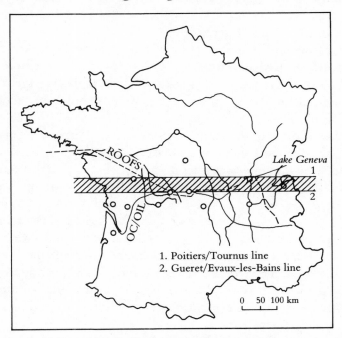

1. Poitiers/Tournus line
2. Gueret/Evaux-les-Bains line

0   50 100 km

Map by Robert Sprecklin in *Acta geografica*, 1982.
Using place names, historical and archaeological sources and
aerial photography, Robert Sprecklin has mapped a fortified
limes about 50 kilometres wide, cutting across the middle of
Gaul. Possibly created by the Ligurians of prehistoric times
against Celtic invasion, then fortified by the Romans against
the barbarian invasions of the fourth century, it later became,
in about the sixth or seventh century, a Frankish march.

neither entirely the France of the *langue d'oc* (in contradiction to
what is usually said) yet standing against the all-conquering France
of the *langue d'oïl* to the north. I should like to know what Bonnaud
thinks of the sort of marcher zone, as it were a fortified *limes*, which
Robert Specklin[139] has curiously located between the north and the

Midi, suggesting that in the Roman and pre-Roman period it cut transversally across the country from the Gulf of Poitou to Lake Geneva, north of the Auvergne which it thus isolated to some extent from the northern territories.

Pierre Bonnaud does not of course stop at this telling example, but proposes similar alterations to our picture of the whole of France. So I shall have further occasion to include in the pages that follow some of the stimulating, intelligent and fresh perspectives from his fine book.

Its author returns to the major explanation he borrows from the prehistorians, namely that prehistoric 'France' was subject to a double movement, one wave from central Europe and another from the Mediterranean. The first spread because of the early superiority of a cereal-growing economy, which can be described as advanced, and which originated in the east: in Bonnaud's scheme, the 'peasant continent' par excellence in the mesolithic era was central Europe, from which new techniques and new men reached the west. The Mediterranean wave, an earlier phenomenon, moved northwards into the empty spaces it found, bringing a way of life based on sheep farming, combined with gathering plants and temporary crops.

So the two Frances we still know today – the north and the south – already existed long before the dawn of history. So too did the former 'basic cells' which Pierre Bonnaud has carefully circumscribed and mapped. According to François Sigaut, INSEE [the French Statistical Institute] estimates that there are

473 'agricultural regions' in the present-day territory of France. [Were there not more than this in the past?] . . . From the Bourbonnais to the Roussillon, from the Aunis to the Bauges, the number of farming systems in the France of the past can never have been fewer than about a hundred. [Please note this statement, to which I shall be returning] . . . Therefore until we have discovered the methods, concepts and scientific means . . . enabling us to apprehend this diversity . . . our generalizations will remain worthless.[140]

We are in other words faced with the same task as the kings of France, as they battled against all the odds to conceptualize and construct the unity of the kingdom.

Cultural anthropology: or family structure versus French unity

Consequently, we shall not easily be able to leave off discussing French diversity, and more particularly that diversity of cultural origin which makes the French landscape so variegated a patchwork. How could France exist with such internal divisions?

In this search for distant cultural origins, anthropology has recently been able to offer much assistance. Not the old-style physical anthropology, measuring skulls and classifying 'races', but the cultural anthropology which has more recently roused the enthusiasm of young (and even not so young) historians.

The key discovery is the family. No doubt, as Jean-Louis Flandrin has rightly observed, it is probably the transformation threatening family life in our own time that has prompted such interest in researching the family, the basic cell that is the *mater dolorosa* of every society.[141] Everything after all starts with the family, and almost everything can be explained by it. What would become of the order in a hive of obedient bees if all the workers decided to marry and have children? As historians, we had already realized this, before the anthropologists and even before the psychoanalysts. But today, thanks to them, we are more aware of it than we were. As a result, we are captivated, if not always convinced, by surveys which start from present-day statistics and maps, and set out to carry us dizzily back into the past.

To understand this approach as practised by Hervé Le Bras and Emmanuel Todd in their book *L'Invention de la France*, a few rules must be explained and these in turn require a few preliminary remarks.

Western families can still be divided, even today, into three categories: the nuclear family, consisting of father, mother and unmarried children, the family reduced to its nucleus so to speak; and two kinds of extended family. The vertically extended family, or *stem-family*, includes several generations – parents, children, grand-children. This is the authoritarian family, under the rule of the paterfamilias, where marriage is strictly controlled and post-poned, with only one child in each generation, the heir, being able to marry, and the others remaining unmarried or seeking their fortune elsewhere. The second type is the *patriarchal* or *community family*: extended this time horizontally, it brings together the patri-arch and all his children, married or unmarried. It contains several conjugal units which join the group as and when they are created, and are tied to it by siblinghood. This type sometimes extends to 'give rise to whole clans or local communities'. The most signifi-cant distinction between these two types of extended family is the average age of marriage: in the first type, it is later, with high rates of celibacy, while in the second, marriage is early and unrestricted, and celibacy rates are low. Thus marriage, 'the dynamic element that reproduces the family system, the basic social event . . . , holds approximately the same place in anthropology as does the class struggle in Marxist theory'[142] – a remark intended by its authors to bring a smile.

These three types of family structure divide Europe into fairly clearly delineated zones: the nuclear family covers the whole of Britain; the stem-family has predominated in the German world, and the patriarchal family in Italy; only France has contained all three at once. Yet again, France is a meeting-place and an epitome of Europe. And in this case something that is a national characteris-tic for her neighbours has become a source of provincial contrasts in France: very broadly speaking, extended families are found in the south and nuclear families in the north, except in peripheral zones like Brittany, Alsace and Flanders (see Figure 10). The extended southern family is usually of the community type, and the extended family in Alsace and Brittany of the authoritarian model.

The interesting thing is that these family types are, and have long been, located in the same geographical areas. They are com-paratively fixed over time, and anthropology here comes up against certain permanent features, 'rigidities', in short the *longue durée* of cultural reality. This does not of course prevent the fringes of these relatively stable zones from becoming in many cases fertile

FIGURE 10
The 45 départements *with the highest percentage of extended families in 1975*

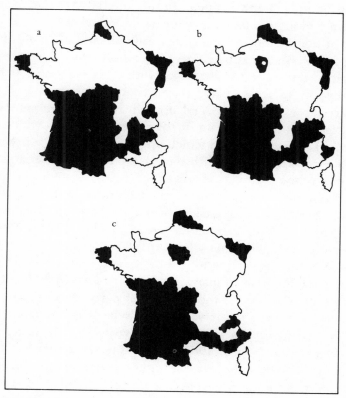

a) farmers
b) rural households
c) urban households

The division, still visible today, between the extended family zone and the nuclear family zone corresponds in general terms to a series of other contrasts identifiable throughout French history: language, literacy, living standards, forms of property ownership and urbanization, and religious and political attitudes.

Map from H. Le Bras and E. Todd, *L'Invention de la France*, 1981.

ground for the structural collapse brought about by accelerating urbanization, or by industrial civilization, which has enormous potential for penetrating and destroying traditional society. When such structural collapse happens, the affected societies on the edges of cultural blocks become the scene of individual despair and alienation, of depression, mental illness, suicide and alcoholism. The longing for security explains why the Catholic church, in its efforts at spiritual reconquest in the nineteenth century, found such fervent support in areas characterized by the authoritarian family, 'that producer of celibates'; and also why, this time among areas of the extended community family, the communist party, which is not 'a party like the others' and which offers a high degree of security, was able to take in hand a disoriented population.[143] What is truly astonishing however is that where the family system has broken down or at any rate been modified, the attitudes that go with it, religious or political, have taken over and prolonged the obstinate undergrowth of long-standing differences. Old splits and contrasts are revived and given a new lease of life.

For it is the fascinating aspect of these family structure zones that they are the basis of many correlations. I have just mentioned the Catholic church and the communist party, each of which has flourished where a particular family type predominated. Even more surprising are the correlations revealed by election results, whether in 1974, 1978 or 1981. In general, the community family zone is favourable to the left; the authoritiarian family zone to the right, and the nuclear families, 'the unstable families' as Frédéric Le Play insisted on calling them, are notoriously shifting ground: they vote first one way then another.[144]

The electoral test is not of course the only one that reveals the frontiers of the 'family zones'. Every reference to the map enables their presence to be sensed, although their influence varies depending on whether one is looking at relations between the sexes, migration trends, attitudes towards the elderly and infirm, number of children, religious observance, prostitution – or indeed crop rotation, inheritance patterns, the spread of architectural forms, witchcraft after the late sixteenth century, or differences in literacy. They provide the geology beneath history, the very diverse infrastructure on which it has been shaped, one that makes it possible for the underlying structures to be detected by the attentive observer. What historian could fail to be astonished to find that in the north, in the wealthy Paris basin and in the Limousin or Poitou, village organization was barely existent, being reduced generally to its most simple expression, while it was more pronounced further south in Dauphiné and Auvergne, and positively flourished in Guyenne, Gascony, Languedoc and Provence?[145]

It is proof once more that France is divided because the past has so decided – a slap in the face for the short-term historical perspective. Hervé Le Bras and Emmanuel Todd have expressed their surprise, wonder and indeed amusement at this. They claim that the division goes back at least to AD 500, to the days of Clovis, and the establishment, following the barbarian invasions, of several ethnic zones. Are they right?[146]

Cultural anthropology can only be of assistance to historians if, starting from the present day, it is able to produce documentary evidence going back through the centuries. I can imagine research of this kind providing a series of re-readings of history. Take the Paris basin for instance. On today's map, it is on the whole a stronghold of the nuclear family. And we duly find the nuclear family clearly identified around Meaux, the very heart of the region, in the sixteenth, seventeenth and eighteenth centuries, by the research of Micheline Baulant, who even speaks of the countryside around the town as having 'fragmented families', (*des familles en miettes*,[147] the title of Georges Friedmann's successful book, *Le Travail en miettes*). And the fragility of this family type, its 'unstable' nature clearly emerges in a society where there was no form of social protection. If a family was broken up by the death of one of the spouses, it meant immediate isolation, desolation, economic collapse and disaster, making life impossible. Micheline Baulant points out that hasty remarriage after the death of a partner was frequent, as if both men and women looked to this as their necessary rescue. 'Nicole Picard had her eighth, ninth and tenth children respectively in June 1739, August 1741 and May 1744; [within this space of time] she had managed to be twice widowed and twice remarried'.[148]

Going even further down the ages, we may imagine a continuity running perhaps as far back as the Middle Ages, something which would challenge the accepted view that the nuclear family is the result of the modern development of economy and society. The case of England is persuasive since Peter Laslett claimed over ten years ago that the nuclear family may have been the norm there as early as the sixteenth century;[149] and Alan MacFarlane has more recently claimed that the extended family was uncommon in England in the Middle Ages. The nuclear family may thus have been entrenched for centuries across the Channel.[150]

If it could be proved that the same was true of the area around Paris in those far-off days, the eleventh and twelfth centuries, we should better be able to understand the early expansion of the feudal system between the Loire, Seine and Somme. An expanding feudalism would have been able to take advantage of the lesser resistance offered by a family type already fragmented and undoubtedly more malleable. Feudalism's origins would not be explained entirely by the repeated and almost exclusive use of land as currency and reward for services: we would have an explanation not only in terms of land, but also of people, customs and cultures.

South of the Loire by contrast, the extended family (whatever its form or the reason for its extension) may have stood firm and, with the strength born of solidarity, resisted the rise of 'feudalism', hindering its progress by safeguarding individual properties (the *alleux*) and defending local freedoms, both those of the towns and of the village communities. Here too a difference emerges between what happened north and south of the Loire: a difference with far-reaching consequences since the nuclear family, 'unstable' and renewed with every generation, is by nature less rooted in tradition, more open to change and 'modernization'. The north therefore changed earlier; by the same token, it stood up less well to a trial of strength in which the state was soon the opposite party. For there was constant rivalry between family and state.[151] Seen from this perspective, should one regard the fragmenting of the family in England as a consequence of the violent impact of the Norman conquest after 1066?

Such suggestions, classing the nuclear family as fragile and open to outside forces, are no more than hypotheses, although they seem to be backed by some convincing evidence. But the American sociologist, Richard Sennett, has after all argued the opposite: that the nuclear family was a powerful obstacle to social mobility.[152] And Georges Duby thinks that 'it was the development of capitalism that broke up the traditional family, precisely so as to free people for labour'[153] – which would suggest that it was a late development. Clearly on this subject we shall not be able to draw any very certain conclusions until some survey evidence is forthcoming from customary regulations and the inexhaustible legal archives. When a bourgeois of Reims notes in his diary in 1632, 'Grandfather wants this marriage for me. I have replied "it's not my grandfather who is getting married, it's me" '[154] – should we think that this is a language new for the time, the 'modern' attitude of a man of the seventeenth century? Or is it simply that of a man who, having been born in Champagne, enjoyed a certain traditional independence within the family?

The fact remains that such anthropological research, though hardly yet begun, already points to the great impact the past has on the present, facing one at every turn. I can well understand Hervé Le Bras and Emmanuel Todd who, reviewing the spectacle of these powerful age-old divisions within France, concluded that 'by rights, France should not exist', that from such a heterogeneous collection of peoples and civilization, France had somehow to be 'invented'.[155] And indeed France did have to overcome obstacles and divisions, dragging along with her a mass of stagnant, contradictory and weighty histories, as heavy as the earth.

CHAPTER THREE

Distance: a variable measurement

Until now I have been considering distance as an invariable. But of course it does vary, the true measure of distance being the speed at which people can travel. In the past, they moved so slowly that distance imprisoned and isolated them. The France of the 'hexagon', a unit of only modest dimensions by today's standards, was still in those days an immense expanse, a seemingly endless succession of roads and obstacles.

In his *Panegyric of Trajan*, Pliny the Younger talks of Gaul as 'almost limitless'.[156] So it still was in the days of Louis XI: the province of Burgundy alone in the time of Charles the Bold, whichever way one crossed it, was ten or twelve times the equivalent of the whole of France in the 1980s.

Small wonder then that the so-called Hundred Years' War never at any time covered the whole of the territory; neither did the Wars of Religion (1562–1598) although they lasted over a third of a century. Distance alone could be barrier, defence, protection and prohibition, as the emperor Charles V found to his cost. Twice he was thwarted by this nameless enemy: in July 1536 when he invaded Provence only to collapse outside Marseille, his army exhausted after a series of lengthy marches and missed rendez-vous.[157] The second time was in 1544: having opened up the route along the Marne by capturing with ease the little fortress of Saint-Dizier,[158] and then following the narrow river valley as far as Meaux (whose arms stores he looted) he again ran out of strength and was only too happy to patch up the peace of Crépy-en-Laonnois.[159] History repeated itself with his son Philip II: after his terrifying victory over the French constable Montmorency at Saint-Quentin on 10 August 1557,[160] the way to Paris lay open before him. The old emperor, in retirement at Yuste in Spain,

FIGURE 11

The Wars of Religion in France: localized rather than countrywide

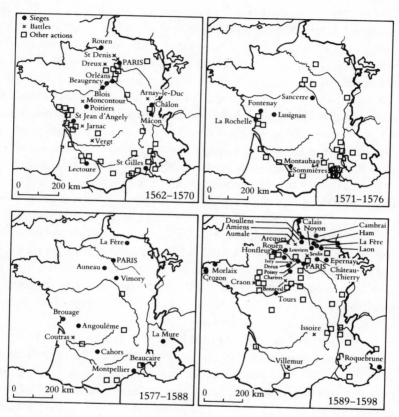

- ● Sieges
- × Battles
- □ Other actions

Rouen
St Denis ×
Dreux × ● PARIS □
Orléans
Beaugency ●
Blois □ Arnay-le-Duc
× Moncontour × Châlon
● Poitiers
St Jean d'Angely Mâcon
× Jarnac
□
× Vergt
□
St Gilles
Lectoure ●

0 ── 200 km ──
1562–1570

Sancerre ●
Fontenay
● Lusignan
La Rochelle ●
Montauban
Sommières

0 ── 200 km ──
1571–1576

La Fère ●
● PARIS
Auneau ●
● Vimory
Brouage ●
● Angoulême
Coutras ×
● Cahors
La Mure ●
Beaucaire
Montpellier ●

0 ── 200 km ──
1577–1588

Doullens ── Calais
Amiens ── Noyon ── Cambrai
Aumale ── Ham
Arques × ── La Fère
Honfleur ── Rouen ── Louviers × Senlis ── Laon
Morlaix ── Ivry × Dreux ── PARIS ── Epernay
Crozon ── Poissy ── Château-Thierry
Craon × Chartres
Bonneval
Tours □
Issoire
×
Villemur × ── Roquebrune

0 ── 200 km ──
1589–1598

These maps show only 'major engagements', based on the account by Henri Mariéjol in Lavisse's *Histoire de France*, and thus give what is obviously a simplified picture. It is clear enough, however, that these engagements were not all simultaneous, and that events were localized rather than affecting the entire national territory. Even the final phase, in Henri IV's time, was chiefly confined to the north of the country.

Reproduced from F. Braudel, *The Perspective of the World*, Fig. 33.

anxiously wondered whether his son was about to march on the French capital: surely he knew that it was virtually impossible? The victorious army in fact went hardly beyond the field of battle.

The logic of distance had scarcely altered two and a half centuries later: Napoleon's impressive French campaign of 1814, using young troops, would have been unthinkable if distance had not still been an obstacle. While the allied armies were advancing slowly along the valleys that converged on Paris, Napoleon used the breathing space to make a series of forced marches from the Aisne to the Marne and Aube valleys; moving more quickly than his opponents, his mastery of distance enabled him to surprise and disconcert the enemy and to survive – until the massed weight of the allies forced him back towards Paris. Talleyrand had foreseen the weakness of these tactics. In reply to the marquise de la Tour du Pin's questions, he replied: ' "Oh don't talk to me about your emperor. He is a finished man." "What do you mean finished?" I said. "I mean", he replied, "that he is a man who will soon be hiding under his bed!" I put a thousand questions to him, to which his only reply was: "He has lost all his matériel. He has reached the end of the road. That is all there is to say".'[161] The matériel in question had consisted of one cannon, a few caissons, some ammunition, one carriage – and men.

In 1870, the Prussian army used the railway, which was a great innovation. Even so, looking back on the drama of France's defeat in that war, Marshal Foch, who had taken part in it as a young officer, still insisted that if he had been in command, he would have chosen to go on fighting, falling back if necessary as far as the Pyrenees, using the territory of France to its utmost limits. Even in 1914, the enemy advance was carried out at the pace of the foot-soldier, which is why the long French retreat to the Marne was possible. In May and June 1940 by contrast, a motorized army overwhelmed our country in a few weeks.

France in the past then appears as a territory so vast as to be difficult to cross, difficult to supervise and difficult to control. Great events tell us so, but perhaps even more eloquent are the everyday happenings, the run-of-the-mill incidents of ordinary life. I might tell for instance the story of the desperate flight of the connétable de Bourbon, pursued by agents of the king in 1523: he managed against the odds to disappear into thin air, after crossing the Rhône – a major barrier and closely patrolled if ever one was. Another incident, though less dramatic, seems to me even more revealing: an escapade by the duc d'Epernon in 1619. An intriguer and desperado since his stormy youth, when he had been one of the favourites of Henri III, the duke, now older (he was born in 1554) but no wiser, held the post of governor of Metz. The king had placed a ban on his leaving the town. But what was one more act of rebellion to such a man? On 22 January 1619, he set out before daybreak with a train of fifty gentlemen and forty armed guards; 'then came the trusted officers and a few valets, all on horseback, and finally about fifteen pack mules with the baggage'. The purpose of this little jaunt was to release the queen mother, Marie de' Medicis, who was a prisoner under heavy guard in the château at Blois. It thus meant crossing France from east to west and what interests us here, rather than the politics involved, is the course of the astonishing journey: it was a comparatively rapid one, for in spite of the winter, the pot-holed roads, the unavoidable halts, the difficult river-crossings, the slow pace of the mules, and the need to steer clear of big towns like Dijon which would immediately have reported on the travellers to Luynes or to Louis XIII, the daily distance covered was about 40 kilometres. The extraordinary thing is that this quite sizeable band of men was able to pass unnoticed, for a whole month, loose in the huge kingdom like a needle in a haystack. They crossed the Loire by a ford between Roanne and Decize, the Allier at Vichy by a bridge, and during the night of 21 to 22 February, the queen mother escaped by climbing out of her bedroom window.[162]

I must confess that stories like this intrigue me, as somehow allowing a direct view of everyday life. Take Louis XIV's special envoy to Madrid, Nicolas Mesnager, who was hurrying to Spain in the spring of 1708.

> I arrived here [in Bayonne] on the night of the 30th, [he writes] after nine days travel. The poor roads and several disorganized staging posts are the reason for this slow progress. I am about to leave for Madrid. It will take me twelve days to

get there, having failed to obtain mules for one or two stages.[163]

Ninety years later, in 1800, an inspector of the roads set out on a tour of duty: his carriage overturned six times in 500 kilometres, requiring many hours of repairs. No fewer than eleven times it got bogged down in the mud and oxen had to be sent for to haul it free.[164]

I can well believe that nothing was more tiring than endless journeys on horseback.[165] But were carriages or stage-coaches much more comfortable? 'I did not get off to a good start', writes an unfortunate agent of the *Conseil d'Agriculture* sent to find grain reserves in 1794. 'The axle of the stagecoach broke near Senlis and in order not to waste time I went on foot to Compiègne where I took another coach for Noyon'.[166]

Tribulations of another kind met the traveller by river boat. In 1799, General Marbot was to take command of a division of the army in Italy. Setting out from Paris, his path crossed with that of Bonaparte in Lyon, as the latter returned from Egypt to the capital, amid scenes of popular rejoicing. Marbot and his son meanwhile began a disastrous trip down the Rhône by boat. They had to make what was virtually an emergency landing at Avignon and after Aix, they were stopped by the floodwaters of the Durance: the ferry could not get across. There was nothing for it but to wait, losing precious time.[167] Boat travel on the Loire was always an adventure, with a high risk of running aground on sandbanks. In September 1675, Madame de Sévigné 'took boatmen at Orleans' (the fashionable mode of travel at the time) to go to Nantes. 'Oh what madness!', she wrote to her daughter in the course of the long journey. 'The water is so low and I am so often aground that I miss my carriage, which does not have to stop and is getting along famously'. One night she found herself sleeping on straw, in a cabin on the river bank, with her travelling companions. A hundred and fifty years later, in 1838, Stendhal stepped aboard one of the latest steamboats at Tours, en route for Nantes. Ten minutes later, 'we came to a grand halt on a sandbank which is an extension of the Ile de la Loire'. Completely immobilized in the cold and mist, they narrowly avoided a collision with 'a large boat which was coming rapidly up the Loire pulled by eight horses at the trot'.[168] In 1842, a steamboat aground in the Allier in similar circumstances had to be hauled off by six pairs of oxen.[169]

And yet great progress had been made in road-building throughout France since 1750. But how real was such progress to our twentieth-century eyes? Stendhal, precise as usual, notes in 1838 that he has taken only 71 hours and three-quarters to travel from Paris to Bordeaux.[170] But two years later, 'the messengers took fourteen days to go from Paris to Marseille'.[171] As late as 1854, the railway from Paris to the Mediterranean not being completed, troops destined for the Crimean war had to de-train at Lyon and march to Valence to find a railway again.[172] Even in 1917, hard as it may be to believe, French troops on their way to Italy after the allied disaster at Caporetto, found the rail network inadequate: some of them had to cross the Alps on foot,[173] just as they would have in the time of Charles VIII, François I or Bonaparte!

Are such anecdotes worthy of our attention? Or ought we rather to have heeded the statistics which tell us that between 1765 and 1780, the 'great road-building revolution' shortened and sometimes halved distances all over France? I am rather inclined myself to believe that anecdotes give a more reliable picture of the way slow and difficult journeys could affect the whole of everyday life. Such incidents indicate the *limits*, the ceiling so to speak, of what was possible: there would be no revolutionary breakthrough until the coming first of the railways, then of motor cars and lorries, motorways and aeroplanes.

The French patchwork explained

The reader will guess where this is leading: in a world where distances seemed interminable, villages, bourgs, towns, cities, *pays*, regions, indeed whole provinces, institutions, cultures, dialects and all manner of ancient and various originalities – all existed in sheltered cocoons, having almost no contact with one another. They were thus able to develop undisturbed, and even the smallest units were miraculously preserved, a state of affairs encouraged by the monarchical regime's preference for building major roads and arteries, rather than the capillary network of minor roads – not that it had very much choice. The most usual consequence was the continued lamentable condition 'of the little country roads we call *chemins vicinaux*'.[174] In its grievance register in 1789, a small village community in Provence – Châteaudouble, near Draguignan – expressed the following wish: 'that any towns, villages or communities far from the main roads should be permitted to build roads for traffic between one another, each in its own area, for the greater benefit of trade'.[175] At the level immediately above this, the secondary or 'link roads' were little better, according to one speaker at the provincial assembly of the Ile-de-France in 1787: 'During the rainy season', he explained, 'which means about half the year, carters and farmers taking their goods to market in the nearby towns are obliged to double the number of their pack animals or draught teams, which for one thing considerably raises the cost of transport, a cost which the consumer must bear in part, and for another diminishes the profit of the seller or landlord'.[176]

In the Corrèze in 1792, a distance of seven or eight leagues (about thirty kilometres) was considered to be a serious obstacle to communication between villages. Any further, and the linguistic barrier became considerable. The problem was not so much distance *per se* of course, as the ease or otherwise of communication. As a local historian says in his book on the Embrunois published in 1783, while one had to travel several leagues in lowland regions before 'noticing differences in language and costume', 'here [in the high Alps] one has only to leave one little valley and travel to another to see a complete change' in language and customs. This was 'probably because of the lack of contact the inhabitants of one valley have with those of the next, being cut off from them by the . . . obstacle of the mountains'.[177] Likewise, Brittany was a compact island, virtually closed to the French language: sermons were preached in Breton, even in the towns; village schools, when they existed, taught children to read (rarely to write) only in the Breton language, with occasionally a little Latin. Yet there were some Breton country folk, apart from people living close to towns, who 'could express themselves in French'. On the border with Anjou perhaps? No, 'along the coasts'.[178] Breton boats large and small had of course long engaged in active trading as far afield as Spain and the Mediterranean. And how could one do business if one spoke only Breton?

Mutatis mutandis, much the same was true of what is now Haute-Savoie. Eighteenth-century travellers were surprised to find French spoken where they least expected it, in the most inaccessible region – the high mountains of the Faucigny, Chablais, Maurienne and Tarentaise. From about 1720 on, schools had been set up everywhere in the region, sometimes even in tiny hamlets. It had begun as a sort of new fashion: charitable donations, instead of going as in the past to religious causes, were now used to provide Savoyard children with classrooms and teachers. To learn to speak and read French cost a child's parents 6 or 8 *sous* a month (writing came a little extra at 4 *sous*). And the classes were well-attended – forty or fifty pupils. There is nothing mysterious about this enthusiasm: migrant workers, who mostly came from the highest valleys, knew that to find a good situation in Lyon or Paris, or indeed Germany, it was useful to know French which was spoken 'in almost every country in the world', as a report explained in 1750 to the village of Praz near Beaufort.[179]

In short, because they needed to emigrate, Savoyards chose to communicate. Dialects only flourished and above all survived in circumstances of isolation. If they were to be rooted out, as was the desire of the revolutionaries who wished to make French 'the universal language of the Republic', what did the authorities recommend, in Poitou for example? 'The means would be to build local roads between village and village, bourg and bourg, town and town'.[180] Precisely. All the same, as late as 1947 in the high Pyrenean valley of Aspe, the villagers of Lhers near Lascun still had to bring their dead down to the cemetery in Accous 'strapped to a mule', for no road existed.[181]

In such circumstances, it is far from surprising that France was for century upon century an area 'split into fragments . . . almost totally unconstituted, its cells merely juxtaposed';[182] 'an aggregate of microcosms, capable if necessary of self-sufficiency over long periods'.[183] It was 'a mosaic of little "pays", of villages and towns possessing a degree of independence even if they all belonged within the same political and religious whole . . . Some relative cultural autonomy on the part of the mass of people is . . . required to bring about the cohesion of any community, urban or rural, and to provide it with a coherent view of the world, to fortify its people against life's difficulties'.[184]

Within this limited horizon, social ties were of necessity close. As Jacques Dupâquier rightly remarks:

> The vast majority of French people [in the past] were able to put a name to every face they met; and they in turn were known and recognized. They met in church, at the *veillée*, at weddings, at charivaris. They helped each other and kept an eye on each other. A network of marriages, kinship, friendships and feuds enclosed these villages. The French countryside might even have become an aggregate of isolated molecules, if three needs had not combined to oblige the villagers to look beyond the parish pump: the need for money to pay rents and taxes; the need for employment for surplus young people; and the need to marry women who were not their cousins

– since the church kept a watchful eye open and was not generous with dispensations.[185] Staying at home with those one loved, or tolerated, or even detested – but whom one at least knew – was the rule. The reaction of that authentic village figure, the father of Rétif de la Bretonne, was typical. Paris disorientated him: '*Ho, que de monde*! what a lot of people!' he cried, adding 'there are so many that *nobody knows anyone else, even in the neighbourhood, even in your own house*'.[186]

The same fragmentation, *mutatis mutandis*, is to be found all over Europe, whether in the Swiss cantons, in Spain, England, Germany or Italy. The *contado* behind Pisa is a patchwork of communities,[187] as is the string of small localities around Lake Garda, described with precision by Giovanni Zeldin, a historian who has studied their individual lives, led under the shadow of the glorious history of Venice.[188] He actually uses the expression 'vertical history', as if the depths of the past contained a series of mineshafts for historians to plunge into and explore.

118

Diversity and history

Diversity is thus the eldest daughter of distance, of that forbidding immensity that has preserved all our particularities since the beginning of history. But in turn this age-old diversity has itself been a force in history. I am firmly convinced that the deep-seated division of France, making it a collection of isolated units, prepared the ground for all subsequent attempts at domination, whether local or more ambitious. If the dominant superstructure was able to grow and spread so quickly it was because it did not encounter any serious obstacles or concerted resistance at its own level. When the crown succeeded in annexing a new territory, it faced uprising from at most a single province or part of a province; it waged its battles one by one, in different parts of the country by turn. Similarly during the Revolution, the Girondins' revolt of 1793 did, it is true, cover a number of *départements*, but only on the surface. It failed to reach the population at any deep level. The north and east, where the armies were stationed, did not budge. It is not so much the perversity of the multiple as the indifference and inertia of the multiple that has fuelled political, social and religious conflicts in France, wherever they have broken out.

Every nation is divided, and thrives on division. But France illustrates the rule rather too well: Protestants and Catholics, Jansenists and Jesuits, blues and reds, republicans and royalists, right and left, Dreyfusards and anti-Dreyfusards, collaborators and resisters – division is within the house and unity is no more than a façade, a superstructure, a shout in the wind. So many differences result in lack of cohesion. Even today, an essayist has recently remarked that 'France is not a synchronized country: it is like a horse whose four legs move in different time'.[189] I like this excessive image, neither altogether right, nor entirely mistaken. The trouble is that all the divisions – physical, cultural, religious, political and social – are piled one on top of another, sowing incomprehension, hostility, misunderstanding, suspicion, conflict and civil war which, once having been kindled, may die down only to flare up again at the first breath of wind. As one historian puts it:

> France is gifted not so much for battle as for civil war. Apart from 1914, she has had no experience of a long and truly patriotic war. Every one of the conflicts waged by the nation that takes greatest pride in its military renown, have contained elements of civil war. This is obvious of 1939–45, but is no less true of the Revolutionary and Napoleonic wars, of the age of Joan of Arc and the Burgundians, of Henri IV, the Ligue or Richelieu. Even in 1870, there was a party which secretly or openly desired the defeat of the country's leaders.[190]

Must we then concur with Michelet's judgement, going literally to the bottom of the question, that 'The material [of which France is physically composed] is essentially divisible and strains towards disunion and discord'?[191] Or Julien Benda's reflection (terrible if true) that the history of France has in many ways been 'a permanent Dreyfus affair'?[192] Must we admit that France, having only slowly united its territories and peoples, is better fitted to understand internal than external war – as Jean Guéhenno argued vehemently against me one evening when I was trying to defend Péguy's position of 1914? 'That war', Guéhenno later wrote of the 1914–18 war, 'was not my affair'. Fate had forced him into it, but he had never been able 'to believe entirely, deep down', that it 'really concerned me'.[193] I must admit that because of my own past I am poorly placed to understand such views. It is civil war that I find hard to understand. Perhaps it is because unlike Jean Guéhenno, a Breton who put *'patrie'* above 'nation', I think like an easterner, conscious of the unitary mass of France behind him and aware that his own liberty depends on that unity and the vigilance it implies. I am not trying to justify my position, simply to indicate the inherited or lived experience from which it springs.

No doubt it is this experience that explains the emotion aroused in me by the few pages I shall now quote, and which I can never read without sadness. And yet they were written a long time ago, in the sixteenth century, by François de la Noue, a Protestant, and a stout-hearted man if ever one was.

It is June 1562. Queen Catherine de' Medici, the king of Navarre and the prince de Condé have arranged a meeting between Catholics and Protestants, an 'interview' near Toury in the Beauce. The two bands of accompanying troops, composed of 'picked men, mainly lords', one commanded by the maréchal d'Anville, the other by the comte de la Rochefoucauld, have come to a halt about eight hundred paces apart.

And after they had looked on each other for half an hour, each man, being anxious to see one his brother, another his uncle, his cousin, his friend or former companions, asked permission from his commander, which was only obtained with difficulty, it having been forbidden for the men to make contact for fear they should come to insults and subsequently to blows. But so far from this leading to quarrels, on the contrary there was nothing but greeting and embracing by those who could not refrain from showing signs of friendship to those with whom ties of kinship or honour had united them in the past, despite the opposing colours that each side now bore; for the troops accompanying the king of Navarre[194] were dressed in caps of crimson velvet and bore red banners, while those of the prince de Condé had white caps and banners. The Catholics, who imagined that the men of the reformed religion were lost, exhorted them to think of themselves, and not to persist in entering this miserable war in which kinsmen would kill one another. They replied that they hated the war too, but that they were sure that if they did not defend themselves, they would be treated in the same manner as several others of their religion, who had been cruelly slain in various parts of France. In short, each urged the other to peace and to persuade the great to listen. Some, standing a little aside, considered these things more deeply and deplored the public discord, source of future evils; and when they came to think in their minds that all the caresses then being given would be transformed into bloody murders if the commanders should give but a little sign for battle, and that the visors being lowered and prompt fury veiling all eyes, brother would be pitiless to brother, tears flowed from

their eyes. I was there on the side of the [reformed] religion
and may say that on the other side I had a dozen friends whom
I held as dear as my own brothers and they bore the same
affection towards me.[195]

Six months later, on 19 December, came the battle of Dreux. The
opposing troops stood face to face.

Each one then stood firm, [François de la Noue writes]
thinking in his heart that the men he saw coming towards him
were not Spanish, English or Italians, but Frenchmen, and of
the bravest, among whom some were his own companions,
kinsmen or friends; which gave some horror to the deed but
did not diminish the courage. They held themselves thus
until the armies began to stir ready for battle.[196]

How easily this dramatic text could be transposed and applied to
many other equally painful episodes of our past! Not to speak of
our own times, it reminds me of the remark made by an elderly
nobleman who could see the Revolution coming and was predict-
ing the turmoil ahead to a former page of Marie Antoinette's, the
comte Alexandre de Tilly. To his disbelieving listener he said: 'Sir,
we are a nation given to tragedies'.[197]

And what of the present day?

The limitless expanse of the France of the past, divided against
itself, has shrunk with the extraordinary progress of transport, and
become confined and enclosed within a 'hexagon' which grows
smaller day by day. It has not yet made a success – in any real sense
– of the Common Market. It has lost, with its colonial empire
(1962) a super-expanse; hence the nostalgia of its strategic commanders who miss being able to use the airstrips of Chad in the
heart of Africa, whenever they like.

And everything is still changing at a rapid rate: today it takes
only an hour and a half to fly from Paris to Algiers, to the Maison
Blanche airport where, almost fifty years ago (how small it was

then!) I landed in a plane, also very small, which bravely managed 200 km an hour and in order to lose height had to manoeuvre first on one wing then the other. Flying from Paris to Geneva nowadays, in less than an hour you find you have no sooner crossed the Jura, glimpsed briefly, than Lake Geneva is coming up to meet you, ringed round by the Alps and Mont Blanc. Flying from Paris to Perpignan takes one hour ten minutes: you step out to the air and the fragrance of another continent. Is it because they now feel confined that the French – such obstinate homebodies before the last war – have all or almost all begun to travel abroad?

I was writing these lines when the radio on my desk, as if to contradict me, brought me a programme made by France-Culture (8 February 1981) about a shepherd and his flock in the Lozère: strange music, the sound of sheep-bells, a dog barking, a man calling out commands, and the flock travelling past, gradually moving away into the silence. All at the pace of bygone times. France is still, for a while at least, a place where life can move slowly, faster or very fast. The fastest speed, impressive or threatening though it may be, is not yet everything. And what a joy it can be, alone on a mountain side, to rediscover and re-live, as when I listened to the shepherd in the Lozère hills, the time and space of yesterday.

PART II

The Pattern of Settlement: Villages, Bourgs and Towns

It has been and still is France's destiny to live between the contrary pulls of plural and singular: for plural read diversity, as ineradicable as bindweed; for singular read the tendency towards unity, something both spontaneous and consciously willed – but not willed only. Like any other country, France has been pulled in these two separate directions, with the result that most of its sinews have been stretched to snapping-point with the strain.

Historians have to be able to see both perspectives simultaneously, and must therefore be wary of one-sided views. As Hervé Le Bras and Emmanuel Todd inform us with relish, France should not by rights exist, it has yet to be invented. And yet France has long been in existence, it is no myth, and it did indeed invent itself many years ago. Jean-Paul Sartre remarked once in passing that France was 'non-unifiable',[1] which is at once true and plainly wrong: France may have found it difficult to be *one*, but could not, and never has been able to resign itself to being *several*. French cultural and political unity was one of the first examples of its kind in Europe, if not the very first. To this end, thousands of obscure and unconscious forces have been at work, their full measure not always taken by history.

I myself began this book by describing the France

whose 'name is diversity', and did so, I confess, with great pleasure. This is France's most beautiful aspect, the one I love best, and its sheer beauty released me from any potentially depressing reasoning.

But with Part II, it is time to move from the plural to the singular, to cross the divide in search of France one and indivisible, and to seek that unity, if possible, in the realities and forces that lie deepest. For it was not achieved entirely by the 'forty kings who in a thousand years built France'. They were not the only toilers in the vineyard, though they remain the most celebrated.

France, to a degree, is of its own making. For if distance divides, by the same token it also unites, division itself being the constant creator of complementary needs. Between cereal-growing and animal-raising areas for instance, or between grain producers and winegrowers, contact is virtually essential. Likewise when cultural disparities juxtapose 'human groups very different from one another in language, culture, material civilization, and technical achievement',[2] such juxtapositions can be explosive, demolishing all obstacles. In short, different from and hostile to each other though they may be, human groups of whatever size never live entirely within their own shells, hiding behind some impenetrable barrier. In practice, perfect self-sufficiency is nowhere to be found. To survive means making some contact, however small, with the outside world.

According to a report of 1721,

> in the whole of Provence [ravaged by plague which had spread from Marseille] there were only ten villages that the sickness had not yet reached; but . . . their inhabitants were languishing from hunger and other hardships, being unable to obtain the provisions they needed from anywhere, since all the routes were guarded [by soldiers] to prevent anyone entering or leaving, on pain of death.[3]

And yet the galloping advance of what was to be the last outbreak of plague on French soil saw it spread, that same summer, from Provence into Dauphiné and Languedoc. The entire French army was on virtually permanent alert to combat this implacable and stealthy enemy. The only defence against it was to establish road-blocks and cordon off the disease. As a result, the normal life of towns, villages and entire regions was threatened. The same summer of 1721 found the Dauphiné complaining bitterly: the *cordon sanitaire* had cut off its communications with the outside world, literally bringing ruin.[4] A few months later, when the maréchal duc de Berwick received orders from Court[5] to establish a cordon cutting off upper from lower Languedoc, there was similar panic: the estates of Languedoc intervened, brandishing the spectre of 'inevitable' famine for both regions, and managed to have the order revoked.

Am I right in thinking that incidents like this give some idea of the nature of our problem? The ordinary everyday rhythm of French life depended on contacts and communications. The depths of France's history are full of these continuous, silent movements, these regular currents. No one really controlled them; they simply occurred across distance, bringing groups together, binding them to one another.

At ground level, the settlement patterns of villages and bourgs formed the living base on which everything else would depend. These aggregates were reproduced indefinitely, on a model that did not radically vary from one end of the country to the other: villages would be grouped in a circle round the bourg (where the market was held) like little planets around a sun. The whole unit, bourg plus villages, was about the size of the present-day *canton*. Such 'cantons', basic population units, were in turn positioned around a town of some activity, greater or smaller. We are still talking about quite small units, the *'pays'* as we have called them, keeping the terminology used by Lucien

Gallois[6] and the geographers of his time. And the *pays*, with greater or lesser success or determination, provided they were in touch with a town dynamic enough to play a leading role (not always the case), were thus drawn into the orbit of a region or province. The architecture would be completed by the construction – sooner or later, perfect or not so perfect – of a national market, and of a nation.

Even so, for the national market to exist, it would need to have at its service a large and powerful city, endowed with means and favoured by circumstance. Paris, because of its size, became an urban monster very early on; but it did not immediately succeed in carrying the rest of France along with it. The motor might be more or less equal to the task: and the vehicle might follow a jolting course. Is this not perhaps a fair general view of French history as a whole, infinitely repeating itself?

CHAPTER FOUR

Starting from the village

If we accept the existence of a coherent system, a system accounting for the construction of France, our first concern must of course
be to describe and dissect it. Later on, though not in this chapter
which is only a first approach to the question, I shall try to
reconstitute it dynamically and to see the extent to which it was
able to rearrange, I do not say to wipe out, the diversities within
France. It would never completely succeed in this as we already
know: too many threads in the network were short or fragile.
When stretched too far they broke.

The whole of Part II will be a prospecting trip, concerned simply to describe, not at this stage to analyse in depth. It will be a first
outing, a reconnaissance expedition. And since the system occurs at
a number of levels, our first stop must logically be the vast rural
base, with its thousands of villages and hamlets.

Village diversity and beyond

There is no such thing as the typical French village. There are
clearly many types of village: here diversity and the plural reign
supreme.

The reasons are many. In the first place, villages differ according
to their principal activity: it might be livestock farming, or cereals,
or vines, or olives, or mulberry trees, or chestnuts, or apples, or
small-scale industry – or any number of things. To take one example among many, the wine-growing village is instantly recognizable: it 'forgoes land, which is expensive, all the more willingly
since it positively welcomes the dark and cool conditions suitable

129

for cellars; [its] buildings huddle together. A village living by the plough on the contrary will spread itself over the open plain round about'.[7] Elsewhere, the doors of the village houses might open on to workshops where the weaver, shoemaker or upholsterer plied their trades. To this diversity is added that of architectural tradition (houses built in blocks or round courtyards), of building materials, of local features related to the climate or the water supply. So there is the Provençal hill village, with its narrow streets to shield one from the sun and wind; the Lorraine village, with its adjoining houses lining the broad street that also serves as farmyard; and the very different Breton village, scattered and dispersed, its houses isolated on their own farmland – and so on.

The two last examples – the Breton and Lorraine villages – illustrate the problem of concentration and dispersion. It is a problem hard to get to grips with, though often tackled. Probably it is insoluble, by which I mean that its roots, and underlying causes remain largely unknown. Here history in the broadest sense has not yielded up all its secrets.

Take the terms 'dispersed habitat' and 'concentrated habitat'. André Deléage preferred to speak of habitat as 'spaced out' (*espacé*), or 'drawn together' (*rapproché*).[8] And Carl Lamprecht in 1878, writing of the far-off time of the Salic law, referred to the opposition between *Dorfsystem* and *Hofsystem*:[9] the village system and the farm system,[10] assuming that both had probably appeared even before the Salic Franks had settled in the lands south of the Scheldt.[11] The vaguest term of all, and the hardest to pin down, between farm and village, is that of hamlet, which refers at the very least to a few houses, sometimes clustered together, sometimes not. Is the hamlet perhaps, in certain regions – infertile, mountainous or with poor soil – an elementary way of taking over any cultivable land there is, with the farm or farmstead corresponding, as it does in the Aspre in Roussillon where I live, to the occurrence here and there of small plots of usable land? The 1891 census of France listed 36,144 *communes* (towns, bourgs and villages, large and small), but 491,800 'hamlets, villages and sections of *communes*' which were no more than 'geographical expressions . . . and account for the scattered population' attached to certain *communes*. The units of concentrated population thus had on average thirteen outlying settlements around them,[12] though this average is meaningless in itself, given the very unequal distribution over the country of the scattered population. We shall return presently to this point. (Cf. maps in Figure 12)

But it should be made clear first that the contrast between dispersed and concentrated habitat does not always occur as clearly as the image it suggests, that is on the one hand a cluster of houses round a church, and on the other a scatter of isolated farmsteads, each having its own territory. There are at least two (and probably more) types of dispersion: the first consisting of outlying dwellings (mainly farms) surrounding a grouped village; the second corresponding to a scatter of farms and hamlets around what may be a very notional centre.

Even clustered villages, like those of Lorraine, might have outlying settlements, at least a few farms, sometimes even a hamlet. From the fifteenth century, in the eastern provinces, the seigneur of a given village, affected by currency devaluation (and therefore by rapidly falling revenue, since his tenants' rents were paid in fixed cash sums) might have sought and found compensation outside the village boundaries. New farms would thus have been created, either on the seigneur's *réserve*, or on ground of uncertain ownership between two village territories, sometimes by reclaiming abandoned land.

This was what happened in the *Champagne berrichonne* (in the very centre of France) following the 'reclamation of the land abandoned for the whole duration of the Hundred Years' War'.[13] And the pattern would be found too, much later, in the nineteenth century, with the proliferation of capitalist farms under the Second Empire, which in many regions marked the high point of French agricultural activity and of peasant exploitation, given the surplus of farm labour following the excessive increase in the rural population in the early part of the century. Similar patterns are found, for the same or other reasons, in western Picardy, in some parts of Normandy, and 'the plain of Poitou', where one finds quite large villages with outlying farms and sometimes even small villages in between.[14]

131

FIGURE 12
Dispersed population of France (i.e. living in hamlets, villages and 'sections of communes') in 1891, by département

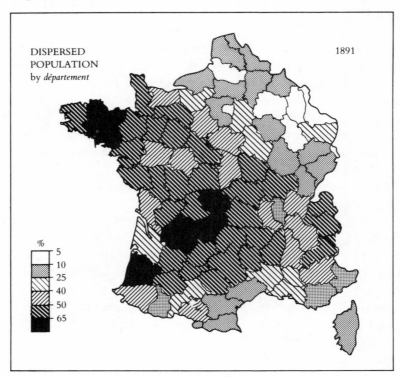

Left: percentages.
Right: absolute figures.
Source: Census, France, 1891 (Bibliothèque Nationale).
Maps by Françoise Vergneault.

In other cases, the situation is rather different: for instance, one might find a fairly substantial village, virtually a bourg perhaps, with an almost continuous ring of farms surrounding it at a respectful distance. Such is the pattern of the Provençal section of the Rhône valley, or in the maritime districts of Provence (leaving aside Haute-Provence which runs into the Alps, and where a scat-

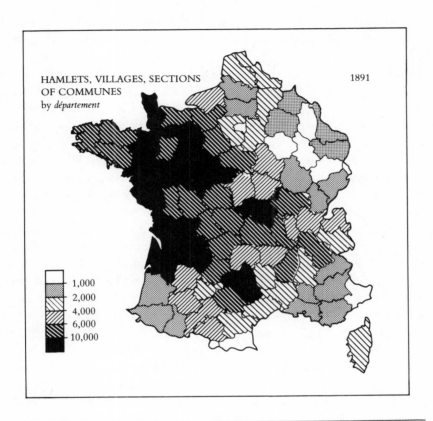

HAMLETS, VILLAGES, SECTIONS
OF COMMUNES
by *département*

1891

1,000
2,000
4,000
6,000
10,000

tered habitat is only typically found in the high plain of Barcelonnette).[15] In lower Provence, the *grange, bastide* or *mas* are different words for the same reality: a property around a farmstead, quite often with the owner's house alongside, a settlement not unlike the *mezzadria* of Tuscany, or even the distant *habitación* of the New World plantations.

The *Atlas historique de Provence* enables one to see this in the case of the large village of Rognes, north of Aix, set back from the left bank of the Durance, 'as if clinging to the denuded barrier of the Lubéron'.[16] Rognes still had a 'grouped population' of 610 in 1954, as against a 'scattered population' of 363, giving a total of 973. The number of inhabitants, which had been larger in the past (1,652 in 1765, 1,561 in 1855, 1,052 in 1952) would be enough in eastern France to promote it to the size, if not the functions of a bourg, and that would also justify its huge territory (8,166 hectares). But whether to call it a bourg or simply a large village need not concern us here. The important thing is the gradual appearance, on its outer limits, sheltered by the east-west running 'mountains' (or rather hills) of Basse-Provence, of a series of *bastides*: five in 1485; fifteen in 1500; and more as time went by. The result was a transformation, of a 'capitalist' nature in fact, and benefiting urban landowners, very like what happened on a vast scale around Florence in the thirteenth century, and what one suspects must have happened in other places, the *Gâtine poitevine* to take but one example, studied some time ago in detail by Dr Merle.[17]

Similar evidence, also in Provence, comes from Garéoult, another large village, about fifteen kilometres south of Brignoles, on which an exceptionally good study has been published.[18] In the sixteenth century, this village was just beginning to 'spread its wings', that is a number of *mas* were appearing on its outskirts. Can we take this to be the normal pattern, detected in this case as it actually began to take place? And do we have the right to generalize from this example? If so, the *mas* and *bastides* would be the result of the dismembering of the village territory, or rather of its extension and of the colonization of marginal land, since *mas* and *bastides* were usually built on the outskirts of the village, on cleared land bordering the meagre sheep-pastures – hence the clear and often all-important interest taken in the operation by the sheep-farmers. Whether or not this is the case, the outlying farmsteads were never independent of the village, whose size meant that it was always a giant compared to these tiny holdings, *granges*, *mas* or *bastides*. And we know from reliable evidence that the isolated farm, here as elsewhere, often corresponded to a 'capitalist' invasion from the nearby towns. The next step was that in order to survive, the 'farm' drew its workforce from the pool of day-labourers living in the village or nearest bourg and who in summer would wait at daybreak every morning to be hired by the local *ménagers* or landowners – just as in Andalusia or Sicily. Hence the apparent paradox that the farm labourers lived in a quasi-urban milieu, and thus had something of an urban culture, while the landowners in many parts of Provence lived out in the country. So perhaps we may conclude that the Provençal example is particularly easy to understand, with its regular rings of *mas* on the edges of the villages.

Elsewhere, the dispersion of dwellings might disrupt the main village, perhaps eliminating more than half of it, leaving only a few hamlets or scatters of isolated farms. Such was the case for wide areas of the Massif Central. On 29 March 1703, at the height of the Camisards' revolt, the maréchal de Montrevel ordered one of his officers to 'go and capture all the inhabitants of the *commune* of Mialet, consisting of seven hamlets including the parish'.[19] This was also the pattern in the *bocage* in Brittany and in the lower Limousin.

The Armorican massif in Brittany consists of a patchwork of hedged fields (*champs clos*), with isolated houses standing in properties of varying size, surrounded by raised dykes planted with trees. These basic units once drew primarily on their own resources: not so long ago, the peasants made not only their farm implements but their clothes and even shoes. At the same time, there would always be a central hamlet or village – sometimes known as the bourg, but the word 'bourg', like the word 'village', does not have a fixed meaning throughout France.

At all events, such a centre would long have consisted of a cluster of houses, generally inhabited by a small number of privileged families, around the parish church: only the weekly markets and the hubbub of the fairs brought life and animation to it. In the nature of things, considerable social distance came to be marked between the privileged residents of the 'centre' and the peasants in the outlying farms. On 26 February 1790, at Châteauneuf-du-Faou in Finistère, a letter denounced the inappropriate appointment of a mayor who was 'a peasant *living away from the village* [my italics] who can scarcely sign his name'.[20] 'The isolation in which the [Breton] peasant-farmer lives', says a document from the same period, 'and the habit of speaking a language [*bas-breton*] which is rarely printed and which few people know well, will prove an obstacle, for a long while to come, to his instruction and to progress towards his civilization'.[21]

Was there perhaps a pattern typical of *bocage* areas, at least in the Maine? According to Robert Latouche,[22] such a pattern could have appeared in the eleventh century, with the population increase taking place all over Europe. But why should there have been such a difference between the Breton west and for instance the plateaux and cereal-growing plains north and east of the Paris basin? Why do we find on one hand a village unit of loose construction, with houses scattered widely around a centre that long remained of only minor importance, while on the other we find large villages with closely packed houses, set in the wide expanses of the openfield?

Robert Latouche argued that the regions which later formed the *bocage* were originally vast expanses of forest, a land *vacua ab omni habitatore humano*,[23] empty of human habitation. In such a hostile environment, Roman Gaul only rarely established its villas, the great manor farms which Fustel de Coulanges studied with such enthusiasm. So the seigneurs and religious foundations, coming later, built on untenanted land, virgin territory[24] – and in difficult conditions, to say the least.

The *bocage* regions of the west were indeed often cursed with clayey soil, itself an obstacle to the creation of large peasant settlements. 'The network of damp hollows divided the arable land into tiny units'; movement was difficult without proper roads, and the clay also hampered the use of agricultural implements – all factors which drastically reduced 'the radius of operation of a farmer around his dwelling'.[25] And on the sunken roads of Brittany, a wheeled vehicle could only rarely get through. 'In mid-nineteenth century . . . in the huge parishes of inland Cornouaille, to travel from outlying farms to the bourg and back meant a day's journey in the bad season, so greatly was progress hindered by the pot-holes in the road'.[26] Indeed some of these were pot-holes in which the traveller ran a real risk of drowning. It is true that 'the building of drains and metalled roads had by the nineteenth century largely reduced the disadvantages of the clayey soil, but . . . by then rural settlement had already acquired its definitive pattern, one that corresponded to the natural properties of the terrain'.[27]

It is indeed this extravagant expanse of heaths and empty countryside that explains the huge size of Breton parishes. (The average
French parish measured 12 or 13 square kilometres – in Brittany
the average was 25). With their 2,000 to 5,000 inhabitants, they
sometimes slip, improperly, into the statistical category of the
town. Crozon for instance had 5,000 or 6,000 inhabitants in the
seventeenth century, but they were dispersed over 100 square
kilometres:[28] certainly not an urban settlement pattern.

The Bas-Limousin – roughly the present-day *département* of
Corrèze – presents similar features. The poor quality of the soil
meant a scattered and isolated habitat, but the responses to identical conditions were different and original. Here every *commune* or
parish is like a miniature archipelago, with islands scattered irregu-
larly around the *chef-lieu* of the *commune*, itself rarely of any size.
Here, rather than the bourg (or even compact village) the hamlet
'constitutes the basic cell of the rural organism'.[29] Sometimes,
explains Alain Corbin, it is made up of 'ten to twenty houses, dispersed in no regular alignment, around courtyards and *couderts*,
communicating with each other by muddy lanes: elsewhere the
hamlet may possess no unity at all, but consists of four or five
farms, all within sight of each other, near a crossroads, or built
along a main road'. Some of these hamlets 'are bigger than the *chef-
lieu*, but do not have the same functions; the *mairie*, school and
church may be severally situated in the different hamlets making
up the *commune*'.[30]

It may seem a strange pattern, but it is also authentic, surviving
evidence of a special rural civilization which was the product and
accompaniment of these little hamlets, or as the old census used to
call them, these 'sections of *communes*'. This was a civilization
where the farmsteads were occupied by patriarchal families, pas-
sionately attached to their independence, one where the hamlet
still practised a collective way of life if for no other reason than that
it owned its own property (which cannot be called communal) –
usually consisting of poor land remaining undivided, used as transit
land by animals, or for clearing and temporary cultivation. Various
amenities useful to everyone were common property: a *lavoir*, a
fishpond, a bake-oven and a mill for grinding rye, the staple of the

peasant diet. In this setting, a tenacious local culture survived, with its own particular features – the *veillées* for example, evening gatherings between mid-September and the beginning of Lent, still ceremoniously held until 1914 and in some cases even until after World War II. These were long meetings, lasting about three hours, and ending only when the receiving householder signalled that it was time to leave, 'by putting ash on the burning embers'.[31]

In such ways there have come down to us echoes of periods long-dead, reaching back into the mists of time. It makes any attempt at explanation all the more difficult: the history we are seeking can only be apprehended, if at all, in its occasional lingering forms. And such units as villages, hamlets, bourgs, isolated farms, are ancient creations, belonging to history in the fullest sense, that is going back beyond the historical into the centuries and millennia of prehistory. Peering this far back in time, we cannot see clearly. We are reduced to hypotheses.

I imagine, along with Pierre Bonnaud, that before all these patterns of rural settlement became established, there were centuries and centuries of nomadic or semi-nomadic wandering: such a restless way of life may not have given way to a more settled existence, in some parts of France, until about AD 800 or 900. Elsewhere, today's pattern may have been preceded by centuries of collective life of a more or less restrictive kind – restrictions which in some places have survived even into the twentieth century.

A recent article by Emmanuel Le Roy Ladurie and André Zysberg[32] throws light on the double significance of a dividing line running either from Eu to Geneva or from Saint-Malo to Geneva. It separates a zone of clustered settlement from one with hamlets and scattered habitat. That this line should once more prove to be a significant split will surprise no one: the whole history of France divides along this frontier; the 1891 census both pointed out and plotted on the map this distribution of the scattered population. But one might wonder why, in the east and north-east, villages with saints' names are rare, indeed almost absent, whereas they are comparatively common in the rest of France. In fact, place-names based on saints are late developments: they first appear in about the eighth or ninth centuries, but become really widespread only after the year 1000, with the first beginnings of modern Europe. The 'non-saintliness' of northern and eastern France may therefore be related to its apparent claim to be an older area of settlement, in short, to its precocious development.

This explanation brings us back to one of the principal arguments advanced by modern scholars of prehistory, one with which Pierre Bonnaud's dialectology also concurs – namely that this large area of the Paris basin was developed very early, from the fourth millennium BC, by peasant peoples from central Europe. They introduced to the region both an advanced form of agriculture, of which the cereal field was the essential element, and the typical habitat of their place of origin – large villages of 50 to 200 inhabitants, with houses close together, as excavation has clearly proved. There is nothing like this in the Mediterranean south, where the first signs of agriculture, early though they are, did not rapidly alter the customs of a population used to a semi-nomadic existence.[33]

The diversity of the rural habitat can thus very largely be explained by the irregularities, the early or late developments, of history in the broad sense. Its geometry is the product of time, and of adaptation to an environment which might itself vary – it being understood that any form of settlement once established tends to perpetuate itself, if necessary accommodating changes and modifications to do so.

The village as model

If we forget the form of the village for a moment and concentrate on its role, the differences are reduced, and a *model* can be suggested: *mutatis mutandis*, it can be applied to the clustered village or the dispersed village, the village of consequence or the mere hamlet – even to the tiny unit of the isolated farmstead.

Every village occupies a given area, what Pierre de Saint-Jacob would call 'a cultural clearing'.[34] It is 'a biological cell which makes possible the *colonization* [in the primary sense of the term] of the factor of production "land" '.[35] In fact this land – *terroir* or *finage* – is more important than the site plan of the houses. The latter might fall into ruins and disappear – something which could and did happen – but the territory remained: neighbouring units, whether towns or villages, would take possession of it.[36]

The village territory, usually about a thousand hectares, operated like a Von Thünen diagram:[37] it was organized according to distance which, being costly in time, labour and money, led to the establishment of successive concentric zones. The crops in the fields nearest home would not be the same as those in the far fields, which could only be reached by a wearisome return trip once in the day. 'The greater the distances from the centre to the extremities of the farmed land, the more sensible it is to relegate to the periphery the land requiring least attention, that is the poorest.'[38] 'Because of the shortage of manure and the poor roads', Paul Dufournet writes of a Savoyard village, 'because of the inadequate carts and the small numbers of draught animals, the land nearest the village . . . was the best cared for and consequently the scene of the fastest rotation.'[39]

The most favoured land of all was simply a border or 'belt' surrounding the houses of the village: this was the zone given over to kitchen gardens, plots and enclosures, hemp-patches and orchards, sometimes but not always protected by walls. In Lorraine in springtime, the villages were surrounded by the 'garlands of white blossom' of the plum-tree orchards.[40] So too were the farming villages around Paris, where blossom would be out on espalier fruit trees trained against the walls of the houses long before it opened on free-standing trees, as we know from a description of Arcueil and Cachan in mid-March 1787.[41]

Always lovingly tended, this zone of orchards and gardens benefited from constant effort: at every free moment, its owners would push open the garden gate to wheel in an extra barrow-load of manure, to prune the odd tree, or to dig over a patch of earth. And the garden was always the natural place to try out new plants. The first potatoes, maize and beans appeared here, long before these revolutionary imports from overseas were to be found in open fields.

Beyond the gardens began a wide zone corresponding to all the arable land – which I shall refer to as the *terroir*, as distinct from the *finage* (the village territory as a whole).

In eastern and northern France, the arable land still formed, in quite recent times, a continuous circle round the village, divided into three *soles* or *saisons*, which replaced each other every year in the system known as triennial crop rotation: wheat (or rye); oats or barley (*les mars*);[42] and fallow land, *les jachères* or *les versaines* as it was known in Lorraine, that is land in theory left uncultivated. The following year the circle rotated and wheat was sown in place of fallow, oats in place of wheat, and the land formerly under oats was left fallow. Not so long ago, before the old system collapsed, the three *soles* could be told apart in summer by their colour: the yellow of the wheat, the light green of the oats and the ploughed earth of the fallow land ready for the October or November sowing. (That is why the fallow lands were sometimes called *les sombres*, the darklands).

In the very wide area where rotation was biennial, the land was divided into two alternating zones only: land capable of being ploughed, or worked by spade and pick, was divided equally between cereals and fallow.

But everywhere, in the past, saw the spread and consolidation of cultivated land as opposed to the waste land and forest, that unfarmed and inhospitable terrain viewed with horror by travellers and economists alike. Ange Goudar imagined that half the country must be left waste.[43] This zone was the third circle, and often the largest. Here a few patches of land might be taken into cultivation but only at intervals of ten, twenty or even thirty years.

Unfarmed land was the equivalent, broadly speaking, of the *saltus*, a word borrowed from Latin agronomists and signifying the opposite of the *ager*, the cultivated land. Historians have developed the habit, good or bad, certainly convenient, of using these two words whose opposition down the ages bears witness to the long-standing contrast they mark. In England the terms outfield and infield serve a similar purpose.

The *saltus* could mean many different things: heaths and hillsides abandoned to natural vegetation; vineyards no longer cultivated but often containing a few surviving fruit-trees, originally planted between the rows of vines and sometimes obstinately bearing fruit; disorderly lines of trees, once planted as hedgerows and then left to grow wild, reaching the same height as those lining the princely avenues of eastern Europe and tended by careful gardeners. More commonly, it meant scrubland, 'thickets, brushwood, tangled grasses'.[44] And most of all it meant forests.

Such wildernesses varied of course depending on climate and soil. In medieval Aquitaine, as it emerged from the Roman period, the *saltus* 'included uncultivated land as well as woodlands offering many resources, marshes, waterways, and coastal foreshores'.[45] In the part of Savoy near the Rhône today, 'land not cultivated . . . includes rock, standing water, gravel, *murger*, naked *teppe*, pasture and brushwood',[46] and of course forests or what is left of them. In the Auvergne, untended land formed a huge encompassing wilderness of scrub, brushwood, thickets, 'with a psychological connotation: the *saltus* remained "the mountain", the wooded zone haunted by wild beasts and fear; the *ager* meant the safety of the plain'.[47]

Communes did not usually trouble themselves greatly about marking the boundaries of the little-used areas separating them from their neighbours. It was only in the autumn of 1789 for example that the inhabitants of the large village of Bonnet (in the Meuse) asked for and obtained a survey and the 'recognition of the boundaries separating the woods of the community of Bonnet from those of the abbey of Vaux', near the valley of the Ornain.[48] Such stock-taking was no doubt becoming the rule during the early years of the Revolution. It was made compulsory, in the upper Loire valley at any rate, in 1790.[49]

In practice, the *saltus* was more significant as an internal frontier between cultivated and uncultivated land than as a boundary with the neighbouring village. Crops not infrequently spread beyond this internal frontier whenever circumstances made it necessary. Land-clearing would then be undertaken. In Languedoc, during the period of comparative prosperity between 1500 and 1640, some of the *garrigues* were transformed into marginal *ager* for vine-growing.[50] And in Provence, in October of the terrible year 1709, following the disaster of a fearfully cold winter and the ruin and

142

dearth that followed, the peasants unremittingly devoted themselves to clearing land and sowing it. Was this a natural reflex? 'I do believe', wrote the *intendant* Le Bret, 'that they will have sown more land this year than in any before, for it is certain that they have been clearing and sowing in the pinewoods that were killed by the cold weather, although the land in these woods is of the poorest and stoniest sort'.[51]

Often, especially in our own times, the opposite might happen. Waste land 'is spreading like a plague'[52] as is clear for all to see, writes Lucien Gachon, a propos of the crystalline massifs of Auvergne: it 'bears witness to the ruin of the rural landscape. Ruined farms and mills are everywhere to be seen and no new buildings are being put up'.[53] The abandoned land, deserted by all, becomes overgrown with gorse, heather and broom. For children on holiday it is a sort of adventure playground, full of discoveries: sheep and goats, nests of wild bees, hazel copses, the advance guard of the expanding forest; wild game, startled into flight from its lair; an adder curled up on the path.

But for the villagers of the past, the *saltus* was a reservoir of free resources which long familiarity had taught them to use. In the Escandorgue,[54] a narrow plateau of volcanic rock south of Larzac and overlooking the Lodévois, it was extraordinary what could be found: litter for animals (bracken and chopped boxwood), grazing for sheep and goats, acorns for pigs; the villagers could gather hazel-nuts, sloes, wild cherries, beechmast, rowan berries, strawberries, mushrooms, wild honey, and any number of herbs for the cooking pot – dandelion, *latcheron à la broco*, *ensaladeta fina*, *bezègue*, *bourrut*, *repounchou*, *lengua de buou*, asparagus, salsify, wild leeks. And there was always hunting or poaching: the local traditional recipe for hare was to roast it, on a spit 'made of hazel-wood, basted with bacon fat melted in a *lambadou*, a perforated tin funnel, well heated . . . served with a sauce containing the animal's blood and chopped liver, and plenty of garlic'.[55]

In short, neither the wasteland of the past, despite its unprepossessing appearance, nor (need I add) the forest, ever went unused. Wild fruits could be gathered there; flocks found part of their food there; pigs were regularly taken into beech and oak woods; all animals – sheep, oxen, horses – spent long months at liberty running almost wild in the heath and forest. In the remarkable marshlands of Poitou, or in Brittany, horses were turned loose and left to fend for themselves. In winter when the ground was frozen, they had to kick it with their hooves to find grass. Stallions were allowed to run with mares, and reproduction took care of itself. The herd would huddle together against wolves under the fierce protection of the stallions. Left to themselves, the animals returned to a state of nature. The Sieur de Gouberville reports in his diary (17 May 1556) as if it was a routine matter, that in order to catch the horses he needed in woods he owned at Mesnil-en-Val, near Cherbourg, he had to organize a hunting party with his friends: 'We caught a black colt for me, which Simonnet and Th. Quatorze brought to the house. We failed to catch Th. Drouet's mare: it rushed Vincent Paris and tried to trample his belly'.[56]

Did herds like this invent their own way of life? In the Vosges, the mountain tops known as the *chaumes*, having lost their tree cover either naturally or by human action, would between April and October become the gathering place for large herds of horned beasts, usually watched over by herdsmen known as *macaires*, mostly from Switzerland. According to one account from 1698, in the *chaumes*, 'cattle are capable of going up to their pastures on their own in the spring and coming down again on their own in October'.[57] Was transhumance something invented by animals before being thought of by humans? As Jean Anglade says of the Massif Central, 'no one knows which came first to the Massif Central, men or cattle'![58]

Wildlife in the true sense was abundant: stags, roedeer, wolves (the latter still a danger as late as mid-nineteenth century and even beyond): only hunting could protect the crops against their depredations. The forests round Paris for instance, where hunting rights were reserved for the king and great lords (who unfortunately did not always exercise them) harboured animals that spilled out into the farmland. On several occasions Phélipeaux, the *intendant* of Paris, reported on the superabundance of game in the forests of his 'department', which were 'horribly full of creatures', with herds of thirty or forty head of deer.[59] Guarding the crops would cost the peasants 'more than the *taille* they pay the king'.[60] Also near the capital, at Segrez (in the Arpajon district of Essonne), the seat of the marquis d'Argenson, 'the people complain of a great nuisance: the animals, rabbits in particular, which eat the vines, grain and every fruit that individuals might have harvested' (25 March 1750).[61] Similar complaints, this-time about hares, were expressed in March 1787, at Limay near Mantes, where the duc de Bouillon had neglected to come and hunt for years.[62] So one can sympathize with Monsieur de Massol, who owned land at Achères, Garennes and Fromanville, between the grassy banks of the Seine and the forest of Saint-Germain, where 'the *bestes fauves* which have been brought in over the last few years . . . have multiplied so much', said the unfortunate landowner, 'that they are ruining my land'. There are no crops. The tenants are threatening to leave and there is no solution. Would the king do him the favour of buying his land? (The term *bestes fauves* in this instance refers not only to the wildness but to the colour of the game – 'tawny' animals like stags, deer and hares – as opposed to 'black' or 'red' game, wild boars and foxes respectively.)

Game was a nuisance all over France. The grievance registers of 1789 often broach the subject. In Brovès, a small village community near Draguignan in Provence, the request was made that the king 'grant permission to every private individual to be able to destroy, at least on his own land, with snares, traps or guns, all the animals that are destroying the crops; that each man also be allowed . . . to keep dogs to guard the herds, without [wooden] hobbles round their necks, in spite of the decree of the *parlement* of Provence'.[63]

Needless to say, whether they had permission or not, the peasants hunted and trapped game. But under the *ancien régime* poaching was a severely-punished offence. The peasant saw the gamekeeper as his sworn enemy, 'a man always despicable because he does no work' as a grievance register in Normandy put it.[64]

145

The forest: jewel among properties[65]

What is easily forgotten today is the economic value of the forest in the past. I have already mentioned its role as grazing for flocks. In addition, its leaves could be collected to feed stock when there was no hay (oak and elm leaves); or to fill mattresses (beech leaves); or to manure land (leafmould, box leaves). The forest provided fuel for cooking, for heating the house and for the voracious furnaces of factories (foundries, ironworks, breweries, refineries, glass-works). It provided the raw material for casks and other cooper-wares, for ploughs, waggons, carts, clogs, countless farm implements, houses, boats and even machines: presses, pumps and treadmills all had gears made of wood.

Every peasant was also a woodcutter and in autumn the available workforce of the village would get together to cut down trees and lop branches. As late as 1900 in the Burgundy 'mountains', after the potato harvest which brought to an end the year's round of agricultural work, 'we would leave before dawn. We would take half an hour to climb the steep paths of the short cuts and arrive well ahead of the others at the clearing. We would shout to our right, "Ho! Auguste!" and Auguste would reply, "Ho!"; or to the left, "Ho! Denis!" and "Ho!" Denis would reply.' Then 'the axes would begin to answer each other: a heavy chop to start the felling, and a light chop, flat-on, to send the tree over'. Meanwhile dinner was keeping warm in a pot covered with hot coals: 'a stew of potatoes and beans with bacon'.[66]

With so many takers, and with so many peasants clearing land, wood very soon became scarce and its price constantly rose. As early as the sixteenth century it was sufficiently sought after for the forest to be a 'jewel among properties'. Pierre Séguier, the descendant of a former family of merchants, who in 1554 became president of the *parlement* of Paris, a canny man who spent most of his life acquiring land bordering on his family estate, had a marked predilection for buying up forests – hardly surprising when one sees from his accounts the substantial income he derived from them![67] From about 1715, the price of wood rose even faster, shooting up in the last twenty years of the *ancien régime*. The heating of Paris alone was by then absorbing over two million tons of wood a year.[68]

So the forests, which man explored more willingly than he does today, were also shaped by him. Too many retrospective observers are inclined to see the forest as nature's bounty, to which man had only to help himself. This is only partly true. The comparatively stable forest boundaries, from the reign of Louis XIV to our own time, tend to be misleading. For in the *longue durée*, nothing stands still. What is more, on 'maps of densely-wooded regions . . . the place-names help to reconstitute a picture of the landscape [of the past] very different from the one [schoolbooks] have taught us to imagine'.[69] Man left a heavy mark on the forest. Even the densest of woods were only allowed to remain so in accordance with his needs and activities. The Argonne forest was left untouched because of its subsoil of gaize, it is true. But what also protected it from exploitation as merciless as that of the forest of Orleans was 'its awkward relief, plus the lack of communications and means of transport which prevented it from being exploited otherwise than on the spot' – hence the number of glassworks.[70] Finally, we should not forget the way woodlands were besieged by the often destructive village economies, which the state from time to time tried to control.

The forest: a world upside down

The forest was also a world upside down, a paradise for bandits, brigands and outlaws. The famous forest of Bondy, near Paris, which the marquis de Sade made the setting for the celebrated adventures of Justine,[71] was only substantially deforested under the Second Empire. There was constant danger in the sinister forests of the Ardennes, where 'prowling thieves' were still feared in January 1715, along the whole length of the 'unavoidable road between Sedan and Bouillon'.[72] Sinister too were the forests between Metz and Saint-Menehould, a frequent repair of assassins,[73] as, surprisingly, were the royal forests of Normandy where it was eventually decided in 1712 to create '*chemins ferrez*', (paved, or in other words main roads) on account of the 'robberies and murders to which travellers are exposed'.[74] And this was in Normandy, one of the most thoroughly policed provinces in the kingdom! The same went on even nearer Paris, if we are to believe the reports (1694) of the lieutenant in charge of controlling crime at the tiny royal seat of Ieure-le-Châtel, a village near Pithiviers. He was in despair because 'despite the great number of murderers and highwaymen he has caught in the forests of Fontainebleau and Orleans, there still remain a very great quantity of them'. Would the authorities please give him the means to carry on his work, since (and here one has to smile) 'he has been obliged to imprison [some] of his own archers on account of their thieving and bad ways'.[75]

Forests near villages, a haven for criminals, traditionally also harboured the salt smugglers, often deserters from the army, who had been lent horses by peasant accomplices and whose exploits consisted of getting as quickly and discreetly as possible from one protective forest to the next. If surprised, they would use their arms only to cover their getaway.

Sometimes though, these salt smugglers grew bold, like one troop which split up into several bands within the same area in 1706, and set out with wagons laden with salt, forcing the villagers and folk in small towns to buy it, under threat of setting their houses on fire. 'They travel with such impunity', wrote the *fermier-général* who was pursuing them near Nogent-sur-Seine in July 1706, 'that they no longer keep to the woods, but go on the ordinary roads, up to the very gates of the towns.'[76]

The forest as refuge

In time of war however, the position was reversed: the forest could serve as a refuge for the weak – one thinks of the Chouans in the Vendée or the Resistance in the Vercors during the last war. In 1814, when the Cossacks arrived in eastern France and, the story goes, slashed with their sabres the beams of the house where Joan of Arc was born in Domrémy, the villagers took to the woods as their ancestors had done during the constant pillaging of the Thirty Years' War. On that occasion, the troubles were so protracted in Lorraine that the peasants, prevented for too long from returning to their houses, lost touch with civilization and became 'wild men of the woods', robbing without compunction officers and soldiers in the king's service. To put an end to it meant organizing man-hunts and holding multiple executions, under the authority of the maréchal de la Ferté-Senneterre in 1643.[77]

Another category of refugees were the poor: beggars, vaga-bonds and outcasts, who for want of anywhere else to go, took to squatting on the 'common land' at the forest edge of village terri-tory. They would settle there with their families, in shacks made of branches, wattle and daub. As a rule the village communities toler-ated these *logistes* (cabin-dwellers) as they were called.[78] But some-times a few of them grew prosperous by reclaiming the forest. Solid houses would appear, and with them began the complaints, lawsuits and threats from the established villagers. This happened in the eighteenth century in the Loire valley in Anjou, where the poor had lodged on the edges of water-meadows, or on the *gâtines*, unfarmed land once reclaimed from the forest and later aban-doned:

> Many of these little groups of cabins put up clandestinely two hundred years ago on common land are today properly built hamlets, whose wretched beginnings one would never sus-pect if they did not have names betraying their origins: for example Les Loges [a word which in the eighteenth century denoted log-cabins in the forest, used by woodcutters or charcoal-burners]; or else names with a colonial ring to them: Le Nouveau Monde [the New World], Canada, Mis-sissippi, Cayenne.[79]

These were poor Americas indeed, unrewarding frontiers for their pioneer settlers.

The village ideal: producing all one's needs

Providing for all its own needs was the usual inclination of the village. As long as it was a certain size (over 500 inhabitants) it could even find enough marriageable girls and boys on the spot to ensure its biological survival. Otherwise neighbouring villages, or more rarely migrants who settled there, would provide new blood. As a rule autonomy prevailed: Romainville, a winegrowing village on the outskirts of Paris was very largely endogamous in the eighteenth century.[80]

The village tended then to live as an isolated unit;[81] it had its own institutions, its landlord or landlords, its community, its commonly owned property, its feast-days, its social life, its customs, its dialect, its fairy tales, songs, dances, proverbs, and its ritual mockery of neighbouring villages. One list from the towns and villages of the Côte-d'Or, tells us some of the unflattering nicknames bestowed on their inhabitants: lily-livers, frogs, pigs, wolves, empty-bags, bran-bellies – the two latter names being conferred upon the people of Is-sur-Tille.[82] The need to make fun of one's neighbour, the jeers and mocking songs, the real feuds which could end in long-drawn-out lawsuits, are all evidence that here was a miniature *patrie*, with all the faults, excesses and enmities to be found between great countries. At certain times of year, fights broke out among the young men of the village, the *tapageurs de cabaret* (inn-brawlers), and blood might be shed. Between 1780 and 1790, a ten years' war was waged between the inhabitants of Livinhac-le-Supérieur (today le-Haut) and those of Flagnac, despite the forceful intervention of the bishop of Rodez. Quarrels like this had barely died out in the Aveyron by 1890.[83]

Hatred or malice are powerful motives for making one's mark, asserting one's identity – hence the large number of quarrels over prestige: who would have the highest steeple, the finest church, the most decorated altar?[84] Hence too the strong desire for independence and autonomy. The village thus sentenced itself to be self-supporting, to depend on no outside assistance. The villagers would all help each other out, whether in building a house, threshing grain, fishing a pool or putting rims on cartwheels: the red-hot iron rim was clamped round the wooden wheel which was then plunged blazing into the village pond: the suddenly-cooled rim would contract, gripping the wheel.[85]

This effort to be independent was based on not insignificant resources: the village often owned common land, pasture and forests; it had its mill for grinding grain, its feudal bakehouse (sometimes bought back from the local squire by the villagers) for baking bread; it had its own presses, for olives, grapes or walnuts, depending on the area. And more than one might expect, it could provide its own *services*, maintaining a diversified secondary sector. In his memoirs, Joseph Cressot remembers the artisans in his native village in about 1900 – a village near Langres which in those days still had its own vines:

> The fingers of my two hands would not be enough to list them all: millers, fullers, master sawyer; shoemakers and clog-makers, wheelwrights, blacksmiths, carpenters and joiners, masons, oil-merchants, weavers, coopers . . . and even a notorious bone-setter.[86]

All these were hard-working craftsmen, 'men of experience': the masons 'knew everything there was to know about building a house, from the choice and quarrying of stone to the fixing of *laves* to the roof'.[87] That did not prevent such artisans from owning their fields and gardens, and keeping a few animals. Indeed how else could they have survived?

Some of them should be singled out as playing a vital role in the village: the blacksmith, likely to be a dominant figure since at least the twelfth century, sometimes the leader of a gang, often rather a sinister fellow, recognizable by the lead rings in his ears;[88] the baker, a late-comer (rarely recorded before the nineteenth century) whose appearance marked the long-awaited triumph of white bread; the inn-keeper, later café proprietor, an essential agent of popular culture, source of information, organizer of special occasions, money-lender and sometimes usurer; 'his house was the

usual meeting place for people who lived in the street or the hamlet'[89] – often a rival centre to the church.

One has the strong impression that these 'active presences' guar-
anteed the village's autonomy, as if it needed in some way to be
defended. The same effort is visible in the hamlets of the Limousin.
Besides their everyday occupations, some people were specialists
contributing to these little communities some particular assistance
or skill: the pig-killer, the *langueyeur* (the man who could diagnose
tape-worm infestation in pigs), the barber, the buyer and seller on
commission, *lou mège*, who knew the medicinal properties of
plants.[90]

If we know the number of artisans or quasi-artisans in a village,
we can make a reasonable guess at its approximate size. In the
eighteenth century, the village of Ermont, 17 kilometres from
Pontoise,[91] whose population was mostly composed of *laboureurs*
(moderately well-off peasants) and winegrowers, plus a few
'*laboureurs-vignerons*' and *journaliers*, that is day-labourers, or
farmhands (also known as *brassiers*), could boast not only several
coopers, but also a blacksmith, a butcher, more than one pork-
butcher, one or two grocers, inn-keepers and *tabellions* (village
notaries), a midwife and a schoolmaster. A list like this betokens
something approaching a bourg or at any rate a large village with at
least 500 inhabitants, including some master-merchants and a few
bourgeois from Paris who owned land there.

Something similar would be true of Saint-Didier-sur-Arroux,[92]
in the Morvan, though in this case one is not so sure. With 3,000
hectares of territory altogether, it is logical enough (assuming 3 or
4 hectares per head) that there should have been between 750 and
1,000 inhabitants: 950 in about 1865, as compared to only 353 in
1975. But in the early twentieth century, the village is recorded as
having about fifty artisans. This seems a lot. Did their presence
indicate that Saint-Didier fulfilled the role of a bourg? There are
indeed four or five hamlets scattered around Saint-Didier and living in its shadow. But without a detailed study, how can one know
for sure? The Arroux valley, a deep trench running north to south
in the dense mass of the Morvan, is quite an important route, but
Saint-Didier lies between Autun (twenty kilometres to the north of

the village) and Toulon-sur-Arroux (fifteen kilometres to the south). Autun, the big town, and Toulon, a large bourg, would have had the little locality at their mercy. One ought of course to relate the village to its surroundings, in this cattle country where livestock fairs were a continual occurrence: Autun in 1813 had 13, one of which lasted a whole month from 31 July. Toulon-sur-Arroux had eight in the same year, but only two were held at Saint-Didier, which was apparently only marginal to these busy livestock fairs, accompanied by the usual subsidiary exchanges which kept small trade alive in the area. A hiring fair for farm servants was however created there, rather late it is true, in 1874. Was Saint-Didier after all simply an ordinary village, a little more isolated than most and therefore obliged more than most to provide for its own needs?

The indispensable link to the outside world

However hard a village tried, it could never be entirely self-sufficient. It would have to sell its surplus at market or at the fair in the neighbouring bourg, if only to obtain the money necessary to pay seigneurial dues, state taxes, or for the *sel du devoir*, the state-monopolized salt which was in itself, while the *ancien régime* lasted, an externally-imposed breach in the village economy. To 'pump up money for taxes' as a report on stock-farming in eighteenth-century Limousin puts it,[93] the peasants would go to the bourg or to town on market days, taking butter, vegetables, eggs, poultry, livestock on the hoof, wool and wood, in long processions by farm cart or on foot. In the bourg, they could buy bread from the baker, and meat which the butcher sold in ready-cut joints: thus the mountain-dwellers from Morzine (an Alpine locality in what is today Haute-Savoie) used in the eighteenth century to go down to Martigny in the Valais (what a journey!), to buy butcher meat. The bourg also provided spices, dressmaking material, tools, iron-mongery; and the money-lender might be open for custom, although increasingly, in the nineteenth century at least, he was being replaced by local notables and inn-keepers in the villages.[94]

In areas that produced too little to enjoy this kind of exchange, the great recourse more often than not was outworking to order, for merchants from the town or bourg. This kind of industry was omnipresent in country districts in the eighteenth century, whether weaving, fulling cloth, or as in Saint-Julien-Molin-Molette in the Forez, milling: a little stream, the Ternay, powered mills of all kinds – for oil, grain, metal work, crushing lead ore, spinning silk.[95]

Another resource was haulage. During breaks in the farming year, the peasant could use his team and carts to become a haulier. It was an activity that led to regular journeys and some extra-ordinary cases of specialization. The 'chartons' (carriers) of Rembercourt-aux-Pots, a village in the Barrois mouvant (directly attached to the king of France) later to be famous for its martyrdom in the early stages of the 1914 war, and possessing a sumptuous church indicating its long-standing prosperity, were already by the sixteenth century taking part in the international trade flow between the Low Countries and Italy.[96] Another example is Orgelet, an old fortress-town on the Jura plateau, with a fortified church, which dispatched hauliers with their waggons and draught-teams all over France. The residents of Cieutat and Ossun, in the Pyrenees, specialized in carrying dairy produce from the Campan valley to Toulouse and elsewhere. Ox-teams from Salles, Belin and Sanguinet brought fresh fish to Bordeaux from Arcachon.[97]

Some transporters were specialists within a small radius, like the middleman known as the tourtahlier in the Basse-Corrèze, who 'would go to town once or twice a week, on a donkey or by charretou, to buy goods on behalf of his customers'.[98] In Savoie, the barlotiers, peasant-middlemen, were still within living memory tak-ing butter, cheeses, poultry, calves and sheep to the weekly market in the neighbouring small town, and bringing back 'messages' for their customers: skeins of spun wool (exchanged for fleeces), cof-fee, sugar, oil. This activity came to an end only fairly recently when weekly bus services began to operate between the mountain villages.[99]

But peasant rolling-stock was always exposed to requisition by the authorities, usually for supplying the troops. No excuse – even the need to fetch in the harvest – could prevail against such orders. In 1695, 1,400 farm carts transported the necessary wheat and oats from Verdun to the army in Alsace.[100] During the summer of 1709, the army in the north commandeered (and endangered the lives of)[101] the peasant carriers, who were sent to Landrecies,

> notwithstanding the bad roads caused by the almost incessant rains. Several horses died, and the others were quite worn out and on their last legs. I learn however that they were forced to take a convoy to Valenciennes, which means these peasants will be in no state, on their return, to take another convoy.

In 1744, the army in the Alps requisitioned the peasants of Dauphiné and Provence as porters.[102]

Villages near large cities, needless to say, gave up attempts at self-sufficiency without much of a fight. They prospered by specializing in dairy products or fruit and vegetables. In the eighteenth century, the central Paris markets were supplied, in the early hours of the morning, by the waggons of market gardeners from neighbouring villages. Peasant holdings nearest to the towns were divided into gardens and worked with pick or spade, ploughs being used only on big farms. There were other profitable lines: stone was the source of wealth for Andelarre[103] near Vesoul; and Ermont, mentioned earlier, specialized, like other villages near Paris, in wet-nursing babies from the capital – poor little creatures who all too often died soon after their arrival, having hardly had time to be christened.

The parishes in the Armançon valley – Argentenay, Lézinnes, Pacy, Vireaux – about ten kilometres south-east of Tonnerre and with direct roads to Paris since the sixteenth century, sent wet-nurses, gardeners, domestic servants, male and female, and wine-carriers who sometimes settled in the capital as wine-shop proprietors. Weddings and christenings were occasions to meet up again either in Paris or in the Tonnerrois.[104]

Movement between villages

People, as well as goods, travelled between village, bourg and town: countless individuals left home. In Provence, it was artisans rather than peasants, men rather than women, the poor rather than the well-to-do, who were tempted to travel, or run away. The 'wild rovers' sometimes stopped, settled down and married, bringing fresh air and new blood to the village system. In the little village between Champagne and the Barrois where I spent my childhood (and which I mention too often) there were, in about 1914, nine 'artisans' to about two hundred inhabitants. Four of them were not native to the village – the joiner, the blacksmith, the saddler and the baker; five had been born there – the wheelwright, the miller, the innkeeper and the two grocers. As for the peasant population proper, its new blood consisted of ploughboys from elsewhere: I know of at least two who founded families there.

Another kind of movement, in the opposite direction, was that of travelling salesmen or artisans coming out to the villages: in one village in the Meuse between 1914 and 1920, there were two butchers (a belated luxury) serving customers on the main square, one on Saturday morning, the other on Sunday – the only days, it is true, when people ate meat. Over the purchase of some humble boiling-beef, the customer, more often a woman than a man, would haggle and take her time, making sure people saw her, taking full advantage of her social prominence – for to be buying meat was in itself a sign of affluence. To the village too came the greengrocer, the knife-grinder, the tinker, the *cossonnier* who collected milk and eggs, and the man most integrated of all into village life, always ready to chat and ask for news of everyone, the so-called 'merchant' but actually collector of rabbit skins, who at the beginning of this century also collected from Revigny-sur-Ornain (Meuse) 'scrap iron, old mattresses, worn-out stoves and pans, odd fire-irons, broken tongs, skillets with holes in them, cracked spades'.[105]

The same sight might be seen in any region of France. In Les Nonières, an Alpine village in the Diois, during the Second Empire,

> spoons and forks [as everywhere else in rural France] were made of tinplated iron which tarnished quickly. Periodically the *estamaïre* [the tinker] would come and set up his brazier under the canopy of the communal bakehouse; on top was a cauldron full of molten tin, from which the cutlery came out bright as new, to the great amazement of the village children who were fascinated by the metamorphosis.[106]

One of my friends who spent his childhood in a village of the Morvan before 1914, remembers the tinker as

> a sort of giant Vulcan, dark and hairy like a great bear . . . He always wore the same combination of odd, patched clothes, worn into holes . . . by the passage of time even more than by the fire of his brazier . . . People knew that he did not drink much, that he never washed, and took off his clothes only when they fell apart; he smelt worse than a billy goat, but was thoroughly honest. 'You'll see how beautiful they'll come out', he would say to me, showing me the tarnished forks and spoons. 'More beautiful than silver ones.'[107]

In Franche-Comté in the old days, the most widespread of travelling trades was probably that of the *pignards de chanvre*, hemp-combers. Hemp was 'retted in the meadows, then stripped by the grower himself, and taken to the paddle-beaters', powered by the waters of the streams, before finally being handed over to the combers,

> poor wretches, often from Savoy, who would arrive in the village to face the jeers of the children and the distrust of the villagers. They would work in teams of three on each grower's stock of hemp. In small villages one team was enough . . . They were poorly paid: in 1812, 15 centimes for a kilo of tow plus food, or 20 centimes without food. In a few days, the village's hemp was combed and shouldering their tools, they would head for the next village.[108]

Other travelling services were provided by the molecatcher or the snake-collector.[109] No so long ago, in the Alps, the Pyrenees, the Massif Central, and many other places, pedlars on foot or with little carts were still plying their modest trades. But is it a sight that has completely died out? In a little village in the *Périgord vert*, south of the Limousin, even today, 'a long blast on a motor-horn, every morning, means the milkman has arrived [i.e. the milk *collector*]. A bugle call? It is four o'clock on Monday afternoon, and the grocer is here. A hunting-horn means the baker, on Wednesday afternoons at three.'[110]

I shall not here embark upon a list (for it would require many pages) of the temporary workers attracted by haymaking, harvest, grape-picking and threshing. The *gavots* from the high Alps used to come down to the plains of Provence, where they soon acquired and kept a taste for wine. And there were the teams of harvesters in the Diois, the *soques*, who took advantage of the staggered harvest timetable at these altitudes to go from one district to another, 'marching at night, so as to be in reach of more work at dawn', singing as they tramped through the sleeping villages.[111] In Viry, a little village in what is now Haute-Savoie, as late as 1845, according to the local priest, the 'gangs' of labourers would arrive at harvest-time, each gang having at its head a man 'who carried all the sickles of his companions in a bundle', to the sound of the haunting chants of harvest songs. Then 'the inns would be open all day long, against the laws of both church and state'. And it was farewell to peace, quiet and piety.[112] Farmhands from the Massif Central too had always gone down to the wine- and cereal-growing Languedoc, which awaited them with impatience. What would Olivier de Serres (1539–1619), lord of Pradel in the Vivarais, have done without his extra harvesters?

> God, the sovereign housekeeper, in his providence has provided [for this, he writes] . . . by bringing down from the mountains and cold places [i.e. the Massif Central] into the plains and warm country an infinite number of people to harvest the grain . . . These poor folk . . . earn their living and enough money to keep them in winter, having insufficient work to maintain themselves at home.[113]

FIGURE 13
Regional trade specialization of temporary emigrants from the Auvergne in the eighteenth century

- ● Chief town of *élection*
- ▬ Boundary of *généralité* of Riom
- --- *Election* boundaries

0   10 km

Montaigut

BOURBONNAIS

Riom

Thiers

FOREZ

MASONS
LONG SAWYERS

Clermont-Ferrand

Billom

LIMOUSIN

IRONMONGERS

Issoire

SAWYERS

LONG SAWYERS

Besse

Ambert

La Tour

CHIMNEY
SWEEPS

RAG AND
BONE MEN

Bort

ODD JOBS
TINKERS

BOATMEN

La Chaise-Dieu

NAVVIES
SAWYERS
ODD JOBS

Brioude

NAVVIES

Mauriac

HAWKERS

SAWYERS

EMIGRATION
TOWARDS
SPAIN

Salers

Murat

Langeac

VELAY

Aurillac

St Flour

EMIGRATION
TOWARDS
PARIS

PEDLARS

COBBLERS
TINKERS

WATER CARRIERS

FLOOR POLISHERS
STREET-PORTERS
BOOTBLACKS

ROUERGUE

GÉVAUDAN

Lot

Dordogne

Allier

HEMP WORKERS

After A. Poitrineau, in *Revue d'histoire moderne et contemporaine*, 1962, ix.

As our last example, let us note the departure, again in the nine-teenth century, of the *galvachers* of the Morvan, drivers of ox-teams who would set off for neighbouring regions in March, not to return with their oxen and carts until November. Traditional fêtes today re-enact the ritual departure of the *galvacher* in his 'blue smock or *biaude*, clogs and round hat'; music is played on old-fashioned viols and it is a good excuse to dance the traditional *branles*.[114]

There were even more extraordinary journeys: among the migrants from the Briançonnais in the Alps, were primary-school teachers, coming 'down from their mountains, a quill-pen stuck in their hats', leaving home temporarily or for good.[115] And I have not even mentioned the itinerants, the Romanies, 'Bohemians' and gipsies, who were more talked about than seen.

All villages were thus obliged to have some links with the out-side world. In 1787 and 1788, a traveller was making a leisurely journey through Basse-Auvergne.[116] Near Thiers, alongside quite ordinary villages, he found a series of strange hamlets, 'formed by the different branches of one family'. They marry amongst them-selves, he reports, share all their property, and have their own laws and customs. They form a sort of republic with a chief, and all indi-viduals are equal. The hamlet of Pinon, founded, it is said, in the twelfth century, consists of four households and nineteen people. The chief or master, elected by the community, is in charge of everything, does all buying and selling, and collects the money. They also elect a mistress who is in command of the women. She is never chosen from the same household as the master. Goods are never shared out. The group owns altogether 'three pairs of oxen, thirty cows and eighty sheep'. Linen, furniture, clothes and shoes are made by the community. Its only outside purchases are iron and salt. So even this fraternity, though a marvellous example of self-sufficiency, was not totally autarkic: even if the need had not existed to pay *gabelle* and other taxes, it would still have been open to the outside world, if only very marginally, in order to be able to buy the iron and salt it needed.[117]

CHAPTER FIVE

Explaining the system:
the bourg

After the village, the bourg (taking the word in its broadest sense: anything from a large village to a small town) was the next step up towards the town proper. Within rural society, the bourg itself often represented the outside world as a whole: administration, justice, trade. Although it channelled only 'the smallest capillaries and blood vessels of large-scale trade' to these remote corners of the countryside, such links 'fulfilled a role in stimulating and enlivening the region out of all proportion to the tiny volume of goods handled'.[118]

This was something that went back a long way: as early as the tenth century, as Georges Duby points out,[119] the bourgs with their dependent villages and hamlets were already recognizable:

> The lowest judicial division [in the Mâconnais] was the *viguerie* (*vicaria*) . . . Centred on a *vicus* (village or bourg), usually located on a main road or near a ford, it would contain about fifteen hamlets within a radius of a league; anyone could travel to the centre, to attend court or to plead his case and come home again within a half-day. This administrative division would also be a geographical unit, its limits set by marshes, forests or hills, in other words the major obstacles to peasant transport. Originally it would have been a population unit (archaeological evidence has shown that its *chef-lieu* is the oldest inhabited centre) and also a religious unit . . . as is indicated by the antiquity of the patronal dedication of its church.

But such a unit would be unthinkable without some exchange of goods at a market or markets, or without the existence of money, however minor its role in those far-off times.

The bourg as model

Indeed there could be no bourg as such unless the surrounding villages and hamlets really made use of its markets, fairs, services and meeting-places. The inseparable complement of the villages,

> it derived its wealth [and justification] from the web of relations it made possible, prospering and expanding only if they did. It would usually have grown up at a crossroads, often at the entrance or exit of a valley, always [or almost always] on the edges of two *pays* producing different kinds of goods, whose inhabitants would come to the bourg to exchange the fruits of their labour. The function of the bourg was encapsulated in the local market, the *halle* shared by all the villages. Only intermittently busy, its animation would subside between market and fair days. Its heart was the market-square, surrounded on every side by taverns which on certain days of the week rang to the sounds of a temporary clientele – easy prey for the shopkeepers and 'men of law',[120]

– and also for wine-sellers, usurers, small-time money-lenders and canny horse-traders.

The bourg or small town was also the place where festivities and solemn processions took place. In May 1583, an alarming drought having struck the region around Bar-sur-Seine, rogatory processions from the local villages made their way as far as the town. The day ended in predictable disorder:

> I must frankly say [a chronicler reports] that these *filles blanches* [girls dressed in white who had just taken part in the procession] most of them chambermaids, drank too much in the evening, and after nightfall allowed themselves to be kissed and went into the cornfields, there to commit debauchery and all kinds of dissolute behaviour.[121]

Excitement on fair days not infrequently ended like this.

The bourg essentially stood for domination: it reigned over a rural district which needed its services – but which also provided its sustenance, for the bourg itself could not otherwise have existed. A string of villages within a radius of about five to ten kilometres, rarely more, were thus dependent upon it. The maximum distance was virtually fixed by the journey a peasant could manage *on foot* (or on horseback or in a farm cart) in order to get from the village to the bourg and back in a single day. On 1 Ventôse of Year V (1797), the newly-created *département* of the Loire held a count of its inhabitants. Saint-Symphorien, a little *chef-lieu de canton* (a smaller equivalent of the English county town), contained 1,936 people, 'of twelve years and over'; around it were four villages: Naux (462 inhabitants), Fournaux (445); Vendranges (275) and Saint-Priest-la-Roche (323).[122] In about 1850, the very small town of Châtillon, 'capital' of the Haut-Diois in the Alps, was *chef-lieu* for some 6,600 inhabitants scattered in ten *communes* round about: Bonneval, Boulc, Châtillon, Creyers, Glandage, Lus-la-Croix-Haute, Menglon, Ravel-et-Ferriers, Saint-Roman and Treschenu. The modest *chef-lieu* had a post office, a tax collector, a brigade of gendarmes, a justice of the peace, a few notaries, a doctor, a weekly market, several fairs, an annual patronal fête (the *vogue*), which was much frequented, many shopkeepers and artisans, 'not to mention the grocers, bakers, café-proprietors and butchers, a wheelwright, a cooper and a few tailors'.[123] In Anjou, the bourg of Durtal fulfilled similar functions for seven villages. Twentieth-century population figures (1962) give an idea of its relative importance: Durtal, 3,102 inhabitants; Baracé, 420; Daumeray, 1,106; Etriché, 887; Huillé, 526; Montigné, 397; Morannes, 1,694; Les Rairies, 810.[124]

Such was the model, reproduced in literally thousands of copies, of the ties of subordination linking bourg and villages. The bourg not only represented social and economic superiority: it was also the seat of the first tier of law and order. Under the *ancien régime*, it would contain a court of first instance at least, the *prévôté*, and would have its own detachment of the constantly reorganized *maréchaussée* (rural police). In the towns, this legal machinery was growing ever heavier and more complex: lawmen of all sorts, advocates, *procureurs*, justices of every rank proliferated there beyond all reason. In the villages meanwhile, the representatives of seigneurial justice played the same role as a present-day justice of the peace. Sometimes over-represented within the same canton, the various judicial orders might find themselves at odds with one another, giving rise to not a little friction.

Every bourg gradually built up its own zone of influence, depending on changing local circumstances. In the Middle Ages, Thann, the *chef-lieu* of a *seigneurie* in the Vosges in Alsace, extended its jurisdiction in 1344 to take in the villages of Vieux-Thann, Erbenheim, Aspach-le-Bas, and Aspach-le-Haut; in 1361, it took on Roderen, Rammersmatt, Otzenwiller and Leimbach; and in 1497, it acquired the right to graze its flocks on the bans of Cernay, Steinbach, Wittelsheim, Lutterbach, Reiningue, Schweighouse, Ernwiller, Michelbach, Bitschwiller; and the extension continued at the expense of the rights of Belfort, Lauw, Sentheim, Guewenheim and Sewen. In the course of its rise, Thann eliminated two possible rivals, Saint-Amarin and Dannemarie. All this success was achieved through its dynamism and a prosperity reflected in successive building schemes: a collegiate church and a new hospital in 1518; the market in 1519; a new town hall in about 1550; and in a provocative display of wealth, the town launched a crossbow-shooting competition, for which magnificent prizes were awarded.[125] Did this mean that Thann had by now crossed that uncertain frontier between bourg and town? Needless to say, the distinction is sometimes hard to draw, despite what our documents tell us. Thus Fécamp and Elbeuf are described as bourgs,[126] and so is Roanne.[127]

Usually a text, a reference or a detail is enough to tell us that a place was carrying out the functions of a bourg. This would be true of Meulan, which controlled a bridge over the Seine downstream from Paris; of Gray, built on the Saône at the point where it becomes really navigable; of Auray, a picturesque settlement about thirty kilometres from Lorient, which has kept its old-world charm and was once the *chef-lieu* of a 'royal *sénéchaussée* covering 19 parishes'; it would be true too of Bar-sur-Aube, of which an official letter (6 March 1720)[128] tells us: 'Although this town is not very significant in itself, nevertheless . . . it is the centre of one of the strongest *élections* in the *généralité* of Champagne and . . . all the peasants of the surrounding country come here to sell their grain and other produce.' (This is all very well but unarguably falls far short of the former splendours of the fairs of Champagne in which Bar-sur-Aube had once played its part.) The same could be said too of Saint-Affrique (in the present-day *département* of Aveyron) and the dozen or so *communes* surrounding it, where in the eighteenth century, despite the departure of the Protestant merchants and craftsmen, a local industry producing coarse cloth managed to survive.

To identify a bourg, it is perhaps enough simply to ask oneself where one would go to find a doctor or a notary, or where the peasants went to market or to a fair. In Rougemont in the Jura at the beginning of this century, the market was still a great event. From daybreak, the travelling merchants would be arriving with their caravans, and putting up their stalls on the main square, alongside those of the pork-butchers (the only local shopkeepers to set out their wares in the open), while there streamed into the bourg 'a variegated throng of gigs, barouches, farm carts and waggons of all kinds, of women on foot carrying heavy bags'. Country women, 'dressed in black . . . and wearing a *caule* [white bonnet] or hat, would settle themselves under the lime-trees to sell their produce: eggs, butter, chickens, rabbits, vegetables'. On trestles covered with blue, green or red cloth, and in the shops round the square, anything and everything was sold: pitchforks, rakes, scythes, household utensils, china, fabrics, linen, sweets and gingerbread, sausages and hams. On fair days, hucksters selling patent medicines would turn up, and so too did the bone-setter and tooth-puller.[129]

Would it not be true to say that the market is still the essential attribute of the French bourg, even today, although the minimum population level to qualify as such has risen (I shall have more to say about this) to 10,000 to 20,000 inhabitants?[130] (In the Middle Ages that would be the size of a large town.) Take Apt for instance, with its 11,612 inhabitants today. Lying between two towns larger than itself, Cavaillon (21,530 inhabitants, 31 kilometres away) and Carpentras (25,463 inhabitants, 48 kilometres away), it exactly fulfils the functions of the bourg of the past. The nearby village of 'Peyrane' has been the subject of a twentieth-century study, whose author is our guide to the Saturday morning market that has been held in Apt for over four hundred years:

> Vendors' stands fill the public squares. Streets and shops are so crowded that it seems as though all the people from the surrounding area have deserted their homes . . . Doctors' waiting-rooms are crowded . . . Pharmacies do big business. To have a prescription filled, you must stand in a line of fifteen to twenty people. Lawyers' offices are jammed. Notaries meet their colleagues and clients in Arène's café, the same café favored by mayors and town clerks. Each café is the headquarters for a special professional clientele . . . [Here and there, in the squares] farmers are selling hares, thrushes, essence of lavender, lavender honey, beeswax,

– and indeed truffles, fruits and vegetables. In such a scene, yesterday and today undoubtedly mingle.[131]

Gondrecourt (Meuse) and its villages in 1790: the evidence of socio-professional categories

Turning from the system to look more closely at a real-life example, I wanted to find one with enough documentary evidence for a fairly detailed inspection. I had thought, on account of Robert Chapuis' excellent study of the Haute-Loue, of choosing that extraordinary valley tucked away in the Jura, which runs along a line from Besançon to Pontarlier, and centres on the lovely little town of Ornans. But its vineyards, industry and trade – notably in salt – and the volume of exchange carried on there (after 1800, Ornans had 24 annual fairs, held on the first and third Tuesday of every month) made the Loue valley, about which I shall have more to say, a rather special case. I was also attracted by the example of

166

the little population centre of Auxonne, a fortress on the Saône and the heart of a tiny *pays* which long maintained its sovereignty, between the duchy and the county of Burgundy. It clung obstinately to its privileges, at least as regards the demands of the king's tax authorities who never managed to get their hands on it, since it fiercely defended its exemptions, and as a further argument against the taxman invoked the 'sterility' of its territory.[132] But by the same token, this was also a rather exceptional example. I wondered about the pays de Gex, but here the Genevan owners of land in the area were a complicating factor in its economy and society. In the end, I chose a less striking and more ordinary example, from which it is consequently more easy to generalize: the canton of Gondrecourt in the Meuse, which at the time when the *département* was created in 1790, stood at the meeting point of several authentic little *pays* with uncertain yet tenacious frontiers: the Ornois, the Blois or Blésois, the Voide, the Vaux, the Vallage and the Bassigny.

Lying in the south of the Meuse *département*, Gondrecourt is the *chef-lieu* of one of its poorest cantons. This is a region of plateaux (the highest point of the *département*, 423 metres, is in the *lieu-dit* Le Buisson d'Amanty). It is a rather cold region: in the late eighteenth century, vines were grown only at Houdelaincourt, Saint-Joire and Tréveray (16 kilometres from Gondrecourt). And vineyards only really developed beyond the northern limits of the canton, where the land dips down along the valley of the Ornain and the climate becomes milder, in Ligny for instance (altitude 220 metres) or Bar-le-Duc (184 metres).

This very ordinary and unexceptional canton lies at the point where two limestone plateaux of different textures come together: to the east the plateau of the Meuse (or the Côtes de Meuse), to the north and west the plateau of the Barrois (or the Côte des Bars). The gaps between them leave room for a series of hollows and it is here, on the clay or marl, that the villages, including Gondrecourt, are built, since it is here that the water, after filtering down through the limestone, bubbles out again in springs, wells, brooks and rivers. A carefully-dammed stream could make a pond big enough to turn a mill-wheel – like the mill in Luméville-en-Ornois which existed as far back as 1261.[133] The limestone also gives rise

FIGURE 14
The region and canton of Gondrecourt

Map by Cassini, late eighteenth century. The superimposed circles indicate the proportional population of the villages.

to many quarries, hence the stone-built villages, surprising to the traveller arriving from *la Champagne humide* where in the early seventeenth century, the houses were still built of wattle and daub and roofed with straw or reeds.[134]

Almost everywhere, the limestone appears in the form of low hills, survivors of erosion. Their tops are covered with forests of beech, hornbeam and oak but with little undergrowth, and the forest itself is thickest in the east: on the Côtes de Meuse, rising towards the river, the forest covers practically everything and it is still possible to get lost in it even today. Between the woods and the low ground there is often farmland on the bare, stony slopes: they literally turn white during ploughing with all the stones that come to the surface. The plough itself, we are told, used to need four, six or even ten horses, and it was useless to pick off the stones, because the next ploughing would only turn up more. The result was clear: while the hayfields were at the same level as the village, the cereal fields were on the slopes above it. At harvest time the great four-wheeled carts, groaning under loads of wheat or oats, would come down to the village with a deafening screech of 'mechanical' brakes locked full on, while somebody held the shaft-horse back by its bridle.

The soil is not particularly rich here. Out of 100 hectares, half at most would be arable (all subject to triennial rotation), a tenth would be unused, about a third would be forest, and the rest would consist of gardens and meadows. After about 1730, it is true, a blessing did reach the region: the potato, which spread here early, as it did in nearby Lorraine.

Life on the whole then was not easy perhaps, but it was possible. The population of the canton, 6,903 inhabitants in 1796 and 8,263 in 1803, reached 11,668 in 1851; thereafter it declined. The count made in 1796[135] (which noted incidentally that 253 of the inhabitants had been mobilized in the army, and 133 were already dead) also gave a breakdown of the population: 1,605 men, 1,629 women, 1,589 boys, 1,515 girls. And it listed the livestock: 3,680 oxen, cows and calves; 1,633 horses and mares of 'bastard' race; 7,181 sheep; 625 goats; no donkeys or mules; 939 pigs. The stock was not of high quality: the horses and oxen were of only modest size, cows were harnessed to the plough, the sheep were small but 'good' (to eat, presumably), and the pigs were bought from merchants at fairs. By my calculations, wheat production works out at about three quintals per head.

As in the rest of the Meuse, there was metal-working in the canton, which consequently had its mines, blast furnaces (six or seven metres high in the eighteenth century), ironworks and ore-mills. But industry did not operate all year round, on account of the excessive amounts of fuel it would take to keep the furnaces working continuously, and of the short supply in summer both of labour and of the water needed to turn machinery. If efforts were made to prolong metal-working beyond the winter, by holding the water at abnormal levels, there was even a risk of flooding the crops. Metal ore, *la pierre à myne*, was not lacking, and wood – always a problem for ironworking since 100 *stères* of wood were needed for 100 kilos of iron – was fortunately plentiful; but it had to be transported. It was forested on the Barrois plateau to the west, and particularly on the eastern plateaux towards the Meuse river: Vouthon-Haut, in mid-forest, had its specialized wood-cutters. It was where the two plateaux met, in the hollow between them, along the valley of the Ornain and its little tributaries, that the furnaces and forges were located, dependent as they were on the mill-races.

All in all, this was a largely forested region, like Lorraine itself, and coming within the area of Lorraine dialects and Lorraine villages. Here were the same rows of large adjoining houses (containing barn and stable as well as living quarters) with their backs turned on the gardens behind, but their massive barn doors opening directly, at the front, on to the broad streets, *les rues à usoirs*, cluttered on both sides with carts, harrows, ploughs, dungheaps. The houses were roofed with the curved tiles known as 'Roman' tiles, although it is not thought today that this Lorraine tradition has anything to do with Rome.

In 1803, Gondrecourt had 1,139 inhabitants; by 1851 there were 1,692. The ring of villages coming within its sphere of influence was limited by the force of attraction (sometimes stronger than its own) of other bourgs and small towns: Ligny-en-Barrois to the north-west (2,800 and 3,234 inhabitants for the same dates); Void

FIGURE 15

Roman roads through Lorraine and the area where 'under and over' tiles in the Mediterranean style are the traditional roofing material

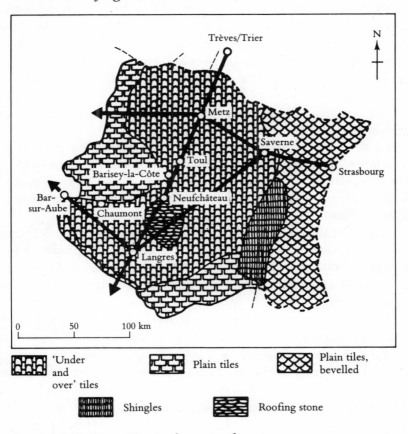

Source: J.-R. Pitte, *Histoire du paysage français.*

to the north, almost exactly the same size as Gondrecourt, and having served in the past as a somewhat inadequate port and staging post near the Meuse; Vaucouleurs, also on the Meuse, and the same size as Ligny-en-Barrois; Neufchâteau (3,380 inhabitants in 1788)

171

again on the Meuse – so the entire river valley was outside Gondrecourt's little empire which reached only just as far as Vouthon-Haut or Les Roises.

West and south of it were Montiers (1,257 inhabitants in 1803) on the Saulx, a little river more enclosed than the Ornain; Joinville on the Marne (2,210 inhabitants in 1788); and lastly Andelot, on the Rognon, a tributary of the Marne, which I mention only because part of the canton of Gondrecourt was at the end of the *ancien régime*, attached to the *prévôté* of Andelot, and through that to the *bailliage* of Chaumont.

The canton of Gondrecourt was at the same time the largest of the cantons in the Meuse (341 square kilometres) and in about 1803, the least densely populated, 24 inhabitants to the square kilometre. The neighbouring cantons – Void, 274 square kilometres, Montiers-sur-Saulx, 199 square kilometres – had a density respectively of 37 and 29 inhabitants per square kilometre. This confirms the rule that the sparser the population, the greater the extent of the bourg-village complex. No doubt it was the large area of the canton that explained the existence of markets in the villages of Bonnet, Tréveray and Demange-aux Eaux, which if I am not mistaken, added their services to the four annual fairs at Gondrecourt.

The clearest sign of a bourg's capacity to act as animating force in a rural area is of course in the first place the relation between its own population and that of the canton of which it is the centre. If we give the former the value of 1, the cantonal population in about 1803 works out at a minimum of 1.37 (around Bar-le-Duc) and a maximum of 11.47 for the canton of Damvillers. Within this classification, the canton of Gondrecourt, at 6.95, is lower not only than Damvillers but also than Vigneulles-lès-Hattonchâtel (11), Dain-sur-Meuse (9.44), Souilly (8.34), Void (8.32) and Montfaucon-en-Argonne (7.8). Although these figures need some interpreting (the canton is a convenient but not ideal division), they say fairly clearly what they mean: when the figure is low, it implies a close relationship and a corresponding division of labour between centre and periphery, and proves that we are dealing with a town whose influence goes beyond the canton in which we have counted it: such is

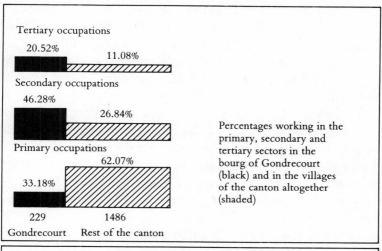

FIGURE 16
The population of Gondrecourt and its canton

Tertiary occupations

20.52%

11.08%

Secondary occupations

46.28%

26.84%

Primary occupations

62.07%

33.18%

229   1486

Gondrecourt   Rest of the canton

Percentages working in the primary, secondary and tertiary sectors in the bourg of Gondrecourt (black) and in the villages of the canton altogether (shaded)

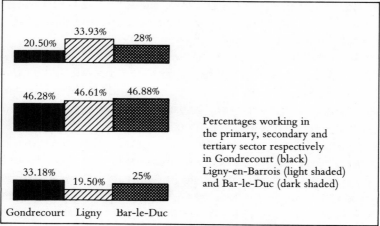

20.50%   33.93%   28%

46.28%   46.61%   46.88%

33.18%   19.50%   25%

Gondrecourt Ligny Bar-le-Duc

Percentages working in the primary, secondary and tertiary sector respectively in Gondrecourt (black) Ligny-en-Barrois (light shaded) and Bar-le-Duc (dark shaded)

Distribution of 'active citizens' into primary, secondary and tertiary occupations.

the case of Bar-le Duc (1.37) and Verdun (1.45) or even of Saint-Mihiel (2.75). If the figure is very high on the contrary, it denotes the illusory prominence of bourgs plunged deep in the country themselves and hardly more than large villages, like Damvillers or Vigneulles-lès-Hattonchâtel.

With a score of 6.95, Gondrecourt does not come off too badly, as is borne out by the socio-occupational composition of its population and that of the surrounding villages. This evidence is available – more or less complete – from the lists of 'active citizens' drawn up in May 1790 by the various municipalities (or 'communities' as they sometimes styled themselves) on the instructions of the Constituent Assembly.[136] All men over 25 and exercising any occupation figure on these registers, which were only supposed to count as active citizens, that is primary electors, those who whether as proprietors or tenants, paid in taxes the value of three days' work, that is about three *livres*. But not only is the figure of three *livres* itself low, some municipalities seem to have completely forgotten their instructions, since the list includes even the names of beggars and – even worse! – a few widows. On the whole, the figures seem to relate coherently to the totals: whereas the total population of the canton (in 1803) was 8,263, the 1790 lists give 1,715 active citizens, that is 20.7% of the whole, a figure which is close to the ratio conventionally assumed between households and the total population (1 to 4 or 5).

Simply as they stand, these lists tell us quite a lot. It is a little surprising for instance that there should only be one baker in the whole canton (living in Gondrecourt naturally). So the villagers made their own bread: every house even after 1789, still had or might have its own oven, and the *mée* or *maie*, a sort of kneading-trough, was still a common piece of furniture. Another surprise is that there were no butchers even in Gondrecourt, apart from one in the large and very busy village of Mauvages. One has to go to Ligny-en-Barrois or Bar-le-Duc to find a proper shop selling meat (five butchers in Ligny, fourteen at Bar-le-Duc). Innkeepers and wineshop proprietors (*cabaretiers*), whom I have lumped together, were not numerous either: eighteen altogether but only found in seven out of twenty-four localities – two inn-keepers in Gondrecourt, one innkeeper and two *cabaretiers* in Bonnet, three *cabaretiers* in Dainville-aux-Forges, one innkeeper and three *cabaretiers* in Demange-aux-Eaux, three *cabaretiers* in Rosières-en-Blois. If you turn to Figure 14 on p. 168, you will see that the *cabaretiers* were only found in the villages on the periphery. So our region was not yet really open to alcohol and wine, nor to the regular consumption of meat. Nor was there a single grocer.

And there was no doctor. One had to go to Ligny to find two doctors (plus two surgeons) or to Bar, where there were three doctors and four surgeons. Our canton could boast only of barber-surgeons and precious few of those: seven in all, two in Gondrecourt, two in Mauvages, one in Charcey (now Chassey), one in Bonnet, and one in Vouthon-Haut. On the other hand – but of course our voting registers cannot tell us this – there were midwives everywhere, as the parish birth registers had always recorded.

The score is less depressing for schoolmasters (*recteurs d'école*): eleven for the twenty-four localities. It would still be a rather low figure if the clergy did not, in all probability, do some teaching as well. For literacy was a long-standing feature of the area: even in a modest village like Luméville, there was a schoolmaster in 1689, as we know from the records of his own marriage.[137] And when in the eighteenth century the registration of births, marriages and deaths required the signature of witnesses (especially godfathers and god-mothers of babies baptized) the men could nearly all sign their names, but never, or hardly ever, the women.[137]

We need not linger over the 'bourgeois' in our lists, who are classified as rentiers (but at what level?): eleven altogether, five of them in Gondrecourt. And we may note that five *chevaliers de Saint-Louis* are named, four of them in Gondrecourt.

One distinction repeated everywhere is that between the many *laboureurs* (well-off peasants) and the *manouvriers* (day-labourers) who might elsewhere be known as *brassiers* (farmhands) and who sometimes owned a small plot of land. Of the 1,715 active citizens in the canton, 491 were *laboureurs*, 478 *manouvriers*. There were equal numbers of both categories, a sign, to my mind, that the well-off peasants themselves were only moderately prosperous (around Metz,[138] there were two *manouvriers* for every *laboureur*). Slight though this social distinction might be, it still existed. Village society was as unequal as urban society; it had always had its 'top dogs'.

Another way of weighing up these village societies is to calculate the respective size of the three sectors known as the primary (essentially agriculture); secondary (artisan manufacture) and tertiary (in which I have included all those who did not work with their hands: lawyers, merchants, teachers, priests and rentiers).

In Gondrecourt, the primary sector accounted for 33.18% of the population (the bourg was therefore quite seriously involved in agriculture); the secondary sector for 46.28%; and the tertiary sector for 20.52%. These figures become meaningful when compared to those of the villages of the canton, which I have lumped together for simplicity's sake: here the primary sector amounted to 62.07%, the secondary to 26.84% and the tertiary to 11.08%. And the last figure is a bit generous, since I placed a few doubtful cases in this category. The essential and obvious points to note are the comparatively low number of people in the bourg, as compared to the villages, who were engaged in agricultural activity; the greater importance there on the other hand of artisan production; and the comparatively large number of people in the tertiary sector. My conclusion is that the organization of territory itself creates inequality and hierarchies. Marx saw the conflict between town and country as the oldest example of class struggle – a masterly insight.

The dissymmetry is even more marked when one moves from the bourg to the town proper, large or small. For comparative purposes, I plotted the social composition of Ligny-en-Barrois and Bar-le-Duc on the same table as the canton of Gondrecourt. The respective proportions in Ligny are 19.44%, 46.61%, and 33.93%; and in Bar-le-Duc, 25.06%, 46.88% and 28.05%. The size of the primary sector in Bar-le-Duc as compared to Ligny is surprising at first sight. It is explained by the presence in Bar of 343 winegrowers whom we can assume to have worked the slopes near the town, now abandoned.

Overall, one of the things I find striking is the amount of artisan production, the importance of activities designed to meet *local* needs. In Gondrecourt, Ligny and Bar, very nearly half the occupied population were artisans. In the villages, even more surprisingly, one villager in four was an artisan (while probably also farming a small plot of land). I am struck by the well-filled ranks of shoemakers, wheelwrights, masons, stone-cutters, weavers of wool or hemp, carters, woodcutters, metal-refiners, nail-makers, *varcoliers* (saddlers)[139] and messengers 'on foot' or 'by horse'.

Without intending to, I have rather neglected Gondrecourt's own history (a poorly recorded one as it happens) since it was not particularly relevant to my purpose. This little town, more like a village in appearance, had taken advantage of a crossroads: Bâle–Reims, Chaumont–Verdun. Its fortifications did not prevent it being twice captured in the fourteenth and fifteenth centuries, and burned down each time. It had the misfortune of lying at the meeting point of three threatening frontiers, those of Champagne which had since 1285 been those of the French kingdom; those of the duchy of Bar (the *Barrois mouvant* alone had come under the French crown in 1302); and those of the duchy of Lorraine. So Gondrecourt had several masters, all eager to possess it, to hold it to ransom and to tax it. The king's tax agents, in Langres, were the most menacing. There were however a few advantages to be derived from this confusion: concerning noble birth for instance, the Champagne custom '*Le ventre anoblit*' (the womb ennobles), was regularly invoked in Gondrecourt, so that a son whose father was a commoner but whose mother was noble could claim nobility, which the duc de Bar would grant, if valid proof was provided, without even claiming from the applicant (as was the rule in the *bailliage* of Bar, but Gondrecourt was exempted) one third of the property inherited from the non-noble father.[140]

Once a fortress, then downgraded, Gondrecourt consisted of 'the high town' with its walls and towers, and 'the low town', more lively, better supplied with water, busy with shopkeepers and deriving prosperity from its Friday market and regular fairs; it was easier to take livestock out to graze from here than it was for the peasants and householders in the high town, who were subject to close control by the gatekeepers. Its fortifications did not make Gondrecourt a key town, only at best a lookout post, surrounded by forests where enemies could move about easily without being seen. In 1635,[141] when Richelieu went to war with the house of Austria, the duc d'Angoulême, who was in command of the French army guarding the *Barrois mouvant*, made sure to leave a small detachment in Gondrecourt, 'because it is a crossing place'. When Louis XIV, in the course of simplifying the defence of the frontiers, had the fortifications demolished (all that remains of them today is 'a tower with a pointed roof'[142] and the grand name of Gondrecourt-le-Château) the military downgrading of the town did not affect its influence in the region, nor the services and activities it sheltered. One document[143] tells us that twenty-nine villages came under the jurisdiction of its *prévôté* (the bottom tier of the judicial system). And its deanery (dependent on the arch-deaconry of Ligny and beyond that on the bishopric of Toul) covered twenty-five parishes.[144] From its distant past the town had inherited a church (Romanesque and Gothic) in which several illustrious men were buried, notably a knight who had fought for François I at Pavia (1525) and the siege of Naples (1528). There was still a *maison des Recollets* there in 1790, when the municipality and the district were officially installed (Gondrecourt having briefly been a *chef-lieu de district*). But these signs and a few others – a dis-affected leper-house, a hospital, a manufactory of good quality serge still functioning in 1700 – did not elevate the little town above a fairly humdrum existence, one that had little significance except in relation to the poor country districts which it dominated, though not to excess, and for which it provided some kind of stimulus.

CHAPTER SIX

Explaining the system:
the towns

Towns form our third tier. We should not expect everything to become clear at this point, as if the system is to be explained from the top downwards. For there have been as many urban identities and roles as there have been towns. And the smallest towns, of which there are so many, may be barely distinguishable from bourgs. Like the latter, they may have been plunged knee-deep in agricultural life, which remained the occupation of the vast majority of people until the Industrial Revolution and indeed well beyond.

The initial problem, in constructing a valid typology of urban systems, is to distinguish between what is and what is not a town. For instance, to a seventeenth-century Frenchman, like Furetière the author of the *Dictionnaire* (1690), it was quite simple: a town deserved the title only if it was surrounded by walls. These made it a world apart, distinct from the countryside around. They were the sign of its independence, evidence of its identity. But there have been perfectly good towns with no walls and on the other hand some walled settlements which hardly qualify as towns. A traveller passing in 1672 through Nuits, the town in Burgundy whose vintages would soon be famous, was not too sure how valid the criterion was. Nuits, he wrote,

> can be called a town because it has walls, moats, drawbridges and a *bailliage*; for otherwise there is but one good main street, which is however inhabited only by coopers on account of the quantity of wines harvested around the town.[145]

179

Indeed the little town's population did not pass the 2,000 mark and then only just, until the nineteenth century, when the *Statistique de la Côte-d'Or* indicates that it measured a mere '400 metres in circumference'![146]

On the other hand, there were plenty of walled villages, which no one would dream of describing as towns. There were several such for instance round Narbonne: Canet, Saint-Nazaire and Saint-Vallier (which even had a double row of fortifications surrounded by a large trench, a *cava magna*). Another example in the same region is Ginestas, whose ancient moats eventually became humble horse-ponds.[147] Nor can there be any doubt what to call Rouvray: famous for its oak forest, it was no more than a village, yet it boasted moats and ramparts until the sixteenth century.[148]

Statisticians are inclined to solve the dilemma by classifying towns and conurbations according to the size of their *concentrated* population: anything over 2,000 inhabitants counts as a town, while under this figure it is described as a bourg or village. This is certainly a clear-cut distinction, possibly a little too much so, since the crucial dividing-line is bound to have varied from period to period. This awkward question will be considered again later.[149]

What counts as a town?

Rather than its walls or the size of its population, the most obvious characteristic of a town is the way it concentrates its activity into as confined an area as possible, cramming its inhabitants closely together – 'so many people in such a small space!' as Ange Goudar was already saying in the eighteenth century[150] – obliging them to crowd through streets sometimes too narrow for traffic, and eventually to build upwards, the only direction where there was any room left, especially if a town wall contained and stifled expansion.

The walls could of course be moved, and sometimes were, like stage sets. As a result, the town could breathe a little more freely. In the newly-acquired space, gardens, orchards and ploughed fields might appear, or later perhaps shooting-ranges. Then streets and houses would start to encroach on this ground, gradually covering everything up. But even when the walls were simply removed, as in eighteenth-century Limoges (thanks to Turgot), or in Caen, Rennes, and elsewhere, the urban area remained compact and concentrated. It would hardly have been either convenient or desirable to move away from the town centre where everything was so close together, and where all decisions were made. In the end the basic constraint on every urban settlement, and the condition of its effective operation, was its concentration. It had to accumulate and bring together shops, markets, houses, artisans and residents.

But the town stood, above all, for domination. and what matters most when we try to define or rank it, is its capacity to command and the area it commanded.

So when in the month of *pluviôse*, Year IV, Carpentras tried to move up in the urban hierarchy by having the civil and criminal courts of the *département* of Vaucluse located there rather than in Avignon, it cited in support of its claim the quality of its roads, 'which make *easy and uninterrupted* communication possible throughout the year [my italics]: [there is a] main road from Avignon to Carpentras, . . . from Apt to Carpentras, . . . from Orange to Carpentras, . . . and from Valréas to Carpentras'. And then there was its location, right in the middle of the *département*, an advantage 'that neither Avignon, Apt nor Orange can offer'. Consequently, 'by virtue of its position, its regular weekly market, and the extraordinary number of outsiders who gather here, [Carpentras serves] as a meeting point for the inhabitants of other *communes* in the *département* and of several neighbouring *départements*'.[151]

Needless to say, geographical location alone would not have been enough to account for Carpentras's influence or superiority over its neighbours. Bonnières, north-east of Paris, near Mantes-la-Jolie, was a mere village of 600 to 700 inhabitants when in 1738, the newly-laid royal road from Paris to Rouen was built through it, to be followed a few years later, in 1753, by the road from Paris to Caen. From now on it was at the intersection of two important routes, and became a centre for trade. But a town it was not.[152]

Towns certainly had to be on a road, or indeed at a crossroads, but for a genuine town to be established, many other ingredients were required.

Any town of unequivocally urban status would be surrounded for instance by a ring of bourgs, more or less under its influence, each of them linking it by extension to the Lilliputian world of the villages. This suggests a fairly simple geometric figure, not always an adequate one unfortunately, especially when we move up to the largest category of towns which are much more complicated.

Every town, large or small, would moreover have around it a supply zone, on which it was dependent, if only for perishable foodstuffs. Every town had its markets, like the 'market in Toulon, which received its fruit and vegetables from nearby producers, who would come in every day, a journey of one or two hours on foot, accompanied by donkeys and mules'.[153] In Tarascon, at the end of the fourteenth century, this supply zone was contained within an entirely man-made landscape.[154] It was the little town's good fortune to lie on the banks of the Rhône, but there was consequently danger of flooding which it averted by building a series of embankments, running from the small mountain north of the town to the edge of the Alpilles chain south of it. Its territory was divided into two zones: between the embankments was a low-lying area close under the town walls, divided into gardens and strips of orchard; beyond the embankments were meadows, fields and *herms*; and lastly, on the hillsides, stood closely-planted vines.

It was these village districts immediately surrounding them that the towns most easily influenced, whether they tried to or not: they dictated the activities pursued there, and even acted as a refuge for populations under threat. Such refugees did not always return home but became absorbed into urban life. Around such Alsatian towns as Colmar or Guebwiller,[155] a belt of villages already moribund by the fourteenth century was absorbed into the town, a process found elsewhere too, round Aix-en-Provence for instance.[156] It was possible for villages to be swallowed up by the towns in all innocence.

But the agricultural zone devoted to fruit and vegetables, just outside the city walls, constituted only the first circle, an inner belt representing the modest beginnings of what was a sort of colonial empire. A town was like a huge stomach, drawing on not one but several successive supply areas and zones of influence, in theory (but in theory only) concentrically disposed: the kitchen garden and dairy zone, the cereal zone, the wine-growing zone, the livestock zone, the forest zone, and the zone of long-distance trade. Within these successive zones were markets, and even towns, which acted as intermediaries. We may recall here Eckart Schremmer's accurate observation: 'Urban markets are the meeting point not only for town–country exchange but also for town–town exchange'.[157] In a similar context, Rudolf Häpke long ago referred to the urban networks in the Netherlands, in the fifteenth century when Bruges was at its height, by the evocative term 'an archipelago of towns'.[158]

Urban domination and expansion were not only economic, but also political, administrative, religious and cultural. In the kingdom of France, the towns fought against the seigneurs, and against (or for) the crown, in order to acquire privileges and liberties. One by one, they seized slices of seigneurial or royal power, and received as gifts institutions that associated them with rule over ordinary people: a *présidial*, a *bailliage* or a *parlement*, depending on their good luck, their size or their pugnacity. One thinks too of the advantages towns could derive from possessing a religious foundation, an episcopal seat, a chapter, a convent or a university. All the more piquant then are these lines from a history of Romans, a little Dauphiné town on the banks of the Isère, a few miles from Valence:

> Whereas Valence, with its university, Grenoble with its *parlement*, its *chambre des comptes*, its *intendance* and the seat of government of the province [of Dauphiné], and Vienne with its archbishopric and *cour des aides*, attracted to them litigants, office-seekers and students in large numbers, Romans [which was poorly off by comparison] strove to develop its industry and commerce. To tell the truth, . . . its administrators several times considered claiming the seat of the *bailliage* of the Bas-Viennois, which had been placed by Humbert II in Saint-Marcellin, but they were never successful.[159]

FIGURE 17
Immigration to Aix en Provence in the eighteenth century

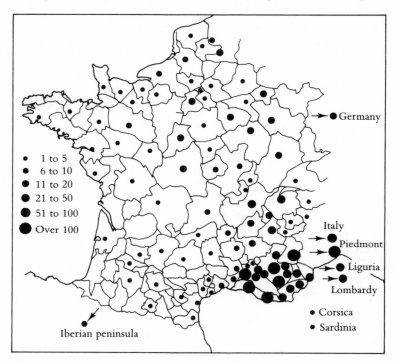

- • 1 to 5
- • 6 to 10
- ● 11 to 20
- ● 21 to 50
- ● 51 to 100
- ⬤ Over 100

Germany

Italy
Piedmont
Liguria
Lombardy
Corsica
Sardinia

Iberian peninsula

After *Histoire de la France urbaine*, ed. G. Duby, III.

In such cases, any new deal of the cards was exceptional –
unfortunately for Romans – since justice and administration were
industries with little unemployment. It was not far short of a disaster for a town to lose one of these institutions so helpful for survival. This happened to Nancy for example when it lost its *bailliage*
during the French occupation (1670–97). If we are to believe the
inhabitants, the town was 'reduced to extreme poverty . . . Few
people were untouched by this misfortune and by the desertion of
all the bourgeois'.[160]

FIGURE 18
Place of origin of married men living in Versailles 1682– 9

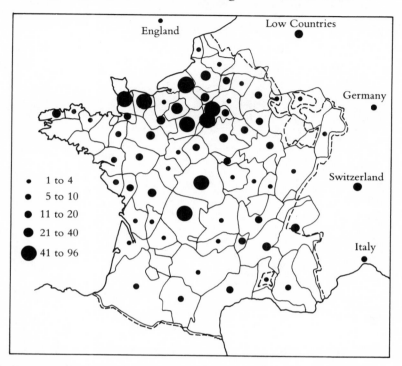

The ambitious building programme at Versailles under Louis
XIV attracted workers from all directions to its building sites.
After *Histoire de la France urbaine*, ed. G. Duby, III.

In determining the furthest-flung circles of influence of a town,
the most important factor was perhaps the supply of immigrants.
The human race is indeed 'the most invasive in the world'[161] and
has always been the one most given to travel. The town was like the
poacher's dark lantern luring the game. It fascinated the peasants in
the countryside around. Nothing is more eloquent in this respect
than a diagram showing the place of origin of immigrants to the
towns. Without this flow of new blood, the towns would have
declined, being unable to match the number of deaths by the num-

FIGURE 19
*Marseille and Rouen: unequal and imperfect exploitation
of the French market as a whole*

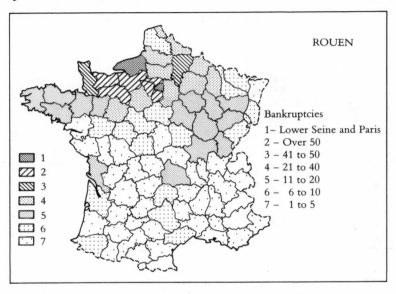

ROUEN

Bankruptcies
1– Lower Seine and Paris
2 – Over 50
3 – 41 to 50
4 – 21 to 40
5 – 11 to 20
6 – 6 to 10
7 – 1 to 5

1
2
3
4
5
6
7

ber of births, which always fell far short. For all towns (large or medium-sized), up to and including the eighteenth century, were 'death traps'.

The places of origin of incomers cover an astonishingly wide area around the host town. Thus the diagram showing immigration to Aix-en-Provence in the eighteenth century (and Aix was only a medium-sized town at the time) extends over a very large area of France. The majority of incomers were artisans, sometimes curiously specialized according to their region of origin, to the point of exercising 'real monopolies on the labour market'. 'Navvies, whether in Toulouse or Périgueux, were likely to come from Brittany . . . , more than half the boatmen in the ports on the Rhône were from the upper Rhône valley, while lime-burners were mostly from the Bresse and butchers from the Auvergne'.[162] In eighteenth-century Paris, carpenters came from Normandy,

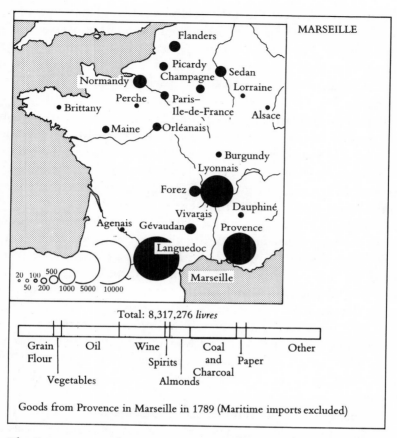

MARSEILLE

Flanders

Picardy
Champagne
Sedan
Normandy
Lorraine
Perche
Paris–
Brittany
Ile-de-France
Alsace
Maine
Orléanais

Burgundy
Lyonnais
Forez
Dauphiné
Vivarais
Agenais
Gévaudan
Provence
Languedoc
Marseille

20 100 500
0 ○ ○ ○ ○ ○
50 200 1000 5000 10000

Total: 8,317,276 *livres*

| Grain Flour | Oil | Wine | Coal and Charcoal | Other |

Spirits | Paper

Vegetables | Almonds

Goods from Provence in Marseille in 1789 (Maritime imports excluded)

The Rouen map is by Pierre Dardel (*Annales de Normandie*, 1954) and is based on bankruptcies between 1740 and 1790. The division by *départements* is anachronistic but convenient. On the Marseille map (by Charles Carrière, *Les Négociants marseillais*, 1973, II, p. 583), goods from the rest of France are estimated by value in *livres*.

masons from the Limousin, wet-nurses from Burgundy, chimney-sweeps from Savoy, water-carriers from the Auvergne, and so on. Any urban centre of any size would reveal similar patterns if examined, whether bourg or town. Bonneville (the capital of the Faucigny, now in Haute-Savoie) held a count in the eighteenth

187

century and discovered that the doctor was from Dijon, one of the two policemen (*sergents de ville*) was from the Bourbonnais, the other from the Nièvre; the baker came from Normandy and the shoemaker from Dauphiné; and there were day-labourers hailing from Carcassonne, the Périgord and the parishes of Savoy. A classic example.[163]

Better documented than the immigration patterns of artisans and general labourers, however, are those of the 'quality' immigration, the future bourgeoisie of the towns, usually merchants bringing both property and ambition with them. It is possible for instance to represent on a map this immigration of the prosperous to the town of Metz in the thirteenth century.[164]

Wider still were the zones that large-scale trade created around active towns (*villes-villes* as André Piatier has called them) since these zones covered large tracts of France and extended far away, along the major trade routes to the Levant, the Baltic, Africa and the New World or the Far East, the routes to which were opened up by the great discoveries in the late fifteenth century. In Figure 19, I have plotted the large sections of French territory drawn into the trading zones of Rouen and Marseille in the eighteenth century. The reader will notice that wide-ranging as these trading areas were, none of them succeeded in capturing the whole of French territory. It is true that the *national market* – that is to say economic cohesion and unity throughout the land – took a long time to come into being. The sheer size of such an area was an obstacle to the unification of trade, despite determined efforts to improve transport, despite plentiful markets and an incredible number of fairs – which were in some sense substitutes for towns and bourgs, or, if held in towns, visibly served to multiply the towns' own activity. Even the very largest fairs – those of Champagne in the thirteenth century, or the Guibray or Beaucaire fairs – concerned no more than part of French territory. France was simply too big a morsel to be swallowed either by the French state or by the capitalism of its most advanced cities – cities curiously located around the edges of the kingdom, as I shall have occasion to point out later.

Some straightforward examples

But rather than theorizing about what towns have in common or about what divides them, would it not be better to consider a few case studies and experiences? Let us begin with the simplest instances, in theory those of modest towns without great ambitions – though I doubt whether there really are any examples of towns simple and readable at first sight. Every urban settlement is bound to live by maintaining a balance between what it receives (or takes) and what it gives (or returns). The balance has perpetually to be adjusted, the point of equilibrium is never fixed. And the particular way a town draws on the outside world while modifying itself internally, the better to attach itself to its surroundings and dominate them, is never simple: its secrets usually have to be decoded.

The point of taking examples will be to confirm or to contradict our theoretical schema, which is only a preliminary attempt at an explanation, a kind of model. And a model is never adequate in itself: it has to be confronted with reality, tested out on the water. If it floats, that is of some significance; if it sinks, then we must start again from scratch.

It will no doubt be important at this stage not only to situate the town in relation to the bourgs and villages – in other words to what it is not – but to situate it in relation to other towns, to throw some light on the local, regional or international 'logics' which distinguish them. Some towns have international standing – world history is constantly knocking at their door, moving them up (or down) in the hierarchy: this town may outclass that one, although nothing in its individual destiny may have pointed that way.

In our attempt to verify (and to complicate) the schema outlined above, we shall therefore look at the towns not so much from the inside, *intra muros*, as from the perspective of urban domination in general, which has to take account both of internal and external factors, depending on the relation between two spheres which are not always easy to define, let alone estimate.

FIGURE 20
Immigration to Lyon 1529–63

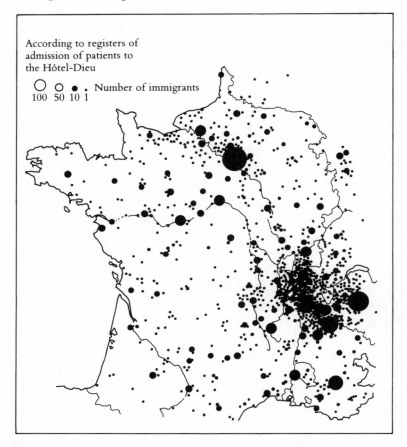

According to registers of
admission of patients to
the Hôtel-Dieu

○ ○ ● . Number of immigrants
100 50 10 1

Map from Pierre Chaunu and Richard Gascon, *Histoire
économique et sociale de la France*, vol I/1, 1977. Immigrants to
Lyon, then the finance capital of Europe, came from all over
France but also from Italy (as far away as Naples), Geneva,
Berne, Cologne, Munich and even the Low Countries and
some towns in the Iberian peninsula.

Besançon and the problem of regional leadership

Few urban sites are more clearly defined, more promising at first glance, than that of Besançon. From the town's site, everything else followed, for better or for worse; geographical determinism is not, in this case, an idle term.

A bend in the river, the extraordinary loop of the Doubs, encloses and protects the town. It does not provide a perfect defence, since the two ends of the loop do not quite meet to make an island surrounded on all sides by water: there is a gap, a potential breach. But, as can be seen from Figure 21, the gap is closed by a narrow strip of mountain (about 360 metres high) with a drop of about 100 metres to the river bend. On these heights, there was probably a rampart in the days of Gaul, then a fortress (completely rebuilt by Vauban, much later) to reinforce the natural barrier. The latter was the product of extremely ancient geological processes. In the Pliocene era, the Rhine ran through what is now the valley of the Doubs, until the intermediate collapse of the Vosges-Black Forest massif forced it out of its course through the Jura and into another channel. So the relief of the Besançon region was carved out by a mighty river, much mightier than the Doubs, one that fragmented and chiselled away at the edge of the Jura. The citadel of Besançon is on the summit of one of these fragments, between the *cluses* of Rivotte, to the north, and Tarragnoz, to the south.

It is not surprising that a town should have appeared very early on such a well-protected natural site. Besançon was the capital of the Sequani, one of the major tribes of independent Gaul, who had contacts with the Helvetii, beyond the Jura, and had as enemies the Aedui, who lived on the other side of the Doubs and the Saône. Caesar in his *Commentaries* notes the importance and the strength of the town's position.

In Roman times, *Vesontio* would have been an important provincial capital, lying at the meeting-point of two routes: the first, leading to Lausanne and Lake Geneva, crossed the Jura by the valley of

FIGURE 21
The town of Besançon and its site

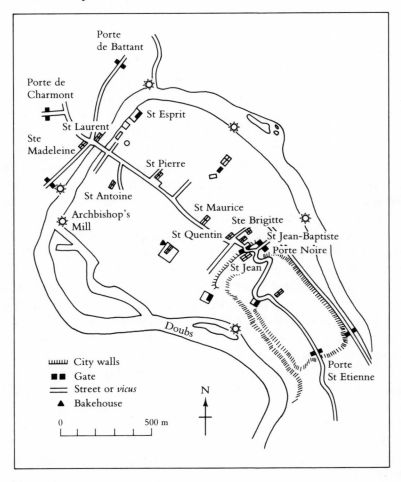

Porte
de Battant

Porte de
Charmont

St Esprit

St Laurent

Ste
Madeleine

St Pierre

St Antoine

Archbishop's
Mill

St Maurice

Ste Brigitte

St Quentin

St Jean-Baptiste

Porte Noire

St Jean

Doubs

City walls
Gate
Street or *vicus*
Bakehouse

Porte
St Etienne

N

0   500 m

After Claude Fohlen, *Histoire de Besançon.*

the Loue and the long *cluse* of Pontarlier; the second left the Saône
at Chalon and ran along the edge of the Jura to Besançon, then to
Montbéliard, Belfort, the Rhine and its *limes*, before reaching
Mainz. This second route, used by the Roman legions,[165] was the

most important road leading to the Rhine, with the exception of the major axis Lyon–Chalon–Langres–Trier. *Vesontio* was unquestionably an important town for trade, even receiving wines from Campania and Latium:[166] excavation of the bend in the Doubs has uncovered the remains of many amphorae. But apart from the existence of a Roman theatre, a forum, the Porte Noire and the *cardo*, which corresponds more or less to the present-day main shopping street, the Grand' Rue, we do not know much about *Vesontio* in Roman times. We do not even know how Christianity was brought there, in about the second century, 'by the nomadic populations of slaves, legionaries and traders', as it was to the rest of Gaul.[167]

Nor do we know how the town fared during the dark ages of the barbarian invasions, or during Merovingian and Carolingian days. It was sufficiently rich to have markets from very early times and to erect many churches, some in the seventh century (Saint-Etienne, Saint-Maurice, Saint-Paul, Saint-Pierre), others in the eleventh (Saint-André, Notre-Dame-de-Jussa-Moutier, Saint-Vincent). In addition to this architectural exuberance, either confirming or promoting it, came the elevation of Besançon to the dignity of an archbishopric, at a date difficult to specify. But it must have been an important event, since in 1041, the archbishop of Besançon, the religious leader of the province, obtained by imperial concession the right to exercise civil power within the town.

So it was as an episcopal city, under the remote authority of the emperor, that Besançon participated in the general movement of western Europe, between the eleventh and thirteenth centuries, towards modern times. Thousands of new towns were founded, while many old towns expanded. It was no doubt because of this general prosperity that Besançon managed in 1290, not without a struggle, largely to free itself from the archbishop's authority, and to set itself up as a *commune*. The charter granted it in that year by Rudolph I made it a free imperial city in whose affairs the archbishop would interfere less and less, a sort of urban republic with the right to levy taxes and pronounce justice, to police itself, even to sign treaties of alliance and (only after 1534 it is true) to mint money stamped with its own arms.

These successes were however to bring drawbacks in the future. Besançon, although still the religious capital of the Franche-Comté, was politically and administratively so detached from the province as to become foreign and irritating to it, 'like chaff in the eye', as the président Froissart de Broissia put it in 1574.[168] Thus the role and the advantages of being capital of the province fell to Besançon's rival, Dole: with a smaller population, a favoured but slightly off-centre position as regards routes, Dole was the seat of the provincial *parlement* (1422) and of a university, and grew in size as a result. As the sixteenth-century historian, Loys Gollut, put it, Dole 'has the finest bridge and the finest tower . . . , the finest steeple, the finest covered market, the finest lettered youth and the greatest and finest number of learned folk in the country'.[169] And the people of Franche-Comté probably felt, in Dole more than anywhere else, that they were on Burgundian soil.[170] These were all advantages lost to Besançon, the imperial city which ended by being walled up inside its prerogatives.

Yet Besançon was the town with the highest population in the Franche-Comté. In about 1300–1350, it numbered between 8,000 and 9,000 inhabitants, counting its 'suburbs'. At the time this represented quite a large town. But where did this community find its means of subsistence? Its ecclesiastical population, the dependencies of the archbishopric, and church estates all probably constituted regular sources of income. And its bourgeoisie possessed land outside the town. These all come under the heading of a sort of parasitical rentierism, early-flowering but destined to last.

There were plenty of artisans: weavers, spinners, carpenters, shoemakers, saddlers, upholsterers, tilers, cutlers, locksmiths. But they all worked for a local clientele, if one excepts the production of white woollen cloth which was exported as far as Avignon or Marseille in the fifteenth century. Butchers, bakers and tavern-keepers all took part in the town market, and the most-frequented shops lined both sides of the bridge leading to Battant, a sister-town which Besançon had created on the opposite bank of the Doubs. In the thirteenth century however, the town derived advantage from the international activity of the Champagne fairs, comparatively close at hand, and acted as a staging-post between

Champagne and Italy, via the Loue valley and the toll at Jougne. So at this time there were wholesale traders and money-changers in town, and some foreign merchants even settled there. But this hour of glory did not long outlast the prosperity of the Champagne fairs, which had already begun to decline by the early decades of the fourteenth century.

Deprived of this external stimulus, hit by the Black Death in August and September 1349, Besançon fell back on its own resources. It then found its salvation at its very gates, in the surrounding territory, a wide supply zone as strictly dependent on the town as a village on its seigneur. This territory consisted of limestone hills, which a sixteenth-century historian describes as 'stony terrain, on a base of continuous rocks, with only a little earth as a covering on top of them'.[171] On such arid soil, only vines could be cultivated. They produced good quality wine, distinguished according to whether it came from the 'high, medium or lower slopes'. Beyond the vineyards were a few fields of wheat, at Saint-Ferjeux or Les Tilleroyes for instance, to the north; and there was a little grazing, as well as the immense forest of Chailluz (over which the town authorities kept a close watch), which provided wood to be floated down on the Doubs.

Its only major source of wealth, 'the true substance of the City'[172] was in the end its wine. Every year, after the wine-harvest, its date fixed by the authorities, the great event was the noisy arrival of the casks of new wine. Even inside the town, in the bend of the river where a large area was still cultivated in the form of gardens, orchards and vineyards, vines predominated – notably in the 'clos' belonging to the clergy,[173] who owned at least a third of all the land within the bend and all but one of the mills powered by the water of the Doubs.

Like all medieval cities, Besançon remained essentially rural at heart: it was invaded by farm animals which wandered through the streets, blocking them to traffic. There was not a house without its own poultry, sheep and pigs (though it was forbidden to keep the latter *intra muros* during the hot summer months from June to September: were they sent to the woods of Chailluz?). Another equally telling sign was that winegrowers, a very active and outspoken group of people, made up half if not three-quarters of the population.

In the end, the town could not find enough grain or meat in the immediate vicinity. For meat, it turned to the inexhaustible grazing lands of the high Jura. Grain was more complicated, and the situation was sometimes critical. When the traditional source of cereal, the Gray region, dried up – because too much had been sent down the Saône to Lyon, or because the Swiss cantons had bought up too much before the new harvest – it had to be sought further afield, at least as far as Alsace. The building of a granary in 1513 was to be a kind of insurance, usually reliable, against the risk of shortage.[174]

It is at any rate clear that in about 1300, Besançon controlled an area barely greater than its own territory. We are not too surprised to find that this essentially consisted of villages and hamlets. The same was true of all towns, whether Toulouse where the vines stood guard around the city walls, or even Paris itself. The suburbs surrounding the towns were after all very like the fringe of gardens and orchards around the villages, though on a different scale. There was no need here for intermediaries, for bourgs to act as go-betweens exerting authority over districts so close at hand and often directly managed by town-dwelling proprietors.

What is surprising on the other hand is that we do not find, further out from Besançon, that ring of bourgs and small towns which were the only means of extending the influence of an urban centre. In fact Besançon had very imperfect communications with Dole, Gray, Vesoul, Salins, Pontarlier and Lons-le-Saunier. It is true that the surrounding roads were terrible for travelling into the mountains of the Jura, and poor in every other direction because of the pot-holes, the mud and the lack of upkeep. To the south, traffic had to face the 'roadblock' of the enormous forest of Chaux, the largest expanse of woodland in eastern France, with its interminable stretches of oaks and hornbeams, invaded every year by some 50,000 to 60,000 head of cattle – a forest that had grown up on the gravel bed deposited by the Rhine as it crossed the flatlands of the Bresse. And the Doubs, a minor river, was not navigable – it was used only by rowing-boats, 'navois', and to float logs downstream.

So there were no waterways, and hardly any good roads.

Besançon had little incitement to turn its face to the outside world – particularly since it had comparative prosperity on its doorstep and was content with it.

In later times, many things would change for better or worse, but the town remained enclosed within its unsatisfactory structures, and dependent on them. In the fifteenth century, thrown back very much on its own resources, Besançon went through a bad patch. The sixteenth century by contrast was a time of liberation and unexpected expansion. The town welcomed the century of progress with open arms. The Burgundian inheritance had been divided in 1477 into two parts, the duchy and the county (the Comté), the duchy falling to the king of France and the county finally (in 1506) entering the domains of the Habsburgs. The people of the Comté served with honour and profit their new masters (the emperor Charles V from 1519, and his son Philip II of Spain, from 1555), so much so that the Comté is said with some exaggeration to have become 'Spanish'. Did not two men from the Comté, Perrenot de Granvelle, and later his son, Cardinal Granvelle, govern not only the Comté but the Empire 'on which the sun never set', on behalf of these illustrious masters?

But Besançon's sixteenth-century prosperity was even more closely linked to unexpected circumstances: the arrival in the city of the Genoese banker-merchants in 1535.[175] They had just experienced a series of misadventures: expelled from Lyon by the king of France in 1528, they had taken refuge in Chambéry in Savoy, only to be expelled by the duke of Savoy, and obliged to hold their Epiphany fair in Lons-le-Saunier. In 1535 they finally obtained from the emperor and the town permission to settle in Besançon. They were to hold their fairs here for thirty years, starting at Easter 1535. What advantage did this have? It kept them in the neighbourhood of Lyon, at the time the centre of the European economy at its highest level. The Genoese from Besançon could carry on business there covertly, through middlemen. I am also inclined to think that the gradual decline of Lyon, from the 1560s, gave them more freedom of manoeuvre. At any rate when they left Besançon in 1568, after an obscure dispute with the town authorities, they stopped only briefly at Poligny, then at Chambéry, and by 1579, their fairs which had become the centre of the European finance and credit market, were established at Piacenza in Italy, although they were still known as the *ferie di Bisenzone*.

By a fortuitous set of circumstances then, Besançon found itself the home of the most powerful financiers of the century. This was no mean gift: the city was as if touched by a magic wand. Up went the Granvelle palace, the city hall, the grand houses of Montmarin and Bonvalot. And in came rich immigrants from Montpellier, Fontenoy-en-Vôge, Luxeuil and Lons-le-Saunier.[176]

In the following century however, the 'hungry' seventeenth century, misfortune returned. War, plague and famine stalked Besançon. Spain, running out of money and motivation, abandoned the province and the city to their own strengths and weaknesses. Conquest by France was thus made easy in advance: it began in 1668, but was halted later that year by the peace of Aix-la-Chapelle, when the French withdrew, abandoning their allies and leaving behind them a welter of bitterness and hate. But six years later, the conquest began again and although difficult, this time it was successfully completed. In May 1674, the army of the duc d'Enghien accompanied by Louis XIV in person, massed before Besançon and the 200,000 cannon balls of the royal artillery overcame all resistance. On 15 May, to avoid being sacked, the city surrendered.[177]

This was a moving but by now commonplace occurrence: a free or almost free city succumbing to the force of a modern state. How many cities all over Europe were devoured in this way! The occupation of Strasbourg a few years later, again by Louis XIV (29 September 1681) is another example. In Besançon, the real drama was yet to come, the establishment of French rule in the Comté. The initial prudence and concessions of the new rulers had little effect: peasant guerrilla wars broke out; public opinion for a while lived in hope or fear of the return of the Spanish. After the brief occupation of Alsace by imperial troops in 1675 in particular, old passions were rekindled. Once the alert was over however, French rule was imposed methodically not to say brutally. Louis XIV's monarchy was by this time a tried and tested machine.[178]

What interests us here needless to say, is the new balance to which the town found itself subjected. It had been doubly annexed: to France of course, but also to the Franche-Comté itself into which Besançon had never really been absorbed. It is true that Spain, in agreement with the imperial government, had in 1664 united the city to the province and had also granted it the extra territory round about, known as 'the hundred villages'. But apart from this territorial extension, the decision had remained a dead letter. Matters would be very different after the annexation to France, rendered official by the Peace of Nijmwegen in 1678.

The royal government immediately made Besançon the provincial capital, transferring to it the *parlement* previously established in Dole, and creating a series of new institutions: a *présidial*, a *bailliage*, and a string of special courts (money, waterways and forests, consular justice). The city also received a university, an *intendance*, a governor and to cap it all a strong military garrison. If the choice of the royal government, in its efforts to put the province in order, fell upon Besançon, it was because this was the most populous, the most wealthy and above all the best-defended and strongest of the province's towns. Once again, the reason had to do with its site.

Even though Besançon in the end derived some profit from its new position, we should not see this as the result of a benevolent policy by a government which, once the conquest was complete, soon wanted nothing from it but obedience and tax payments. The *parlement* was only moved to Besançon in return for a contribution of 300,000 *livres*, exacted rather than freely offered. In 1692, in spite of strong feeling against it, Louis XIV's government introduced venality of office to the province.

The true innovation, following on the heels of the French occupation, was indeed this invasion of the old town by an army of magistrates and ministerial officials, in all about 500 office-holders; with their families perhaps some 2,000 persons: 'only the winegrowers can now boast of being more numerous in the city'.[179] The *parlement* now became the upper, envied tier of a rentier class preoccupied with its privileges, which it readily assimilated to the privileges and interests of the province, since these were now supposed to be represented by the *parlement*, the estates of the Comté having ceased to meet. All this clearly reinforced the town's rather sleepy tradition of easy-going parasitism.

And yet for the first time in its history, Besançon had attained the dignity of a truly regional capital, both serving and making use of a ring of bourgs and small towns closely connected with the life of the larger town. This development was in fact rather slow. It can be traced through a series of evidence. In 1735, we learn that

> Besançon is not a rich or commercial town . . . trade is extremely limited . . . being reduced to the clothing of the inhabitants and the goods and products they need for their own use or family consumption. They buy these from merchants established in the province,

or from travelling pedlars. In 1747, it was the same story. In 1765, Savary's *Dictionnaire de commerce* describes Gray, where the Saône became navigable, as the most active centre of trade in the Comté. But by 1785, everything seems to have changed. A memorandum indicates that trade was by now 'occupying a fairly large number of people' in Besançon: 'one could mention twenty-five trading-houses', plus two or three specialists in wholesaling 'which consists of selling to the retailers in the small towns goods obtained from all over the kingdom in large quantities'. Besançon had at last become a distribution centre for the surrounding bourgs and small towns. Further evidence in this direction is that it had also become an active centre for bills of exchange, 'to which almost all the province turns directly or indirectly for all its needs',[180] and although such dealings were modest by European standards, the town had banking contacts with Strasbourg, Bâle, Frankfurt, Holland and even England. Finally, Besançon launched into industry: hosiery in particular was successfully introduced there.

How is such progress to be explained? By the economic expansion and general rise in prosperity in the eighteenth century for a start; then there were the improved road links throughout the province – unquestionably the best gift the Comté received from the French crown. An official letter dated 8 August 1740 tells us that there were in the province '75,000 *toises* of perfect roads, [so that] one can *now* [my italics] go at a trot in any direction across mountains and marshes which before these works one crossed with trepidation and only during a few months of the year'.[181] By about the middle of the century, a regular mail-coach linked Besançon daily to Dijon with a connection to Paris: and there was also one once a week to Nancy, Belfort, Strasbourg and Bâle.

One should also bear in mind a rather particular circumstance: the Franche-Comté, being 'considered as foreign territory', was surrounded by a continuous customs barrier, vis-à-vis both the rest of France and the Swiss cantons – a case in fact of full decentralization. The result was to put a certain damper on trade, depriving the province as a whole of commercial vitality, 'but its counterpart was a polarization around Besançon',[182] now the heart of a kind of miniature national market.

This market was of no great size though: in 15,000 square kilometres, it only had 340,720 inhabitants in about 1710, of whom 11,520 were in Besançon itself; 5,663 in Salins; 4,115 in Dole; 3,982 in Gray; 3,340 in Arbois; 3,320 in Poligny; 2,540 in Montbéliard; 2,664 in Pontarlier; 2,225 in Vesoul; 1,922 in Lons-le-Saunier; 1,745 in Saint-Claude; 1,632 in Ornans; 990 in Baume-les-Dames; 532 in Orgelet; and 470 in Quingey.[183] If we take 2,000 inhabitants to be the minimum *urban* population, the Franche-Comté has a particularly low rate of urbanization: barely 11.5%. In short, the province was not a pulsating economic area. However by the end of the century, its population had reached 450,000 inhabitants, that is an increase of 32%, and Besançon itself had gone up by 75.6% (to 20,228 inhabitants in 1788). By this date the population in the other Comté towns was as follows: Salins, 6,630 inhabitants; Dole 7,774; Gray, 4,784; Arbois, 5,902; Pontarlier, 3,042; Lons-le-Saunier, 6,500; Saint-Claude, 3,640; Vesoul, 5,200; Baume-les-Dames, 2,080; Orgelet, 1,274; Quingey, 1,846.[184] The document does not contain the populations of Montbéliard, Poligny and Ornans, but they too had increased – the more so since Besançon, growing as it was, did not dominate all these towns equally. As usual, it was better established in the central than in the northern Jura: members of the *parlement* and merchants owned land, ironworks, furnaces and paper-works there. As for the southern Jura, south of a line from Salins to Pontarlier, it almost entirely escaped Besançon's influence.

One suspects however that in this late flowering of Besançon's regional influence in the eighteenth century, there was something artificial, or at any rate unspontaneous, imposed from outside, when one considers how brief it was. For the Revolution was to prove fatal to Besançon: it now lost at one blow its *parlement*, its *intendant*, and its religious communities.

Despite the introduction of watchmaking by Swiss craftsmen in 1793 (it had difficult beginnings and only took off much later), despite the revival of some activities after 1810 and again during the July monarchy, despite the building of new roads and of the Rhône–Rhine canal which promoted trade (but gradually killed off winegrowing, since it brought wines from the south), despite the animation, actually rather artificial, provided by a military garrison, Besançon continued to be a sleepy sort of place, declining relatively to the rest of France. From eighteenth rank among French cities in 1801, it had fallen to twenty-fifth by 1851. 'Detestable and full of civil servants', was how Sainte-Beuve described it;[185] Balzac claimed he could 'explain it in a few words: no other town offers such deaf and dumb resistance to progress'.[186]

In fact, Besançon was dogged by ill-luck. Its chief handicap – the still poor road system – might have been countered by the railway. From 1840, Besançon was anxious to acquire this trump card. But repeated efforts met with failure. It lost out to Dijon and Dole; and the railway network, dominated by the main line, via Vallorbe and the Simplon, which linked Paris to Switzerland, Italy and the Balkans, was to rob Besançon of any major rail link with the outside world. Even in 1960, there was only one through train a day between Besançon and Paris.

This bitterly resented failure accounted for much in the town's poor performance. Although Besançon witnessed sudden and unprecedented expansion after World War II (reaching the fateful figure of 100,000 inhabitants in 1960) it was never able to become a powerful provincial capital. Put at a disadvantage by its poor rail connections and a network of twisting roads unsuitable for fast traffic (there is still no motorway), it also suffered from the well-established pull of other large cities in the area: Nancy, Mulhouse, Dijon, Lyon. Even the area under its administrative control was

FIGURE 22
Telephone links in the Besançon area 1956–8

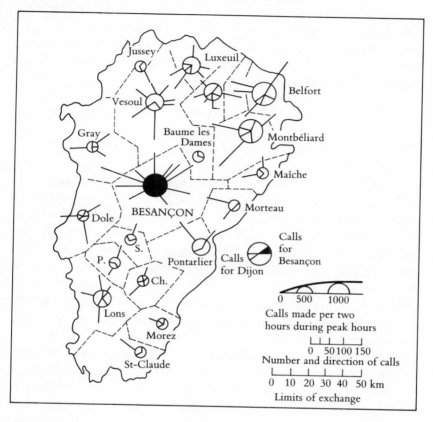

challenged by its rivals, as is demonstrated by a curious map of telephone links in the region, drawn up in 1956–8.[187] Despite distance
and administrative ties, it is a fact that 'Besançon hardly seems any
nearer than Dijon to Dole or Gray, any nearer than Lyon to Saint-
Claude, or than Nancy to Luxeuil, etc'. Born of a remarkable
defensive site, provided with a comfortable income by a series of
chance events, and long sustained by its vineyards, Besançon
throughout almost all its history has had to be content with only
modest prosperity and to abandon any larger ambitions.

Is Besançon's history in the end significant? Can it be seen as 'typical' in any sense? It teaches us one basic and banal truth, namely that it is possible for a town to live – or be forced to live – off its own resources and site, like an overgrown village. And above all, Besançon only emerged from its self-centred existence with the help of outside circumstances: the change was always somewhat artificial and never permanent.

Roanne and its region: a crossroads

Leaving Besançon, if one crosses the Saône and goes through Lyon, one has to go only 86 kilometres further, via Tarare, to reach Roanne, well inside the Massif Central and in a setting completely different from the Doubs and the Jura. This little town will be our second example: picturesque, lively, complicated enough to raise a few problems, but simpler nevertheless than our previous stop. In fact Roanne did not become a town worthy of the name until the end of the fifteenth century, rather late in the day, and the town's fortunes were specifically linked to shipping on the Loire. Here too, external circumstances were all-important.

The Roannais is the northern part of a little *patrie*, like hundreds of others in France: the Forez. It is one praised to the skies by those who were born there or made it their adoptive home, like Honoré d'Urfé, who set his novel *L'Astrée* (1610–27) there, in a sort of terrestrial paradise. Such enthusiasm is somewhat misplaced, the equivalent of claiming that the salmon, the royal fish which used to come up the Loire and Lignon to these remote shores, can be fished there any day of the week.

The Roannais consists of a small plain, thirty kilometres by fifty: in the past it was marshy, unhealthy, 'aquatic', covered with 'great abysms of water'[188] as Honoré d'Urfé himself says. Thousands of hectares consisted of natural or artificial ponds,[189] all full of fish, jealously watched over by their owners and by active poachers who would sometimes *débonder* a pond, drain it in order to make a huge killing of fish (or simply to get their own back on the owner).[190] Add to this the running streams and brooks and the swift-flowing, undisciplined and widespread waters of the Loire, 'fordable almost everywhere' during the summer heat,[191] but liable to overflow its banks later in the year. The flood waters could be two, three or sometimes five metres above normal level (seven in the great flood of 12 November 1790).[192] Cutting a huge swathe through the plain, the main bed of the river, with its sandbanks, islands and unstable channels, was never less than one and a half kilometres across (five at Decize, a town built on an island in the river).[193] And man had added his own touches to these natural conditions, by insisting on digging drainage ditches after harvest and leaving heaps of excavated earth all round the fields; since the plough also accumulated earth at the end of the furrow, the fields were turned into basins in which water was trapped and stagnated.[194]

Roanne, which long remained a village 'huddled around its church' and castle, stood on the left bank of the river, on an ancient fluvial terrace which kept the town ten to fifteen metres above the dangerous waters – so dangerous that they swept away with remarkable ease the wooden bridges that were built one after another. Not until 1854 did Roanne get a solid stone-built bridge,[195] a privilege acquired earlier by Decize and Nevers.[196] Even so, in 1687, of Decize's two bridges, 'two of the finest bridges standing in France', one had collapsed and been replaced by a dangerous ferry, and the other had just lost one of its arches.[197] These were treacherous waters, especially since they often had to be crossed by fording. The reports of officials of the ducal *bailliage* of Roanne mention with monotonous regularity the drowned bodies washed up on the banks, and for every one that was recognized – a guide surprised when taking his flock over the river – many remained unidentified.[198]

Overland communications were inevitably difficult across this waterlogged plain: a few carts pulled by cows, as in the Auvergne; a few beasts of burden or men 'carrying packs on their shoulders'.

Since grain production (wheat, rye, barley and oats) did not even meet local needs, the Roannais was constantly in trouble.[199] In the plain around the small towns, large estates had sprung up, with the help and at the expense of many needy share-croppers,[200] but the results were disappointing because of the poor quality of the land.[201] Apart from a few places with recent alluvial soil, the *chambons*, the plain consisted of sandy or clayey ground which could often do no more than supply brick-works with raw materials. Only grass grew well and not much of that. There is an old saying that warns, 'If the grass on your land can feed you, do not be so ungrateful as to plough it under'.[202]

What was more, the plain's unhealthy nature meant that mortality was high. The low density of the population was the major handicap of a countryside plagued between April and autumn by 'intermittent fevers, to which few of the peasants are immune'.[203] Should the blame be placed on the 'corruption of the air', as they said in the late eighteenth century, caused by the regular practice of draining ponds to grow crops on them, then flooding them again three years later? Malaria certainly thrived here, and during the hot summer months, the rich would leave for the neighbouring hills.

For on three sides, the Roannais is ringed round by quite high country: to the east the Beaujolais hills, which go up to 1,012 metres; to the west the Madeleine hills (1,165 metres); and to the south the plateau or *'seuil'* of Neulise (500 to 600 metres) across which the Loire plunges in a tunnel of gorges up to 200 metres deep. (It was recently decided to build a dam here in order to control the river's always unpredictable flooding).[204] This plateau divides the Roannais from the true Forez (with Feurs and Montbrison). If you are in a car and leave Feurs travelling north, the road suddenly plunges downwards and roadsigns in several languages tell you to brake with care. To the north, the Roannais is only distantly bounded by the 'hills of the Charollais–Brionnais towards Iguerande and Saint-Bonnet de Cray',[205] and the way is open, relatively unbarred, into the lowlands of the Bourbonnais.

The two mountainous regions to the east and west give the Roannais its originality. Their overflow population of day-labourers (who came to help the farmhands of the share-croppers to dig ditches in winter), shepherds, winegrowers and migrants of all kinds, enabled the plain to restore the balance of an economy always short of labour. But in their mountains, these rough men, independent smallholders, lived a marginal life, with their own fierce loyalties: thus they were 'fanatically' attached to their priests during the years of the Revolution, and firmly opposed to conscription under the Empire. And who would care for the task of going up to smoke out the refractory priests or peasant deserters to whom these highlands afforded 'inaccessible retreats'?[206]

A distinction should be made, though, between the Madeleine and the Beaujolais hills. The latter have no vineyards on the Roanne side. The Beaujolais grapes grow on the rather steep eastern slopes overlooking the Saône, whereas on the Roanne side (a series of gradual slopes: one can hardly see the top from the town especially if there is low cloud), the hills are mostly wooded, with meadows surrounded by thick hawthorn hedges. These slopes to the east of the town, better suited to herds than to crops, have long resembled a *bocage* country, one that is not on the whole very fertile. Was this why the textile industry successfully established itself here in the nineteenth century, from Cours to Amplepuis and Panissières? Or was it because of the ease of communication with Lyon?

The sheer slopes of the Madeleine hills, clearly visible to the west, are very different. Down their steep hillsides tumble a number of fast-flowing streams, their near turbulent action carrying downhill the alluvial soils which have no doubt helped to push the Loire towards the Beaujolais hills: thus the Roanne plain is somewhat asymmetrical either side of the river, and the town, choosing the west side, took the better part. These short streams have hollowed out narrow gorges in the Madeleine hills, accompanied by paths of difficult access. In the old days the *bandoliers*,[207] highwaymen, found a natural haven here for their misdeeds.

But up to a height of about 400 metres, this slope, exposed to the rising sun and favoured with quite good soil, was covered with a wide band of closely-planted vineyards: these provided the livelihood of the large villages whose wines had a certain reputation: Renaison, Saint-Romain-la-Motte, Saint-Germain Lespinasse, Saint-Forgeux, Noailly, known as *le garambeau*, 'of a fine raspberry-red colour', the white wine of Pouilly-les-Nonnains, 'sweet and fruity'. The comments are taken from a debate about wine imagined by a seventeenth-century priest.[208] If one had to choose the best? 'Well', he concludes, 'we would bow to the arbitration of the couriers and postillions who travel on the road from Paris to Lyon [running of course through Roanne], who are fine connoisseurs and who are in any case perpetually thirsty by profession', and would like nothing better than to adjudicate a wine-tasting.

In the eighteenth century, the large bourg of Renaison became the chief marketing centre for this Roannais wine, by then being exported on a massive scale to Paris, 'where it is known by the name of Armaison wine', an official report tells us. 'Highly coloured, it is sought after to tint the white wines of Anjou and elsewhere. Its quality is mediocre but it passes for a good *vin ordinaire* if handled carefully'.[209] It is true that in Parisian eyes, the wines of Roanne had been dethroned by those of Beaujolais, which were commercially distributed from about 1720.[210] Exports of wine nevertheless helped the trade balance of the Roannais, and the vineyards continued to develop until mid-nineteenth century: in 1809, production reached 130,000 double hectolitres.[211] As in Besançon and elsewhere, it was 'the coming of the railways [which] caused decline', because of the impossibility of competing with the wines of the Midi.[212] But even today, although reduced in size, the vineyards have not disappeared.

The vines of the 'Roannais hills' do not grow above a certain altitude. Above them is the forest with its stands of oak, beech, and chestnut – today increasingly challenged by plantations of conifers, regarded as more profitable. Higher still, the forest gives way to bare summits, rather like the *chaumes* of the Vosges, vast grassy spaces where 'reeds abound and waters stagnate', to form here and there '*nouillères, boulières* where the cows . . . are knee-deep in mud'.[213]

Nowadays the decline of demand for beechwood clogs or charcoal, the semi-dereliction of the local vines and the general drop in the peasant population have all been bitter blows for the hillsides and mountains which are steadily losing their inhabitants. Now the plain is doing better, its value increased by modern agriculture and thriving industry. If you cross it today, the plain is what is known as *bocage d'embouche* (fattening fields), made healthier by drainage, planted with trees: here are large houses, with four-sided roofs, walls of cob, and doors and windows framed in the yellow local stone.

The Roannais, past or present, should not of course be judged simply on its merits but also in relation to the general circulation of trade within France – a circulation which brought benefit to the town rather late in the day and finally made its rather special fortune. For the two complementary halves of France, the south and the north, come together at the Loire. The Roannais lies at the point of contact – so exactly that northern dialects are spoken in the north (including Roanne) and southern dialects in the south!

The two halves of France exchanged commodities, people, cultural goods. Two major routes were used from quite early days: one following the Rhône–Saône corridor, by Arles, Avignon, Orange, crossing the Rhône at Lyon by the Pont de la Guillotière, built before 1190, then continuing along the Saône valley towards the Rhineland, Champagne and Paris; the other running through the Allier valley: merchants coming from Aigues-Mortes or Montpellier would go by Nîmes, Alès, Le Puy, Montferrand and on to the north.

Later, in the fourteenth century, a further road via the Haute Loire came into use, a third route, again going by Le Puy, then to the Forez, passing through Saint-Germain-Laval (thus missing Roanne) and linking up with Nevers.

A network of transversal roads linked up with these north–south axes, westwards to the Auvergne and eastwards to the Saône valley.

Say roads and you say towns. As soon as the roads became frequented, in the fourteenth century, towns began to emerge in the hitherto unpromising region of the Roannais, each protected by a castle or occasionally a monastery. And without too much difficulty, they obtained their charters: soon, with or without walls, they were setting up markets, and accumulating populations of 1,000 to 3,000 (quite sizeable for the period): Villerest, Saint-Haon-le-Châtel, Saint-Germain-Laval (a crossroads), Cervières, Saint-Just-en-Chevalet, Le Crozet, Néronde and last but by no means least Charlieu, the earliest and most active of these settle-

FIGURE 23
How Roanne captured the Charlieu traffic

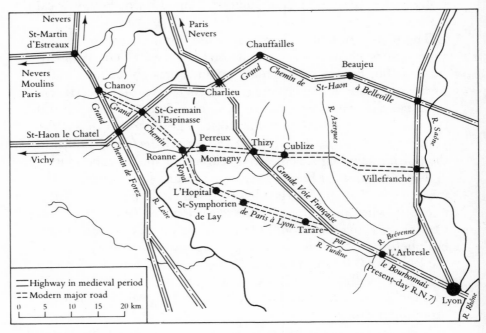

ments, situated on the right bank of the Loire and at the crossroads between the 'Great French Highway' from Lyon to Paris, and the transversal road linking the Loire to the Saône at Belleville. Charlieu, on the edge of the Brionnais region, with its Romanesque churches, still retains some traces of its former splendour, if only in the twelfth-century narthex, the remains of a long-lost abbey church.

Roanne, or the triumph of transport

Among all these small towns, Roanne was still only a village in the fourteenth century, probably containing fewer than 400 inhabitants. It was not until the end of the following century, after the

Hundred Years' War, that its first career began. It did after all have one important advantage: it was near here that the Loire, emerging from the Villerest gorge, through the high Neulise plateau, became navigable, began to 'carry boats'.[214] It was an advantage that Jacques Coeur (1395–1456), Charles VII's financier, soon spotted: with his interests in the iron, copper and silver-bearing lead mines of the Roannais, of which he had become overlord, how could he fail to be attracted by the position of Roanne, since he wanted to send mineral ores to his smelters in the Berry, the Orléanais and Touraine? It was through his good offices that bargees and boat-builders from Berry were sent to Roanne – a group of incomers whom some have seen as the ancestors of the turbulent, quarrel-some and violent boatmen who have such a place in Roanne's history.[215] But perhaps we should not put too much weight on the episodic intervention of Jacques Coeur.

Roanne's take-off – which in fact happened later – had two very clear causes.

The first and essential one was the steady and very slow development of the long-distance links between Lyon and Paris, that is between the Rhône, Loire and Seine. Roanne's growth kept pace with the expansion of these links between the essential poles of French economic life – Paris, for centuries the commanding pole and insistent magnet; Lyon, entering upon its modern destiny when in 1463 Louis XI granted it the privileges of its fairs. The connection would not reach (comparative) perfection of course until the building of the Briare canal (1642), two centuries later: this canal eliminated the need for portage and overland transport between Loire and Seine.

The second cause was the acquisition by Roanne (for reasons as it happened independent of its own wishes) of the Saône–Loire link over the Beaujolais hills. Until the fifteenth century, this had run from Belleville (the river port of Beaujeu, on the Saône) across a series of cols to Charlieu, whose early importance as a crossroads has already been mentioned. But in the fifteenth century, Villefranche eclipsed Beaujeu as the centre of the Beaujolais and, becoming the bridgehead between Saône and Loire, activated a new route through the cols, which this time led to Roanne. Before

FIGURE 24
Roanne in mid-eighteenth century

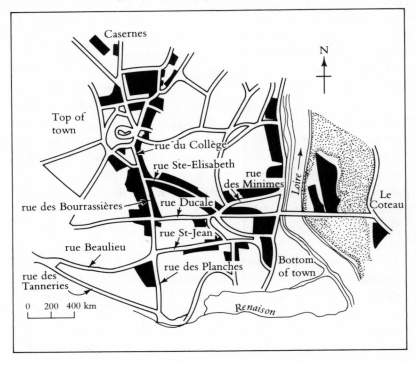

long, the Lyon traffic, instead of taking the *Grande Voie Française*
(the Great French Highway) running directly to Nevers and Paris,
would be going to the river port of Roanne, which meant improving the road through Tarare, completed by 1449 (see Figure 24).[216]

It is hard nowadays to imagine the difficulties of the old road, as
one drives down the RN7 which follows more or less the same
route along the valleys of the Rhins and the Turdine, their meeting
point, the col des Sauvages, being the watershed between Loire and
Rhône.[217] In the past this was an 'uncomfortable [road], not so
much because of its height but because of its irregular gradient,
taking one now downhill, now uphill', writes Elie Brackenhoffer,
a seventeenth-century traveller from Strasbourg whose diary of

the journey has survived. The marquis de Fontaine, French ambassador to Rome, who shared with him the 'carriage with glass windows', drawn by six white horses which were quickly spattered with yellowish mud, was obliged after Tarare 'to harness eight oxen to the carriage to get along better'. This was in 1644. But even on the eve of the Revolution, in spite of all the road-building progress of the eighteenth century, oxen still had to be harnessed to the stage-coach to cross the 'mountain' of Tarare![218] So the problem of transporting goods between the Rhône and the Loire may be imagined: it verged on the heroic.

But could the same not be said of shipping on the Loire? Who would think, seeing it today contained within its many embankments, its edges littered with sandbanks, vegetation, flotsam and flood debris of all kinds, that in the past it was a turbulent river, yet one covered with all kinds of boats? 'The Loire has never really been navigable', one historian rightly remarks.[219] 'The thriving river-traffic on the Loire', concludes another, François Billacois, 'had much less to do with the promptings of nature than with the ambitions of men'. One cannot but agree.

For much was at stake: the upper Loire valley handled the bulk of France's north–south trade, by land or water. Up the Rhône valley came ironware, arms, fabrics (cotton, wool, silk), haberdashery and the thousand and one products of the south – almonds, filberts, oil, figs, olives, lemons, grapes, corks, and barrel upon barrel of cheese. Then there was the produce of the Levant, including cotton, and goods from Italy. And since anything was possible in a transit centre like Lyon, one might even find cloth from Amiens being brought down the Saône and reaching the Loire at Roanne to be distributed, like other goods, by river boat.[220] Add to all this the produce of the Auvergne, shipped down the Allier: stone from Apremont or Volvic, millstones, bricks, tiles, paper from Thiers and Ambert which was exported via Nantes as far afield as Spain in the seventeenth century, straw, wine, timber, fruit, charcoal, coal from the mines of the Bourbonnais, and even Vichy water, which was much prized by Parisians as early as the seventeenth century.[221]

Going the other way, upstream, there was little traffic, and most

of it was light: madder, charcoal, kegs of herring, fabrics, sugar and coffee from America. Salt from the Atlantic coast did go up the Loire however, and even a little way up the Allier. And wheat, another heavy commodity, was also shipped, of necessity, whenever a serious harvest shortage had to be met in one place or another. Since the Roannais ran short of grain every year, it would appeal for supplies to be brought along the Loire routes which had access to Poitou, the Beauce and the Auvergne; appeals might even be made to the Atlantic ports. Thus there was a bad harvest in 1652, but

> no sooner had the ice melted on the river Loire, in January 1653, than there arrived so many boats laden with grain, rye, wheat, peas, beans, pears and conserves . . . to feed the people, that there were some in every port on the Loire, from Orleans to Royne [Roanne] coming [the produce that is, not of course the boats] from the kingdom of Poland, it is said.[222]

In 1529, 1531 and 1543, when Lyon was suffering from food shortages, wheat from the Beauce was shipped as far as Roanne then transferred to farm carts.[223] In 1709, there was widespread penury: and the same routes saw grain being taken from Orleans, in flotillas of boats, to feed the army in the Dauphiné.[224]

In the other direction, grain from the Levant unloaded at Marseille was sometimes taken to Roanne to be sent on to Paris, as happened in 1710. This consignment gives us an opportunity to estimate the volume of overland freight between Lyon and Roanne.[225] It seems best simply to reproduce the essentials of the document containing the precise data, but one has to read it carefully (it is rather like those arithmetic problems that used to catch one out at primary school in the old days). I shall insert a few necessary glosses, in brackets and in italics.

> The parishes [*that is the villages*] near Lyon, on the side nearest the mountains [*i.e. to the west*], normally provide 600 drivers who can only take one load a week to Tarare [*that is, a third of the way*] because they take six days to cover loading at Lyon, travelling from Lyon to Tarare and

FIGURE 25
'Chaland' or barge on the Loire, sailing upstream

Note the sail; the fixed tiller (*la piautre*); the *arronçoirs* (serrated wooden batons to hold in place a large oar or pole for rapid manoeuvres); and the *guinda* (capstan) for hoisting the mainstay. After G. Biton, *Bateaux de Loire*, 1972–6.

unloading [*in fact as the reader will see, they were transferring goods*] at Tarare, then returning to Lyon, and the seventh day is Sunday, when they do not work. So 100 drivers [*i.e. 100 wagons*] load up every day in Lyon, each of them carrying on average 8 quintals, *poids de marc*.[226] So the 100 drivers are taking 800 quintals, which makes 374 *setiers* of grain, at 230 *livres* per *setier.* A similar number, 600 drivers, operate daily between Tarare and Saint-Siphorien [*sic*] and from Saint-Siphorien to Roanne. Therefore every week, 2,244 *setiers,* that is 187 *muids,* are transported from Lyon to Roanne. And on the road from Belleville to Poully-sur-Loire [*sic*], an average of 150 *setiers* of grain travels every day, that is 900 in a week, which makes 75 *muids.* The total (187+75) is 262. But since there are sometimes holidays, when the drivers stop work the same as on Sundays, we should reduce the quantity of *muids* to an estimated 250.

If the reader has had the patience to read through every word of this, he or she will have noted that what we have here is a regular and abundant form of freight operated by peasants: 1,800 teams of oxen, travelling slowly (about 14 kilometres a day) relaying each other every seven kilometres; that is over every kilometre of the road there would be over 20 wagons going up or down, that is one every 50 metres. And we complain nowadays that we have to overtake or meet too many lorries on the roads! What did the traveller in a carriage or the driver of the stage-coach think in the old days?

As for the quantities of grain carried, the document estimates them as 187 *muids* (Paris measure) per week travelling from Lyon to Roanne. If we say 180, to allow as suggested for holidays, we get a figure of 9,360 *muids* a year; at 18 hectolitres to the *muid,* this works out at 168,480 hectolitres, approximately 140,400 quintals or 14,000 tonnes – a figure representing the maximum freight that could be carried on the road when it was operating at full stretch. The first lines of the document in fact reveal that 3,200 *muids* (Paris measure) were stocked in the south, but that they would take several months to arrive in Paris where they were impatiently awaited, in this year of dearth. For since alas, overland transport between Lyon and the Loire was 'the most difficult, it was this that governed the quantity of grain arriving every week in Paris':[227] a mere 250 *muids,* in spite of using two parallel roads.

The figure of 14,000 tonnes a year is of course merely an order of magnitude, since not all the goods in circulation weighed the same as grain, volume for volume, and in any case it is not clear that the road was constantly being operated at full stretch. But neither is this totally improbable, since it represented what would today be called a bottleneck. In particular, the reader should not protest that this figure is too low, since it represents the equivalent of 6 or 7 ships of average tonnage, and was being carried, what was more, on a hilly road before the improved surfacing techniques of the eighteenth century. Did the improvements increase the flow of traffic? We may presume so, since in times of war during the eighteenth century, both Provence and Languedoc used the Roanne route to Paris rather than risk capture at sea by the English.[228] But is it merely coincidence that the first railways built in France by private industrial initiative (1823–8), even before the introduction of the steam engine (1831), were those linking Saint-Etienne to Lyon and Saint-Etienne to Roanne via Andrézieux? After all, as was explained to the shareholders of the first railways in 1826, this represented 'the surest way . . . of realizing at last the long-awaited benefit of a link between the Loire and the Rhône'.[229]

Much easier to visualize in retrospect is traffic down the Loire. Thousands of boats plied to and fro, all flat-bottomed to avoid the nightmare of every boatman, running aground on the dangerous sandbanks or colliding with a rock or submerged tree in the river bed. Even marking channels with stakes did not guarantee safety: they had to be marked over and over again, since every flood disturbed the river bottom. On some stretches, where the Loire broadens out or divides into tributaries and islands, 'so that it is at once everywhere and nowhere',[230] a special craft, the warping tug, went ahead of the boats, guiding them by singing out and planting tall stakes of hazel or elder.

Most of the boats on the Loire, built of deal (*sapin*) and variously known as *sapines, sapinières, salambardes* (a deformation of Saint-Rambert, the boat-building centre on the upper Loire) or *auvergnates* (if they came from the Allier), travelled downstream only. The crew would disembark – returning to Roanne on foot – and the boats would simply be broken up on arrival and sold off for firewood, or, as the *Annuaire statistique de la Loire* for 1809 says, 'sold to be taken apart and used for carpentry and joinery'. To bring them back upstream would have cost 400 to 500 *livres* per boat, whereas each one, originally bought for 300 to 500 *livres*, would fetch 100 *livres* in Paris. They were not very sturdy in any case, being hastily assembled and 'often sold by the dozen, piled up one inside the other'. They would not have stood up to many trips.[231] By contrast, boats destined to be sent both upstream and downstream were carefully built of oak. These were the *gabares*, a very ancient type of vessel, also known as *gabariotes*, *camuses* or *chenières*, but the word *chalands* prevailed by the end of the eighteenth century. These narrow craft, 9 to 15 metres long, each with a large sail, generally travelled upstream in convoys of three, five or six, attached together. The leading boat – the 'mother', was the only one to use her rudder and to hoist the sail very high, the others setting their sails progressively lower to aid the action of the wind. A string of *allèges*, flat boats about five or six metres long, would be towed along behind, and the whole formed an impressive procession.[232] But when a squall blew up, on 14 September 1709, the last two boats in the string 'took off the stern of the third last', which sank.[233]

This river traffic, subject to many risks, dangerous in winter because of flooding, impossible in summer when the water was too low, took weeks to get anywhere, even travelling downstream, whether on the Loire or the Allier, and the crew, who had to manoeuvre continuously, were subjected to a prison-like routine, not to mention having to sleep packed like sardines in the master's vessel,[234] on piles of straw. The only moments of respite were halts to go ashore before nightfall, or even better the walk back home, when the trip was over, a time of relaxation, merry-making and extravagant spending.

As a rule then, shipping went down the Loire. But there were hundreds of trips the other way – perhaps fifty a year as far as Roanne, as against several thousand trips downstream from the upper Loire and the Allier. In 1789, a conscientious geographer, J. A. Dulaure,[235] reported seeing in port in Roanne boats with 'enormous' sails, 'laden with goods from Nantes or other towns along the Loire, which will be carried overland from here to Lyon'. But this upstream traffic, which used human haulage besides sails, was extremely slow and often came to a halt waiting for a fair wind.

As a result, colonial products from overseas 'often take longer to travel the 100 leagues up river in these open boats than they have spent crossing from America to France' and might spoil, according to one Sinson, of Orleans, who argued that animal haulage should replace men on the towpaths of the Loire as it had on the Rhône. This was quite impossible, stated a long memorandum in reply. Serious obstacles made it impossible for horses to follow the banks of the Loire; embankments stood above the river almost everywhere, some with a five- or six-metre drop. And the ramps were neither numerous enough nor broad enough: men might risk using them, but horses certainly could not.[236]

It was the peasants from land bordering the Loire who hired themselves out in winter as hauliers. Some of them also worked as extra crewmen, but the true boatmen made up a closed society, virtually self-contained, as little communities often were under the *ancien régime*. So they were free with their insults for the hauliers, ('landlubbers', 'bird-catchers', 'muddy-bums') who returned the compliment, calling the boatmen 'windbags', 'whoresons' and 'wet-bums'.[237] Was this a class struggle or merely a war of words?

The large number of charges laid before the *bailliage* of Roanne[238] is at any rate sufficient evidence that the boatmen's world was a violent one. It amounts to no more than a catalogue of minor offences, true, (exchanges of blows, insults) but the 'river folk' figure disproportionately. They were also capable of rebelling against the public authorities and, as a late document remarks, 'of meeting force with force'.[239] That they were in addition 'deceitful, untrustworthy, unreliable and shiftless', is not impossible. Elie Brackenhoffer of Strasbourg had been warned about them: they lay in wait for the traveller, and vied with each other to cheat him. In dealings with them, it was best to specify everything in advance – food, wine, halts along the river, whether the skipper was to be on board or not. And the golden rule was never to pay until the end of the trip. But when at last Brackenhoffer, taking the advice of a trading-house in Roanne, hired the boatman who had ferried Louis XIII the year before, he recognized afterwards that 'we had no occasion to observe [the faults] of our boatmen, for their attitude was trustworthy and correct'.[240]

At all events, travellers crowded into Roanne, not so much it seems to get to Paris more quickly (this could not be counted on: in 1737, while a post-chaise took five days to get from Lyon to Paris, the trip in a *cabane* from Roanne to Orleans alone, in good weather, took three days)[241] as to avoid the fatigue of horseback or coach travel. On the *cabanes*, the light boats specially built for their use, they found comparative comfort in the form of what we should call cabins, constructed on deck. Important people did not at any rate disdain this form of transport. In 1447, King René[242] travelled up the Loire from Angers to Roanne on his way to his county of Provence, in 'a long procession of boats draped with hangings and decorated with banners, bearing princes and courtiers, or trans-porting tapestries, plate and furniture'. In 1481, 'his mortal remains travelled, incognito, on their last voyage, in the other direction, from Roanne to below the Ponts-de-Cé, to reach his fair city of Angers'.[243] Other illustrious travellers included Louis XI, coming from Le Puy in 1476; François de Paule in 1482; Charles VIII in 1490; Louis XII in 1498;[244] the marquis of Saluzzo in 1539, who took with him to make the voyage more agreeable, a 'consort of viols';[245] Henri III and Catherine de' Medici, during the sum-mer of 1584; Charles-Emmanuel of Savoy in 1599;[246] Henri IV, who was on his way back to Paris after abandoning operations in the war against Savoy, in January 1601. Not to mention Louis XIII, Richelieu and Madame de Sévigné . . .

Passenger traffic and freight both expanded in the eighteenth century. One reason was that the thirst of the Parisians extended demand to the vineyards of the Roannais and Beaujolais which were exporting respectively 30,000 and 50,000 hectolitres a year. Not all these casks of wine passed through Roanne: Beaujolais and Burgundy wine was also shipped from Pouilly-sous-Charlieu, from Decize, Digoin and even from villages and bourgs along the Loire, all known as 'ports', though actually no more than embarkation points. But Roanne had appropriated by far the greater share of this traffic.

The second reason, an all-important one, was that shipping could go upstream from Roanne to Saint-Rambert after 1728, when the gorges of the Loire across the Neulise plateau were rendered navigable. This was the culmination of a long series of projects, (the earliest dating from 1572) and of a lengthy programme of works carried out by one Pierre de Lagardette, who seems to have been backed by a consortium putting up the considerable funds needed for altering the course of the river: buying up the mill which was blocking a narrow passage in the gorge, negotiating with a dozen others so that they left navigable channels clear, removing dangerous rocks and trees from under the water. All in all, a difficult, lengthy and risky undertaking. The order in council authorizing the enterprise dates from 2 May 1702, and 'it was only in 1725 that [the works] were registered as being well and truly executed and completed'.[247] In theory the contractor was supposed to extend the alteration of the river upstream from Saint-Rambert, as far as Monistrol. But Pierre de Lagardette was never to complete this part of the contract, which he declared, rightly or wrongly, to be impossible. This led to many protests, offers of service and even an offensive by certain traders. I like the story of the boatbuilders of Saint-Rambert, who were moved in their fury to build two boats at Monistrol, one of which was washed away in a violent flood, though the second did reach port safely in Saint-Rambert on 14 May 1756, in order to demonstrate (to no avail at all) that the journey was possible.

But to return to our problem: extending navigation above Roanne to Saint-Rambert had at least two objectives. In the first place it meant the exploitation of the hitherto untouched forests around Saint-Rambert, and thus the chance to concentrate in this little port the activity of the boat builders who soon had the near-monopoly of building all the craft used for the *entire* river traffic on the Loire. This meant at least a thousand boats a year and more later: 1,500 on the eve of the Revolution, if my calculations are not too wild, and possibly 2,800 by 1822, if we accept the figures of the young historian Denis Luya.[248] These boats reached Roanne either empty or carrying wood and, increasingly, coal. The latter was taken from the Saint-Etienne coalfield in carts or on the backs of pack animals, as far as Saint-Just, the little port downstream from the bridge at Saint-Rambert, where it was embarked. Empty or laden, these boats all paid 40 *livres* toll on entering Roanne where the toll-owners had planted a row of stakes across the river, with a chain barring the channel through which the boats passed.

The *sapinières*, which carried a maximum load of 15 tons of coal, were strengthened on their arrival, to carry extra capacity, up to 20 tons. Such trans-shipments confirmed Roanne's prosperity. The whole, wine and coal together, amounted to an enormous volume of freight for the time: over 2,000 boats, perhaps 40,000 tons.[249] The coal was particularly in demand at the Sèvres porcelain manufactory, and travelled to Paris via the Briare canal.

Capitalism and feudalism

We should not however imagine that Roanne enjoyed extraordinary prosperity in the eighteenth and early nineteenth century. It remained a small town (6,992 inhabitants in 1800, plus an adjoining village of 810, Parigny).[250] Having no walls – which is an indication of something, if not a decisive factor – it did not enjoy the 'title of town', noted J. A. Dulaure in 1789;[251] 'it is still called a bourg today, though people add [it is true] that it is the finest bourg in France'.

What can be said with certainty is that controlling an essential route for national traffic did not turn Roanne into a major centre of trade. Like any town, it contained a range of occupations, and could also boast lawyers, doctors and various degrees of merchant. There were even a few wholesalers, the inventories of whose property after death should make it possible to estimate their wealth, and in 1700, there were a dozen or so commission agents who, it is true, merely received goods dispatched by firms in Lyon, and generally sent them on to Paris.[252] Finally, Roanne contained a few grand personages, occupying honorific posts, but remaining rather marginal to the real life of the town. The offices of aldermen, created and sold by the king alongside the existing consuls in 1657, occasioned no enthusiasm among the rich citizens. Was this why the town was so poorly governed, indeed hardly governed at all – always flooded with mud, its streets badly paved and in need of

222

repair? Or was it in this respect simply like most other towns of the period?

The historian's curiosity is naturally drawn retrospectively towards the transport sector. Is this not where in theory the wealth and capitalist innovations of Roanne should have been concentrated? Yet even in this, the heart of the town's activity, there were few outstanding success stories. The town's rise had brought some change to the life of the boatbuilders and to the boatmen. An elementary form of capitalism took its gentle course here. Thus the merchant-carriers were distinguished from the master-carriers, the latter working on their boats alongside their crewmen, the former owning several boats run by factors and bargees. With the further prosperity of the eighteenth century, transport firms were created in a rather hand-to-mouth way, to the advantage of small-scale capitalists. One family who benefited from the general climate, the Berry-Labarres, are a typical example. They owned both boats and boatyards. Pierre Berry-Labarre and a few fellow-merchants were in 1765, 'the businessmen who alone handle almost all the trade which can take place' between Saint-Rambert and Roanne.[253] Does 'trade' here mean the purchase or only the transport of coal, which was the chief freight on this stretch of the river?

Either way, a monopoly would have been of significance. It is not entirely a coincidence that a bill of exchange mentioned in official documents happens to come from the business circle of this powerful family. But power and success provoked enmities and challenges. On 25 September 1752, some master-carriers took possession of certain boats carrying coal belonging to the firm and gave notice that they meant to sail them to Paris themselves. A minor incident, but a significant one.[254] The Berry-Labarres did not have complete freedom of movement and met some stiff opposition. Furthermore, even in the absence of statistics, one cannot avoid the impression that any capitalist who emerged from this shipping world remained at a modest level. Indeed freight was never a very profitable sector under the *ancien régime*.[255] If there were any exceptional fortunes, we need to seek them at some other level.

Pierre de Lagardette, about whom little is known, was a more thoroughgoing capitalist than the boat owners. From the start, his undertaking could count on considerable capital, of the order of 500,000 *livres*, provided by a large group of financial backers (forty in 1792, when the firm was wound up and claims were lodged). What was more, yearly expenditure on maintenance of the river (including the marking of channels which was indispensable) came to over 4,000 *livres*, and quite a number of tollkeepers were required to collect the tolls. These varied in the region of 50,000 *livres* a year: a modest income, it might be thought, compared to the capital invested, which had been tied up unproductively for several years while work was in progress. The income brought in was not more than 8% by the roughest of calculations. But we do not know all the 'secrets' of the affair which seems to have had many ramifications. A chance reference in some documents tells us for instance that a certain Vernon, '*subdélégué* of the *intendance* of Lyon', in November 1765, was one of the proprietors of 'the new shipping', that is something like a shareholder in it. And another even more precious detail is that Pierre de Lagardette was no mere toll-gatherer: he bought coal at the gates of Saint-Etienne and shipped it to Roanne – incidentally contravening thereby a by-law stating that all coal produced within a radius of two leagues around Saint-Etienne had to be kept there.[256]

In short, the so-called 'new shipping' project, more far-reaching than it looks at first sight, was a prosperous and many-sided undertaking, and one understands why Lagardette and his associates were not greatly anxious to get on with the expensive and hazardous development of the Monistrol–Saint-Rambert section of the river. The firmest evidence of their power is perhaps their victory in a battle – on this very issue – against someone not without importance himself, Pierre de Rivas.[257] This former shareholder in the mines in Brittany (output from which had fallen considerably) had settled in Firminy and wanted to load the coal from his mines into boats at Monistrol. The result was a quarrel with the new shipping company, whom Rivas took to the king's council. He accused the company of making feeble excuses for not fulfilling its commitments. There was a procession of experts and reports, clearly biased towards Lagardette. Rivas did not get his way, despite arguing the case for developing not only the coal mines but also the abundant resources of the forests round Monistrol, as yet untouched, which could have replaced as boat-building materials the forests of Saint-Rambert, now exhausted by fifty years intensive use; the Monistrol forests could also have provided the royal navy with the tall trees it needed, which could have been floated down to Nantes. Rivas's efforts failed, despite his unquestionable determination and sturdy spirit of enterprise: he had for instance installed in his Firminy mine, when it was flooded, a machine of which he was extremely proud – actually a steam pump on the Newcomen model, somewhat simplified.[258] And this was in 1759 – well ahead of its time.

Can we call the ferry from Roanne to Nantes and Paris, created for the benefit of the duc de la Feuillade in 1679[259] and almost immediately farmed out by him, another example of big business? The ferry had no monopoly, but since might is often right, every time it left Roanne, twice a week, it shamelessly bagged a full load of passengers and freight, thwarting its competitors, the usual transporters, by a few impudent manoeuvres. But the resentment and hostility of the injured parties was such that the ferry gave up in 1697. In 1736 however, the contract was revived by Alexandre Yvon, who was moreover an owner of the Briare canal and a competitor of the ferry-owners of Nemours and Montargis. This battle of the Briare, Orleans and Loing canals only distantly concerns us, but it reveals the extent of the business empire of Alexandre Yvon who was not, incidentally, a native of Roanne.

All in all, Roanne and the surrounding area in the eighteenth century were far from being taken over by capitalism, which was then only in its beginnings. For evidence that the inhabitants of Roanne remained sunk in the past, one has only to look at the behaviour of the duc de la Feuillade, who acquired the dukedom of the Roannais in 1666. The title brought him a string of estates, dues and privileges which his ambition and self-interest wholeheartedly exploited. That he should have managed not only to preserve but even to strengthen them, to revive in all their ancient vigour certain prerogatives long since lapsed, is after all revealing. In Roanne itself for instance, he was entitled to harbour dues, and to dues on crossing the Loire (farmed out at 5,350 *livres*); to a *droit de grenette*, a duty levied on all grain sold in the town market; to a *droit de greffe* on the *bailliage*, even to prison dues, and a quarter of the tithes of the parish; he further had the right to sell his wine in the town a month before everyone else, and to oblige the residents to grind their grain in his mills. A league away from Roanne, he owned the château of Boisy with its land and sharecropped farms, plus seven or eight fishponds. Then there were his winepresses, where the village winegrowers were obliged to press their grapes. This is only a summary of an interminable catalogue, details of which are revealed in the records, whenever the duke or his agents took action, protested or lodged claims, as in 1705–6 for instance, when they took on the commission agents in town, or when they built or bought several mills in order to re-establish the milling privilege. Such successful aggression throws a harsh light on the situation in the Roannais. Feudalism seems to have coexisted quite cheerfully with capitalism here.[260]

Inside the town

A sketch of the socio-occupational composition of the little town at the end of the *ancien régime* is provided by a convenient monograph which offers ample food for thought (see Figure 26).[261] If the population is divided into the three sectors (tertiary, secondary, primary) we get the following figures, approximately: 13.5%; 54%; 20.5%. The total does not come to 100% because of the impossibility of a complete census. But the figures do reveal a rather curious structure:

1. The presence in the 'tertiary' groups of a class of office-holders and members of the legal profession who ruled the roost: merchants and inn-keepers only represent 7% of this group.

2. A large majority of artisans: 54% (of whom 19% were bargees).

3. In the primary sector (swollen by the inclusion of day-labourers whom I have put in this category), peasants and winegrowers account for only 7%, which seems to prove that Roanne was somewhat, or even substantially distinct from the farming world that surrounded it. This poses quite a problem. Was it because of the

town's late development? Or because of the constant demand for labour in occupations related to river and even road transport? The privileged, as owners of real estate, nevertheless exerted a strong influence on a good share of the land surrounding the town. Roanne was not one of those towns like Mulhouse, which had given up investing in the countryside around.

4. Lastly, on the eve of the Revolution, there was clearly some specialization by district: artisans and day-labourers were mostly to be found in the north, in the Casernes (barracks) district, and on the southern and western periphery, at the bottom of the town and round the docks. The privileged lived between the top and the bottom ends of town; merchants, commission agents and bargees on the island of Roanne. The town adapted itself to its various tasks.[262]

Roanne in the nineteenth and twentieth centuries

There are many gaps in our brief survey of the former activity of Roanne and the Roannais, notably concerning the balance between the rural and the urban. Further exploration in the mass of erudite publications and unexamined documents would have made it possible to go much further. But do we really need to in the context of the present discussion?

Perhaps it would be best to end this attempt to situate the particular case of Roanne by looking quickly at what became of the town and its region after the old river traffic disappeared,[263] that is either after 1838, the date of the completion of the Loire canal, which would long be a faithful servant to Roanne (though today its traffic is in steady and disastrous decline), or after 1858, when the building of a railway bridge brought the rail network to the town.[264]

These events did not harm the general prosperity of Roanne. It remained an important centre of communications, just as it had after the opening of the Givors canal linking the Saint-Etienne coalfield to the Rhône (1761) and after that of the canal du Centre (1784–90) between Digoin and the Saône. The town's population

227

FIGURE 26
The changing socio-professional pattern in Roanne

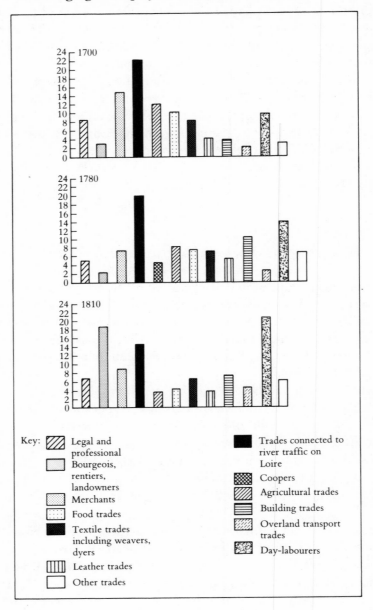

Key:
- ▨ Legal and professional
- ▢ Bourgeois, rentiers, landowners
- ▨ Merchants
- ⣿ Food trades
- ■ Textile trades including weavers, dyers
- ⫿⫿ Leather trades
- ▢ Other trades
- ■ Trades connected to river traffic on Loire
- ▨ Coopers
- ▨ Agricultural trades
- ▤ Building trades
- ▨ Overland transport trades
- ▨ Day-labourers

has moreover grown quickly. Today, within its much wider town boundaries, Roanne contains 100,000 inhabitants or more, over ten times its population of 1800. What is more, the nineteenth century saw it extend its grip over its district, a fairly restricted district it is true: what was left by the ring of rival towns that surround Roanne on all sides, at a distance of about 60 kilometres: Saint-Etienne, Lyon, Mâcon, Moulins, Vichy, Clermont-Ferrand – a set of immovable objects. The district was limited in size then, and poor as well, but during the nineteenth century rural industry grew up there. Labour was cheap – to the satisfaction of the Lyon capitalists responsible for the spread of cotton- and silk-weaving, and to that of the small-scale employers of the Roannais. And this was a skilled workforce – had not the country people, as in so many French villages, been working hemp for centuries? In summer, 'the most disgusting of smells' would spread through the plain, 'in the season for retting the hemp and spreading it out to dry'.[265] Moving from hemp to cotton, first in the eighteenth century, then more rapidly in the nineteenth, was not such a break with the past: fingers had remained nimble.

This was of course an archaic type of industry, not so very far removed from the woollen industry in thirteenth-century Florence and Tuscany.[266] But this proto- or pre-industry proved to be long-lived. The proximity of food markets to these country workshops made life easier for them and created prosperity or at any rate a comfortable balance. The 'bosses', disturbed or horrified by workers' unrest in the industrial towns, were in no hurry to concentrate or to mechanize the industry. And electricity came to their

---

Note, within an overall context of expansion: the growth of the tertiary sector and the bourgeoisie; the sharp fall in agricultural work; the comparative (and absolute) drop in the number of boatmen; the steady expansion of overland traffic; the slight rise in the numer of artisans (building trades included); and lastly the striking rise in the number of day-labourers, who were the largest single group by 1810, a sign of the proletarianization of ordinary people, as wealth in the town increased.

aid, making it possible to decentralize energy sources and thus to keep the workshops dispersed. So modernization did not come quickly; especially since circumstances gave a fillip to the activity of the Roannais. Thus the annexation of Mulhouse by Germany in 1871 made our little town the leading manufacturer of canvas and brightly-coloured ginghams. Indeed the Roanne textile industry saw its best days between 1870 and 1890. Later, it managed to withstand the depression of 1929. Hosiery – knitted fabrics – began to appear there and Roanne quickly became the second producer in France, after Troyes.

Rather surprisingly, structural crisis did not begin to affect Roanne until after 1955. Then, whole sectors of the old economy collapsed, bringing dismay and consternation. And yet, taking advantage of its administrative functions, of a booming tertiary sector, and of new engineering industries located in or near the town, sustained perhaps by the euphoria of its past success, Roanne still managed to survive quite well. Today, the overall crisis which is devastating France, and the rest of the world as well, has arrived there too: this time the crisis is not only economic, social and political, but is also a crisis of attitudes. What the future holds no one knows. But problems are already appearing.

Thus, among other things, the perennial problem of transport routes, already present in the fourteenth century, is posed once again. History is repeating itself: there are three competing north–south routes: the Allier route, via Clermont-Ferrand; the Bourbonnais route via Roanne and Tarare to Lyon (that is the Loire route); and lastly the Saône–Rhône route which has taken a lot of traffic from the other two in the twentieth century and is still forging ahead. Then there is the still uncertain future of the transversal routes from Nantes to Lyon, and from Bordeaux to Lyon, via Clermont-Ferrand, as well as competition from bigger towns. We do not know the end of this story, and it is hard to make predictions. But perhaps we should place our confidence once more in the vitality of Roanne and the Roannais.

Laval, or the twin triumph of industry and long-distance trade

I originally intended, on leaving Roanne to its fate, to take the case of Brive-la-Gaillarde, on the other side of the Massif Central. I could at the same time have mentioned Tulle and Ussel: Brive would have been the lowland town, Tulle the next stage up in *bocage* country, and Ussel, near the Millevaches plateau, an example of a mountain town. In the end I decided not to; partly for reasons of space, but also because Brive-la-Gaillarde as its name suggests (*gaillard* means 'confident, valiant') was a solid, almost untroubled town, that is one without problems: it was somehow too self-confident, too sure of the protection of its double walls, of the profits it effortlessly derived from its trade routes and the renown of its fairs which in the eighteenth century could assemble up to 5,000 head of cattle; it was also too comfortably assured – given the fertility of the surrounding country – of the landed income of its nobles and bourgeois; and lastly, it was too cramped by the straitjacket of its craft guilds.

So I have arrived sooner than I expected at Laval, in that awkward region of lower Maine, on the high right bank of the 'pretty, dark'[267] and deep river Mayenne, at the point where the Vieux Pont, the old bridge, crosses it, looking up to the old castle and the new castle. This is an old town, with its cluster of complicated monuments, daring the passing historian to summon up everything he can (or cannot) remember about medieval and early modern art. At any rate, Laval is a very *French* town. Italian towns are often prettier; and if they care to be, magnificent. But French towns are invariably steeped in the character of the particular countryside that surrounds them, supports them and *to some extent* explains them. In the France of the past in particular, the town was first and foremost, the result of its countryside.

Laval, which had perhaps 10,000 inhabitants in the seventeenth century,[268] stands in the centre of a narrow basin, richer, or at least less poor than the regions round about, with the advantage of some chalky soils; lime-kilns made an early appearance here.

231

It lies on the edge of Brittany, once a province of *franc salé*, that is exempt from the salt-tax, the *gabelle*; consequently salt-smuggling prospered here for centuries, in 'this land of brushwood, interspersed with woods and ponds', where 'thickets of holly or broom could hide a man a few paces [from you, and where] the mossy ground . . . stifles all sound'. This land of the *faux-sauniers* – the salt-smugglers – would become a natural stamping-ground for the Chouans during the Vendée war. But how, pleaded the priest of the tiny parish of Landivy, could the region avoid being drawn into smuggling, since it formed 'almost a peninsula between Normandy and the "foreign" province of Brittany'?[269] True, Laval did not maintain any regular links with those outlaws[270] the *faux-sauniers*, except that, as a frontier town, it had to provide, more often than it cared to, billets for troops and garrisons – which troops and garrisons almost without exception swelled the ranks of the smugglers. It was after all regular practice for soldiers, even honorable officers, to allow themselves to be tempted by the profits of salt smuggling. Despite repeated ordinances from the king, prescribing heavy penalties (being sent to the galleys for instance in 1682)[271] they engaged in it almost openly. In 1693, twelve eye-witness reports spoke of small companies of troops, between 20 and 70 armed horsemen, such as 'the cavalrymen of the Mestre de Camp Général regiment, taking by force the horses of the ploughmen to go and look for "unofficial" salt in Brittany, attacking the archers of the *gabelle* office, . . . and even passers-by on the pretext that they looked like *gableux* (tax-collectors)'.[272]

Even when it caused no incident, this military presence was a nightmare because of the problems of lodging and food supplies. The arrival, in May 1693, of six cavalry companies caused panic in Laval and the surrounding cantons. How was this mass of voracious men and horses to be supplied with bread, forage and oats? The *intendant* Miromesnil feared popular unrest and asked the king to pay part of the contribution exacted from the parishes which provided fodder for the horses. He even considered, if matters grew worse, bringing oats 'from beyond the river Loire'. As for grain, which the inhabitants were always afraid would run short, 'the panic' was the greater since there were still nine battalions in the area – which meant a consumption of 1,000 sacks of flour a month. It would nevertheless be necessary, the *intendant* concluded, 'to make people open their granaries in both town and country. We shall try to prevent any incidents by all reasonably possible means'. But a few days later there were indeed incidents and the *intendant* had to authorize requisitions.[273]

The popular feeling aroused by supply problems was natural: this wide area, intersected by fast-running streams and scattered with low hills, was made up of cold soils, generally barren if left to themselves:

> Many of these fields yield barely four or five harvests in twelve years; they need a seven-year stretch of completely unproductive rest, during which they grow broom which is thought to restore their fertility. Wheat yields are low. Fields which have been prepared at great expense yield only 3 to 5 for 1, one reason why farmers prefer to grow buckwheat, which yields 30, 60 or even 100; this cereal provides the food of the people who cannot obtain wheat or even rye [more widely grown than wheat] which is always sold at very high prices.[274]

'We can only sow wheat', says a report to the Committee of Public Safety, 'on a quarter to a third of our land every year, in normal circumstances, and these days generally less than a quarter, because we are so short-handed.'[275] Chestnuts were a possibility of course, but could they always be found? It was also possible to ship in grain from Nantes along the Loire, Maine and Mayenne. Vines we must rule out: their presence in the Laval area was negligible. It is true that apple trees had since the fifteenth century been used for producing cider, which was not merely a poor man's drink in this region. But a bad harvest, as in 1741,[276] sent cider prices almost as high as wine: at the Hôtel-Dieu, the authorities served the inmates wine – well watered no doubt – rather than cider. Real wine did of course reach Laval from nearby Anjou, and from the Orléanais, to the tune of 2,000 *pipes* a year (each of 4 to 5 hectolitres), making a total consumption of 8,000 to 10,000 hectolitres for 10,000 inhabitants – not bad for a town of cider and water drinkers.

As for livestock, there were hardly any sheep, but plenty of cattle and small local horses – four oxen or four of these little horses made a ploughing team. And game was abundant: hare, rabbit, partridge, woodpigeon, rail, quail and snipe.

The agricultural situation scarcely improved over the eighteenth century. In the Year III, the potato was 'still in its infancy,' says one report, 'since it has been successful only in gardens and the best land, or on ground manured at great expense. It is still sufficiently uncommon to be used as food for humans only.' Artificial, that is rotated grasslands, too were only just beginning, although their area had tripled during the previous twenty years, but for want of fertilizers they were confined to good land and were then 'cultivated by the spade'. The only plentiful products were flax and wood. And the report concludes: '[cider] apples and pears are our principal fallback'.[277]

All in all, the agricultural balance-sheet was not impressive. The peasant had no choice but to be a sharecropper: 'the greater part of our land is farmed on a shared basis, that is the farmer takes half the produce for his own use and gives the other half to his landlord',[278] a landlord who almost invariably lived in town.

So Laval was unlikely to become rich from its land. Did it owe its prosperity to the many roads which met there – leading to Rennes, Angers, Le Mans (and beyond to Paris or Orleans), to Mayenne and Caen, to Alençon across the high and difficult country of the Perche? No, because not one of these roads was any good. The Le Mans–Laval–Rennes highway was not in service until 1772. And the local roads were terrible, even between neighbouring farms. 'Nowhere in western France was isolation as total as it once was in the lower Maine.'[279] Travellers before 1772, who included Madame de Sévigné, chose rather to go via Angers and Nantes. 'Transport was on horseback, and sometimes on the backs of men'.[280] There was of course the Mayenne, which was navigable as far as Laval and even beyond. But downstream from the town, there were twenty-two locks and a number of mills. The latter were perennial obstacles here as everywhere else, and the locks sometimes failed to work.[281]

It should be added that here as in Roanne, if one were to

describe a circle of about 70 kilometres radius round the town, it would touch several rival towns, which acted as repulsive poles so to speak: Angers (73 kilometres away, 143,000 inhabitants at the last census); Le Mans (75 kilometres, 155,000 inhabitants); Rennes (72 kilometres, 205,000 inhabitants), whereas Laval today has a population of only 54,500.

All in all, who could fail to be surprised not so much at the present importance of Laval, nowadays making the most of its *préfecture*, its varied industrial sector and land improvements which have turned it into a quite successful grazing region, but by the town's achievements as early as the seventeenth century?

To what can these comparatively precocious achievements be attributed? To the fact, first of all, that a poor and subservient hinterland surrounded it and was attracted into Laval every week, from the seventeenth century, by three markets, on Tuesdays, Thursdays and Saturdays, plus five annual fairs. In addition, within the area of its *élection* and linked to the town were no fewer than twenty-one fairs[282] (four in the 'bourg of Ballée, two at Grez-en-Boire, three at Sougé, eight at Montésurs and four at Cossé'). The *arrondissement* of Laval at the beginning of the nineteenth century by no means corresponded to the old *élection*, but one finds somewhat to one's astonishment, that it had no fewer than 67 fairs at this time.[283] These were evidently livestock fairs, where the Laval district sold to neighbouring districts the cattle and horses it had reared. This trading certainly contributed to the good order and healthy condition of Laval's affairs: at about the same time, the fair ground was extended after ministerial permission, to take over the land and the building 'of the convent of the ci-devant Benedictines'.[284] In short, Laval could hardly fail to dominate the surrounding territory, as the figures testify: in 1831, the town had 15,830 inhabitants, the canton 24,669, and the *arrondissement* 114,577 (that is 13.8% of the *arrondissement*'s population lived in the town).

But Laval's prosperity was accounted for above all, by its industry, linked to the circuits of long-distance trade and strengthened by the poverty that reigned in the countryside. As one historian points out: 'It was this poverty which kept the manufacturers going: necessity forced the poor man to ask a low price for the work on which he depended'.[285] We are in one of those many regions where cottage industry eked out the inadequate incomes of the peasantry.

Everything appears to stem from the very ancient establishment (traditionally dated with suspicious precision in 1298) of linen manufacture, said to have been brought to the town by the Flemish craftsmen who accompanied Béatrix de Gavre, the wife of Guy de Laval, ninth of that name.[286] It was certainly a very timely arrival: the lower Maine had always produced flax and hemp, whereas the meagre and poor-quality wool of its sheep enabled only a coarse cloth to be produced there.

In reality, linen did not prosper in Laval until the seventeenth century. But then it took off with a vengeance: thousands of weavers set to work and the merchants quickly became rich. The boom was unquestionably caused by the opening up to European industry of markets in Latin America and the West Indies. Even unbleached linens which Laval sold to Troyes, Beauvais, Caen, Lyon and Rouen for bleaching, were mostly destined for the New World. Laval wholesalers sending linen directly to America used the services of pedlars and carters who would deliver woven pieces to Saint-Malo or Nantes, from which they were mostly sent to Cadiz, the point of departure for the big American supply fleets. On the return trip, the carters would bring to Laval timber, planks, beams and iron: for the lower Maine was full of ironworks and blast furnaces. Linen thus helped to make Laval into an iron market.

Towards the middle of the eighteenth century,

> every year, 20,000 to 25,000 lengths of woven linen are sold for cash in the Laval linen-market. Each length contains at least 100 ells [Laval measure], whether unbleached linen still to be bleached, or grey linen for jackets and linings. The unbleached linen is sold at between 26 and 100 sous per ell . . . and grey linen at 20 to 50 sous. There are about fifty trading houses in this line at Laval. They have recently begun to make linen and cotton handkerchiefs here, as in Cholet, but those of Laval are of better quality.[287]

If we translate this into modern measures, Laval was producing between 2 and 2.5 million metres, at an average price of three *livres*, yielding an annual turnover of six or seven million *livres*. And unlike other French textiles, the woollen *etamines* of Le Mans for instance, Laval's linen production rose steadily until the Revolution.[288]

The shop window for this thriving activity, which animated the entire town as well as the villages and bourgs round about, was the new market hall built on the Gast in 1732. The *tissiers* (weavers) would come here every Saturday, carrying their roll of linen on their shoulders; the customer, perched on a bench, would unroll it and examine it closely; he would then pass his purchase on to a 'bleacher'. There were numerous bleaching laundries around the town, on the left bank of the Mayenne or along the Jouanne, adjoining the meadows which gave the linen 'a marvellous whiteness'.[289] Their owners were often merchants or wholesalers themselves; they would buy linen on their own account, bleach it and sell it again. They also bought on commission (about 6 to 8%) for merchants in other French towns.[290]

Handling the finishing processes (in this case bleaching linen, elsewhere fulling and dyeing woollen cloth) was one way the merchants could control the market, while keeping for themselves the most profitable operations, acquiring the last instalment of value added and the substantial profits of retailing. Laval wholesalers were in touch with wholesalers in other major cities; they also accepted all the risk, hoping for the habitual high profits made on overseas trade. They were quite prepared to send brothers, sons or cousins off as agents to Bayonne, Cadiz, Port-Sainte-Marie or Lisbon (the earthquake which destroyed that city in 1755 caused them losses of 300,000 *livres*),[291] to Canada, Martinique, Santo Domingo or even Guinea.[292] They formed consortia to share the risk of sending goods and money on ships leaving Saint-Malo to trade in the American islands or the South Seas, at the time of the war of the Spanish succession, or on the ships taking part in Duguay-Trouin's punitive expedition against Rio de Janeiro in 1711.[293] Or else they bought shares in the French Indies Company, and took part in due course in the crazy speculation in the Mississippi Company. From time to time there were bankruptcies, but they were relatively infrequent, for these speculators, if they can be so called, remained prudent.

Need we dwell longer on these businessmen, since they are so like any other businessmen in France or Europe, comfortably installed at the pinnacle of capitalist activity and consequently of local society as well? They inevitably occupy the foreground of history, and it is not hard to follow them into their counting-houses and their daily business, riding out with their wives to their country houses, or waiting on market days for their sharecroppers to come in on their orders with supplies for their town houses. Their attics and cellars were well-stocked with wheat, rye, buckwheat, salt meat, fruit, firewood. They were also early purchasers of office and, even more, of noble estates, at any price.[294] As money opened all doors, their sons and daughters entered the ranks of the nobility.

In Laval however, unlike the pattern in most towns, these privileged men, whether ennobled or not, almost all remained faithful to trade. The Le Clercs, the Marests, the Guittets, the Bersets, the Delaportes, the Bussons, the Duchemins, the Renussons, the Pichots and so on, known by the name of their properties (Pichot de la Graverie, Guittet de la Houllerie, Berset de la Coupellière), lived fairly simply. Their still patriarchal families stood shoulder to shoulder (and not only on the occasion of a bankruptcy when the family came to the rescue to save the honour of the clan). Their houses, in the old town centre, became more ornamental and were 'modernized' in the eighteenth century to make them more comfortable, but these families went about soberly dressed and had few servants.[295] A doctor who came to live in Laval in the late eighteenth century noted that both rich and poor ate frugally: soup, plenty of soup, cabbage or leek, and little meat. The workers drank water, 'and cider on special occasions', the rich drank cider as a rule. Wine and fancy dishes were only 'for ceremonial meals'.[296]

All the same, the small group of wholesalers occupied all the leading positions. How could it have been otherwise, when the organization of work both in the town and in the surrounding countryside made them the keystone of the whole industry, creating immense differences in social status, to their advantage? The

Laval linen trade, an observer explained at the end of the seventeenth century,[297] 'depends on three sorts of persons': the thirty
wholesale merchants, who control the trade; the five hundred master weavers who buy the thread and put it out to be worked; and
over five thousand workers, 'the richest of whom has not 100 *livres*'
worth of possessions'. In fact this overall classification could cover
a multiplicity of situations. In theory there were no guild regulations in Laval to limit the number of masters and men. Anyone
could bring his work to market and sell it freely. But in practice
there was a system of dependence, from the wealthy master-
weaver, owning several looms, perhaps a laundry, who could buy
raw materials for cash and who sold the products of his workmen,
to the weaver who worked in his own workshop with one or two
journeymen, who was anxious to sell quickly so as to be able to buy
raw materials and was often at the mercy of the master-spinners,
'known as cancers, because they gobble up and suck dry master-
weavers who are in difficulties'. And there was a gulf too between
the workman who was fortunate enough to own his own tools and
to have wife and children working with him, in conditions little
different from those of a modest master-weaver, and the poor man
who had to hire himself out for wages, or more likely worked at
home part of the time because he was also a peasant. Every village,
every farm in the Maine was the scene of cottage industry. This
being so, how could the protests of the master-weavers who in
1732 tried to alter the ritual conditions of sale in the newly-built
market hall, be other than doomed in advance? What went on in
Laval went on everywhere else where a pre-industrial workforce,
mostly rural or living on the edge of the town (in Laval in the
Coconnière district) found itself in dispersed order and up against a
compact group of urban merchants. This was the pattern in Reims
as in Rouen, in Amiens as in Le Mans, near Laval where an industry
in light woollens, *étamines*, had been set up in the late seventeenth
century.

Laval, surrounded by its poor countryside, was a good example
of a structure adapted to take advantage of the creative benefits of
long-distance trade – though there were disadvantages too. Who
would provide the money the weaver needed for buying linen on

the Craon market (where the best quality thread was to be found)?[298] Who would provide the indispensable credit during the long wait for financial return unavoidable in long-distance trade? Who would invest the capital required to build a laundry? And what if there was a glut – which sometimes happened? The system would come to a halt, but the hardest hit would be the unemployed journeymen weavers.

The Laval industry seems to have prospered until the end of the eighteenth century. It then began to meet serious competition from abroad, in the shape of the linen cloth of Silesia, woven from excellent Polish thread and employing a workforce as humble, as exploited and even worse paid than that of the lower Maine. Worse followed with the French Revolution and the almost complete collapse of foreign markets in the New World, not to mention catastrophic events like the Vendée war. Created by long-distance trade and perishing by the same means, Laval's first fortune went into eclipse for a while.

Caen: urban model or point of reference?

Though large, Caen was only in the second rank of French cities. Paris, Rouen, Nantes, Bordeaux, Marseille, Lyon, Lille, Strasbourg, Toulouse and several others had long outstripped it. All the same in 1695, it had 26,500 inhabitants, a very creditable number; in 1753, there were 32,000 (three years earlier, the town walls had had to be demolished to provide more space); and in 1775, 40,858; but the figure fell back to 34,996 in 1793, with the disturbed early years of the Revolution.[299]

Surrounded by a fertile countryside, Caen at any rate provided a livelihood for many artisans, plus several industries of repute; it had a port, on the Orne, fifteen kilometres from the mouth of this little coastal river, at exactly the point where it became tidal, and where the even smaller Odon joined it. But the Orne became silted up and in the seventeenth century, Caen's shipping practically came to a standstill, the town being visited only by coasters of 200 tons and then only during the high equinoctial tides. As a rule the port saw only barges of 30 to 50 tons which sometimes sailed as far as the lower reaches of the Seine.[300] The town's shipping would only revive with the creation of a canal parallel to the Orne, inaugurated in 1857.[301]

In spite of its still comparatively modest dimensions, or possibly because of them, Caen, as described in detail in Jean-Claude Perrot's massive study,[302] opens up some extremely useful perspectives for urban history in general. The period concerned – the eighteenth century – also has the advantage of enabling us to view it at a watershed, since the town had not yet entirely shaken off the legacy of previous centuries, yet was already subject to the constraints of new choices. Caen's slow development is another advantage: such a gradual pace made it easier for contemporaries, as well as for us, to appreciate what was happening. Hence the title of this section 'Caen: urban model or point of reference'.

The reader will not be surprised to learn that Caen created a classic series of Von Thünen-type circles around itself, that is successive, concentric, economic zones. These divisions of the surrounding area are explained by its consumption needs, each linked to successive supply zones which had of necessity to be close at hand, since transport was so slow and problem-fraught. Caen's appetite did not of course compare to the monstrous belly that was Paris. All the same it was sufficient in itself to account for the concentric zones around this capital of Lower Normandy.[303]

The first circle, 'the kitchen-garden zone', began with the gardens or meadows *intra muros*. It spread into the territory outside the built-up area but within the town's bounds, and extended to a dozen or so villages located less than a league and a half out of town, encompassing an area of over 5,000 hectares. This zone, a sought-after one because of the proximity of the town's markets, was divided into mini-properties whose owners made a fairly decent living. It was entirely to be expected that this zone would devote a large share of land to cereals: daily consumption of vegetables was modest – only some 5,000 kilos. Milk consumption too was low: 2,000 litres, milk being only a supplement to diet, or else sold to pharmacies to make up medicines. Cereals, the staple food, thus found their way into this zone which should, in a strict appli-

241

cation of Von Thünen's scheme, have been one of kitchen and dairy produce.

The second circle, massive by comparison (66,700 hectares) corresponded to the rich, often clayey soils of the vast Caen hinterland, almost entirely devoted to wheat-growing, between the Seulle to the west, the Dives to the east, the Channel to the north and the forest of Cinglais to the south. This wheat-growing zone kept to triennial rotation and horse-drawn ploughs; it was only to the south-west, where the *bocage* began, that barley, rye and buckwheat replaced wheat, in the Domfrontais for instance.

Further away still began the grazing lands and the sparse forests.

Caen's wheat supply then was largely taken care of, and almost always in surplus. It hardly ever failed, even in a poor year, so the town never bothered to build the public grain-stores which almost all urban authorities throughout Europe kept fully-stocked in this period. In 1771, consumption was about 535 grammes per person per day, which is a good ration, giving an *annual* total for the town of 81,000 quintals. Eleven weekly country markets were held in rotation in the bourgs of the *élection* (covering a total of 131 *communes*) and these fuelled the daily procession of carts and waggons towards the town. Supplies[304] rarely broke down; this did all the same happen in 1725, 1752, 1789 and 1790.[305] But when there was a shortage, the public authorities had no difficulty buying grain elsewhere: they had only to apply to Le Havre; and there was always Dutch or English grain waiting in the Channel to be landed. So the town enjoyed great security and equilibrium – and the situation could only get better, since in the eighteenth century the quality of grain generally improved: the specific weight of wheat thus increased in Caen by 10% between 1740 and 1755. At the same time milling improved with the use of economical millstones in the seven town mills which ground almost half the total grain consumed. Since the bread ration was assured – not everyone ate white bread, but they did eat bread made from wheat-flour – so, essentially, was the existence of the townspeople.

Supplies were assured too even of other goods, which can hardly be called luxuries. Demand for meat and fish (over 30 kilos of meat per person per year) certainly outstripped supply from the direct

FIGURE 27
Caen and its surroundings

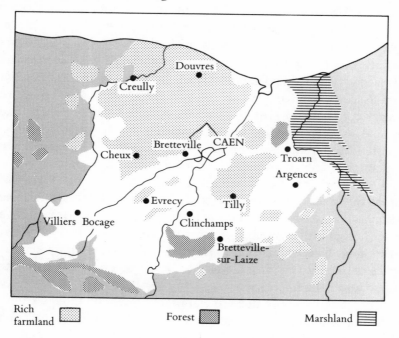

Between the Channel, the Seulles and the Dives – largely a
cereal-growing area. To the south-west, *bocage*; forests south
and east of the Orne. From J. C. Perrot, *Genèse d'une ville
moderne. Caen au XVIIIe siècle.*

Caen hinterland, almost entirely devoted to cereals, except on the
marshy banks of the Dives. But not far away was an extra source
of meat, the *bocage* country from which cattle, sheep and (in
smaller quantities) pigs were habitually exported. And the sea was
close at hand for fish, while the Orne was rich in salmon, shad and
lamprey.

Similarly, if vines were absent (unless we mention the 'presump-
tuous and struggling little vineyard' on the Argences hills?)[306] cider
was abundant. It took the place of wine and in previous centuries

had supplanted beer, ale and perry. In 1733, the taverners of Caen ordered forty times as many jars of cider as of wine (42,916 to 1,005).[307] Such a heavy demand required continual processions of two- and four-wheeled carts into town, laden with kegs of cider – frequent and heavy loads which made the bad roads even worse. Indeed this transport was so onerous that the pays d'Auge took to distilling its cider and sending it in the form of spirits. *Calvados*, which seems to have been invented in 1713,[308] was able because of its price, to bear the cost of transport, despite being carried by pack animal, an even more expensive form of transport than carts. It was in all likelihood responsible for the growth in Caen of what quickly became an alarming incidence of alcoholism.

Like wine and grain elsewhere, cider and grain here saw their price fluctuate in related directions. In 1772, the poor apple harvest would, according to the *intendant* of Caen, 'necessarily have an effect on grain consumption, for the people eat more when they drink less'. Similarly in 1778, 'shortage of drink will help keep the price of grain up'.[309] In 1779 and 1781, the mechanism worked the other way round.

There is perhaps no need to elaborate further on the question of food and drink. Compared to many other towns, such as Roanne or Laval, Caen enjoyed enviable security.

Like any other town of course, Caen provided a living for the many artisans and shopkeepers who ministered to its daily needs. Here as elsewhere, some of the artisans were in the craft guilds, others were free; some handled everyday work; others, more insecurely placed, catered to the 'opulence or luxury' of a wealthy clientele; a change in fashion could bring them to the brink of ruin.

But, and this is the interesting thing, industry (pre-industry or proto-industry if you prefer) became established in the town. Four waves of industry succeeded each other in the eighteenth century: woollen cloth of both luxury and ordinary quality; hosiery; canvas; and lastly lace-making. I have used the word 'wave' which is perhaps excessive, to indicate that these industries replaced each other rather than being added to each other. Each in turn thrived, declined and finally collapsed, something which might have been the result of normal industrial cycles. But were there perhaps special factors at work in Caen to frustrate any large-scale manufacturing development?

The establishment of an industry generally corresponded in the past to one of two possible situations. The first possibility was that it would go to regions with food surpluses, which exerted an almost irresistible attraction for workers. 'In some ways', Jean-Claude Perrot writes,[310] 'the location of industry in "food centres" in the old days was obeying the same imperatives as its location near coalfields in the industrial era'. The second possibility was almost the opposite: industry developed in regions where an excess of population relative to the food supply created a cheap local workforce. Examples are the industries of Roanne, Laval or the Normandy *bocage*, notably the extraordinary copper-working centre of Villedieu-les-Poêles.[311]

Caen falls into the first category. But was this the one most favourable for industry? Certainly the establishment of industry there was not easy. And this was not on account of the state, nor because of crushing fiscal burdens (as sometimes happened elsewhere). Nor was it because of unbending hostility on the part of the guilds; nor for lack of local capital. The brake on industry, for there certainly was one, lay it seems in the very wealth of the surrounding countryside and its social as much as economic consequences. In several ways, 'the rich farmland of the Caen region', as Jean-Claude Perrot puts it, 'really did prevent Normandy's agriculture from becoming the handmaid of industry'.[312]

In the first place, it refused to provide the town with a supply of cheap and plentiful raw materials. Hemp and flax were very little grown and of only mediocre quality (thread for lace-making was imported from Holland or Picardy). Wool too was both mediocre and expensive, so English wool had to be bought in. This drawback affected the whole of lower Normandy, whereas the less fertile countryside of Haute-Normandie willingly met the industrial demands of Rouen and other nearby towns.

Secondly, if the region around Caen was densely populated (70 or 80 inhabitants per square kilometre, sometimes even 100) and if there was some emigration to the town, this rural population was nevertheless well nourished, had plenty to occupy it and tended to stay at home. The urban labour market consequently remained limited and rather inelastic, from at least the end of Louis XIV's reign. What might we not do, exclaimed an inspector of the Manufactures in 1764, 'if we could have the abundant supply of labour we have so long desired!'.[313] As for supplementing their incomes by cottage industry, the peasants were sufficiently well off not to be looking too hard for it, or else to accept it only at high rates. Between 1715 and 1724, three quarters of the looms in the royal manufactory lay idle, for want of spinsters. In 1766, the village women would not come forward, 'unless they are paid much more than in the past for their spinning'.[314]

A further consequence of this agricultural wealth was that it attracted investment away from the town. Capital was placed in land (about 40%), in real estate and in *rentes*, securities preferably on land; little of it was spent on offices, hardly any in limited partnerships or commercial loans (0.5%). Industrialists and merchants themselves only invested 40% on average of their personal wealth in their professional businesses, the rest being in real estate and *rentes*. If one of them found himself in difficulties, he would sacrifice his portfolio of *rentes* first, and never, if he could help it, his real estate.[315]

All this was for reasons only partly economic. Land and income from land were of course profitable in this rich countryside, while industry was never, in the pre-industrial era, a sector of high profits. Industrialists did not make fortunes unless they were also wholesalers, as in Laval, and were thus able to launch their products on to the profitable but high-risk circuits of long-distance trade. And through living quietly off the land, mental attitudes became established, hostile to any adventure and wary of the trouble and uncertainty caused by risky investments.

Such was the case at Caen, where land-owning was all-pervasive, all-commanding and lulled the town to sleep. Jean-Claude Perrot goes so far as to speak of 'regional hibernation',[316] a strong expression perhaps, but a telling one. Caen offered few openings for the new needs and temptations. A few of its speculators risked their money in mines, and a few lawyers or servants of the king took an interest in the new economic ideas. But they met little echo. Even in textiles, the sector in which its production was most directly concerned, Caen paid small heed to the technical innovations which after 1750 were officially encouraged all over France. Compared to Rouen, always on the watch for the revolutionary new processes coming out of England, and ready to engage in industrial espionage, Caen was always about fifty years behind. Its merchants only communicated with foreign countries through the large fairs at Caen and Guibray. In France itself, their radius of activity only sporadically extended beyond the zone covering Brittany, Normandy and the Paris region; they knew little of the south and east of the country. Only a very few individuals on occasion invested money in a shared maritime project: the mania for long-haul trade which raged in France did not affect Caen until the very end of the century. In a pamphlet on 'the advantages of seaborne trade' published in 1781, Le Vanier, a bourgeois of Caen, but formerly a captain in the slave trade, commented on the failure in 1775 of the Gaultier bank, the only merchant bank in Caen. Why had it not made intelligent use of the deposits and loans on which it offered interest of 4%? 'I confess that I cannot comprehend such inactivity', the captain wrote indignantly. It could have been used to fit ten to twelve ships.[317]

Perhaps so, but how was one to budge a town so peacefully and reasonably attached to its habits, and to the advantages of an 'income-bringing situation'?[318] Could it not boast of the wisdom of its physiocrats, when it was happily living off the fat of its own land, looking hardly any further than the horizon to be seen from the towers of the Vieux-Saint-Etienne, or the splendid Abbaye-aux-Hommes and Abbaye-aux-Dames? No doubt Caen cared little that its radius of influence eastwards barely extended across the Dives. On the other side of this small river, the attraction of Rouen was all-powerful: Rouen was a big city in the full sense of the term, over-endowed with monuments and riches, looking to the outside world and to the high seas.

It was Caen's misfortune, in short, to be too comfortably off; to have been deprived of the difficulties that provide stimulus; and never to have faced any real challenge.

Big cities in the true sense

A register based on surveys by the *intendants*[319] in 1787–9 gives figures for the urban populations of the kingdom. Here is the ranking order of the top twelve cities:

1. Paris: 524,186 inhabitants (probably an underestimate).
2. Lyon: 138,684
3. Bordeaux: 82,602
4. Marseille: 76,222
5. Nantes: 64,994
6. Rouen: 64,922
7. Lille: 62,818
8. Toulouse: 55,068
9. Nîmes: 48,360
10. Metz: 46,332
11. Versailles: 44,200
12. Strasbourg: 41,502.

Among other towns with over 30,000 inhabitants were Orleans, 35,594; Brest, 33,852; Montpellier, 33,202; Tours, 31,772; Troyes, 30,706; Reims, 30,602. The reader will have noted how high Bordeaux comes on the list: then at the height of its prosperity, it outranked Marseille. But that is merely a point of detail.

If we compare this table to the total population of France (some 29 million inhabitants) the urban structure of the country seems modest in comparison with that of England or Holland. Paris represented between a fiftieth and a sixtieth of the whole. The top twelve towns all together accounted for 1,249,890 persons, or one twenty-third of the total French population. Today Paris and its conurbation account for one fifth of the country's population.

As a result, the big cities of the past allowed ample room for the establishment of hundreds and hundreds of minor towns and bourgs, visible evidence that *ancien régime* France had an incomplete urban structure.

But how were these twelve exceptional cities (*villes-villes* as André Piatier calls them, super-towns if you like), distributed within what seems to us the limited area of French territory? Four of them were ports: Rouen, Nantes, Bordeaux, Marseille. Another four lay on France's continental frontiers: Lyon, Strasbourg, Metz and Lille. Let us set aside Nîmes, which was near the sea without being too closely associated with it. Three inland cities remain: Paris, Toulouse and Versailles. The last-named can be eliminated: we can attach it to Paris. As opposed to the capital, Versailles was merely an annexe, tied to Paris by everything that mattered, even by the continuous stream of hired carriages, the enragés, rushing at breakneck speed along the Versailles road.

All in all then, the towns on the periphery predominated, whether they lay on the coastal or the landward frontier: 9 out of 12, which between them contained half the population (626,436) of the top twelve towns. These frontier cities were both in France and out of France. Rouen, Nantes and Bordeaux were linked to the Baltic, the North Sea, the Channel, the Atlantic, America (Canada, the West Indies, Portuguese and Spanish America) and the Far East. Nîmes was on the edge of a Languedoc which itself spilled over its boundaries. Marseille has been called a Barbary and Levantine city; it is more properly a Mediterranean city. Lyon, attracting trade from Germany and the Swiss cantons, was for many years, and this accounts for much of its prosperity, an Italian outpost, a sort of 'Milan' in France. Lille was connected to Flanders, Holland and England, that is to the most progressive forces in Europe from the seventeenth century onwards. And if Strasbourg is poorly placed, at the end of the list, it is because, from being an international city as it was when Louis XIV annexed it by force in 1681, it became a regional capital and was absorbed into Alsace, which became French before the city did. This decline may also have come about because Germany looked towards Amsterdam, and engaged in exchange with Lyon and Italy rather than via the Strasbourg area. The German economy was thus of as little help to Strasbourg, as it was to Bâle. Metz has still to be accounted for (but I shall return to it):[320] it looked towards Germany and the Netherlands, but above all it was an enormous 'military capital', from which France surveyed the Rhineland – a wide-open battle-field and constant preoccupation.

The only major inland city, apart from Paris, was Toulouse. Despite the desperately unequal importance of the two towns (both in the past and today) bracketing them together does, on reflection, have a certain logic. These were after all the centres of gravity of the two great sedimentary basins of France, the Paris basin and the Aquitaine basin. Toulouse was favoured by its geographical position, between the Massif Central, the Mediterranean, the Pyrenees, Spain and the Atlantic. A rich cereal-growing region nearby gave it equilibrium. The Garonne can be compared to the Seine, though the comparison is not to its advantage. And the city had for centuries dominated the composite and culturally rich world of Languedoc. If history had run in its favour, its language, like that of the Ile-de-France, might have conquered great areas, beyond the Rhône as well as towards the Atlantic. Was Toulouse a Paris that did not succeed? And is it today having its revenge, with its industry and the 600,000 inhabitants of the conurbation?

Such ideas will no doubt seem incongruous. But do they not bring us to the essential question – that is once again the coexistence of two Frances, the *oïl* and the *oc*? Was it Paris which subordinated and stifled Toulouse from a distance, just as it overshadowed Orleans and Reims, northern rivals in which the history of France might have found its centre of gravity?

Could it not also be said that besides the north and south, there were two other Frances, the inland and the peripheral, in constant conflict or at any rate opposition to each other? France is not the only example of this repeated opposition between an inland city and one on the frontier, the latter more easy-going, allowing itself to be carried along wherever its career and the world takes it. What of Moscow and St Petersburg, Madrid and Seville (or Cadiz); Berlin and Hamburg; Vienna and Trieste?

In France, the seaward periphery was a ready focus for dissidence, something unmistakable to the point of being spectacular in the case of Marseille, in as much as Marseille was a very old city, enjoying a prosperity all its own, having created well-established liberties and clans, and having come late in time into the French complex. Indeed it long refused to call itself French. Rouen, Nantes, even Bordeaux (except during the Fronde or the Girondin episode) were more obedient cities. They nevertheless remained cities apart, whose preoccupations, interests, adventures and vital terrain would virtually never be those of the capital and of the great landmass of the French interior.

Paris's only rival on the periphery – but only rarely conscious of being so – was Lyon, 'the second . . . and perhaps the most important [city in] the kingdom', as her city fathers nevertheless claimed on 10 February 1706,[321] the city of fairs, of jingling coin and credit, of financiers from over the Alps, across the Rhine and from Switzerland. Lyon was the meeting point for business, and for many years the financial and capitalist pole of the kingdom, far enough away from Paris not to suffer unduly from the capital's vigilance and ill humour. But at the end of the eighteenth century, Paris, with its prosperous *Bourse* and the growing mania for 'business', less visible but more sustained than in Law's day, took over, or rather stood poised to take over control of France's money markets. All the same, the rivalry between Lyon and Paris simply set one inland city against another. What a pity for the country (or for the historian, a backward-looking observer with curious questions to ask) that there was no real duel between land and sea, pitting Paris against say Rouen or Nantes! Oddly enough, this was something history spared France.

Paris: a city like the others?

In spite of what economists, geographers or essayists say or predict, I do not believe that the *'ville-ville'* even today can entirely escape from its geographical setting, and thus from the rules and the fate governing lesser towns. It merely gives the appearance of standing above the normal context – towns, bourgs, villages – although it is certainly caught up, increasingly and more than the others, in relations between city and city. Today, every city speaks directly to the outside world, listens to it and follows it, but even today cities have their roots and cannot pull them up and live as they please. This truth may be easier to perceive by seeing how the Paris of the past, always a monstrous city to contemporary observers, nevertheless obeyed the general rules of historical urbanization. That Paris stood at the crossing of the ways, that the geography of river systems favoured it, are simple truths which can be checked by looking at any atlas: here are the Yonne with its floating logs, its boats laden with wine-casks; the capricious Marne, with dramatic changes in the speed of its flow (would the boat sail safely between the pillars of the bridge?); the smooth-flowing Oise; and the Seine, that complicated and lazy serpent which nevertheless reaches the sea in the end. I am not sure that Lyon, whatever people may say, ever derived such advantage from the linking, for its benefit, of Rhône and Saône.

Like all towns, Paris grew up from a crossroads: a north–south axis (originally the rue Saint-Jacques plus the rue Saint-Martin) and an east–west axis, benefiting the 'right bank' and embodied in the rue Saint-Honoré. Later on, two new axes paralleled the first: the boulevard Saint-Michel plus the boulevard Sébastopol in the first case and, running at right angles to these, the long rue de Rivoli, on which work began in 1800. It is on these axes, the old and the new, and near their intersections, that we still find today the great architectural monuments to the Parisian past. They testify to Paris's early predominance.

The French state was the watchful engineer, or the good fairy, which prompted and made this destiny possible. Into Paris, an exceptional and privileged city, money flowed and accumulated, was put to every use and spent sumptuously. The money of the whole realm – political money above all – went to feed its successes and its parasitism. The money-changers of eighteenth century Europe knew moreover that if one drew on Paris one could easily obtain payment in cash, as one could on Venice at the same time, in the Age of Enlightenment.[322]

This profusion of money, and this monstrous parasitism were excessive, measured on the scale of the country as a whole. But then all cities enjoyed financial superiority; the cost of living was always higher there than elsewhere. Even Châteauroux, such a modest town in 1800, had a cost of living higher than anywhere else in the region.[323]

Like other cities but more so, Paris was also the point of convergence for waves of immigrants: beggars, vagabonds and destitutes would at times virtually besiege the town. Nothing stopped them, not even the indescribable brutality of the Paris police, too few in numbers and driven to panic by their impotence to control the rising tide of beggary which might slide at a moment's notice into criminality. This was the dark side of the history of Paris, indeed of the whole of France.[324]

Paris, like all towns, was constantly at odds with itself, clearest evidence of this being specialization by district. There was a hierarchy of urban space, with artisans' workshops and the lodgings of the poor and very poor being pushed out to the Saint-Marcel and Saint-Antoine districts (the faubourg Saint-Antoine was until the end of the First Empire the home of an archaic form of artisanal industry, controlled by merchant capitalists on the old model).[325] Since at the same time the city was destined to expand at an abnormal rate, along with the French state itself, and since in the eighteenth century 'masonry' was taking it over, great upheavals resulted. The centre of gravity gradually moved westwards, as there grew up on both right and left banks of the Seine new quarters for the rich,

airy and spaciously built. After 1737–40, the enclosing of the main sewer which had made the Seine noxious, enabled building to take place in the north-west, towards the Roule and Monceau. Financiers invested in houses outside the boulevards, in the rue de Provence or the rue d'Artois; rues Chauchat, Taitbout and Laborde, were all built up. On the left bank, the *quais*, the Invalides and the École militaire provided work for expansion towards the Gros Caillou and Grenelle.[326]

Faced with an all-conquering aristocratic West End, the poor East End expanded too, housing as best it could the uninterrupted flow of immigrants. The newcomers gathered together according to their provinces of origin, recreating their communities. In

the faubourg Saint-Marcel [for instance] incomers from Burgundy settled in the rue Saint-Victor and the rue d'Orléans, and on the *quais*. Here they rubbed shoulders with immi-

253

grants from Lorraine and Champagne, but also with Normans. The Limousins preferred the rue Saint-Jacques and the place Maubert, while the Auvergnats lodged in the rue Mouffetard and the rue de Lourcine, alongside Picards, Flemings and Dauphinois.[327]

These *quartiers* were like so many urban villages, where people could recognize their own 'pays'. Before the big building programmes of the 1960s, certain Parisian streets were still a meeting place for Bretons, Auvergnats and Savoyards, and even today their traces have not completely disappeared.

The nearby and even distant countryside did not escape the shadow of the capital, which was responsible for a high rise in the price of neighbouring land. This explains the prosperity of Montreuil with its orchards, or the presence of profitable vineyards both in Romainville and on the slopes of Suresnes and Ivry. One night in February 1704, about twenty soldiers armed with 'loaded' guns, rushed the guards at the toll gate of Saint-Michel; each one carried on his back a *'bachou'* of wine (a small open-topped cask, used as a hod). The police report on the incident explains that 'tavern keepers in the faubourgs Saint-Marcel and Saint-Jacques are at present using this method of smuggling in by night much wine from the Villejuif vineyards'.[328] But was there a spot around Paris where vines were *not* growing, wherever the soil and the situation were even half-suitable? These suburban vineyards were probably the biggest in France – certainly the ones which produced the highest income per hectare, more than the finest vintages of Burgundy, Champagne or Bordeaux according to some 1817 figures. We shall return later to this question. It was the city which gave rise to such anomalies in the surrounding area. The most ordinary of wines were after all sure to be drunk in large quantities in suburban drinking haunts, which sold at low prices wine that had not paid the *octroi*, the tariff charged at the city gates.

Travellers approaching Paris could not fail to notice the change in the landscape. Such were two Dutchmen who, in December 1656, had just left Beaumont-sur-Oise:

On leaving this little town [they noted] we began to

realize that we were approaching Paris, on seeing the quantity of fine houses scattered as it were all over the countryside. The villages we passed through were bigger and better built than those we had seen hitherto. And they are justly described as the lifeblood of the city which they surround, for it is from them that it derives the greater part of its sustenance[329]

– a heaven-sent text for substantiating a Von Thünen schema. So too is the comment of a woman who was travelling, not without some apprehension for her own safety, round revolutionary Paris in 1790–92. She fell into raptures about La Villette 'which borders the city limits and is regarded as a mere village . . . This place is busier and more inhabited than most of our third-rank towns in the provinces'.[330]

All these places were in thrall to the great belly of Paris. In order to live, in order to eat, the capital had to organize the countryside around. 'The economic domination of Paris over a radius of 40 to 50 kilometres, representing a day's journey on horseback, was already a fait accompli a century before the Hundred Years' War', writes Guy Fourquin.[331] From earliest days, Paris extended the domains of its religious foundations and scattered the surrounding landscape with its châteaux and country houses. Then there was investment by the city-dwellers, for whom land was a source both of prestige and of revenue. In the seventeenth century, these investments encouraged the establishment around Paris of large firms. All towns probably did much the same at the time.

What distinguished Paris from the rest were the abnormal demands of a society dazzled by the luxury of the royal court: people fell over themselves to copy it. In about 1700, Paris was no longer content to have on the doorstep plenty of wine, 'vegetables and herbs in abundance'; it had to produce 'figs, pomegranates, oranges and lemons, medicinal herbs, flowers of all kinds. The gardeners round about . . . have learnt the art of maintaining, even in the dead of winter, asparagus, artichokes, lettuces and other things which are found elsewhere only in summer'.[332] Glasshouses had already begun to appear. And in protected gardens – those of the Marais for instance before it became an aristocratic quarter in the

FIGURE 28
Some of Paris's supply routes at the end of the Middle Ages

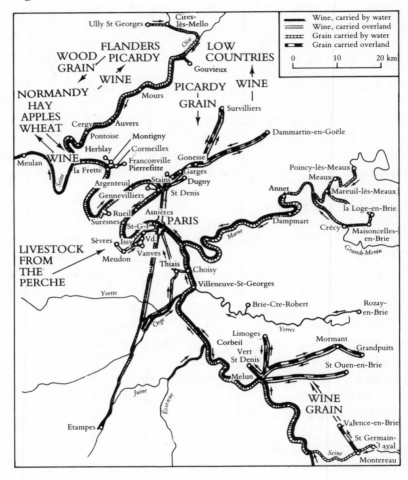

This map strikingly demonstrates the essential role played by the rivers and their 'ports' in keeping Paris supplied with wine and grain (both heavy commodities). Overland routes joined a waterway as soon as they could. Map from R. Fossier, *Le Moyen Age*, III, 1981.

seventeenth century – the first fruits of spring were grown.

Once outside the *barrières*, the city limits, one was immediately surrounded by fields, crops, orchards, villages and peasants. On 29 July 1830, the duke of Orleans, the future Louis-Philippe, seeking refuge no doubt, after hearing that the Tuileries palace had been seized by rebels, left Neuilly where he happened to be, with 'Heymès, who had just been introduced to him, for Raincy, which he reached by going *across the fields*,[333] and arriving at night'. The next morning, the parliamentarians who came looking for him to offer him power did not find him at Neuilly; they had to go to Raincy to bring him back.[334] When Jean-Baptiste Say or Michelet went beyond the *barrières* in their wanderings, they found themselves virtually in the countryside; the people they met were genuine peasants. And when in 1815 the Allies first threatened and then reached Paris, and the population of the suburbs flocked into the city, these fugitives too were authentic peasants. The comtesse de Boigne and her mother going out in their carriage found the outer boulevards round the capital 'crowded with the population of the environs of Paris. They were on foot, pell-mell, with cows, sheep and their pitiful baggage, [and inclined] to irritation against anyone who appeared better off. One could move only at walking pace. Our carriage received not a few insults'.[335] Unlikely though it might seem, exactly the same scene was repeated in 1870: 'When the Germans approached', noted a doctor, Professor Achard, 'although many families left Paris, the residents of the suburbs flocked into town with their handcarts and animals. Many of these countryfolk, as people called them, were lodged in the new but unoccupied houses lining the recently-built avenues'[336] – something Haussmann had certainly not foreseen!

We can easily recognize from such descriptions the first supply zone in Von Thünen's scheme, the one which provides the town with supplies for its daily markets. It was a particularly wide zone, as befitted the size of the capital city.

But what about the other zones surrounding this abnormal town – the cereal-, meat- and timber-producing zones? They look much the same here as elsewhere, I would say, except that the ring of bourgs with their markets was in this case a ring of towns.

An unpublished document[337] gives an idea of one of these broader circles in the eighteenth century: its circumference runs through Pontoise, Mantes, Montfort, Dreux, Melun, Nemours, Meaux, Rozay-en-Brie, Coulommiers, Provins, Nogent, Montereau, Sens, Joigny, Saint-Florentin. Along this line, with more or less good reason, each town had its place according to whether it provided Paris with wood or hay, livestock on the hoof, charcoal, oats, labour and above all wheat. One has to go even farther afield to reach the outer limits of the Parisian sphere of influence, marked by a series of large and fairly large towns: Orleans, Troyes, Châlons-sur-Marne (or rather Vitry-le-François, a major depot for grain from the Barrois and Lorraine which would then be sent by boat down the Marne to Paris), Reims, Compiègne, Amiens, Rouen and Chartres. At about this distance out, give or take a little (and the limits varied over time too) the influence of Paris began to wane or even vanished – except for draught animals or beasts for slaughter who had the advantage of providing their own transport.

That there was a certain correlation between Paris and these rings of towns is proved by a prolonged episode in French history, the sieges of Paris towards the end of the Wars of Religion (1562–98), since these 'secondary' towns took advantage of the misfortunes that paralysed the capital: they served as a refuge for unemployed artisans, or for merchants and bourgeois fleeing the rigours and dangers of the siege. And it was also from the zone contained within these necklaces of towns that Paris drew most of its immigrants, notably its domestic servants. Two towns served as staging posts on the way into the city, Versailles in the west and Troyes in the east (for immigrants from Lorraine, Burgundy and Champagne).

Note that the material dictatorship of Paris was, broadly speaking, exerted only over the Paris basin, between the Channel and the Loire, Picardy, Lorraine and Normandy, and to a lesser degree the borders of Brittany. This large area was totally subservient to the capital, which kept other towns at a lower stage of development than they might have reached if left to themselves.

That does not mean to say of course that the effect of Paris was confined to this vast zone. Its material life depended on it. But the many-sided influence of the capital city, political and cultural in the broadest sense of both terms, constantly exceeded these limits. For centuries on end, Paris has constructed, influenced, interfered with and sometimes thwarted the overall destiny of France as a whole.

The village-bourg-town schema in our own times

In conducting this first survey across the France of the past, I hope to have given sufficient indication that there was a network of persistent elementary connections without which the fabric of France – or of any other European nation – would have had neither coherence nor strength. Bear in mind that the village-bourg-town system survived the collapse of the Roman Empire and stood up even better to the cataclysmic Hundred Years' War. It has also survived – at least in my view – the most fantastic test of our history, the half-century following 1939 and the monstrous acceleration of what Jean Fourastié has called the 'thirty glorious years' (1945–75).

I would cite as evidence for this, the work by André Piatier and his team. Studying the 'structure of the territory' of present-day France, they have divided up the surface area of a *département*, the Loiret for example, into zones of urban attraction, by a concrete description of the space within which Orleans, Montargis, Pithiviers or Gien etc. are able to impose their goods and services, their middlemen and wholesalers, their shops, their solicitors, lawyers and doctors. It should be noted that these areas overlap to some extent, that urban zones are in conflict with one another at their outer limits, and that this leads in the end to 'the creation of a hierarchy of towns based on the intensity of relations they have established', as well as a 'functional hierarchy' of agglomerations depending on their 'exchange systems', predominantly urban (as around Orleans) or predominantly rural (as around Pithiviers).[338]

Such conflicts between towns do not contradict the model I outlined earlier: they make it more dynamic, shake it up a bit and perhaps displace it. But there is still a system there. Can we not see it at work in the magnified example of present-day Paris? On its distant frontiers, it promotes one town at the expense of another – Tours rather than Orleans, Le Mans rather than Angers. [339] The zones of influence may be modified but the fabric of relations persists.

It is not only on the level of the towns that the schema is being modified in this way (though remaining fundamentally in position): in recent years, the rural base has undergone massive change. Rural France changed more between 1945 and 1975 than it did between Louis XIV and Poincaré. My native village (along with a thousand others) altered at a stroke: gone are the horses, tractors have taken their place; gone are most of the crops, but there is more grazing; gone are the smallholders trailing in the wake of better-off or wealthy farmers. The population has shrunk by half. All the same the links survive, although the network now has a wider mesh. A larger schema, but one not unlike the old, is settling into place.

On this point, Henri Mendras has conveniently provided me with supporting evidence of a compelling kind, in a collective study called *La Sagesse et le désordre*, published in 1980. Mendras sets out to present 'an optimistic vision of France, as a better balanced country, one more conscious of its position, of its true problems and of the changes required, [but] in the end a more equitable country than it realizes itself; as the Englishman Peter Wills puts it, "France is more equal than she thinks".'[340] But while this opinion is certainly acceptable to me, it is not my main reason for referring to this important book. It is because I have found in it, from the pen of a sociologist accustomed to working with present-day material and with concrete reality, evidence to support my propositions. As he sees it, whatever the transformation it has undergone (an effective one in every domain), there still remains a rural France vigorously standing up for itself and successfully adapting to the demands of the present. It is true that the French population rose from 42 million to 53 million between 1945 and 1980, and that this surplus population undeniably benefited the towns most of all. 'But we should not regard today's society through yesterday's spectacles'.[341] That is, we should not cling on to the old criteria, like the sacrosanct limit of 2,000 inhabitants, over which a locality becomes a town whereas under this limit it is a bourg or village. Indeed this limit was probably already out of date in the eighteenth century and even more so by the nineteenth.

Today the limit has to be set higher, at about 10,000 to 15,000 inhabitants, perhaps even higher still. And we find that towns of over 15,000 inhabitants accounted for 56% of the French population in 1946; and 58% in 1975; the rural population (in *communes* under the 15,000 level) was respectively 44% in 1946 and 42% in 1975 (in *absolute* terms however, it went up, as did the overall population). 'As a result', Henri Mendras concludes,

> the notorious 'French desert'[342] does not exist and never has existed. We find ourselves at the end of the twentieth century with some 22 million rural residents, more or less the same as at the end of the eighteenth century, after the considerable overpopulation of the nineteenth. And the *composition* of the territory as divided into *pays* centred on small towns . . . remains everywhere almost unchanged in essentials. . . . The agricultural villages have lost population, but to make up for this the small towns [modern versions of the bourgs] have seen their population increase.[343]

Still on their old sites, the villages are still working their land, sometimes better than in the past, now that the tractor has replaced the farmhand or the team of horses.

So a balance remains, a structuring of space, in which as Michel Rochefort puts it, 'the unit of definition is [still] not the town but the [overall] organization to which it belongs'.[344] If there has been an enlargement of the intermediate layer, if the bourgs have grown more important, 'it is because industry [large-scale industry and modern agriculture in fact] has in turn generated a *neo-tertiary* sector',[345] that is a new tertiary sector more extensive than the old. The villages and the 'town-bourg', today as in the past form a sort of cooperative structure in which the bourg 'carries out the functions that any single village would be unable to handle' on its own.[346] 'The *tertiary* sector is the cement of this union, whether in the shape of commerce or services (housing, health, finance, communications or administration)'.[347]

André Piatier goes even further.

The *tertiary* [sector] he writes, existed long before the *secondary* [industry], and it was this which fashioned the towns. However far back in time one goes, the town has always been the centre of meetings and exchanges. It was seen as a focus for cooperation and relations between all those who lived in the surrounding area.[348]

Let us keep in mind this notion of the *tertiary* as an early phenomenon, long preceding present times. It corresponds to what I have been trying to say. For with the tertiary, we are again in the presence of a hierarchy. As the town's weapon, it was the instrument of the town's superiority, its raison d'être. The bourg of the past already housed an active tertiary sector. The present situation is merely a former reality writ large. There is ample logic in this: except at the self-sufficient level (and even then sometimes), *being*, survival, invariably means that some command and others obey.

PART III

Was France invented by its Geography?

To ask this unexpected question is one way of rephrasing Vidal de la Blache's query, 'Is France a geographical entity?'[1] More obviously, it means raising once again the ambiguous problem of geographical determinism. I remain convinced, whatever people may say, that the debate aroused by this subject has not yet been fully aired.

Admittedly, the geographers stopped fighting this battle long ago: in their view, the decisive element is not physical geography – the earth, nature, or the environment – but human history, and man himself – man in fact as prisoner of himself, as both inheritor and continuer of the acts and deeds, techniques and traditions, of all those who have preceded him on his own territory, shaping its landscape and locking him into a series of retrospective determinisms of which he is, however, rarely conscious.

Personally, I have always found the massive weight of our distant origins both convincing and terrifying. They are indeed a crushing burden. But does that mean that every aspect of the complicated genesis of France must be attributed to the past, to history? That would simply be to pluck France out of its geography, out of its position in space, to 'de-spatialize' it. And it would be absurd. France is indeed the result of a prodigious accumulation of history, but that accumulation took place on a particular site

263

and on no other. The unusual and rather special position that France occupies, along the articulations of the European continent, the fact that Europe surrounds it on all sides, are matters that have been of importance. As Vidal de la Blache rightly remarked, and he was thinking of France, 'the history of a people is inseparable from the country it inhabits . . . One should start from the idea that a country is a storehouse of dormant energies whose seeds have been planted by nature, but whose use depends on man'.[2]

This sentence fits well into what Lucien Febvre described as Vidal de la Blache's 'possibilism'.[3] A *possible* France, other *possible* Frances: these are formulas I find attractive. But shall we be able to identify them successfully? Or shall I in the end, like the geographers, be forced back on history as the only possible explanation for the genesis of France in its present unified shape? In order to find out, I have selected three themes around which the argument can be conducted – three themes, I need hardly say, out of dozens of possibilities.

CHAPTER SEVEN

On not exaggerating the role of the French 'isthmus'

The first debate that calls for attention is the question of the French 'isthmus' – an expression coined, if I am not mistaken, by French geographers themselves, certainly used by them, especially in the past. Already a narrow continent – is it even a continent at all, or merely an extension of the great land mass of Asia? – Europe becomes even narrower towards the west, squeezed between the northern seas and the series of basins making up the Mediterranean to the south. A number of isthmuses, following the meridians, link two different worlds, distinguished as much by their history as by their climate, and whose contrasts attract each other with explosive force: the 'Russian' isthmus, between the Black Sea and the Baltic; the 'German' isthmus, from the Adriatic or the gulf of Genoa to Hamburg or the Netherlands; and lastly the 'French' isthmus, or rather isthmuses, since the Mediterranean–Atlantic link, running through the Naurouze Gap and along the canal du Midi (built 1666–81), has as its parallel the Rhône-Saône route, prolonged either down the Seine or the Rhine. The French isthmuses are the shortest. The Russian isthmus is 1,200 kilometres long; the German isthmus 1,000 kilometres (and it has to cross the Alps); whereas the French isthmuses measure '700 kilometres from the mouth of the Seine to the Rhône estuary, and only 400 kilometres from the Bay of Biscay to the Gulf of Lions; and there are no mountains barring either route'.[4] As Ernst Curtius rather curiously put it: 'the northerner can satisfy his nostalgic desire for the Mediterranean in France', for here, 'unlike in Germany, there are no Alps to cross in order to reach the inland sea'.[5]

Thus French territory benefits from a shortening of distances, an 'isthmic pinch', as Maurice Le Lannou has half-seriously called it,[6] which brings together on French soil north and south, Mediterranean and Atlantic. Is this the essential originality by which France's territory is defined?

Of the two French isthmuses, only one can really be called a European isthmus. The route through the Naurouze Gap, much frequented in Roman times, does indeed link the Mediterranean to the ocean via the Garonne, but has only occasionally been of international importance, except in the sixteenth century when English wool travelled along this short cut (in particular along the old Roman road from La Rochelle to Nîmes via Cahors)[7] towards the Mediterranean and Florence; it may also have been used, though I am not too sure about this, during the sixteenth-century vogue for Toulouse woad, a dye-product which would later be driven out by indigo from overseas.

If the Rhône route was the more important, this was not because it was more convenient – it was the longer of the two – but because it ran from the Mediterranean to the countries of Northern Europe, where southerners encountered a contrasting world; and because the same thing happened in the opposite direction: on the shores of the Mediterranean, the nordic temperament came up against one completely different. This had been so from time out of mind, since the days of prehistory. The importance of the link would become greater when it connected the two vital poles of the early European economy, created during the Middle Ages: northern Italy and the Low Countries. The 'electric' current between these two poles brought animation to this route through France and consequently drew attention to its many advantages: the Rhône corridor is after all linked to the waterways of the Saône, the Loire, the Seine and its tributaries (the Yonne, Aube, Marne and Oise) as well as to the Moselle and Rhine.

Where waterways were absent, wheeled traffic or pack animals provided the necessary links in the chain: from Lyon across the edge of the Massif Central to the Loire; through the Côte d'Or, beyond Dijon, between the Saône and the Seine; through the porte de Bourgogne from the Saône to the Rhine. Waterways and overland routes together formed a vast network, making possible the conquest and use of the whole of French territory. Roman roads penetrated the entire area in the interests of 'colonial' exploitation of products from Gaul. Roman legions attached particular importance to the eastern branches of the network, which made it possible to reach the Rhine frontier at Trèves/Trier or Cologne, look-out posts over restless Germany, or to travel via Boulogne to Britain, which was by AD 85 well on the way to being subjugated.

Paul Vidal de la Blache was one of the first to point out the importance of this corridor across France: it was, he writes,

in very ancient times [that] the influence of the Mediterranean–North Sea connection took concrete form on French soil. This influence was geographically expressed and consolidated in the trade routes, the long-distance channels of communication. The major trade route in France, a line running from Provence up to England and Flanders, displays remarkable stability. The principal fairs of the Middle Ages, those of Beaucaire, Lyon, Chalon,[8] Troyes, Paris, Arras, Thourout[9] and Bruges, are all aligned along this axis. The role that that almost immaterial thing known as a trade route can play in the creation of a political unit is demonstrated by many examples: Italy did not emerge as a political entity until the Appian and Flaminian Ways had been joined to connect both ends of the country. Within the network of major routes in Great Britain, Watling Street, the road from London to the Severn, was the axis round which England was built.[10]

The suggestion contained in this rapid survey is that France found in the all-important axis linking the Rhône, Saône and Seine (or Rhine), one of the reasons, if not the overriding reason, for its emergence as a political unit. That being so, the first witness to take the stand, so to speak, should be the Rhône itself. It is here that I shall begin the search for 'a possible France'.

The Rhône in the old days, before 1850

We shall of course take evidence from the Rhône as it used to be, wild and turbulent, a headstrong river, 'irregular to the point of extravagance',[11] of which Vauban said it was 'incorrigible'. But that river belongs to the past, now that technology and the demands of the economy in the shape of a huge programme of works, barely completed even today, have transformed, domesticated and tamed it.

In the old days, powerful and swift-flowing, it carried along with the cold and torrential waters of the Alpine snows and glaciers, a great rolling mass of sand, mud and pebbles – those round stones one often sees in country lanes or paving the streets of towns in the Rhône valley, painful to the feet of beasts and men alike. An engineer of the *Ponts et Chaussées*, Charles Lenthéric, wrote in 1892 that

> an attentive observer, sitting in a boat that makes no sound, can perfectly well hear, if not see, all these movements [deep beneath him] and can distinguish the splashing of the surface water from the continuous rattling made by the successive impacts of these millions of pebbles rolling along on top of one another.[12]

It will come as no surprise to learn that the Rhône was a powerful force for erosion: its meanders hollowed out the concave banks, creating *mouilles* (troughs)[13] of deep water there, while leaving *maigres* (sandbanks) on the opposite side. Thus between high and low water, bars of shingle and sand were formed, straddling the river like dams, unstable dams what was more, where boats could at any moment run aground. When the river was low, it barely covered such bars, and shipping became impossible for 70 days of the year. By contrast when the river ran high, shipping was likely to be carried away by the current. In the narrow corridor between Tournon and Pont-Saint-Esprit for instance, over a stretch of 90 kilometres, boats would be borne rapidly downstream, making it dangerous to pass through the too-narrow arches of the famous bridge, which no captain approached without apprehension. The strong current was, by the same token, an obstacle to upstream traffic. Even the coming of the steamship in later years did not entirely solve the problem: on difficult stretches, tugs were power-less and ships had to be hauled upstream.[14] Another problem was that strong winds, including the redoubtable *mistral*, were funnelled down this narrow corridor. What did boatmen do when this northerly wind blew hard? They hove to in the lee of the mid-stream islands (fortunately numerous in those days), or else tied up firmly to the bank, waiting for the storm to subside.

And yet this dangerous river had been crowded with boats for centuries. Since Roman times (and no doubt earlier) skiffs and cargo boats (*scaphae* and *naves onerariae*) had been going up and down the Rhône. Innumerable companies of boatmen are men-tioned in Roman inscriptions, their numbers further swelled since the Rhône's tributaries (the Saône of course, but also the Ardèche, Durance and Isère) had all had their own river traffic for centuries past.

This shipping was maintained, with only minor modifications, until mid-nineteenth century and indeed almost to our own day. It stoutly resisted even the coming of the steamship, whose timid beginnings date from 1829. As a result, until 1850, the Rhône offered the constant picturesque spectacle of hundreds of tradi-tional flat-bottomed boats, of different sizes and names: *pénelles* (for transporting horses), *cyslandes* or *sisselandes* (boats built in Seyssel), *rignes*, *sapines* or *savoyardes* (up to 70 metres long), *chenards* or *chênes* (oak-built on the banks of the Saône and usually used for carrying grain). Compared to the shipping on the Loire, these boats were gigantic. For passenger traffic, on the other hand, there were ferries or 'water-coaches', no more than fifteen metres long, in which people sat on benches as in a stage-coach. Other, smaller ferries, known as *rapides* could be rowed if necessary, while the bigger ones simply 'allowed themselves to drift with the current'. The little ferries, also known as *barquettes*, had a capacity of up to 250 quintals; they could travel from Arles to Lyon 'in seven to eight days, and take six to sail from Avignon to Lyon, whereas the large [cargo] vessels, which are the standard shipping on the Rhône, take about a month to load and the same to go up' from Arles to Lyon. Going downstream was much faster: just two days from Lyon to Avignon. But even downstream there could be a considerable difference between travelling in summer and in winter.[15]

While it was faster than going up river, the trip downstream, *la descize*, was also much more dangerous. All travellers feared it. In 1320, before going down to the river port of Lyon, which was packed with boats bound for the fair at Beaucaire, Petrarch attended church in Fourvières to commend himself to the protection of the Holy Virgin.

Speed had its attractions of course. 'The Rhône, which descends with great swiftness' remarked a later traveller, leaving Lyon for Avignon in May 1704, 'is most convenient for those who wish to go to Languedoc or Provence'[16] and, he might have added, to Italy as well. But accidents were not infrequent. Madame de Sévigné was shipwrecked in 1673; an Englishwoman, Mrs Cradock, who was travelling during low water in winter in 1784, ran aground on a sandbank, from which she was rescued 'only with difficulty', and took over a day to travel from Lyon to Vienne: it had taken 32 horses to free her boat.[17] In autumn 1799, General Marbot, travelling to join the army in Italy, escaped a number of groundings, despite the low water, but as the boat approached the Pont Saint-Esprit, the *mistral* began to blow:

> The boatmen [writes the general's son, who was accompanying his father] could not get us to shore. They lost their heads and fell to praying instead of working, while the current and a furious wind were driving the boat towards the bridge! We were about to hit the pier of the bridge and sink, when my father and the rest of us picked up boathooks and thrusting them forward just in time, reduced the impact of the boat against the pier we were approaching. The shock was so severe that it made us fall back on to the seats, but our fending action had altered the boat's course and by a near-miracle of good fortune, it slipped through the arch.[18]

There was no such risk going upstream – but it was very hard work!

Words can 'never adequately describe . . . the incredible labour done by those men'.[19] Four or five barges, sometimes more, would be attached together in a convoy; the leading vessel, more stream-lined than the rest, was a sort of flagship, with a cabin in the stern where the crews assembled to cook, eat and sleep. Meanwhile on the towpath, usually along the left bank of the river, were massed teams of horses, of up to fifty at a time: twenty-eight or so harnessed to the fore cable and twenty to the aft cable. 'What magnificent horses they were!', writes one enthusiast, 'I do not think that any so big and strong could be found today'.[20] In the early nineteenth century, there were 6,000 of them working on the banks of the Rhône. In Lyon, they were housed in the stables of La Mulatière,[21] a sort of marshalling yard which dispatched them back downstream on *pénelles*, floating stables, in order to return to their work on the towpath.

The 'sailors on land', who handled the towing, had heavy duties to perform: they took care of the horses (checking them on departure, shoeing them if necessary, harnessing them in groups of four, with special reins or *renards*, to the towing cable, then guiding them according to instructions from the captain in the leading boat); they had to handle the *maille*, the long hempen cable attached to the mainmast of the leading boat, to guide it over obstacles, and to dis-engage it when it got tangled in 'willow thickets' on the banks. On certain stretches, the cable and the *renards* had to be unrolled to a length that might be as much as a kilometre. At Donzère for instance (which the boatmen called *la montagne aux singes*, Monkey Mountain) the horse-teams had to climb to a height of 60 metres above the river, while the convoy of boats continued its slow pro-gress down below. As an extra problem, it was from time to time necessary to transfer the horses to the opposite bank when the towpath broke off. This meant cramming the animals into special ferries to get them across the river before they could start hauling again. The operation of course obliged the boats of the convoy to cross the river under their own steam. On 2 May 1764, a *chêne* going downstream laden with grain, hit the leading boat of a con-voy that was just changing banks, broke in two and sank.[22] Some-times the convoy was carried away by the current: the ropes had to be cut hastily before the horses were dragged into the river.

The boatmen hardly ever left their vessels: for them there was no long walk back home along the Rhône as there was along the Loire or the Allier, although boats were sometimes broken up and sold on arrival in the down-river ports. The population of boatmen was not large: about 3,000 to 3,500 in 1811,[23] all natives of certain localities along the river (for there were once river sectors worked by certain boatmen, just as there were coastal sectors worked by certain seamen). In Givors, Le Rocher de Condrieu, Serrières, Andance and Bourg-Saint-Andéol, 'there were successive dynasties of these tough men, who had the river in their blood'.[24] They were men apart, fearless and loud-mouthed, whose clans would join forces to buy one or more boats. They had a distinctive appearance – gold earrings, long hair plaited into pigtails; their own language, quite different from that spoken on shore; and their own feast-day, St Nicholas, on 6 December. They also had their own cooking methods: for instance they would cut up into a pot all the different river fish at their disposal (these were many and excellent), pour a good Côtes-du-Rhône over the lot, and flambé it like punch – this was their recipe for 'matelote'. And along the river special inns were virtually reserved for them.[25]

To these men must be added the equally numerous 'sailors on land', who have already been mentioned, and the bustling throng of dockers, porters and longshoremen, as well as the boatyard workers of Seyssel, Lyon, Vernaison, Givors, Vienne, Condrieu and Andance; not to mention the builders of the *chênes* on the banks of the Saône, or that other special group of men the loggers, who steered enormous trains of logs (60 to 80 metres long and 14 or 15 metres wide) down the Arve, the Isère or the Durance. Logs were not floated loose on these turbulent waters.[26]

It all added up to a huge distribution system, capable of handling a massive volume of traffic, despite the countless difficulties of the journey.

Unlike shipping on the Loire or Seine however, traffic on the Rhône did not spread to the river's tributaries. These were either unsuitable for navigation or could not use the same types of vessel as the Rhône.

The only exception – in part at least – was the Saône. Despite the spectacular floods which every year submerged the broad meadows on either side, despite the melting of the ice which occasionally transformed it into a furious torrent, smashing bridges, sinking boats, breaking up barges, sweeping away riverside dwellings,[27] the Saône was for most of the year a comparatively peaceful water-course, with an abundant flow, and navigable below Port-sur-Saône. But it was not easy to make the transition between the two rivers. Not only did one often have to trans-ship, but since the residents of Lyon had built houses right down to the river bank, there were no towpaths left for haulage. Instead, a special guild of Lyon boatmen pulled the boats up by hauling on cables fixed to the bridges, the hauliers themselves standing in the boats. Their guild was an aggressive and obstructive one, able to exert exorbitant power over what must have been a major bottleneck in the French isthmus. It therefore commanded respect, and others simply had to bow to its wishes and demands.

By the standards of the past, the Saône–Rhône combination represented a large volume of traffic (the Rhône carried about four times as much freight as the Loire; in fact it was comparable to the Rhine, 'its Siamese twin').[28] But with both waterways, Rhône and Saône, running along a north–south axis, this was a linear and incomplete shipping system, without extensions sideways. The upper reaches of the Rhône, eastwards from Lyon towards Geneva, were navigable only as far as Seyssel. Some links were possible, it is true, with the river traffic on the Durance or Isère, by trans-shipping. But one has to think in terms of other types of transport, waggons, mule-trains and carts, radiating out from the Rhône into the Massif Central, Languedoc, Provence, Dauphiné, Savoy, Lyonnais and even the Jura. The carter, a vivid figure, 'one hand holding the reins, the other a whip, in his blue smock, gaiters, corduroy breeches and multicoloured cap, with his cape blowing in the wind',[29] was an essential link between the river traffic and the hinterland, completing the transport system of the Rhône corridor.

It was during the early decades of the nineteenth century that the system reached its peak, with something like 400,000[30] or 500,000[31] tons altogether going up or downstream, upstream cargoes amounting to about a quarter of the downstream. If we take an average cargo to be 40 tons, that would mean in theory 10,000 trips a year, if not more. The shipping office in Valence however reported that 'between 1 April 1809 and 30 March 1810, 2,250 laden vessels went downstream, plus 15 empty boats; travelling upstream there were 1,468 vessels and a few empty boats'.[32] So any calculation is fraught with uncertainty. As for overland freight, this probably represented only a small proportion of what was carried by water, but again we have only estimates.[33]

There was certainly brisk trade in both directions. The Rhône carried all the purchases made by northern provinces at the amazing Beaucaire fair. At Arles, river boats took over from sea-going vessels carrying Mediterranean produce. And along the way, goods were taken on board from various towns on the Rhône, often light in weight but high in price. In fact almost anything could be carried on the Rhône, sometimes the most extraordinary objects, such as the statue of Louis XIV, intended for the place Bellecour in Lyon, which went the long way round from Paris to the Mediterranean, via Le Havre and Gibraltar, in order to reach Lyon more conveniently,[34] (only to be wrecked at La Mulatière, where it had to be fished out of the river!); or like the furniture and trousseau of Marie-Caroline, daughter of the king of the Two Sicilies, when in 1816 she married the duc de Berry.

Heavy goods, as one might expect, took pride of place: iron, stone slabs, bricks, tiles and above all those cargoes that had become essential since the Middle Ages, grain, wine and salt. Grain travelled up or downstream depending on the fluctuations of the harvest and of demand. Consumers, here as everywhere else, depended primarily on local production, but transfers between regions were frequent. Foreign grain on the other hand appeared only when there was a widespread shortage. But as we know, this was not infrequent. For their wine supplies, towns had long been content with the produce of local vineyards. But with the rise in consumption in the eighteenth century, traffic in wine from reputed vineyards became established on a larger scale. Salt, that essential commodity was a major concern both of the state and of the large capitalist firms which shipped and sold it. Strings of boats went to load from the great salt-pans of Peccais or Les Saintes-Maries-de-la-Mer and supplied the salt-stores at various points along the river. Some boats went upstream as far as Seyssel where the Rhône ceased to be navigable. The river divided Seyssel in two: on the French side was an industrious village, whose boatyards built the *sisselanes* mentioned earlier, sturdy vessels made of pine timbers; on the Savoy side was a customs post and a large depôt from which salt was dispatched to Regonfle, Geneva's lakeside port.

The salt trade was the pump that primed the Rhône shipping in general. In July 1701, some businessmen thinking of organizing a passenger service in *barquettes* between Lyon and Seyssel, three times a week, were anxious to avoid their boats 'having to go back upstream empty, at great expense and no profit'.[35] So what did they request? Permission to 'transport from Peccais to Seyssel, seven or eight thousand *minots*[36] of salt at the standard price'.

Trade, transport, trans-shipping and warehousing were responsible for the string of busy towns that grew up along the Rhône, on sites protected as far as possible from its dangerous waters. Some of these towns became magnificent, if history smiled on them: Arles survived long after the splendours of Roman Gaul; Avignon, for long years one of the centres of Christendom, was then at the height of its brilliance. Even minor towns had their moments of glory. But on the eve of Revolution, two towns eclipsed all others: Beaucaire in the south, with its famous fairs dating back to at least 1315, their bustle and hubbub attracting as many as 100,000 merchants, buyers and visitors; and Lyon to the north, also the scene of monumental fairs, in this case centres for credit as much as for trade. Indeed Lyon sought, unsuccessfully, to draw the whole kingdom into its orbit and even to set the rhythm for that imperfectly tuned orchestra, the European economy.

The French isthmus and the unity of France

But to return to our problem, the Saône–Rhône corridor did play a considerable role in stimulating French life: its course was punctuated by monuments, cities, and animated regions. 'Why are there so many abbeys, priories and monasteries in Burgundy? people ask. And such magnificent ones? The role played by history and geography is obvious. But one is tempted to add that the splendour of nature played its part as well', writes Henri Fesquet.[37] Even more obvious are the advantages brought by trade, from which the Franche-Comté, the Lyonnais, Dauphiné, Languedoc and Provence also benefited. Along the entire axis, history plunged deep roots into the soil.

All the same, must we conclude, as Vidal de la Blache suggests, that all this movement and animation, all the swift journeys downstream to the Mediterranean and slow journeys back up, the pulsebeats of Mediterranean life travelling north, the converging and diverging streams of traffic, actually played a *unifying* and determining role, both culturally and politically, in French life? One might think so *a priori*. But what does the judicious voice of history say?

The isthmus was unquestionably a major axis in Roman times, an umbilical cord; but it was one serving the Empire, serving the major roads, towns and prosperous regions created by Rome along the banks of the Moselle and Rhine. The isthmus was marginal to Gaul. Lyon was a turntable of all Roman trade, it was linked to Cisalpine Gaul, to the Mediterranean, to western and northern Gaul, and was an essential staging post for the legions on their way to the Rhine frontier. But did that not make Lyon a mere colonial capital, a control centre, the site of law and order?[38]

The situation is even clearer at the time of the busy Champagne and Brie fairs in the twelfth and thirteenth centuries. Reachable by sea (Venice's *galere da mercato* came to Aigues-Mortes) or by the Alpine passes used by the carriers of Asti, the Rhône corridor was still favoured to some extent, but it lay on the outer edge of the

FIGURE 29
Roman roads round Lyon

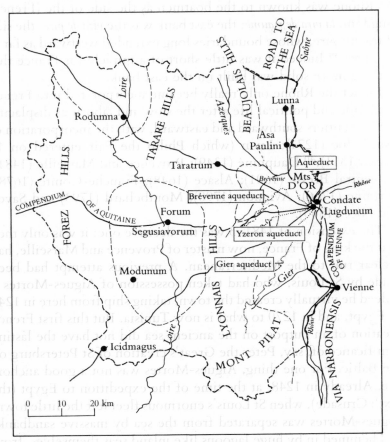

Lyon was a turntable for trade and political administration
within the Roman Empire, lying as it did at the intersection
of the major Roman roads to the Rhine, to Cisalpine Gaul, to
the Mediterranean, and to northern and western Gaul.
Map from *Histoire du Lyon et du Lyonnais*, ed. André Latreille,
1975.

kingdom which was at this time bounded to the east by the 'four rivers': the Scheldt, Meuse, Saône and Rhône. The west bank of the Rhône was known to the boatmen as the side of the (French) kingdom, *la vira de riaume*; the east bank was the *vira de pire*, the side of the Empire, whose boundaries long extended westward as far as the river.[39] Indeed it was little short of a miracle for France that nothing more solid was built on the east bank.

In fact the Rhône only really became incorporated into French economic and political life after the slow and laborious displacing of the frontiers southward and eastward, with the incorporation of Languedoc (1271); Lyon (which Philip the Fair entered on 13 March 1311);[40] Dauphiné (1349); Provence and Marseille (1481–3); central Bresse (1601); Alsace (1648); Franche-Comté (1678); Lorraine (1766); Avignon (1790); Montbéliard (1793) and Savoy and Nice (1860).

The extension of 1481–3 was the decisive one: it was only then that the king of France, now master of Provence and Marseille, had a clear run to the Mediterranean. A previous attempt had been made by St Louis, who had taken possession of Aigues-Mortes – indeed he virtually created the town, taking ship from here in 1248 to Egypt, and in 1270 to what is now Tunisia. But this first French creation of an outpost on the ancient sea did not have the lasting significance of, say, Peter the Great's creation of St Petersburg on the Baltic. For one thing, Aigues-Mortes was not a good anchorage. Already in 1248, at the time of the expedition to Egypt (the Sixth Crusade), when St Louis's enormous fleet left the little town, Aigues-Mortes was separated from the sea by massive sandbanks and hemmed in by huge lagoons like inland seas themselves, from which it was possible to escape only by an interminable series of channels. As for the magnificent town walls, these were built after the death of St Louis by his son, Philip the Bold, by then at war with the Aragonese. An unsatisfactory port and, what was worse, a poor centre for trade despite the efforts of the crown, Aigues-Mortes could not compare with Montpellier, Nîmes or Marseille. In 1248, whether from prudence or because he had no choice, Joinville took ship from Marseille and joined the king only at Cyprus.[41]

So it was not until late in the day that the fabulous Saône–Rhône route began to play its full role in a French context. In the view of one geographer, Pierre Gourou, 'Lotharingia and the Germanic Empire sterilized the Saône–Rhône corridor as far as France was concerned, in spite of the route's longstanding activity and in spite of the thriving and attractive civilization established along its banks (Burgundy, Lyon and Valence)'. 'There was nothing "geographical" about this sterilization', he goes on: 'it was something entirely historical'.[42] Note this categorical distinction, and the accusing reference to events far back in the past: the creation of the 'imperial' portion for Lothair, eldest son of Louis the Pious, at the treaty of Verdun in 843, over a thousand years ago; and the extension of the Empire as far as the Rhône under Otto and his successors.

The crucial factor in the end is that the Rhône had very early become a *frontier* within medieval Europe. This being so, how could the so-called French isthmus have had a national role, lying as it did for centuries on end *outside* French territory or virtually so? Consider the magnificence of Avignon in the fourteenth century, when the Papacy was established there: the renown of the city, which was also a capital for the first stirrings of humanism, was ecumenical, or putting the same thing another way, European, rather than simply French. Similarly Lyon, during the prosperity of its fairs in the sixteenth century, was first and foremost an annexe of Italian trade, a European city.

Can we consequently say that the Rhône missed its French vocation? Or perhaps that France failed to move in early enough to exploit fully the possibilities of the Rhône route?

Another factor was at work too. The French isthmus was not, as we have seen, the only usable isthmus in Europe; and except in Roman times (indeed even then) or in the days of the Champagne fairs, it was not always the most heavily used. From the thirteenth century, the preferred route taken by European trade was unquestionably fast becoming the German isthmus, with its galaxies of towns: in the south, Genoa, Milan, Florence and Venice; on the central stretch, Augsburg, Bâle, Strasbourg, Nuremberg, Frankfurt and Cologne, cities stimulated by the development of the German silver and copper mines; finally, on the North Sea were Bruges, Antwerp, Hamburg and indeed London. The Alps, with their active population of peasant-carriers, whose sledges made light work of the winter snows, were by no means an obstacle but very often a stimulus to trade.[43]

That is why, compared to Genoa, a monumental and historically weighty city and the active pole of an early-developing and all-pervasive capitalism; or compared to Venice, the centre of the Levant trade and linked by trans-Alpine routes to Germany, a town like Marseille, for all its energy and vitality, was simply not, in those days, in the same league.

Let us visualize for a moment all those powerful cities in Italy, Germany, the Low Countries and England, so many inter-linked metropolises, forming between them what has been described as the 'economic backbone of Europe', the key zone in a pre-capitalist and capitalist Europe, a network of inter-connected routes. If Italy and Germany both took such a long time to become unified politically as nations, it was precisely because of this profusion of cities, early-flowering, independent, extremely rich and taking good care to preserve their liberty. France stood somewhat aside from this European development: for the isthmus running through France derived its principal energy not from the towns of Languedoc, nor from Marseille, nor from the ports of Provence, but rather from the good will and self-interest of the Italian cities, the obligatory starting point for any effective economic circuit at the time.

All in all, the leading role of the German isthmus on one hand, and, on the other, the establishment in the late thirteenth century (1298) and early fourteenth, of a regular sea link between the Mediterranean and the North Sea, via Gibraltar,[44] kept France somewhat isolated from the mainstream of trade and the benefits of the modern capitalism then taking its first steps. This is a reality to which we shall have to return, especially since it is not given much prominence in the standard historical explanations. Yet it is surely something of extreme importance. France, although certainly restless and stirring (perhaps because of its very backwardness?), did not succeed in breaking into the privileged geography of European capitalism. Was it France's own fault? The consequence of some 'congenital' failing? Or did European capitalism, not to say international capitalism, neglect or worse exclude France, without even clearly formulating such a desire?

The Rhône as frontier-river

In the end then, the Rhône was frontier, barrier, division, obstacle – 'the enemy' as Daniel Faucher has even called it[45] – because of its dangerous and turbulent waters, and its extravagant behaviour, but also because of the actions of men and the hazards of history. Rivers are normally considered to be features uniting rather than separating, destined to be crossed whenever it has been man's interest, or even pleasure, to do so. Such was not the case of the Rhône.

Its waters could be crossed of course, and were every day. But this required concerted action between the pairs of 'twin' towns that faced each other from either side: bridges, boats or *bacs à traille*, cable-ferries,[46] all had to be maintained. On Cassini's eighteenth-century map, there are about fifteen bridges between Geneva and the sea. There were plenty of these 'twin-towns': Givors and Chasse; Vienne and Sainte-Colombe; Andance and Andancette; Tournon and Tain l'Hermitage; Valence and Saint-Paray; Avignon and Villeneuve-lès-Avignon; Tarascon and Beaucaire; Arles and Trinquetaille.[47] Sometimes it was the town on the west bank (*le Riaume*) that became more important than its partner, sometimes the one on the east bank (*l'Empi*). The very number of such twinnings – dictated by economics – even inclines one to think that for merchants and local inhabitants, crossing the river was even more important than going up or downstream.

But politics did not allow such culpable weakness. There were some rivers of course which politics or mere administrative competence crossed without any trouble. While the Seine and Loire might be able to link their two banks (as is proved by the 'bridge-provinces' on the Loire alone: the Nivernais and Orléanais, Touraine, Anjou and Brittany),[48] other rivers were more like barriers: the Rhine, the Rhône, even the Saône. Neither Provence nor the Comtat-Venaissin, neither the diminutive principality of Orange, nor Languedoc, neither the Vivarais nor the Lyonnais

281

really crossed the Rhône. Savoy – that is to say the duchy of Savoy when it still owned the pays de Gex, Bugey and Bresse, all of which passed to France by the treaty of Lyon (1601) – did not extend beyond the Saône. And Burgundy, web of roads that it was, scarcely crossed the river.

In 1707, the maréchal de Tessé found himself in Dauphiné at the head of an army assembled after the disaster at Turin (see Chapter 10), and fearing an enemy attack in Savoy. At any rate, he consoled himself, Languedoc was unlikely to be a target, since 'the Rhône is not a river that can be taken by surprise'.[49] And indeed, despite its busy shipping, the Rhône was felt to be a 'natural' frontier, like a geological fault or the moat surrounding a fortress. Any state or pseudo-state straddling the river was unthinkable. The kingdom of Provence did, it is true, capture the Vivarais, on the right bank, but the liaison did not last long. In any case, the river flowed between very different kinds of country. Shall I confess to an almost obsessive impression I still have even today, from my fairly frequent journeys between the Alps and the Massif Central via Pont-Saint-Esprit? In spite of the vines which accompany the traveller on both sides of the river, crossing it does feel like entering a different world.

Such contrasts and oppositions endured even after the king of France became master of both banks and stitched together what have been described (with a little exaggeration) as 'the two edges of a wound'.[50] Either side the river, people and provinces hated or at any rate quarrelled with each other. This was no peaceful coexistence. Even if hostilities between village and village or town and town were not entirely 'unremitting',[51] even if there were some harmoniously twinned towns, quarrels, resentment and legal disputes were the rule.

There could (or should) have been no dispute as regards ownership of the river itself. The king of France had long since proclaimed himself sovereign proprietor of the waters of the Rhône and all they embraced. Thus in 1380, well before he became comte de Provence, the king of France declared that 'all the islands in the Rhône and the other rivers of Languedoc belong to him by virtue of his sovereignty and by royal right'.[52] Louis XI was equally cate-

FIGURE 30
Islands in the Rhône

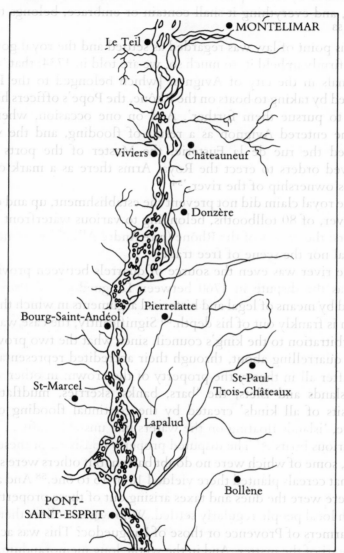

The many islands in the bed of the Rhône, marked on
Cassini's map (late eighteenth century), between Montélimar
and Pont-Saint-Esprit, were so many obstacles to shipping.

gorical in 1474 (that is several years before he inherited Provence): he declared by letters patent that 'the entire Rhône, so far as it shall reach, and everything it shall contain or embrace, belongs to the king'.[53]

This point of law was regarded as settled and the royal government firmly upheld it, so much so, we are told in 1734, that 'when criminals in the city of Avignon [which belonged to the Pope] escaped by taking to boats on the Rhône, the Pope's officers had no right to pursue them further'. And on one occasion, when the 'Rhône entered Avignon as a result of flooding, and the water reached the rue de la Fusterie, the Master of the ports even received orders to erect the Royal Arms there as a mark of the King's ownership of the river.'[54]

The royal claim did not prevent the establishment, up and down the river, of 80 tollbooths, belonging to various waterfront landowners: the waters of the Rhône (pace André Allix)[55] were neither neutral nor the scene of free trade.

The river was even the source of quarrels between provinces, such as the dispute in 1760 between Languedoc and Provence, waged by means of legal and historical arguments in which the historian is frankly out of his depth.[56] Significantly, the case was sent for arbitration to the king's council, since what the two provinces were quarrelling about, through their accredited representatives, was after all in theory the property of the crown: in other words the islands and islets, the 'bars, banks, skerries, mudflats and deposits of all kinds' created by the continual flooding of the Rhône, 'islands floating on the waters like unstable rafts . . . [or] precarious boats'.[57] The disputed property consisted of these very lands, some of which were no doubt barren, but others were so fertile that cereals planted there yielded 10 or 15 to one.[58] And above all there were the dues and taxes arising out of these properties on which local people regularly settled. Who was to collect them, the tax-farmers of Provence or those of Languedoc? This was actually the heart of the matter. And in the whole long memorandum, I can find only one 'trans-fluvial' reference: it concerns the boatmen of Villeneuve-lès-Avignon who were the only people entitled to cross the river at Avignon.

It is of no great significance that the king's council eventually pronounced in Languedoc's favour, permitting it to extend its jurisdiction to the east bank, or rather to the edge of the alluvial land on the 'Empire' side. The royal judgement was no doubt influenced by the fact that Languedoc had been annexed to the crown over two centuries earlier than Provence. It could therefore claim priority. As a result, the *parlement* of Toulouse benefited from certain prerogatives and precedents in lawsuits relating to the Rhône, to its banks or the islands.

It is thanks to another quarrel, this time a more important one – virtually setting state against state – that we are able to read (among other prolix documents) a Memorandum or opinion by Monsieur de Vauban, dated 22 March 1686, now in the Archives Nationales. The essential issues are set out in Figure 31.[59] The plan consisted quite simply of obliging all significant shipping on the Rhône, up or downstream, to use the arm of the river which ran under the steep slopes of Villeneuve-lès-Avignon, thus directing it away from the port of Avignon, city of the Popes, and foreign rival, on the opposite bank. Diverting the river's waters however was no small undertaking and in the end the project came to nothing. Vauban incidentally, seems to have been half-expecting this: 'Not enough work has yet been done' he writes, 'at the foot of the Saint-André rock, one of the places where the hauliers would have to go' – on the Villeneuve side of course. All the same a series of groynes had been built to try to divert as much water as possible towards Villeneuve and its 'canal'. 'The Rhône and its islands all belong to the king', the memorandum says, 'and since the groynes do not touch [the Avignon side] the Pope's people will not be able to say a word and the Rhône can entirely be diverted to the Villeneuve side'.[60] A curious sentence, reaffirming yet again that the waters of the river and its islands belonged to the French king. The Pope would be left only the banks on the Comtat-Venaissin side.

Vauban's memorandum incidentally provides a few details on the bridge at Avignon: 'twelve feet wide, 500 *toises* long . . . [it is] in no way suited to the passage of waggons or heavy loads, [and that] is one of the greatest mistakes that can be committed in this kind of work'. The Pont-Saint-Esprit further north, which was '400 *toises*

285

FIGURES 31 and 31a
Plans for engineering works on the Rhône attached to Vauban's Memorandum of 1686

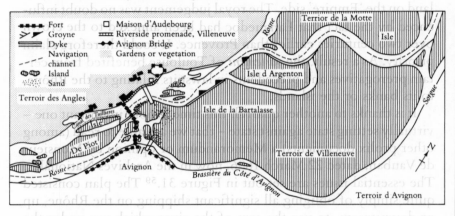

The normal flow of the river, followed by shipping, is represented by a dotted line. The plan was to make shipping use the right (or north-west) bank by Villeneuve, instead of the left (or south-east) bank, by Avignon, which belonged to the Pope. In order to achieve this, it was or would be necessary:

1. To divert the current, by means of dykes constructed between A/B (see Figure 31a) blocking the arm of the river that encircled the 'isle de la Bartalasse'; between C/D, between that island and the 'isle de Piot'; and E/F. It would also require transverse groynes, diverting the water towards the right bank, and the enlargement of the Canal de Saint-Pierre and the Canal des Tuillères. No sooner had this work begun than problems cropped up, including unforeseen consequences such as erosion of the riverbanks and the formation of sandbanks in mid-stream.

2. To create a towpath on the Villeneuve side (see detail Figure 31a). This had already been done between the Avignon bridge and the Maison d'Audebourg (which used to front directly on to the river). But a major problem remained: a cutting would have to be made for the towpath, at least 5 yards or 15 feet wide, in the tall rock on which the

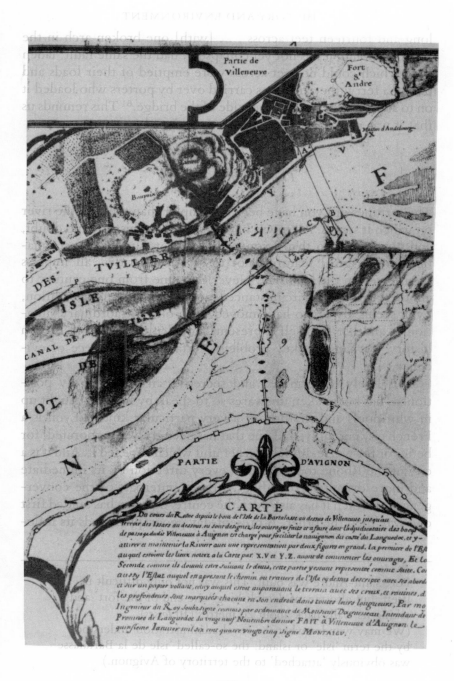

long and fourteen feet across . . . [with] one broken arch in the middle, though it has not yet collapsed', had the same fault: laden carts which could not get across were emptied of their loads and put on a ferry; the cargo was carried over by porters who loaded it on to another cart on the other side of the bridge.[61] This reminds us that it was not so easy after all to cross the Rhône.

The fortunes of Lyon

The fortunes of Lyon have been no simpler than those of the river on which it stands. All towns have complicated histories no doubt, and none more so than Lyon: its wealth, its sudden transformations, its original features, not to say peculiarities, all impress themselves on the historian. Never the same from one century to another, driven by circumstances more than by its own volition, Lyon seems always to have moved from one extraordinary situation to another. In itself it presents a difficult problem in French history, perhaps the key problem, certainly a key piece of evidence.

This lively, determined and secretive city, awkwardly positioned, has been taken unawares so to speak by history, caught up in whirlpools and rhythms of a very particular kind.[62] Lyon is a French city certainly, and one that has been truly incorporated, for better or for worse, into the larger unit which annexed it. And it is a city of the Rhône too, pulled in every direction by its immediate and more distant surroundings – the counterpart of the convergences of which it has also been the centre. So Lyon has tended first one way then the other. A present-day geographer finds its influ-

---

Fort Saint-André was built. This was not only difficult in itself, but also meant demolishing 'one end of the fort' and taking its walls back about 20 metres (10 *toises*).

(We may wonder what the royal administration understood by the term 'isle' or island: the so-called 'isle de la Bartalasse' was obviously 'attached' to the territory of Avignon.)

ence 'paradoxically more noticeable in the Massif Central than in the Rhône corridor itself'.[63] It is true that Pierre Estienne, for reasons both old and new, underestimates the importance to Lyon of the Saône–Rhône axis, a point to which I shall shortly return.

One of the strangest things about Lyon, to tell the truth, is the astonishment, hesitation and irritation it provokes in the observer who cannot get the measure of it however hard he tries, who finds its contours hard to represent, who is obliged from one moment to the next to alter the line of the horizon or the colours of his palette. He sets out of course to explain it by the usual norms, according to some local, regional or national 'logic'; but every time he has half-formulated an explanation, it eludes him, or runs into complications.

To begin with local logic, Lyon lived from day to day off the surrounding countryside, of course: its bourgeoisie owned land, vineyards and houses there. But the countryside did not measure up to its big city neighbour: the Lyonnais let its capital down, acting as a brake on its development. What a difference from the country round Toulouse, or the Ile-de-France, with which indeed there is no comparison!

Any 'regional logic' there might be also turns out to be somewhat disconcerting; it certainly does not provide us with the key to the mystery. Lyon is unquestionably a regional capital, powerful and vigorous, and has been so since its return to strength in the sixteenth century. Today its influence and preponderance extend to a circle of towns some distance away: Roanne, Dijon, Chalon-sur-Saône, Besançon, Geneva (the hereditary enemy), Grenoble, Saint-Etienne, Vienne (in the past) and Valence (today). But for a clearer picture, we need more detailed studies like those of André Piatier (see Part II above), surveys of the state of commercial and financial links between Lyon and these other towns – at once its handmaids and its rivals.

As for national logics, with a few exceptions to prove the rule, I see these as on the whole hostile and negative. Neither the French economy nor the political authorities have wanted, been able, or known how to encourage the influence of Lyon as a powerful pole of attraction within France.

In short, the French economy succeeded in diverting the Saône–Rhône isthmus towards Paris. It favoured the direct Paris–Lyon link by the old Bourbonnais road (now the Route Nationale 7). What was more, traffic coming from Paris would, on reaching Lyon, leave the Rhône and head straight for Italy (Turin and Milan). After Chambéry, it went by the Maurienne valley, the only major way across the Alps, thanks to the easy Mont Cenis pass, at 2100 metres. This was essentially a diagonal route, stopping off at Lyon on the way, true, but crossing rather than following the Rhône axis. In any case, on a national scale there was probably simply no room for two command posts at once, for two very big cities to exert simultaneous supremacy. Paris prevailed over Lyon for the simple reason that it was and remained the capital city, the natural and obligatory destination for converging movements, as well as for money levied by the state, with the result that there was a constant oversupply of specie in the capital.

And yet Lyon had long been more important, economically, than Paris. The city on the Rhône had been promoted well above its station by the prosperity of its fairs. In the sixteenth century, Paris with its retail traders looked rather small beer compared to the wholesale trade and financial transactions taking place in Lyon. But after the seventeenth century when France's economic life had slowed to a crawl, the great days of the fairs were over. And by the time the economy revived again in the eighteenth century, the fairs were out of date and the resurgent economy promoted Paris: little by little the capital city stripped Lyon of its financial supremacy. By the end of the age of Enlightenment, the process was complete. By fair means or foul, Lyon's rival had carried off the prize. The rivalry continued and increased in the nineteenth century. Today Lyon has lost all its finance capital to a metropolis whose voracity knows no bounds. Is there any chance of a reversal of the process, now that we are seeing the first stirrings of reaction by the Lyon *Bourse*, following the creation in 1983 of the 'second market', and the quotation on the Lyon exchange of a few new companies? It is too soon to say. The businessmen of Lyon still appear to be very reticent. This illustrates, in a financial context, the problem of making decentralization work.[64]

It is when we reach this point, I imagine, that we begin to under-stand Lyon's destiny better, indeed it becomes almost visible. Lyon was fated to find its proper rhythm and the conditions for its expansion only at *international* level. It depended on a 'logic' of very wide radius; it needed outside help. Its fairy godmothers were all foreigners.

This had already been true when the Romans, as rulers of Gaul, founded the city of Lyon in an area inhabited by small tribes too weak to oppose the conqueror – on neutral territory so to speak. The new town would be the centre of a 'colonial' exploitation of Gaul for the benefit of the empire beyond the Alps.[65]

History never repeats itself in completely identical terms, it is true. But the exceptional flowering of Lyon in the late fifteenth and sixteenth centuries was clearly the result of a similar process. Its fairs were, if not created (they had existed since 1420) certainly given international standing by the privileges granted by Louis XI and his policy of destroying the fairs of Geneva (1462–4).[66] The Medici settled in Lyon in about 1467, and success followed success in the sixteenth century: it was by now the leading centre of the European economy, just as several centuries earlier the celebrated fairs of Champagne had been. But it was the Italian bankers – Flor-entines, Lucchese, for a while Genoese – who were both the instigators and the beneficiaries of this burgeoning prosperity: through Lyon, they could exploit the rest of France, acquiring the surpluses of a trade balance perpetually in their favour. Was this not suspiciously like the exploitation of Gaul by the Romans many centuries earlier? 'Foreign supremacy', Richard Gascon writes, 'became overwhelming [at this time], bordering on monopoly and leaving the French with little more than a subordinate position as brokers . . . a function which had steadily been reduced in impor-tance as banking organization developed'.[67] Louis Bourgeois, in his lively book on Lyon during the first half of the sixteenth century (1491–1551), entitles one of his chapters: 'A state within a state: the Florentine "nation" '.[68] The richest trading family in Europe did indeed live in Lyon; but it was a Florentine family, the Guadagni, whose name had been gallicized to Gadagne. The Ital-ians formed a close-knit and powerful colony, not more than about eighty families in all, who kept themselves to themselves, married their children to each other and avoided intermarriage with the local people – a typical example in fact of behaviour common among capitalists of all periods.

Lyon's dazzling fortune, whether created by the Lyonnais themselves or by their foreign residents, fascinated France and the French kings. Surely everything was possible for the city on the Rhône, we are tempted to think; it might even have become the capital of the kingdom in the sixteenth century. During France's extravagant foreign policy initiatives – crossing the Alps, wasting energy on the Italian wars – Lyon was the regular marshalling centre for men, matériel, cannon – and credit. The city both held a commanding position in this perpetual war and made money out of it. And since everything went hand in hand, it experienced the splendours of the Renaissance and might have been as brilliant a cultural capital as Paris. Everything was indeed possible, if only in the time of François I, the most Italian of French kings and perhaps the most sympathetic to Lyon. Did such an exalted promotion for the southern city cross his mind in 1538, as he travelled down the Rhône to Aigues-Mortes to meet the emperor Charles V, at a famous interview? Staying in Lyon on the way, he had been charmed once again by the city. Unfortunately, the dauphin was taken ill there with a sudden chill after a game of tennis. The royal journey continued towards the south, but the young prince had to be taken ashore at Tournon, where he died on 10 August. 'Thus departed this fair young soul', as Brantôme wrote.[69]

Was it because of this incident, this evil omen, that Lyon failed to obtain the crown it might have claimed? I doubt it. The promotion of Lyon to capital could never have been the result of a formal decision, only of a de facto primacy. Lyon lost the contest, which indeed it had barely entered, for another, very obvious reason. Europe in the middle years of the sixteenth century was beginning to look northwards and to the Atlantic, away from the Mediterranean and the Italian wars. It was Lyon's loss when these wars were ended by the treaty of Cateau–Cambrésis (1559). This treaty, against which the warlike nobility of France protested so bitterly, wiped out French supremacy south of the Alps. Henri II gave up

Piedmont and Savoy, which had been occupied in 1536 and where France was beginning to put down roots. The frontier was moved back to the Lyon area itself, amputated now of a large extension eastwards. Let us imagine for a moment that France had emerged victorious at Turin or Milan: Lyon might have been confirmed as the centre of the prosperity of all Europe. In sum, the city's eminence lasted as long as victory beyond the Alps remained in the balance between Habsburg and Valois.

Lyon's decline, then, became visible in a number of ways over time, and was brutally presaged by the 1557 bankruptcy. But the city was not excluded overnight from the world of money markets and credit in which it had served such a long apprenticeship. It was gradually losing Europe, true, but it still had France. During the economically depressed seventeenth century, it controlled the prudent and sometimes unemployed capital of French investors, attracted to Lyon by the advantages of carrying over loans between one fair and another – 2% from quarter to quarter – and no less by the gold guarantee offered by the fair: all bills of exchange had to be paid for in *écus d'or en or*. This routine dealing, a series of short term investments at a time when, we must remember, plain lending at interest was still forbidden, kept the financiers of Lyon in business: they were masters in their own house and balanced their books merely by juggling with the figures in their ledgers. It had settled into a routine, providing a steady rentier income.

But Lyon also remained an assembly point for merchandise and an outstandingly creative centre in the active industrial sector, which may have compensated the city for its financial decline. Its manufacturing activities certainly ensured that Lyon goods were to be found in all the markets of Europe, particularly since Lyon had very early chosen to specialize in silk, a luxury industry. And luxury by definition meant foreign markets. For its expanding industry, Lyon was obliged to recruit a workforce that had constantly to be renewed; it was something of an achievement in fact to find the endless supply of labour required to keep the looms busy, whether skilled workers or unskilled assistants. An explanation of Lyon that penetrates below the surface must this time dig down to the roots and realities of this industrial activity.[70] Was

Lyon's workforce replenished by the poor neighbouring regions, the Alps and in particular the Massif Central?

The prodigious efforts of the Lyon silk manufacturers were aimed, whether in France or abroad, at an aristocratic clientèle. Feats of ingenuity were performed to provide it with sumptuous silks of original design, launching fashions in Europe that changed capriciously from one year to the next. Lyon's anxiety – or rather need – to export meant that foreign merchants stayed on in Lyon, particularly since there were still plenty of opportunities for them, whether at the fairs, as importers of food supplies or of raw silk, as money-changers or speculators in precious metals and currencies. Their doings and concerns, their possible links with foreign competitors are reflected in the correspondence from Lyon. Ever on the alert, the Lyon industrialists took fright when Turin began silk production in its turn, when Zurich began to manufacture silk crepe (1707), or when the Italians began to make perfect copies of Lyon silk designs, using bundles of samples. The only effective means of defence was to invent new designs quickly, so that imitations would be outmoded before they appeared on the market. To this end, the Lyon silk producers kept whole teams of specialist designers on their payrolls.[71] The six months court mourning declared in May 1705, on the death of the son of the duc de Bourgogne, caused panic in Lyon: stocks would be left on manufacturers' hands. And 'all the merchandise will be completely lost, since the six months mourning will mean the vogue for their fabrics will be over'. In normal times, they might have been sold abroad. But such a thing was unthinkable in wartime. There was no easy means of communicating with foreigners, 'who have in any case imitated our designs to help their co-religionists'.[72] When the French army was preparing in 1706 to take Turin – an operation which did not succeed – the merchants of Lyon requested that the Italian city's silk workshops – employing workers hired in Lyon – be closed down.

So Lyon continued to have one foot outside France, so to speak, and to depend on its foreign contacts. It was driven to this by its economy, its situation and its circumstances. Sometimes circumstances were particularly favourable. The First Empire and the

Continental Blockade would place Lyon once more at the centre of overland communications within Europe, broadening its zone of influence. Once again, curiously enough, Lyon found itself located at the crossroads of Europe: commanding the road to the Alps, the gateway to the Mediterranean and connections to the Rhine, the Swiss Cantons, and even Holland. But the Empire collapsed in 1814–15; the revival speedily came to an end and Lyon fell back into a state of dependency and vulnerability. When the first steam shipping appeared in the 1830s, it had only to chalk up some early success on the Rhine for German routes to steal a share of Lyon's freight traffic.

I shall return perforce to the extremely important history of Lyon – which I leave now only to come back to the central problem posed by this chapter: the genesis of France itself.

But without offering a complete explanation of Lyon's past, I think I have at least indicated the different levels on which its activities were simultaneously conducted. It was Lyon's fate to stake everything on these activities one after another, as much out of necessity as by choice. If I am not mistaken, what Lyon required in order to fulfil its true destiny was that outstanding career which France could not offer it, and which the Rhône corridor, where population, exchange and the means of production were concentrated, did not seem disposed to yield up to it. Fortunately Lyon could number among its vital resources, the prodigious industrial activity which enabled it to survive and bide its time. For Lyon has often had to bide its time – indeed it could be argued that it is doing so at the moment, in our own day. Such at any rate is the view of Jean Labasse[73] (1982). He maintains that Lyon will never again be an international city – it is no longer one at present – unless it proves capable of transcending the Rhône–Alpes economic region in which it seems in danger of being imprisoned, and unless it manages to shake off (but is this possible?) the secondary, subsidiary role in which Paris has cast it.

The present day: from Rhône to Rhine

The present day finds us on the brink of a complete transformation of traffic on the Rhône, as revolutionary as the adoption of the steamship in the last century. Note the acclaim with which the press has celebrated the domestication of this wild river, following the inauguration on 19 March 1980 of the Vaugris dam, which marked the completion of the Rhône improvement scheme between Lyon and the sea.

It has taken 32 years for the project to come to fruition, beginning with the Génissiat dam in 1948. Altogether 18 dams have been built, thirteen power stations, thirteen locks and 64 powered plants. These marvels cannot console us for the loss of the real Rhône of yesterday. But we should at least have the grace to say that they can also be very beautiful in their fashion.

Along the 300 kilometres of this exceptional 'riverway', ultra-modern shipping is beginning to appear: self-propelled barges of 3,000 horsepower, 80 metres long, with a capacity of 2,000 tons and a draught of over 3 metres, not to mention small cargo vessels coming directly in from the sea. The river has been tamed and set to work for us. And this is only the first stage. It is planned to instal hydroelectric equipment on the upper reaches of the Rhône, between Lyon and Geneva, with a completion date little more than five years ahead, if all goes well. It is also planned to connect Marseille to the Rhineland, by using the calm waters of the Saône (a fairly straightforward undertaking once a few obstacles are eliminated such as the Saint-Laurent bridge at Mâcon, through whose arches shipping cannot pass when the river is in flood, but to which the citizens are very attached), then by completely rebuilding the Rhône–Rhine canal (from Saint-Symphorien); at present it is virtually unusable on account of its narrow width and large numbers of locks.

The overall design of the programme is exceedingly ambitious: Marseille would become one of the outlets for Switzerland and southern Germany and might find itself if not equal to, at least in

FIGURE 32
Twentieth-century development projects on the Rhône

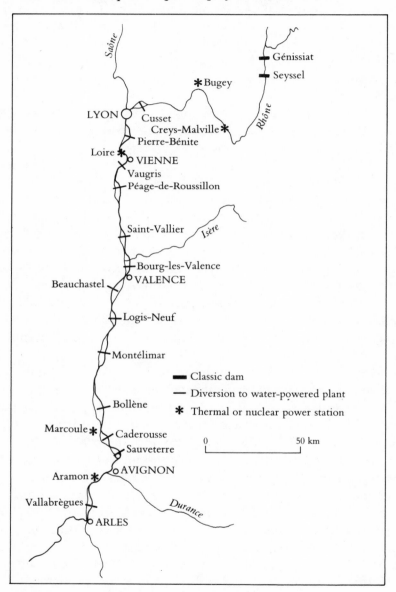

Dams, plants and power stations (some nuclear).

the same league as the great northern ports – Hamburg, Rotterdam, Antwerp, Rouen, Le Havre. It would also be logical to expect some industrial development of the Rhône's hinterland – in other words, some regional spin-off. After all, the Rhône is now equipped to produce 13,000,000,000 kilowatt-hours.

Nevertheless, there are a number of reservations to be expressed:

1. The great Rhône waterway is now open over the 280 kilometres between Lyon and Fourques (4 kilometres from Arles). Along this busy stretch of the river in both directions, travelled 7,356 vessels in 1979: a large figure at first sight, but cargoes were only moderate in size: 463 tons on average (heavier loads go upstream, 589 tons, than downstream, 243 tons), that is a total freight of 3,402,014 tons, of which 1,879,174 consisted of oil products. In 1980, the overall tonnage went up slightly, reaching 3,554, 527 tons. In 1981, (the fourth quarter is an estimate based on the first three), the total came to over 4 million tons: so there was some progress, but only on a modest scale. Rotterdam on the other hand – which is of course the largest port in the world – handled 300 million tons of freight in 1979 and 250 million in 1981. 250,000 river boats dock there every year. And 'of these 250 million tons of freight, 122.7 million were loaded or unloaded by barges'.[74]

Why then is traffic on the Rhône comparatively modest? Is it because of competition from other forms of transport, the pipeline from Fos to Bâle for oil (50 million tons) plus the roads and railways? The Paris–Lyon–Mediterranean railway line has a brilliant record and the TGV (ultra-fast train) does the trip from Paris to Montpellier in five hours. The Mediterranean has been brought nearer to Paris, but it is an achievement that has nothing to do with the waters of the Rhône. If the Rhône seems such a poor relation, it is because it remains difficult of access; because Marseille (handling almost 100 million tons of freight) uses it very little; because Lyon is in the habit of sending goods for export by road or rail; and above all because the Rhône valley is far from comparable to industrial Germany, for which Rotterdam is the thriving outlet.

In fact even the present 4 million tons of traffic on the Rhône is not all accounted for by long-distance freight. A good proportion of it consists of exchanges up and down the river, of short-distance trips – all very useful to the dwellers on the banks of the Rhône no doubt. But the investment in technical equipment cannot be justified without large-scale and long-distance freight. Are we to believe that this will follow on completion of the programme? That the Rhône traffic will then move out of its infancy? Or will the result have been an even greater burden of unproductive investment?

2. Let us suppose that all the projects are completed – although at present that is a long way off, whether we are talking about the hydro-electric installations on the upper Rhône, or the grand Rhône–Rhine scheme which seems to be at a complete standstill at the moment[75] – let us suppose anyway that they all go ahead: nothing has been planned in the way of improving one branch (in my view an essential one) of the Rhône isthmus, namely the network linking the Saône to the Seine by the canal de Bourgogne or the old canal du Centre and the Briare canal. And yet it would seem logical to make the most modern network of navigable waterways in France extend to the capital city. If this does not happen, it is to be feared that the Rhône route will once again turn out to be *marginal in relation to French territory*, that it will be a European highway, rather than revitalizing as a matter of priority the French economy as a whole. Some of our motorways are certainly used by English, German, Belgian and Dutch travellers as a means of transit between their native countries and Spain or Italy, but above all they serve our own national needs. Am I wrong to think that the Rhône installations should *also* be connected to the heart of France itself? Not that I have any desire to see all-out centralization in France. Still less do I wish to prevent France being completely open to Europe. But a major European communications axis provided by our territory should not simply be a means of transit through France, it ought to have ramifications into the whole country. Such is not, it seems, the view of the planners – essentially for economic reasons: it would require very considerable investment. Another factor is no doubt the decline in water-borne freight, which is unquestionably in crisis at the moment.

Present-day traffic on the newly-improved Rhône is itself disappointing. But is this not precisely because it is not connected to a large enough economic unit? Jacques Fléchet, the president of the French lightermen's association declared unhesitatingly on a visit to Rotterdam in September 1982, that

> France's waterways must be connected to the European network. The outposts represented by the French ports on the Rhine and Moselle are inadequate. The Seine and Rhône should be linked up to Europe: Marseille, Le Havre, Rouen, Paris and Dunkerque cannot remain merely local ports as regards their river traffic. They must become European ports, enjoying the same advantages as their competitors in northern Europe: that is homogenous waterways reaching thousands of kilometres inland by the year 2000.[76]

So at least I am not the only person to think that one should not say the Rhône, Lyon, Marseille without also adding the Seine, Paris, Rouen, Le Havre.

3. I wrote the above lines hoping for some success, for some miracle to take place on the Rhône. The miracle seems to be taking its time and the economic crisis is no doubt one reason. Among geographers, critical pessimism seems to be winning the day. Pierre Estienne does not once refer to the 'French isthmus', only to the 'Rhône–Rhine axis', 'corridor' or 'passage', 'which constitutes a great but discontinuous trench'. We are a long way from the imperturbable and unduly confident reflections of Vidal de la Blache. Estienne's pessimism supports the argument I have been advancing: that the Rhône axis was essentially a frontier, marginal to the creation of France. Pierre Estienne goes even further, but is he right? I must say I hope not. 'Must we conclude', he says bleakly, 'that the Rhône–Rhine region is a myth and that calls for a canal between the Rhône and the Rhine are a mockery?'[77] I should like to think that the future will prove him wrong.

CHAPTER EIGHT

Paris, the Ile-de-France and the Paris basin

I do not deny the importance in many respects of the French isthmus, in particular the immense role it has played in diffusing cultural influences for which it has provided a channel since pre-historic times. Today it is the route taken by France's major traffic flow. I am simply arguing that it did not play as formative a role as was once thought in the genesis of France's unity.

The most convincing proof of this, briefly, is that that unity was created elsewhere, between the Somme and the Loire, in the area centred on Paris, with a radius the distance from the capital to Orleans or Rouen, an area that included not only the Ile-de-France but the Orléanais and parts of Champagne, Picardy and Nor-mandy: in other words a rather particular France. There can be no doubt that it was from this nucleus, this centre, that everything began. French unity was created 'outwards from a central point'.

> Thus the centre of France, the least original part of the coun-try, took over all the rest [wrote Michelet in his *Journal*]. This central part embodies to the highest degree the French char-acter. Here the race is more mixed, the land is more flat, and nature is more boring: three things conducive to a *vocation sociale*. The Ile-de-France took over France; and France the world.[78]

It is true that before 1789, 'only the old provinces around Paris identified themselves with France'[79] and that the monarchy had a freer reign than elsewhere in the area of the Cinq Grosses Fermes, the tax-farms unified by Colbert in 1664. But I hardly think that such submission originated in something that could be described as a 'social vocation'. Nor do I believe that the banks of the Oise, for example, or the Loire valley are 'boring'; on the contrary.

It is true though, that they created France. Francis Huré even fancifully imagines 'a royal cell, the Ile-de-France, and its male nucleus, Paris, both possessed of a voracious appetite and accomplishing, at whatever cost, a genetic programme which was to lead to the French "hexagon" '.[80] The result, as we know, was a flagrant dissymmetry.

Scepticism about the genetic programming is quite in order: the process was far from being as simple as this. No long-term calculation really lay behind it. Chance and latent factors played their part, it must be said. And yet the results are there: by the time the first stones of Notre-Dame were laid, in the late eleventh century (1072), the wheels were already in motion for the rise of Paris, already a monster town, and soon to be the most populous in Europe.

One initial problem must be dealt with: in this vast centrifugal movement, did everything begin in the very centre, in the city? Or in the central region as a whole? Or was it both? Let us start with the central region, broadly speaking the Paris basin.

The primacy of the Paris basin

The Paris basin represents over a quarter of the present-day territory of France; it is its largest single plain, the richest and perhaps the most varied, whatever the view of Michelet, who was thinking not of the economy but of the landscape when he spoke of 'the monotonous countryside of Champagne and the Ile-de-France, . . . those towns of chalk and wood [where] the soul is filled with boredom and disgust'.[81]

Of the *généralité* of Paris (which represented a large area of the Paris basin) it was said in the seventeenth century that 'the whole of its territory is useful for something; since where wheat and other grains do not grow, there is wine; and where there is neither grain nor wine, there are fruits, pastures, woods, forests and walnut-trees'.[82] According to Davity (1625), 'the land round Paris is not lacking in grain, nor in wine, nor dairy goods, hay, fruit or vegetables, nor in water, which is to be seen on all sides, and that is what makes Paris marvellously well provided for'.[83] And one could long continue in the same vein.

Present-day geographers would willingly echo these positive judgements, though with some serious reservations about the less favoured regions south of the Loire, between the river and the Massif Central. But they would insist on the exceptional advantages of the limestone plateaux surrounding Paris – with soil through which the rains filter naturally, where ploughing is never held up by standing water, and where in times of drought, moisture is drawn up by capillarity to the surface to save the plants from dying. What is more, these plateaux – the Beauce, the Brie, the Soissonnais – still retain a surface covering of silt, that extra soft soil which in various parts of Europe attracted the first *agricultural* populations of prehistory, because ploughing was so easy.[84]

All these explanations contain some truth. But they do not really hold the key. It is true that the Paris basin experienced exceptional density of population by the standards of what was later to become France. And overpopulation is a major explanatory factor. But it has itself to be explained. What we are seeing are its consequences not its causes.

The overpopulation in question was already present when Roman Gaul collapsed, and was no doubt the reason why Roman civilization survived in the Ile-de-France longer than in other regions, until the eventual defeat of the Roman Syagrius (by Clovis in 487). And this may have been significant: an extra hundred years of organized Roman rule was not negligible.[85]

Overpopulation meant a plentiful supply of manpower: it was on the Ile-de-France and its neighbouring regions that the extraordinary 'transnational' venture of the Carolingians was based. This dynasty had long been careful not to divide up or fracture the unity of the region at the heart of their empire, the very mainspring of their strength. J. Dhondt even claims that the division of the region in 837 did indeed destroy the living source of their might: this may be going too far.

Edward Fox's thesis is more sweeping, more brilliant – and even more debatable. He argues, along with several other historians, that the Arab invasion which came to an end on the field of Poitiers (732) was stopped only by the heavy cavalry used for the first time by the Franks in the days of Charles Martel. This was also the time when the heavy plough (with wheels but no mould-board), to be followed quite soon by triennial crop rotation (wheat, oats, fallow), was becoming established, allowing full use to be made of the rich arable lands of the north. And lastly this period saw the adoption of the stirrup, an indispensable piece of equipment for a heavily armed horseman. Thus 'the Carolingians . . . suddenly found themselves in possession of two new and complementary advantages, the stirrup and the possibility [by growing oats] of feeding an unprecedented number of cavalry mounts',[86] 'powerful horses, thanks to which cavalry acquired in battle under the Frankish kings an importance unknown in Roman strategy'.[87]

For all these reasons, it was logical that the Carolingians should have withdrawn to the northern regions, where oats were grown and horses bred. So Fox rejects Henri Pirenne's old unilateral explanation. It was not Islam that temporarily banished the western powers from the Mediterranean: the latter withdrew northwards of their own accord, in search of 'the deepest and richest soils in western Europe, where even today more wheat grows to the hectare than in any other region of the world'. Matters were finally decided, Fox argues, by 'the soil in the Seine and Thames [valleys] which the new plough opened up to agriculture'.[88]

These arguments are certainly worth considering. Who would deny the importance of heavy cavalry? It opened up a long era in European military history. At the spear point of a galloping cavalryman there was concentrated an irresistible force which William McNeill provocatively compares to that of 'the heavy tanks of the 1940s'; 'even a few score of armoured knights could turn the tide of battle'.[89]

But to return to our space between the Loire, Seine and Somme, let us look more closely at the probable dates of these changes, closer still at the exact origin of these northern agricultural practices, which surely pre-date Charles Martel.

Once again, the explanation refers to a time when everything was already happening. It assumes and describes an advanced form of agriculture and the large peasant population that resulted, but does not explain how these came into being.

Yet in an ancient country like France, no population problem can be understood without reference to the *très longue durée*, the very long term, stretching back in time, well beyond the bounds of traditional history. The crucial events occurred in fact millennia ago, millennia about which we now know more, thanks to recent advances in prehistory.

Before historical times, the area which would later be France witnessed two waves of incoming population, broadly speaking, one from the Mediterranean, the other from the depths of central Europe. For the moment we are more concerned with the second wave, the decisive contribution of central Europe to the Paris basin where these peoples eventually arrived – the future France of *oïl* if you like. The great landmass of prehistoric central Europe was the 'peasant continent' par excellence, and has left linguistic traces behind it 'from the Yenisyei to Finistère'.[90] Within this vast expanse, various peoples can be distinguished moving westwards in successive waves, incorporating as they went other populations either subjugated or caught up in their wake. They brought with them cattle-breeding and cereal cultivation. In the fourth millennium BC, they introduced to the Paris basin, which the depredations of previous populations had partially denuded, an effective form of agriculture centred on grouped villages. The population quickly expanded, encouraged by the natural properties of these wide-open plains. With further immigration from the east, the accumulation of people increased still further, culminating in the Celtic expansion of the first millennium BC. It was now that there appeared the open field, the first version of the 'medieval openfield with regular crop rotation'.[91] This was nothing less than the living construction of Gaul, the first version of France if you like, as it began to take shape.

Prehistory thus seems to reveal a first stage in unification, based on an area destined to give birth to a second. Or does this explanation seem too good to be true?

But why Paris?

Why, though, did the centre from which France was constructed take up residence on one particular island – the Ile de la Cité – on a particular bend of the Seine? Why not at Melun for instance, which also has an island on a bend in the river and lies in equally fertile countryside? Why not at Senlis or Reims, or even Orleans where the political centre of France in its early days seemed sometimes to be located? The Loire, as an instrument for the later unity of France would have been just as good as the Seine; it was navigable downstream, as goes without saying, and thanks to the west winds, boats could travel upstream as well. But then Orleans was boxed in between the forest to the north and the stagnant waters of the Sologne to the south.

Why not Rouen then? For Michelet, 'Paris, Rouen and Le Havre (which was created by François I in 1517) are one and the same city, of which the Seine is the main thoroughfare'.[92] Rewriting history with our imagination, there is nothing to prevent us displacing the centre of France towards the Channel and setting it down in Rouen, enlarging this already prosperous town, which would not begin to feel the disadvantage of its rather confined site on the river until much later. The career of London, at the mouth of the Thames, is after all an English example of the same kind of success. In short, it was not 'necessary that Paris should be in Paris'.[93]

So to say of its site that 'although it was not consciously chosen, it turned out to be very well chosen'[94] is surely something that could equally well be said of any other city that might have won this mysterious competition. It is true that Paris is well situated, near the major traffic routes of the Seine and its tributaries, the Yonne, the Marne and the Oise: an unending stream of grain, wood, casks of wine, boats carrying monumental loads of hay, free-floating logs, all arrived at the city's quaysides.

But the French capital had one major disadvantage: it was landlocked. The fact that it lay far inland was to prove of great consequence: it drew the rest of France inwards too – unless that is, we are to conclude that France chose this option, which remained so long in the balance, and imagined, wished or accepted itself to be an inland unit.

And yet on its western coastline, facing the ocean on which the destiny of the modern world would be decided, France had many advantages: it had sea-ports, sea-going peoples and populations whose poverty might have made them willing to try anything.

> Here was a substantial manoeuvrable mass [as Pierre Bonnaud rightly says] for colonization on a grand scale, much more than England had at its disposal. There is no point objecting that the French showed little taste for emigrating: the royal government was not in the habit of waiting for volunteers and did not scruple to use press-gangs, forced 'transportation', or deportation as a penal measure.[95]

True; but the royal government itself saw the world through continental eyes.

To try to imagine a different destiny for France is one way of trying to understand what history did have in store for it. This is what Michelet was doing to some extent, without taking his thoughts to their logical conclusion, when he wrote in his *Journal* in August 1831:

> Le Havre, . . . on the north jetty. The Ocean [sic] calm, the coastline not very imposing. Ebb tide. The Ocean is English. It made me sad to think that this sublime field of liberty belongs to another nation . . . Whatever the state of our ports now, it is obvious from the countless numbers of churches in Normandy that in those days France's energies lay more to the west. England in the eleventh, twelfth and thirteenth centuries was invaded several times and it seems that in those times France had the upper hand on sea.[96]

Personally I doubt this. I would also question whether the ocean was the 'field of liberty'; it stood for wealth and therefore for inequality. But that is not the real problem. If we are to visualize a different France, we must imagine the Paris basin, the matrix of France, re-oriented northwards and westwards, having the focal point of its ambitions and action in Rouen, not in Paris or Orleans. France's maritime vocation which foundered almost before it was glimpsed, is something about which questions can be asked throughout French history. Is Paris – 'the bottomless pit' as Vauban called it – the real villain? Yes and no. For Paris is as much consequence as cause.

What is certain is that the predominance of the France of *oïl* set on the country the seal of a near-catastrophic distortion and dissymmetry. But would it have been otherwise if France had been centred on Rouen, or Lyon, or Toulouse? Every national unit is a superstructure, a kind of net cast over regions very different from each other. The net is controlled by the hand that holds it, the privileged centre. Inequality thus emerges of its own accord. I wonder if there has been a single nation in the world not marked by dissymmetry.

It remains to ask whether it would have been possible (I do not think so myself) to do without the unitary state, possible for the regions to have lived sufficient to themselves. They were for a while autonomous and powerful, then, logically, they ceased to be so. I believe there is a certain logic in nations.

CHAPTER NINE

The frontier: a crucial test

To have somewhere to live is to begin to exist. France had frontiers and a place to live even before it formally existed. These frontiers, inherited, conquered or reconquered, marked out an enormous area if it is measured, as it should be, by the slow pace of communications in the past. In this respect, France was for a long time a 'monster', a 'continent' in itself, a super-state, an over-sized political unit, not unlike an empire,[97] uniting regions which were consequently hard to hold together and which had to be defended both against threats from within and, no less, from external dangers. The whole enterprise required an unbelievable outlay of strength, patience and vigilance. Ange Goudar in 1756 could say of Louis XIV's wars:

> France, after its victories on land, became a country of fortresses which had to be manned by many garrisons: the frontiers of the monarchy were extended and the keys to the kingdom multiplied in number. From now on there was no difference between peace and war, since the army, having been enlarged on account of the new conquests, required the same number of soldiers [in either case].[98]

The frontier has always devoured French history, draining its energies and 'the most liquid of finances'.[99] Ange Goudar was right when in the same year 1756, which saw the beginning of the Seven Years War, he wrote:

> Our *regular troops* are no longer in proportion to those of any government in Europe. In this sector of our administration there is a surplus ruinous to the state. The armies of Holland and England combined add up to scarcely more than 40,000

men. Whereas we, even in peacetime, maintain over 150,000. We have 110,000 too many soldiers by comparison with these states.[100]

His figure does not seem an exaggeration since, at the beginning of Louis XIV's personal reign in 1661, the infantry alone numbered '218,000 men . . ., of whom 26,000 [were] soldiers in garrison'.[101] The figures varied with circumstances of course. But we should add to the numbers in the army proper all the peasants who were requisitioned, the navvies ('pioneers'), militiamen, entrepreneurs handling the purchase and transport of grain or horses, and the press-gangs in pursuit, often brutal, of new recruits who were almost always difficult to round up and all too likely to desert. The cost of the army also had to cover the enrolment of mercenaries when required, as well as equipment, arms, horses and artillery.

If 'Holland' (that is the Low Countries) and England spent less on their armies, it was because England was protected by the sea and Holland by its small size and its rings of fortresses.[102] France was obliged to pay the price for its immense size and its land hunger, a sort of peasant craving which nothing could satisfy.

The persistence of frontiers and boundaries

The word frontier (*frontière* in French) comes from the adjective *frontier*, meaning 'facing, fronting'. It appeared very early since it is to be found in Godefroy's *Dictionnaire de l'ancienne langue française* (1881–1902) with the following quotation from Guiart (early fourteenth century): '*Li navré vuident les frontières*', 'the wounded left the front line' (to join the rear).[103] When used as a noun, the word necessarily supposed two enemies, face to face, either side of a line separating them.[104] In this sense it had to contend with a number of other terms *fins* (from the Latin *fines*), *confins, mètes* (from the Latin *metae*), *bornes, termes, limitations*. Finally it supplanted them and came to have as its principal meaning the external boundaries of a territorial state.

States tend to act like individuals. Men insist on staking out their home ground, as animals in the wild defend what they consider to be their territory. Vauban told Louvois in 1673[105] to advise the king to extend, as any attentive landowner would, 'his *pré quarré*' (literally square patch; in other words his property) along the northern frontier, where the positions recently acquired by the French were enclaves, isolated in Spanish territory. 'Believe me Sir, preach always the squaring not of the circle but of the patch; it is a fine and fair thing to be able to hold your possessions in both hands'. Staking out, marking boundaries, establishing claims – all territorial states obstinately sought this kind of security. All of them, whether they were in their infancy or in their old age and battle-scarred by painful experience, were fascinated, obsessed and haunted by the 'Great Wall of China' complex. The unfortunate fate of France's own Wall of China – the Maginot Line – will long continue to carry disproportionate weight retrospectively, clouding analysis.

Fortifications were not only related to fear, anxiety and forethought, they were also evidence of wealth and strength. There were even fortifications built for prestige. They went hand in hand with the growth of France as a political unit, testifying to the increasing might of the state. This was already happening well before Vauban's time: it was the Capet monarchy that erected the keep of the Louvre, built the castles along the Epte and Seine valleys, as well as La Roche-Guyon facing the Château-Gaillard.

Any administrative boundary, and *a fortiori* any political frontier, once properly marked out, has a tendency to persist and become fixed for all time. Its trace seems to be extraordinarily difficult to wipe out. Such was the case in France of the many diocesan boundaries, based on the former territories of the Gallo-Roman cities: they lasted undisturbed from their origins in pre-Carolingian times or thereabouts, until the 1789 Revolution.

The durability of state frontiers is plain to see. The territorial divisions of colonial America, laid down in Madrid or Lisbon, effectively drew up in advance what would be the map of the independent states of the twentieth century: indeed these states had frontiers before they even came into being – frontiers that were sometimes paradoxical, and not always appropriate. Similarly we have seen with our own eyes how the new African states, on gaining independence, have remained within the old colonial frontiers, whether these were suitable or not; whether this was to their disadvantage and provoked conflict, or whether to their advantage, as in the case of Algeria, whose newly-independent state inherited not only the inter-African links of colonial Algeria, but also the Sahara and its oil.

History thus tends to provide frontiers with roots, as if they had been caused by natural accidents; once incorporated into geography, they become difficult to move thereafter.

All the same, frontiers originally needed time to become incorporated into the soil. Thirty years ago, I planted cuttings of Canadian poplar round my house in Savoie. Now they have taken over and look like forming a barrier. But thirty years is nothing in the creation and durability of a frontier. It was not much more than thirty years ago that the frontiers fixed at Yalta were carved on to the living body of Europe. It will be at least a hundred years before anyone can be sure of their definite duration.

The treaty of Verdun (843)

The essential feature of the sacrosanct treaty of Verdun (August 843) was probably the fact that its provisions lasted so many hundreds of years, becoming consolidated through the blind complicity of time.

It was over a thousand years ago after all that the unwieldy Empire of Louis the Pious was divided among his three sons: to Louis went 'eastern Francia' (that is Germany); to Charles the Fat, 'western Francia', the early version of France; and between the two, the impossible domain of Lotharingia fell to the eldest son Lothair, who assumed the title of emperor and received with his portion the two capital cities, Aix-la-Chapelle in the north and Rome in the south – linked by an absurd strung-out corridor of territory about 200 kilometres wide and 1,500 long.

This 'isthmic' folly bestrode the Alps and was prolonged into Italy beyond Benevento. The negotiators of the treaty, the 'experts' as Roger Dion calls them,[106] had designed it to maintain the fiction of an Empire. And if they granted Louis the German the city of Mainz and a portion of the left bank of the Rhine – a generous gift – it was so that he should have some vineyards at his disposal!

All these circumstantial (and therefore in theory fragile) reasons do not, needless to say, explain the incredible longevity of the clauses drawn up at Verdun. For France was to remain, for centuries on end, bounded to the east by the frontier known as that of the 'four rivers', Rhône, Saône, Meuse and Scheldt (although it barely reached any of them except the Scheldt). The fragile zone of Lotharingia, it is true, lasted less than a century; but it was absorbed in 936 into a Germany soon to become the Holy Roman and Germanic Empire, and by now displaying a vigour superior to that of the last Carolingians and the first Capets. It was therefore the 'Germanic' frontier that France faced across the line of the four rivers.

This was not, as it happened, a restive frontier – at least so long as the French monarchy had its hands full on the Atlantic and Channel coasts (the quarter from which English attacks came). What was more, the Germanic frontier was on both sides embedded and entangled in the extraordinary mosaic of feudal powers, subdivided into a thousand little states. But that did not prevent the eastern frontier being very much alive. Despite all the conflicts and wars, attacks, litigation and legal quarrels between the feudal princes – or perhaps because of such incidents – the local populations who were the victims of such carryings-on were well aware of the frontier line. The Biesme for instance, is a little stream running through the Argonne, whose only claim to fame arises from the glassworks along its banks. But in the treaty of Verdun, it had the honour of being chosen as the boundary, for a short stretch, between the kingdom and the Empire (then in Lothair's portion), and therefore of being the boundary between the dioceses of Verdun and Châlons-sur-Marne. The local inhabitants, when asked in 1288, could perfectly well distinguish '[the lands] this side

FIGURE 33
The division of Charlemagne's empire by the Treaty of Verdun in 843

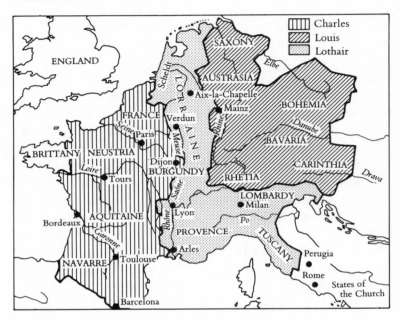

After G. Berthier de Sauvigny, *Histoire de France*.

of the said course, which are in the Empire, and those beyond the said course which are in the kingdom of France',[107] evidence that the frontier of the kingdom was a reality for the people who crossed it or who lived nearby. Even today, the Biesme separates the *département* of Marne from that of Meuse, and since the *départements* correspond to dioceses, it also continues to divide the diocese of Verdun from that of Châlons.

But all this is merely a description rather than an explanation of the longevity of the frontiers. We are told that the treaty of Verdun was a 'compromise between the rival claims of the three sons of Louis the Pious. What preoccupied the parties to the division most was the equality of their shares. They chose as frontiers water

courses, that is lines of demarcation that were purely geographical'
– and also convenient.[108] I accept these remarks by Gaston Zeller,
or the similarly geographical comments of Roger Dion. But in the
end, if the division became meaningful, if it became fixed in time,
was this not because linguistic frontiers were already, in the ninth
and tenth centuries, becoming entrenched along the lines they still
have today, over ten centuries later? The political arrangement was
thus confirmed on the ground by pre-existing cultural realities.
We ought therefore to restore to the Strasbourg oaths (14 February
842, eighteen months before the treaty of Verdun) the importance
they used to receive in traditional history books. In front of their
assembled armies, Lothair's two brothers bound themselves by an
oath, pronounced by Charles the Fat in a 'Germanic dialect', by
Louis (later known as the German) in a Romance dialect and by the
troops in their respective languages. Thus on either side the ribbon
of Lotharingian territory, we can witness the pre-birth, the first,
tentative emergence of *two* national communities, each slowly taking shape, and identified by its language. It is too soon of course to
speak of nationalities or of precise linguistic boundaries. But the
Seine is after all already the Seine even at its source, at Saint-
Germain-La-Feuille. And in 1914, we French and Germans were
still fighting for possession of Lotharingia.

Four crucial years: 1212, 1213, 1214, 1216

An example of the slow-motion history that governs the outline of
frontiers is provided in an article by Yves Renouard,[109] on a later
period. He argues that the political map of western Europe was
'drawn' once and for all in the course of four decisive years, 1212,
1213, 1214, and 1216 – four years which were to fix for good a
situation and a balance of power that had developed slowly over
time.

As the thirteenth century opened, four super-states stood poised
to spill over their frontiers: Spain under the Almohads, having
rolled back its northern frontier and having achieved the unity of

North Africa and a large part of Spain under the banner of Islam; secondly the Angevin empire of the Plantagenets which combined England, part of Ireland and the long seaward-facing sector of France, from the mouth of the Bresle to that of the Bidassoa; thirdly an Occitanian empire which was potentially being created or foreshadowed by the agreement between Toulouse, Zaragoza and Barcelona, and which nursed the ambition of acquiring Provence across the Rhône; and finally the potential super-state created by the victory of Philip Augustus who, after breaking through at Château-Gaillard, entered Rouen without bloodshed on 24 June 1204, and was theoretically poised to control the northern seaboard.

But one after another these super-states failed in their ambitions: they remained enmeshed in the toils of the old frontiers, like a runner becoming entangled in a knot of cables across his path. And their falls were sudden. Almohad Spain was crushed by Christian forces at Las Navas de Tolosa (1212). In 1213, Simon de Montfort triumphed at Muret, over the count of Toulouse and Peter II of Aragon. In 1214, admittedly, Philip Augustus was victorious on the battlefield of Bouvines against the coalition fomented by John Lackland of England. This was a high point for French dreams of grandeur: John was in trouble; the English barons forced from him the concessions of Magna Carta (1215) and in the following year appealed to the son of Philip Augustus, the future Louis VIII (the Lion), who landed in England. But once more the ambitious edifice crumbled: on John's death, the barons rallied to his son Henry III, and Louis had to return to France.

So these episodes all ended the same way. The old frontiers stood the test: they would endure. Perhaps this was because Europe was already, by the beginning of the thirteenth century if not before, a coherent universe, a combination within which political individualities had been created. They all kept each other at bay, immobilized by reciprocal pressures. We should accept Walther Kienast's contention[110] that there was from *very early on* within Europe a sort of balance of power before the term was coined, a machine that broke any attempt at hegemony, at 'universal monarchy', to use an expression from the sixteenth century. Failed empires litter the eventful history of Europe.

These immobilized giants in fact reveal the existence of deeply-rooted forces. Take, in the first place, the battle of Las Navas de Tolosa in 1212: here, Christian civilization, still clinging on in the Peninsula (and even in Muslim Spain, with the Mozarab Christians)[111] forced the retreat of the massive presence of Islam, another civilization but one whose advance had run out of steam and energy in the Iberian peninsula.

Then there is the clear case of England and France. After 1066 and the Norman conquest, England ceased to be an island, and did not have either the intelligence or the good fortune to become one again until 1558 – and then only unwillingly – when François de Guise recaptured Calais (the English ought to put up a statue to this man who unwittingly laid the foundation for their future greatness). During the Middle Ages, France and England (or at least their ruling classes) were experiencing essentially the same adventure: the Plantagenets, as their name implies, were French princes. And yet notwithstanding the princely feuds, the remarriage of Eleanor of Aquitaine, the short-sighted heroics of Richard Coeur de Lion, the mistakes or cowardice of John Lackland, or the prudence, cunning and good fortune of Philip Augustus, underneath the surface, an England was taking shape, and a France was taking shape. When Philip Augustus captured Rouen, he cut in half the long, sinuous, sea-based empire of the Plantagenets. By getting rid of Louis, the future French king, England succeeded in sending France back across the Channel. Either side of the straits of Dover, the breach signalled the birth of an original national unit, a cultural entity; as such, slow to mature but assured of a long future.

The Albigensian crusade, an explosion within Christendom and not, like the other Crusades, outside the Christian world, posed similar but even more complex problems. The result is however plain to see. To outward appearances, order was restored: the heresy was vanquished and in 1271 Languedoc was attached by inheritance to the French crown. Yes, but at the end of this war between two civilizations, the frontier of the land of *oc*, while in theory absorbed, in fact persisted: a long wound which would never heal, a key problem in French history which has never found and will not admit of, any perfect solution.

France's 'natural' frontiers

All this helps us to tackle more effectively the thorny and perhaps false problem of France's so-called 'natural' frontiers – those of ancient Gaul, the earliest prefiguration of France: namely the Rhine, the Alps, the Mediterranean, the Pyrenees, the Atlantic, the Channel and the North Sea. Under Rome, these frontiers were consolidated. And it was in this huge area that Gaul continued to exist under its Merovingian and Carolingian masters. It managed to preserve its territory intact not only in the south as far as the Pyrenees (where it expanded to take in the Spanish marches), the Alps, and Italy (where Lombardy was one of Charlemagne's conquests), but also in the Rhineland and along the interminable sea coast – where Viking raids from the ninth century on caused havoc and devastation but eventually died down without having necessarily been the unspeakable catastrophe historians have described. In short, Gaul succeeded for centuries in maintaining the near-integrity of its territory, long enough at any rate to assimilate it to its destiny, to bring together its populations and civilizations and teach them to co-exist.

In his history of France, Henri Martin does not hesitate to write that 'the new France, the old France and Gaul are one and the same moral person'.[112] We may pass over the expression 'moral person', which is not one I would have chosen; the obvious point being made is that there has been a continuity, a succession of realities, taking over from and in turn determining each other.

But we should not imagine either that the conquest of the limits of ancient Gaul, of 'our' so-called natural frontiers, has always been the guiding principle of French expansion, some sort of genetic programme to which our country's rulers have one after another conformed, with a clear vision of the territory to be reoccupied. The policies of the French kings were contingent, pragmatic, trusting to luck. Any success called for justification (never in the same terms twice) and created new temptations.

In the first place, strange as it may seem, ancient Gaul was for a long time absent from the country's historical memory – simply forgotten. Medieval historians and chroniclers presented France's past as a jumble of princely chronicles, adorned with absurd origin myths. Nicolas Gilles's book *Les très élégantes et copieuses annales et croniques des très chrétiens et très excellens modérateurs des belliqueuses Gaules* (which appeared in 1492 and of which many editions were produced until 1621), despite the mention of 'Gaules' in the title, contains nothing about Gaul or the Gauls, and is all about the kings of France and their origins, which are derived from the golden legend of Priam, Hector and Francion, the supposed Trojan ancestors of the Franks!

For the French of those days, the famous phrase *Nos ancêtres les Gaulois* ('our ancestors the Gauls') did not exist. For them, writes Ferdinand Lot, 'our country's history began with the arrival of the Franks', under Francion. 'They did not even ask themselves who had inhabited Gaul previously . . . or rather they replied: the Romans'.[113] Etienne Pasquier was the first to realize (1560) that some genuine ideas about Gaul and its inhabitants might be gleaned by studying Caesar's commentaries. It is hardly an exaggeration to say that this was when the Gauls entered French 'history'. For this we must thank Etienne Pasquier and a few of his contemporaries (notably the astonishing La Popelinière), the founding fathers of a history that was no longer *chanson de geste* or legendary chronicle, but research based on documents.[114] Alas, this new history, the fruit of French humanism, died soon after birth, and the hostile reaction of the seventeenth century, running 'against the grain'[115] of the model devised by the new historians, once more introduced a smokescreen. As late as 1714, the scholar Nicolas Fréret was imprisoned in the Bastille for trying to prove that the Franks were Germans! And the defendant had expressed his views only within the walls of the Academy of Inscriptions and Belles Lettres.[116]

In the circumstances, with such ignorance about Gaul, how could anyone have referred to the natural frontiers which it had indeed possessed? Before the declarations of the revolutionaries, little was heard of these frontiers and any allusions we can glean are but scraps of evidence, a few pebbles by the roadside.

In 1444 for instance, first Charles VII (although still engaged in war with England), and then his son, the future Louis XI, led their troops through Lorraine, Alsace and as far as Bâle, after a series of conspiracies and commitments, with the secret objective of ridding France of undesirable soldiers and at the same time of blocking the expansionist ambitions of the duke of Burgundy, Philip the Good, who for his part had dreams of reconstituting the kingdom of Lothair created by the treaty of Verdun. On this occasion, Charles VII maintained that the kingdom of France had long been deprived of its natural frontiers which ought by rights to reach to the Rhine, and that it was time to restore its sovereignty there, since the territories 'being this side of the river of Rhine . . . used to be the property of and belong to our forbears the kings of France'.[117] In the context of the period, the 'forbears' in question were the great Frankish kings, Clovis and above all Charlemagne, the hero of the medieval chronicles and *chansons de geste*, whom the French kings described as their 'progenitor'. At the end of his life, Louis XI even started a sort of cult of the holy Charlemagne, and 28 January was declared a holiday in all the towns in France in his honour. It was in the fifteenth century too that a curious ceremony first began: 'At every coronation, the new king of France would send to Aix-la-Chapelle the pall used at the funeral of his predecessor, for it to be spread out on Charlemagne's tomb'.[118] This ceremony was observed until the death of Louis XV in 1774. So one understands a little better a remark by Gaspar de Saulx[119] who in his *Mémoires* regretted that Henri II's journey to the Rhine in 1552 led to the conquest only of the *Trois Evêchés*, the Three Bishoprics. Why not Alsace and Lorraine too? 'It would,' he says, 'have meant the restoration of the kingdom of Austrasia', the heritage of one of the sons of Clovis, which was later on several occasions reunited with the French kingdom. Rather than the natural frontiers of the Gaul of antiquity then, it was the prestigious memory of the Frankish kings and the great emperor himself that the kings of France summoned up whenever they had to defend their rights of inheritance, so to speak.

To the rather slim number of references to natural frontiers we can further add only a curious allusion in 1558 and a clear formulation in 1642.

The curious allusion comes from a little-known Lorrainer, Jean Le Bon, who wrote 'When Paris drinks the Rhine, all Gaul will have its end' (*sa fin*), to be read as meaning 'France will have its frontier'.[120]

As for the clear formulation, this comes in Richelieu's will: 'the aim of my ministry', the cardinal is supposed to have said, 'has been to restore to France the boundaries that nature allotted it . . . to make Gaul coincide with France and, wherever the ancient Gaul existed, to restore the new'. One cannot complain of any ambiguity in this text. But it is well known that Richelieu's will was apocryphal and, what is more, translated from Latin. As evidence it can only partly be rescued by noting that it must after all have been written by someone in Richelieu's entourage and that the formula it contains therefore originated in the very centre of French policy-making. Maybe so. All the same, before 1642 one does not find any comparable text anywhere, while after 1642 we have to wait for the proclamations of the revolutionaries before we encounter once more the language attributed to Richelieu.

Since France under the monarchy did not in fact use the convenient argument about natural frontiers, and since it nevertheless proceeded to annex a number of territories, how then did it justify such conquests? In most cases, the French were content simply to seize and annex without bothering to give any pretext. But the exception proves the rule.

In 1601, France seized from the duke of Savoy the territories of Bugey, the pays de Gex and Bresse. Henri IV declared to his new subjects: 'It stands to reason that since your native tongue is French, you should be subjects of the king of France. I am quite willing that the Spanish language should remain the property of Spain, and German that of Germany, but French ought to be mine'.[121]

But this argument, which does have a certain commonsense appeal (I do not say either that it is just, or that it justifies the action) was not put forward as it might have been when the Franche-Comté, originally occupied in 1674 by the king of France (in fact by an army of Swiss mercenaries) was reconquered and annexed to the kingdom in 1678, at the peace of Nijmwegen. Nor was it heard during the annexation of Lorraine in 1766, on the death of Stanislas Leczinski. And what could possibly be said when in 1648, France moved into Alsace, a region where German dialect was spoken? No justification was offered for this occupation by force, which did not greatly interest French public opinion at the time. In 1659, at the profitable peace of the Pyrenees, France annexed, in the shape of Roussillon and Cerdagne (Cerdaña), a substantial portion of Catalonia. And on this occasion a convenient reference was briefly made to the ancient frontiers, to 'the mountains of the Pyrenees which had in ancient times divided the Gauls from Spain [and which] will in future also mark the division of these two kingdoms'.[122] But the mention of Gaul was fortuitous. During the talks held subsequently to fix the frontier, first at Céret (March–April 1660), then at Lluvia (November 1660), where they were concluded, the arguments invoked on both sides were purely legal. Neither the Pyrenees nor Gaul was mentioned.[123] When, a century later in 1752, the marquis de Paumy inspected the Roussillon frontier, he recalled in his report that

> The boundary was therefore [in 1659] based on the summit and the orientation of the Pyrenees, [and it was agreed that] the slopes of these mountains which faced the Roussillon interior would belong to France, while the slopes facing the provinces of Spain would belong to that Crown, and that the rule of watersheds would be observed, as it was on the Alpine frontiers.[124]

This was obviously a rationalization after the event.

In the end, the theory of natural frontiers did not triumph until the justifications advanced by the revolutionaries after 1789. 'Nature' was after all fashionable in the Age of Enlightenment. The argument swept all before it. 'France', declared Abbé Grégoire in 1792, 'is a unit sufficient to itself, since everywhere Nature has provided it with barriers which make it unnecessary to seek enlargement, so that our interests are in agreement with our principles'. The sentiment was repeated by Danton on 31 January 1793, shortly after the annexation pure and simple of Belgium. 'The boundaries of France are fixed by nature. We shall reach them in all four directions: towards the Ocean, the Rhine, the Alps and the Pyrenees'.[125]

Concerning the Rhine, the Germans only contradicted the French late in the day. In 1746, Frederick II of Prussia even made a declaration which rings very oddly (in French ears at least): 'One has only to take a geographical map in hand to be convinced that the natural limits of this monarchy [the French] seem to extend to the Rhine, whose course appears to have been expressly designed to separate France from Germany'.[126] Not until the *Lieder* of Ernst Moritz Arndt (1813) was the German reaction formulated: 'Der Rhein, Deutschlands Strom aber nicht Deutschlands Grenze', the Rhine, a German river, but not Germany's frontier.[127]

I do not therefore believe that the quest for France's natural frontiers was the guiding principle of French foreign policy. But setting aside all the arguments, discourses and official speeches, the fact remains that France's continuous expansion, a constant worry to the rest of Europe, was a reality. I would quarrel neither with Augustin Thierry, Henri Martin, nor Albert Sorel for drawing attention to the continuity of this policy: the Revolution simply pursued (though making rather a mess of it) the policy of the *ancien régime*. Ever since Henri II's 'journey to the Rhine' of 1552, France has been tormented by the urge to bolt the door against eastern Europe.

The sea: reached without haste, never mastered

Studies devoted to frontiers rarely mention the sea. Such is the prestige, or the superstition, attached to terra firma! And yet if a frontier means a break, a discontinuity in space, what traveller, leaving Calais, or arriving in Dover, could fail to think that he was leaving one frontier and meeting another? 'Man is a land animal', Vidal de la Blache stated firmly.[128] Charles Darwin, Englishman and exceptional traveller though he was, 'having gone round the world [in 1831] on board the *Beagle*, claimed that one only went to sea if absolutely forced to'.[129] Yet the sea exists, the coastline exists, and sailors and fleets exist too. And so do maritime frontiers, the most unarguably natural of all. The problem, in the context of French history, is to ascertain how men or history have dealt, over the centuries, with the interminable coastline of France.

In fact, apart from a number of glorious episodes, French achievements on the sea have scarcely been equal to those on dry land. The scales tip very much the other way. Caught between land and sea, France, as I have already noted, inclined towards the former. 'The French have no knowledge of the ways of the sea', remarked Philip Augustus regretfully, after taking possession in 1204 of the rich and sea-faring province of Normandy, thus clearing the way towards a maritime horizon previously all but closed to him by the Plantagenets. In the same year, 'as if to prove him right, [the French] themselves admitted, at the time of the attack on Constantinople [with the troops of the Fourth Crusade] that "they did not know as well how to manoeuvre on sea as they did on land" '. The quotation is from Geoffroi de Villehardouin.[130]

It is true that it was not until 1246 that France possessed an anchorage, or 'window' on the Mediterranean in the shape of Aigues-Mortes. Outside Normandy, the French in this period could therefore count on few sea-faring peoples. Was that why, in the following century, they lost from the start the battle of Sluys (24 June 1340) and with it the precious mastery of the sea – a disaster which left France open to English attack in the early days of the Hundred Years' War? Moreover if the situation improved on sea in 1369, it was not thanks to Charles V or Du Guesclin, but to the galleys of Henry of Trastamara, king of Castille; these had been armed to come to Du Guesclin's aid and with their bombards (a new invention) annihilated the English fleet in the roads of La Rochelle (1373). This success made possible 'the recapture of Poitou, the Saintonge and the Angoumois'.[131] In December of the same year, Charles V appointed Jean de Vienne admiral of France. Under his leadership, a fleet was created with 'modern' units, and expeditions were successfully launched off Brittany and against the English coast, causing great alarm in London. Aided by Castilian and Portuguese vessels, the French navy was an effective and sometimes victorious one at this time. But the situation quickly deteriorated; Jean de Vienne resigned his post and in 1396 was killed by the Turks on the distant battlefield of Nicopolis.

When France had regained its lost ground and, with the acquisition in 1481–2 of Provence and Marseille, completed its Mediterranean seaboard (Languedoc had already been united to the crown in 1271), a problem arose from the simple fact that the French coast was now divided into two quite different maritime sectors: on one hand the Atlantic, the Channel, the North Sea – the high roads of the future, soon to be sailed only by roundships – and on the other the Mediterranean, the scene of ancient trading achievements and home of the slender galleys which, despite a few brilliant exceptions, were no longer to play a serious role on the ocean after the last years of the sixteenth century.

France therefore needed two fleets. As a result everything had to be either multiplied – or more often divided – by two. Spain, facing the same problem (but with the advantage of having ocean and Mediterranean meet at Gibraltar) was soon (1617) looking with favour on the plans of the duke of Osuna, viceroy of Naples, and began using galleons on both the Atlantic and the Mediterranean.[132] Subsequently the ship of the line, a compromise between the longship and the roundship, came into use everywhere. But this simplification did nothing to help the French problem, which was aggravated by the hesitation invariably displayed by the authorities as to whether to concentrate their forces, either in one sector or the other, as it would sometimes have been advantageous to do. Thus in 1692, at the time of the La Hougue disaster, 'if the Toulon fleet had been able to join the Brest fleet, Tourville would have had over 80 vessels at his command, more than enough to overcome the 99 English and Dutch ships when one considers the quality of his fleet'.[133] The same fatal dispersion recurred in 1805, during the abortive plan to invade England from the Camp at Boulogne. France's maritime might was thus affected by a sort of structural weakness. Only a firm lead given by the state could have obliged the country to make the enormous effort required. A lead of this kind was rarely displayed. Both Richelieu and Colbert effectively worked to build up the fleet, but neither Louis XIV nor, above all, the Regent (who liquidated both the navy and the merchant fleet), nor Louis XV were aware of what was at stake. In fact, between the treaty of Utrecht (1713) and the treaty of Paris (1763), for the long space of fifty years, 'France's only navy was in Monsieur Vernet's paintings'.[134] Corrective action by Louis XVI (whose real hobby was the navy, not locksmithing, writes Alain Guillerm) unfortunately came too late.

Admirably located, in the centre of Europe, for continental wars, France was a victim of its geographical site where the navy was concerned. The French state was either unwilling or unable to develop to their full extent the advantages apparently bestowed upon it by both nature and history. Of its natural advantages, Pierre Gourou writes, 'there was not a country in Europe possessing such a fine stretch of coastline, varied and well-endowed. What an abundance of good harbours, lying at the mouth of great avenues leading inland!'.[135] As for historical advantages, by taking possession of Normandy, Brittany, Aquitaine, Languedoc and Provence, France acquired a collection of genuine sea-faring populations. Jean de Vienne's ships sailed alongside those of Castille and Portugal, as well as with the Basque corsairs. And the uniting of Brittany to the French state (which became definite in 1532) linked France to the leading sea-faring people of Europe in the sixteenth century. But all these gifts remained desperately under-used!

The handicap of 'the two seas' was not really the only reason. In order to conduct, or even to conceive a grand maritime policy, France would have had to disengage, as a condition *sine qua non*, from the perennial hornets' nest of war on land; to have had – like England – only one battlefront and that a maritime one; only one military budget, that of the navy. To make a choice of this order would have required good judgement, good luck, and tenacity – and the power to resist a bellicose aristocracy always ready to set off on the roads of Europe. Emile Bourgeois's still thrilling *Manuel historique de politique étrangère*[136] describes how France hesitated dramatically between land and sea, always coming down on the wrong side. Even in 1740, the aged Cardinal Fleury, at the very end of his extremely long life, energetically opposed the imminent War of the Austrian Succession. But to tell France not to fight on land was like telling it not to exist. And in any case, would Europe have allowed it to abstain?

So France's potential sea power was too often unemployed, underemployed or thwarted. French sailors, left to themselves, signed up on foreign fleets which were always short of crews. Whenever French shipbuilding revived, they flocked back home, deserting the ships of Spain, Malta, England and especially Holland, 'with displeasure to have been abroad so long and an extreme desire to serve the king usefully for the rest of their lives, praising God to see that after such long neglect of shipping',[137] France had stirred herself at last. Colbert's naval construction brought 30,000 French sailors back on to French vessels – the figure may have been exaggerated by the French ambassador at The Hague. But large numbers undoubtedly did return home.

The demands of war on land were not however solely responsible for this state of affairs. Pierre-Victor Malouet,[138] who before becoming a delegate to the Estates General and the Constituent Assembly, had served in the navy (for a longish stretch, seven years, as naval *intendant* at Toulon, where he had been appointed on 1 November 1781), put his finger on the essential obstacle which was never overcome by French policy:

Colbert himself [he writes] despite the superiority of his intelligence, was in too much of a hurry to achieve the great results of maritime power before consolidating its foundations. He knew better than anyone that it is only through large-scale export trade that one can build up a naval force and recruit to it. Everything he did to establish and encourage manufacture proves it to us; but hardly had he created a merchant marine than he appropriated its forces for war and the prodigious development of this short-lived power perished for want of nourishment; whereas our rivals, who had been two centuries ahead of us in their preparation of naval forces, were able to maintain and increase them.

So it was an economic failure – why not even call it a capitalist failure? Malouet indeed goes on to say:

Maritime trade cannot prosper under a regime of absolute power and under the weight of taxes provoked by demands for luxuries as well as those of a virtually constant state of war. Only an industrious freedom to speculate can create a class of wealthy capitalists without whom we shall never obtain that commercial activity which multiplies and sends abroad the products of the interior; we have not yet seen in our national councils nor in our nation's habits that spirit of enterprise and economy necessary to create and maintain a large merchant navy, the only solid foundation of maritime might.[139]

True enough, if a little over-stated. But one could go further: what France failed to become, for any length of time, was the leading economic power, that is the centre, of Europe. Apart from the 'continental' century of the Champagne fairs – if then – the centre of Europe, where wealth collected, was never to be France. Without this all-important privilege, I will not say that France failed to obtain anything at all, but it certainly lacked the essential elements: abundant economic production, plentiful credit, thriving business, accumulated capital, a large volume of seaborne trade – in short the power and the means to sustain a long term project. Speaking of Richelieu's positive achievements on sea, Ange Goudar rightly said: 'It would have taken a century to turn France into a great maritime power'.[140]

A perceptive witness wrote from Toulon on 26 October 1761:

France will never be powerful, or feared, or respected by her neighbours if she is not mistress of the sea and . . . an army of 20,000 men on this liquid plain would bring her more honour and profit than 200,000 men on land. In the end, whoever controls the sea controls everything.[141]

It was a role France was never able to play to the full.

CHAPTER TEN

Two case studies: Metz and Toulon

Examining case studies from the past can be a solution to a difficult research problem, cutting short endless investigations. Our frontier problem may come into this category: it covers the entire history of France and incorporates such a mass of known facts that no historian could ever master it unaided. In such circumstances, case studies, however limited and unreliable, can be a welcome resource. And if, predictably, they do not succeed in solving the problem, they do at least offer us the pleasure of seeing at close quarters what everyday life was like on the frontier in the past. This can be an instructive exercise.

So as not to indulge in too much sightseeing and storytelling, I shall confine myself to two excursions. The first will take us to Metz, on the landward frontier; the second to Toulon, on the sea. We shall learn something that is never sufficiently understood: what a burdensome, complicated and difficult task it was to govern and defend France. Especially since the defenders were often operating in the dark. The future always held shocks and surprises.

The north-eastern and eastern frontiers

Why Metz? Most of France's frontiers are of the kind that can almost without a pang of guilt be described as 'natural': the sea, the Pyrenees, the Alps, the Jura – frontiers defended by natural features, making lighter the task of men. In 1940, during the unprecedented military collapse of France, the Alpine frontier held firm.[142]

France's most artificial and dangerous frontier runs from the North Sea to the Rhine. It is a frontier that has been fabricated and refabricated by political leaders, by military commanders, by engineers, and by the many hazards of history. The Rhine, which seems to close it to the north-east, has nothing in common with the Channel. Its appearance of affording protection is illusory. And in any case, France's political frontier did not extend to the Rhine until 1648, and then only in Alsace, while along the rest of its course, from Bâle to the sea, French presence has been episodic only: from 1795 to 1814, or from 1919 to 1930,[143] when the left bank of the Rhine was occupied by the French and their allies.

This fragile frontier to the east and north-east has also been the most sensitive and uneasy, perpetually on the alert against the threat posed by aggressive and formidable neighbours. The latter learned that this was where the house of France had to be attacked to have a chance of forcing an entry. Charles V provided the first demonstration in 1544: setting out from Luxembourg, he went as far as Saint-Dizier, which he captured, then advanced along the Marne to Meaux, at the very gates of Paris. The exercise was repeated in 1557, 1596, 1636, 1708, 1814, 1870, 1914 and 1940. So when people say that history is irreversible by definition and never repeats itself, we have a right to be sceptical. History often lacks imagination. It can be set in its ways.

This frontier was like all frontiers dating from before the nineteenth century. It should on no account be imagined as a clear-cut line on the modern model: the linear frontier, 'sharp and abrupt' as Ernest Lavisse called it,[144] with its double row of customs posts, only dates 'from yesterday. As late as the treaties . . . of Louis XV, we can see by the large number of *enclaves* and *exclaves* by which states overlapped each other, that the concept of the frontier line did not yet exist'.[145] In 1771, two French surveyors, Chauchard and Jolly were detailed, under General de Grandpré, to map out the frontier from Dunkerque to Landau, in northern Alsace. They had to work over a strip of territory three or four leagues wide.[146]

So the frontier was always a broad band, and usually poorly marked. The consequences may be imagined. Enclaves and exclaves (which are the same thing viewed from different sides of

FIGURE 34
France's eastern defences

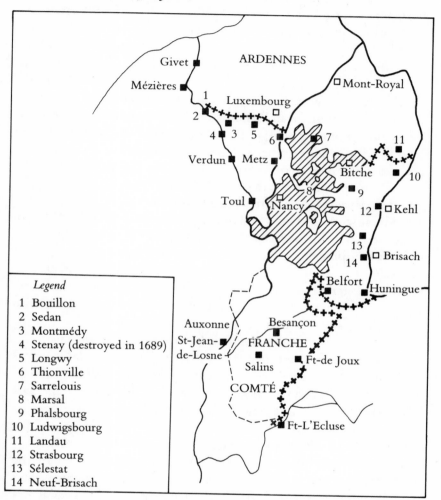

Legend
1 Bouillon
2 Sedan
3 Montmédy
4 Stenay (destroyed in 1689)
5 Longwy
6 Thionville
7 Sarrelouis
8 Marsal
9 Phalsbourg
10 Ludwigsbourg
11 Landau
12 Strasbourg
13 Sélestat
14 Neuf-Brisach

Along the 'sensitive' frontier running through the Ardennes, Lorraine, Alsace, and the Franche-Comté, many forts were lost or saved during the interminable wars of the seventeenth and eighteenth centuries. After Colonel Rocolle, *2000 ans de fortification française*, 1973.

course) often consisted of villages, groups of villages, bourgs or even small towns – a fortified position inside enemy territory was a permanent look-out point on to the other side. Enclaves and exclaves could only survive from day to day thanks to a *modus vivendi* allowing free passage and practised by both sides – as article 16 of the Peace of Nijmwegen even formally stipulated, concerning the frontier between France and the Spanish Netherlands. Inevitably there were conflicts, incidents, miniature wars. The tax farmer of the domains in Flanders in November 1682, was anxious (put yourself in his place!) to forbid the subjects of the French king who lived in frontier villages from 'going to drink at the inns [in the nearest villages] of Spain [sic] . . . on the pretext that the drinks are cheaper there than in the inns subject to His Majesty's taxes; they therefore habitually go [over the border] which causes considerable prejudice [to His Majesty's said taxes]'.[147] I am afraid, replied the *intendant* Demadrys, that this is allowed by the peace of Nijmwegen. However, since war was on the point of breaking out again, the Spanish in 1689 themselves forbade free movement across the frontier. Be that as it may, the *intendant* explained on that occasion, we shall do the same on our side, with His Majesty's permission of course.[148]

Could this sort of thing not have been avoided, we may wonder, by drawing the frontiers geometrically, as was done in later times? Probably not, because force of habit was a powerful obstacle. There was also a certain amount of interested duplicity on the part of the states involved, along this uncertain north-east frontier, in particular by the French crown. Along the whole length of the frontier, the crown made good use of the thousand pretexts for quarrels and disputes arising more or less inevitably out of the imprecision of the frontier line, out of confusion over feudal dues and allegiances, uncertainties over disputed vassallage, and not least out of the delight taken in legal niceties by the men of law. The latter were hardly likely to let such good occasions slip. Here was material for a long-running farce, as the lawyers manoeuvred in the interests of shaky claims, resorting to all sorts of sharp practice under a cloak of injured legal respectability. The French authorities, writes the historian Nelly Girard d'Albissin, 'avoided

FIGURE 35
Vauban's 'pré carré'

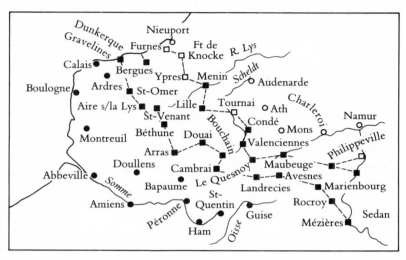

After Colonel Rocolle, *2000 ans de fortification française.*

any treaty on the boundaries – texts were difficult to wriggle out of – preferring instead the infinite possibilities of juridical extension permitted by feudal institutions, a policy which reached its apogee at the time of the *chambres de réunion*'.[149] These sittings, in particular the one held at Strasbourg in 1681, coincided with France's increase in power after the peace of Nijmwegen (1678). In the aftermath of the treaty, there was therefore a great temptation to find some pretext to seize Strasbourg and its bridge over the Rhine. After all, the imperial armies had twice, in 1675 and 1676, obtained from the city fathers free passage over the bridge at Strasbourg. And twice they had surprised Turenne's army from the rear.

But whether clearly drawn or not, the frontier always posed more or less the same defence problems, and these virtually dictated an undertaking that was frighteningly expensive, yet always precarious. Modern fortifications, reinvented in the early sixteenth century by Italian engineers, had spread throughout

Europe, where all the essential elements of siege warfare were soon entrenched: bastions, cavaliers, demi-lunes and crossfiring posts became common coin. Vauban's century began before the marshal himself (1633–1707) had even been born.

Between the North Sea and the Rhine, the frontier consisted broadly of two sectors.

First of all, from Dunkerque to the Meuse (Givet, Mézières), stretched what is sometimes called 'the iron frontier', very largely conceived if not built by Vauban, and christened the 'pré carré' by Colonel Rocolle, in memory of the marshal.[150] In fact the king himself seems to have been the prime mover behind this massive undertaking. It consisted, as the map in Figure 35 shows, of a double line of fortified towns.[151] A third line, further south, was composed of the old fortresses on the banks of the Somme, the former frontier of the kingdom. The latter, of old-fashioned design, would have been quite inadequate in themselves. But on the eve of the battle of Denain (1712), Louis XIV, who had entrusted Villars with the last army France now possessed, explained to him that he intended, in the event of defeat, to retreat across the Somme. 'I know this river well', he told him, 'it is very difficult to cross; there are some forts, and I should count on reaching Péronne or Saint-Quentin, there to assemble all the remaining troops, in order to make one last stand with you and either perish together or save the state, for I shall never allow the enemy to approach my capital'.[152]

This enormous complex was not a continuous line, like the Roman *limes*, the Great Wall of China, or even the Maginot Line, but it was strongly defended by a scatter of forts. Their aim was to block, delay, harass and divide any potential invader.

From the Meuse to the Rhine on the other hand, that is from Mézières to Landau, there was no such densely fortified system. The situation was thus the reverse of France's position in 1940, when we had fortified the 'second sector', from Montmédy to the Rhine, but left unprotected by any Maginot Line the *pré carré* of Vauban's time: with sad results.

It is true that in Vauban's day, a great natural barrier protected the frontier between the Meuse and the Rhine (except to the south where its weakness was at once historic, political and strategic). This natural barrier, stretching from Givet to Bitche, consisted of the Ardennes, a low-lying plateau of ancient rocks, infertile, marshy in places and covered with a dense forest of trees growing closely together though not very high, with only a few clearings, a few 'miserable towns'[153] (Luxembourg, Arlon) and even more miserable villages. Between Mézières-Givet and Luxembourg, the forest formed a considerable obstacle: the major deforestations of the nineteenth and especially the twentieth centuries have still not made much impression on this vast woodland. Note however, for anything was possible, that in May 1794, General Jourdan set out from Arlon and crossed the southern Ardennes to join the army in the north, thus enabling him to win on 26 June the decisive battle of Fleurus.

It is infinitely easier to cross this major obstacle by way of the two narrow breaches in it formed by the Meuse and Moselle valleys (similar, though on a less grand scale, to the 'heroic trench' cut by the Rhine through the schist massif of the Rhineland, of which the Ardennes forms the western part). It was along these two valleys that there lay the fortified towns: Verdun, Stenay (razed to the ground in 1689), Mézières, Bouillon and Givet on the Meuse; Metz, Thionville,[154] Mont-Royal on the Moselle. If one also bears in mind the strongholds built along the Chiers and Sarre, tributaries of the Moselle, there is only one zone that appears particularly weak, the stretch from Sarrelouis or Bitche to the Rhine, practically as far as Landau. It was through this breach that France was invaded in 1792 and 1814.

These various points of strength or weakness along the eastern frontier were closely watched, especially since the French were hemmed in from the rear, to the south, by Lorraine – in theory independent, undoubtedly hostile and constantly manoeuvred from outside. Within this large political unit – stretched out between Champagne, Burgundy, the Franche-Comté, Alsace and the archbishoprics of Trèves and Luxembourg – the territory of the Three Bishoprics, Metz, Toul and Verdun (or, as it was usually called, the *généralité* of Metz) formed a kind of archipelago in the middle of a sea. 'We are in the midst of Lorraine', the aldermen of

335

Metz explained yet again to the king on 3 May 1707. 'There is not enough within the territory [of our] country to feed . . . the inhabitants for three months. And all the wood used for buildings, all the grain and the necessities of life come to us from Lorraine'.[155] Lorraine was therefore a neighbour which had to be tolerated and humoured, as the source of all sustenance. But it was also a constant danger: a moment of inattention, and the enemy might with a single bound reach Nancy and dig in. So the safest thing for the French to do, if war threatened, was to occupy Lorraine, to live in it as if in conquered territory, seizing the forts, levying the taxes normally levied by the duke, blatantly creating new ones, selling offices, appointing new office-holders on annual stipends, and so on. Thus Lorraine was occupied from 1633 to 1661; from 1670 to 1697; and from 1702 to 1714, that is for 57 out of 81 years! The danger from the south was thus averted, if not eliminated.

Why Metz?

The importance of Metz was that it lay at a comparatively weak and therefore sensitive spot on the frontier. Louis XIV, whom we very mistakenly think of as spending all his time in the Louvre or Versailles, stayed six times in Metz. Vauban told him, 'The other forts in the kingdom protect the provinces, but Metz protects the state',[156] in other words, France. 'To hasten the entire fortification of this stronghold', Vauban declared, 'every good Frenchman ought to bring a hodful of stone and earth'. Turenne was equally categorical:

> Metz alone can serve as a recourse in time of misfortune or after a military defeat, to provide refuge for an army, succour the surrounding areas and protect all communications to the rear. This fort alone, properly organized, would be able to stop all the forces of the Empire put together.[157]

– the Holy Roman Empire he meant, which might one day send

massive forces against Alsace and Lorraine, through the Palatinate and Luxembourg.

During the period I chose as suitable for a case study, roughly from the Dutch War (1672) until the end of the War of the Spanish Succession (1714), Metz was in fact out of the direct firing line. This comparatively peaceful spell was the result both of precautionary measures and of chance: for instance the occupation of strategic points like Luxembourg in 1684 or the scorched earth policy applied methodically to the towns and countryside of the Palatinate in 1688 and 1689 – a dreadful military imposition which did not even have the desired military results. So when it came to the War of the Spanish Succession (1702–1714) – the most dramatic of all Louis XIV's wars – the Metz sector was of only secondary importance. Fighting went on in the Netherlands and in Vauban's *pré carré*, on the right bank of the Rhine as far as Bavaria, on the Danube, in Italy, in Spain – and Metz was marginal to all these operations. The only alerts were caused by a few attacks by imperial 'hussars', who now and again 'devoured' the plains, reaching villages only two or three leagues from the town, where Lorrainer informers were on hand to guide them.

This being so, instead of Metz – which, although always on the alert, did nothing but watch the enemy from a distance like the heroes of *Tartar Steppe* – would I not have done better to choose Ypres, or perhaps Lille, a city which became French only in 1668 and was then fortified according to plans designed by Vauban himself? Fortifications or not, Lille was captured by Prince Eugene on 23 October 1708 and occupied by the Dutch.[158] But the allies were brought up short by other forts in the *pré carré* and were unable, after the slaughter at Malplaquet (11 September 1709) to advance on Paris, since it would have meant leaving behind them a still powerful French army which did indeed, on 12 July 1712, crush them at Denain. In short, Lille was in the thick of some dramatic episodes which testify to the tenacity and in the end the success of the French war effort. But by choosing Lille, I should have found myself (as will be the case in my second sample, Toulon) dealing with the exceptional circumstances of wartime. The advantage of Metz is that it can tell us about the ordinary, everyday, monotonous defence effort – fortifications, supplies, troop and garrison movements, reconnaissance expeditions – continuously called for, merely to guard the frontier. There is more to be learnt from Metz than from Lille. At least I believe so.

War in slow motion

Metz was 'a head and place of deposit'[159] or as we should say, a supply base, at once warehouse, point of arrival and of dispatch. Matériel, rations, horses, carriages, money and men flowed constantly into the town. But the chief problem was always the movement of troops. For the townspeople of Metz in the past, as they watched the soldiers arriving, departing or taking up quarters in the town and its surrounds, the army was by no means an unobtrusive visitor. We learn from the *Recueil journalier* (daily record) of a Metz lawyer that in about November 1683, that is before the renewed outbreak of hostilities,

> they began . . . to sound the alarm in Metz, when the troops were about to arrive. And so that people would know which gate they were coming in by, the bell sounded once after the alarm had been rung, to indicate that they would come in by the Porte Saint Thiébault gate, twice if they were coming by the Porte Mazelle, three times if it was the Porte des Allemands, four times for the Pontiffroy, and five times for the Pont des Morts; and they began to hoist on the belfry of the big church a white flag or standard when it was the infantry and a red one for the cavalry.[160]

It was, I believe, on the great bell known as La Mutte[161] hung in the municipal belfry in 1605, that these warnings were sounded.

Of these troops, some were just 'passing through', having been sent sometimes very long distances, depending on the degree of urgency, to fight in Flanders or Alsace. Understandably, they were preferred to the billeted troops, who caused great commotion every year when the dreaded time came round for winter quarters.

Then, whether there was a war on or not, the town was regularly swamped with foot-soldiers, cavalrymen and horses, all in search of lodgings.

To accommodate troops in winter, the town could offer (since the homes of the privileged were exempted) only 2,400 houses for requisitioning. These dwellings were small and cramped; fewer than forty of them even ran to an upper storey. The housing crisis was of course the same in Metz as in other garrison towns: 'the troops come here in great numbers and . . . the places to lodge them are very small'.[162] Somehow they had to be crammed in.

One report in May 1693 tells us that 'this winter there were few townspeople in Metz and Verdun who did not have at least six cavalrymen or soldiers billeted on them all winter and [even] the poorest had three'.[163]

Just imagine what it must have been like to have three soldiers billeted in the cramped shop of an artisan! In 1691, the gravediggers (the poorest of the poor) from the parish of Sainte-Croix in Metz were in despair: 'none of us [has] more than a little room in which we lodge', they said, a room that 'has to be given up to the discretion of the military whenever . . . they pass through'.[164]

There were times when even the privileged were obliged to open their doors, exemptions notwithstanding. In 1707, the clergy, led by the bishop of Toul himself, set an example. This discouraged grumblers and undermined protests, but it also had the effect of deterring seekers after office, who very often, in Metz as elsewhere, only made this considerable financial investment if their office, profitable or otherwise, exempted them from lodging troops.

Troopers billeted on the townspeople might of course be insolent and thoughtless. If underpaid, they became dangerous. Soldiers were invariably pilferers, and were prepared on occasion to traffic in billet papers,[165] to deal illegally in tobacco or to smuggle salt,[166] an activity endemic all over France. The military authorities tried to keep them under control and sometimes handed down punishments. But without much conviction, since the soldiers had good cause for discontent: above all the non-

FIGURE 36
Size of garrisons in Metz military zone

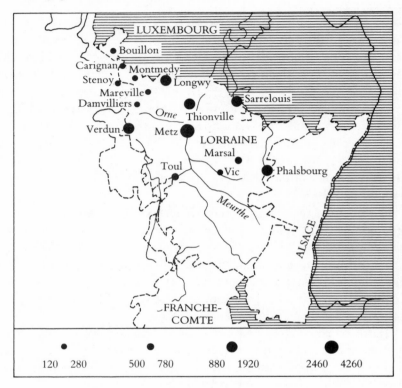

The circles indicate the number of men garrisoned in each
town, calculated from the number of daily rations issued.
From G. Duby, *Atlas historique*.

arrival of their pay, the 'prêt', and the inadequacy and poor quality
of the food. In 1710, the bread provided for the garrison in the citadel of Metz was sold at an excessive price 'per ration', and was
made 'half of barley, half of oats'.[167]

Riots were always on the point of breaking out. The *intendant* of
Metz, Saint-Contest, was at dinner on 14 January 1712, when there
appeared in the street and in the courtyard of the house 'three hundred soldiers of this garrison'. He addressed them, learnt that their

pay was late, 'that they had looted that morning all the markets and several shops'. They were now in front of him, 'sword in hand . . . throwing stones and lumps of ice and preventing my servants from leaving'. Law and order was eventually restored. 'A few of the officers of the garrison, hearing the noise, came and chased them away, giving the mutineers a hiding'.[168]

As a rule, the town was comparatively calm, with both the municipal authorities and the police of 'archers' keeping order and seeing that the curfew was observed. But in the countryside, it was very different, especially near battle lines where the enemy was close. Here anything was possible. The same *intendant* of Metz was well aware of the dangers inevitably threatening the surrounding area: 'All our [frontier] villages', he explained, 'will always be liable to be pillaged and burned, without possible remedy'. The only solution available to the victims was to pay some form of tribute or protection money to the enemy.

> I forbid people to pay tribute, [Saint-Contest reported] but I am convinced that behind my back they have already offered it and will soon be paying it in this *généralité*. And I even find people of distinction who say to me frankly: 'What do you expect us to do, to let ourselves be pillaged and our houses burned? We prefer to pay tribute'.[169]

The troops of the French king behaved no differently, needless to say, whether on foreign or friendly ground. The struggle between soldier and peasant was quite simply a class struggle, waged unremittingly. The soldier usually won, but the peasant sometimes took his revenge. In Lorraine, were the peasants of 'la Vosge' savages? Or had they turned savage? They were, an obviously biased document tells us,

> known as ruffians . . . whenever they could, they attacked the King's officers and men as they went to and fro during the winter and it was necessary to punish several of these wretches by torture on the wheel and afterwards, given their large numbers, to grant an amnesty to the rest.[170]

What the report does not say is why these peasants had left their homes to attack the soldiers. They were no doubt in the same case as the peasants of the Palatinate, so cruelly devastated (by French troops) in 1688–9, where

> ruined peasants . . . are on the road here and there around the Donnersberg,[171] a high mountain range, seven or eight leagues long between Ebernburg[172] and Keyserslutter[173] and about three or four leagues across, covered with woodland and reachable only by very narrow paths, where the peasants have built large shelters, and to which all the people of the plain retreat at the slightest alarm, with their livestock. Those who have nothing to lose, to the number of four or five hundred, often go out in small bands of seven or eight to search for food in the nearby villages.[174]

Metz, though always on the qui-vive, was not of course exposed to direct attack, as a mere village might be. But it could never drop its guard, and had constantly to be reviewing the state of the troops in the garrison, identifying (and remedying) any shortages among the soldiers, whether of shoes, linen, or indeed arms, checking whether the officers were not too young for their command, or whether a given battalion was in a fit state to move.[175] On 25 August 1702, 'there are not two hundrted soldiers properly armed, so the Rouergue battalion stationed at Metz will have to stay there', just when it was planned to send it to Marsal, a small fort in Lorraine. The same comment was made the next day, on the Forez battalion also stationed at Metz: 'Many of these men are undersized and in poor shape. It did not seem one could pick out 150 men from this battalion'.[176]

The fortitications were another worry: they had constantly to be repaired and completed. Palisades would hastily be erected, and the surrounds of the gun batteries cleared to give them a free range of fire: so gardens, orchards and perfectly good fruit trees were destroyed. Armies of peasants were also requisitioned. For the derisory wage of five sous a day,[177] (whereas it cost 25 sous to hire a horse)[178] they were set to work with pick and shovel both inside and outside the town, to cut down unripe corn in case the enemy should try to live off it at harvest time,[179] or to fell trees along the roads through the forests, to forestall ambushes.

The authorities also had to cope with new recruits in need of uniforms, newly-formed militias, invalids, and prisoners, not to mention general administration, supplies, stores, the organization of the indispensable convoys, and the nightmare of paydays. A never-ending stream of chores, tedious but urgent, had to be performed every day. Supplies in the stores had constantly to be checked and replenished: they included match for muskets, rope (much used for making bridges), shot, gunpowder (the saltpetre came from Luxembourg), as well as all the necessary containers (casks for carrying lead for instance). How were these problems to be solved with what was to hand? Could the few local rope-makers meet the demand? Shoes were not such a problem, thanks to the many shoemakers. To provide steel, a blast furnace and ironworks were built in Metz in 1706 – a sensible solution one might think, but the tilt-hammer made such a noise that the townspeople protested loudly. There was at once talk of moving the works.[180]

In one respect the authorities at Metz were fortunate: horses, which the army required in large numbers both as saddle and draught animals, were easy to come by: Alsace and Lorraine were the best-stocked of French provinces in this respect. Horses were despatched from Metz to Italy, if the army needed them. There was still the considerable problem of feeding them, whether the horses were stationed inside the garrison or, even worse, attached to troops on the move and needing fodder sent to them. 'I am on my way as fast as I can', the *intendant* at Metz wrote on 18 May 1702, 'to levy as many oats as I can find, quietly [i.e. as discreetly as possible] and at the cheapest rates'.[181] But, he asked, should the convoys be sent to the Meuse, that is towards the royal army in Flanders, or to the Moselle, that is towards the troops in Germany? The cavalry stationed in the town was also asking for huge quantities of hay, and the horses had to be found forage quarters, just as the men had to be found winter quarters.

It was of course rations for the men that always posed the biggest problems, although it was less easy to reduce the horses' pittance than the troops' rations. Everything was difficult. Meat, since there were no markets close at hand, came from Franche-Comté, Lorraine and Switzerland.[182] Buying grain was straightforward only in years of good harvest – 1699 for instance[183] – but here as elsewhere, even in the fertile Meuse valley, good years were infrequent. The harvest failed completely in 1698 and already by the autumn, no grain was available in the region. The Jewish merchants of Metz, acting as a consortium under the leadership of Cerf Lévy and Abraham Schaub,[184] bought 17,000 sacks of grain at Frankfurt and offered them to the *intendant* of Metz, Turgot (grandfather of the economist). The contract fixed the price at 22 *livres* per sack, so the whole consignment was a matter of 374,000 *livres*. The *intendant* hesitated: should he sign the contract on his own initiative, given the urgency of the situation, without waiting for instructions from Versailles? In the end he decided to sign and asked the controller-general on 9 October 1698,[185] to be so good as to 'ask His Majesty to approve the pressing motives which made me act so boldly rather than entrust to chance the subsistence of his subjects and his troops'. When one remembers the hundreds of examples of the congenital caution of *intendants*, who were always anxious to cover themselves, one appreciates the more Turgot's courage and the desperate plight his 'département' must have been in. Of course, in Metz as elsewhere, there were always people who had cornered grain, but since they were well protected – usually being agents in the king's service – they caused more damage to consumers than to the local authorities.[186]

To organize on this scale, one can imagine the quantities of transport required: boats on the Moselle, boats on the Meuse from Void, Commercy or Verdun. On the Meuse, more frequented than the Moselle, there were however too many mills; cargoes got soaked as the boats passed through the mill-races, so that at Namur[187] or Liège, the flour obtained from grain brought by barge was often bad.[188] Most supplies travelled not by water but overland in the four-wheeled waggons of Lorraine, brought from Verdun or the countryside round Metz. They were requisitioned from the villages by the hundred. In July 1675, 1,500 waggons from near Metz carried 750 *setiers* of grain to Saverne.

Twenty years later, 800 waggons were used to transport grain, originally from Champagne, between Verdun and Metz.[189] The next year, 1,500 of them arrived at Saverne, each carrying twelve sacks of oats.[190] Supplies were brought to Bonn, when it was briefly occupied by the French, in a fleet of 70 barges (each receiving 500 *livres* for the return journey from Metz to Bonn); leaving Metz on 6 January 1702, they arrived at the garrison on 11 January, bringing gunpowder, shot, tools, 4,000 sacks of earth, and moulds for making 'French calibre' shot for muskets. A second convoy stopped a few days later at Merten, near Trier, 'where the cargo had to be loaded into 350 waggons'.[191]

All this cost money of course, and plenty of it. Sacks of cash were loaded into carts, for the benefit or at the expense of the 'extraordinaire des guerres', the wartime budget. But for every one of these carts mentioned in our documents ('40 sacks each containing 1,000 *livres* in new *écus* and half-*écus*, one sack of 1,000 *livres* in reminted 4-sou coins, 8 sacks of 500 *livres* in reminted 4-sou coins')[192] ten or twenty probably went unrecorded. The Mint in Metz, which had since 1663 stopped minting coin for the town and was now only issuing royal coin, flooded the market with small change destined for the soldiery. Hence the regular consignments of silver Spanish coins (for melting down) which arrived at the Mints of both Strasbourg and Metz. It had been decided to issue this coin to prevent what had become regular invasions by foreign money in small denominations, especially the *escalins* and *demi-escalins* from Holland or Spanish Flanders. In return, since bad money chased out good, and since the frontier zone was like a sieve, gold coin had been leaving the kingdom for Germany and the United Provinces. Hence the proposal put to Saint-Contest in 1706, to mint 50 million *escalins* in Metz.[193] Alongside the specie there was of course a mass of paper in circulation – *assignations* distributed by the state to suppliers or moneylenders. It was up to them to get these cashed, not always a simple matter. Military expenditure was a bottomless pit.

Besieged by these incessant demands, the *intendant* was rendered great service by the Jewish community in Metz – over 800 households in 1712,[194] 4,000 to 5,000 people in 1697.[195] Its representatives were almost without exception reasonable and experienced men, unrivalled at buying grain or livestock, advancing loans or providing information. They made fortunes in Metz comparable, in the most striking cases, to those of the *Hofjuden* of the German princely courts.[196] One of their particular requests was for passports to go to Paris, or better Versailles, which in normal circumstances were refused them: their aim was to seek out correspondents there on whom they could draw bills of exchange, or obtain credit, and they also hoped to approach the controller-general. Their strength lay in their network of relations: they could draw bills of exchange on Lyon as well as on Amsterdam or Frankfurt. But their growing numbers worried the town authorities: convents complained they were being surrounded by Jewish houses.[197] 'Would it not therefore be appropriate', the *intendant* Saint-Contest was asked in January 1702, to take action to 'prevent any new Jews settling in future in the countryside of this *département*'?[198] 'I do not think', he replied, 'that it would at present be appropriate to expel anyone . . . It would mean the ruin of the region where money is already scarce. But I believe it might be a wise precaution to prevent more settling here in future, because there are already only too many of them'.[199]

But where was the war?

I did warn you: the war was elsewhere. In Metz, we are far from the front line. There were certainly a few raids by 'hussars', houses were burned and peasants robbed or killed in the villages of the 'bishoprics'. There were also from time to time alerts, operations, even some carefully-planned manoeuvres. And there was always a feeling of being on the qui-vive: after all, anything might happen. The marquis de Créqui for instance had to hurry to Trier, which the French were occupying and the enemy besieging. But the town was betrayed by the garrison and capitulated to German and Lorraine troops on 11 August 1675. Five days later, by 16 August, fugitives who had been too quick off the mark were already turning up in Metz: 'We have been seeing at all hours of the day soldiers returning here in their shirts, having been stripped of everything by the peasants in the woods where they were hiding'.[200] Later, when the evacuation was complete, the mass of men who fell back on Metz was in an equally piteous state. The German and Lorraine victors had not respected the terms of the capitulation, according to which cavalry and infantry would be free to leave on foot and unarmed:

> Notwithstanding this, when it came to leaving the town, the duke of this place [Lorraine] had them all stripped, officers and men alike, so that they arrived here the following Monday, 9th [September], in the most pitiful state in the world; most of them were in their shirts, barefoot, bare-headed, some having nothing at all on their bodies but straw tied round them, others had sacks or old rags, others had hay inside their shirts to protect them from the rain and cold. Once they arrived here, they were lodged in the stables erected on the ramparts and elsewhere, where they were given their rations (*l'étape*)[201] . . . The capitulation treaty of Trier having been violated by the enemy, and the Trier garrison therefore being no longer obliged to observe its terms, it stayed here instead of going on to Vitry,[202] and [the authorities] had clothes, hats, boots and shoes made at Metz so as to restore those who made up [the garrison] to a condition to be able to serve.

The episode did not end on this semi-comic note. On 18 September, the soldiers who had escaped this adventure, properly clad once more, were reviewed. But among them were some of those who had betrayed Trier to the enemy. 'After having set aside forty cavalrymen and dragoons, . . . they were made to draw lots, so that five who had the misfortune to draw black tickets, were instantly hanged and strangled'.[203]

This detail, which will seem cruel to us, was alas commonplace at the time, particularly in Metz. The town had the gloomy privilege of receiving men condemned by the summary military courts, but who had not been executed immediately. 'The royal prison of this town', says a memorandum by the gravediggers of the parish of Sainte-Croix, 'is always full of deserters, galley-slaves and other army men, being the last place and headquarters to which all prisoners are brought from Alsace, the Rhine, and the forts on the Sambre, Meuse and Moselle'.[204] The gravediggers were complaining that they were not paid to bury these unfortunates, 'most of whom die from contagious diseases' in their horrible prison – which was so cold that the prisoners' feet were frostbitten, and where water was available only from an inaccessible well (until the installation of a 'fountain' in 1691).[205] One day in March 1695, an attic full of straw caught fire: was it an accident or revenge?[206] Such prisoners were likely to exchange prison only for the king's galleys. On 2 February 1691,[207] a chain-gang was formed to take to the galleys sixty of these prisoners, mostly young and fit men, 'of tall stature', we are told, almost all of whom had been sentenced to the galleys for life, as deserters. They came from every region in France. At the top of the list were five prisoners, whose noses and ears had been cropped and who had also been branded with the fleur-de-lys.

Should we feel sorry for Metz?

Life in Metz was far from normal: the town certainly suffered from its exhausting role. Troops were unwelcome and trouble-some guests to supervise, and the proximity of the frontier brought both worries and responsibilities. The town's expenditure regularly exceeded its theoretical income of 100,000 livres.[208] So it ran into debt. But then what town in France was not in debt at the time? And the expenditure did after all provide work for a large labour force, if only in the upkeep of the fortifications, or the security and policing of the town.

The large sums of money paid out on the spot by the royal administration were also a godsend to merchants, artisans, local businessmen and moneylenders. All the guilds prospered, there were plenty of butchers and the shoemakers could not complain. Even the town's eight bookshops were deemed insufficient to meet demand[209] – except by the local booksellers' guild naturally, and also by the authorities who feared an increase in their number and a rise in the sale of forbidden books, especially since 'the town of Metz . . . being on the frontier and inhabited by people who have been of the R.P.R [i.e. Protestants],[210] there is much more opportunity to traffic in [such books] and break the law than there would be in any other [town]'. A sure sign that business was thriving, Metz gave employment to eight royal notaries and thirty-eight local notaries, known as 'amends'.[211] And it was rich enough to attract a number of Swiss immigrants.[212] Yes, Metz was making a living, and not a bad one.

It also had its privileged circles, including a powerful group of high-ranking officers, as well as the members of the *parlement* founded in 1632. Both the bourgeoisie and the *noblesse de robe* drew the bulk of their income from their vineyards in the neighbouring countryside. In fact the town had closed its market to all wines except those produced in the immediate neighbourhood, even trying to exclude some from the nearby villages.[213] It claimed that there was good cause to do so:

> The land surrounding the town of Metz is a region of hills, with sandy soil and vineyards and cannot produce anything else. The only property of most of its inhabitants consists of share-cropped vineyards. The richest among them . . . are [simply] those who own the largest number . . . The wine this land produces is not of exquisite quality. It is praised only by those who harvest it. It is weak in quality and colour, rather bitter and [has] a local flavour so it is not good enough to be sent anywhere else.

This was a further reason to oppose the demands of the syndic of the estates of Burgundy who was indignant that wine from his province was not accepted for public sale in Metz. But given the superior quality of even the poorest burgundies, to have done so would have been the ruin of the Metz vineyards. Why should Metz not have the right to restrict its market to its own wines, as Bordeaux, Beaune, Mâcon, Vitry-le-François and Saint-Dizier all did?[214] Neither foot-soldiers nor cavalry had particularly delicate palates. It was perhaps on their account that distillation of wines and residues also made great progress around Metz and in Lorraine.[215] Can you think of a garrison town anywhere in France towards the end of Louis XIV's reign without its supply of alcohol?

Metz did of course have its share of poor people: here as elsewhere, humble folk went hungry when grain was scarce and prices rose. In 1699, the town recorded '4,225 poor people, among whom there are a great many who seek to conceal it'.[216] But then what town under the Sun King did not have its poor, concealed or otherwise, not to mention beggars from outside who had forced their way in? After 1676, the town had taken precautions in this respect and decided that 'the said poor' should from now on be 'forbidden to beg'. Those who were 'natives of the town and district' would be shut up in the Saint-Nicolas poorhouse where 'they would eat in common'.[217] As for the 'foreign poor', they would be given alms and 'put outside the town with orders not to return to beg there, on pain of flogging, while a fine of five hundred *livres* would be imposed on any townspeople who supported or concealed them'. These were commonplace measures – whether they were effective is another matter. Begging in the seventeenth century was of tidal proportions and however prudent or severe the towns were, none of them was exempt from it.

For Metz, war was an everyday matter, a way of life, with its inevitable inconveniences and certain advantages – particularly since real war generally remained far from its gates and was in any case more threatening to the surrounding countryside than to the town itself. In the Europe of the *ancien régime*, war did not interrupt trade, even with the enemy. So whether it was war or peace made little difference to Metz, even in the reign of Louis XV, when the town prospered and was transformed under the 'enlightened' command of the maréchal de Belle Isle. It was modernized, with grand open squares and new buildings, becoming more beautiful and costing even more. But then it was already costing a fortune at the end of Louis XIV's reign!

Our second excursion: to Toulon

There are three possibilities for a case-study on the coast: Brest, France's stronghold in Brittany, overlooking the Atlantic; Dunkerque, 'built from nothing' by Vauban, a window cunningly opened on to the North Sea;[218] and Toulon, the only French naval base in the Mediterranean. I have chosen Toulon, at a particular moment in its history, during the summer of 1707,[219] when the town was blockaded by an Anglo–Dutch fleet anchored off the Hyères islands, while the army of 'Monsieur de Savoie' (the duke of Savoy) was on its way to attack the poorly defended fort, firmly expecting to enter it without firing a shot. So it was under double threat from land and sea. This time I have not avoided exciting events, and we can even say that, as in the classical theatre, the unities of place (the besieged fort of Toulon) and almost of time (a few days in the summer of 1707, from 26 July to 24 August) have been observed. But the issue was not simple. Toulon lay at the centre of a vast plan of attack conceived in London, The Hague, Vienna and Turin, and directed not only at Provence but at the whole of France.

Nature has been generous to Toulon. The town has a double harbour: the main bay opening on to the sea between cape Sepet and cape Brun, is a vast expanse of water, a kind of antechamber or holding harbour; while the inner bay, a smaller one, round which the town and its shipyards are built, had at this time two docks, each surrounded by walls, and even an extra one to the east, the Mourillon inlet where ships were traditionally careened.

Overextended by the Royal Navy's systematic calls on it, the town was nevertheless in 1707 as it had always been, cramped and squeezed inside its walls, chronically short of space. In 1543, it had consisted of only a few hundred houses and 5,000 inhabitants[220] at most, when François I surrendered it (after evacuating the townspeople) to Barbarossa's fleet and army: the port was subsequently occupied by over a hundred galleys, countless accompanying vessels and thousands of men from 29 September

1543 to the end of March 1544.[221] The old town walls were by then already a straitjacket without being a protection.

After 1589, the walls were demolished – would the town be able to breathe now? Yes, but only briefly. For several years there were trees and open spaces inside the new walls, then the gaps were filled in and houses at once spilled over into five or six suburbs, the *borcs*, which were equally close-packed. Improvements later made to the ramparts at Vauban's suggestion did not remedy the original cramped layout. By the beginning of the eighteenth century, the town still consisted of a maze of absurdly narrow streets, winding their way to dead ends or dangerous alleyways, with open sewers and noxious smells everywhere. The incredibly narrow houses – one room to a storey – rose vertically into the air and were propped up by external pillars, themselves supported by beams overhanging the streets and the heads of passers-by. There was nowhere to assemble the troops, apart from one open space known as the Battle Field, and where on 25 July, as the enemy was actually arriving, 'M. le marquis de Vausse, captain of the coasts, and the chevalier de Grimaldi, lieutenant of galleys, fought [a duel] and were both killed, each by a sword thrust, one through the heart, the other through the body. They were cousins german'.[222] It would have been difficult for them to draw swords anywhere else in the town.

The town can have numbered no more than 10,000 inhabitants in 1589, 20,000 in 1668 and 30,000 on the eve of the Revolution. During the summer of 1707, with the three regiments of the regular garrison billeted on the townspeople for want of a barracks, it contained some 60,000 people, if we are to believe a not entirely reliable letter.[223] This population is described as including many loud-mouthed women, prompt to take fright, many children, not a few prostitutes, and numerous beggars whom the towns 'chasse pauvre' (anti-beggary patrol) tried in vain to move on. There were the soldiers of course; and the sailors and seamen on shore leave – quarrelsome men, quick to draw the boarding-knives they wore in their belts, 'loose-living', fond of gaming, resistant to discipline, reckless – and sometimes extremely brave.

Around the town lay magnificent countryside, dazzling to the traveller: gardens, flowers, olive and orange groves, palm trees, vines, villages, fields of wheat – a paradise. But behind it rose mountain upon mountain, baked by the sun, stripped of vegetation, 'bald hills hemming the port so tightly in' as Vauban[224] put it. During the torrid months of July and August in that year of 1707, drinking water, which the town drew from the Ragas spring, ran terribly short both for men and horses. 'I thought', wrote one of the defenders, 'that I would only have to fight the enemy and their supply lines . . .'[225] [but] there is a third [battle] which we had not foreseen, which is the water shortage'. There were a few wells inside the town, but their water, tainted by the sea, was salty and brackish. Sentinels had to be posted at all of them, 'to prevent men and horses from drinking it'.[226] All things considered, the natural setting was beautiful but basically poor, little suited to feed the military, and inhabited by watchful peasants who had no burning loyalty to the king of France. Indeed when they came to work on the fortifications, 'after a couple of days they desert, as do all those called up for militia service, who are unarmed'.[227]

It is true that in Toulon the military commanders, generally imported from the north, were not always able to make themselves obeyed. It required a knack not possessed it seems by the writer of one letter on 20 July: 'I have never seen a nation so rebellious as the people in this part of the world. You give orders in vain, they don't do a quarter of what they are asked'.[228] But the old comte de Grignan, a local man and lord lieutenant of Provence, had no trouble with the Toulon population.

The reason was that Provence, like all the peripheral territories, was a province apart. French rule had not yet been imposed here. The crown had inherited Provence in 1481–3 but two centuries later it still did not really control it. The cities, Marseille in particular, but also Arles and Aix, had their privileges and a certain independence. It is true that when the duke of Savoy invaded in July 1707, the people did not collaborate with him as he had expected. He had even dreamed of a Protestant uprising. The province remained looking on, neutral and unmoved. The nobility did not stir, nor did the clergy; the peasants waited to see what would happen. But in any case, the maréchal de Tessé, commander of the French troops, had already warned the king from the start of the campaign, while he was still in Dauphiné, that one should not 'count on the people' of Provence: even if they were loyal, they had neither guns nor ammunition.[229]

What was more, in 1706, the year before the attack on Toulon, things had not been going at all well for Provence. Marseille, always quick to complain, claimed that the 'piastres' necessary for trading with the Levant, were no longer arriving directly there by sea: instead 'they all come from Lyon where they have been sent from Bayonne and Oléron, via Bordeaux and Toulouse'.[230] Perhaps this meant that the Mediterranean routes had become dangerous because of the naval operations along the Spanish coast? But the real calamity that hit Provence was the torrential rain and flood brought by a disastrous winter. The Rhône had overflowed, flooding Arles and Tarascon, and causing immense damage. Arles complained loudly, but it was not the only town in need of help, especially since it was privileged, 'exempt from *taille*, from billeting of troops and from salt tax'.[231] The disaster was widespread: 'there is not a single parish in all the province that has not been damaged. The waters have washed away the seed corn and even the soil', that is the arable land, and 'in the places where it has not been washed away, it is covered in stones and sand'.[232]

The same year 1706 had been equally calamitous for Louis XIV's armies. The War of the Spanish Succession had scattered French troops all over Europe, and as defeat followed defeat, they had been withdrawn to the frontiers: in 1704, after the defeat at Blenheim, Bavaria had been lost and the French army had crossed back over the Rhine; in 1705, the English had brought to Barcelona the archduke Charles, rival of Philip V, and provoked an uprising in Catalonia; Marlborough's army, after victory at Ramillies on 23 May 1706, had seized Belgium (i.e. Spanish Flanders) and had come face to face with the iron frontier, within sight of Lille and Dunkerque; shortly afterwards, on 7 September 1706, the marquis de la Feuillade was defeated under the walls of Turin; the Milanese, with its French garrisons, was lost in short order, and Piedmont had to be evacuated without delay. In Spain, the recapture of Madrid (3 August 1706) and the successes of the maréchal de Berwick had brought some relief to a desperate situation which nevertheless remained worrying.

So the old king was no longer invincible and his armies were 'beginning to get used to defeats and disorderly routs'. Early in 1707, just before the fine weather returned, Michel de Chamillart, controller-general of finance since 1699 and secretary of state for war since 1701, 'admitted he was incapable of organizing the new season's campaign'.[233]

Meanwhile the troops evacuated from Italy had fallen back towards the Alps, in a line from Savoy, which they still occupied, to the city of Nice which the French had taken in April 1703 (though the citadel held out until January 1704), along with Villefranche, and Antibes; thus they held the entire county of Nice facing the col de Tende.

On 31 January 1707,[234] the king appointed the maréchal de Tessé commander of this 'Alpine' army, despite the damage the marshal's reputation had suffered from two recent setbacks: the raising of the sieges of Gibraltar (1705) and Barcelona (1706). Leaving Grenoble, Tessé arrived on 28 February at Briançon, which he made his command post.

This man was to play the leading role in subsequent events: was he the character we find depicted by Saint-Simon – an odd fellow, both boastful and quixotic, whose letters made the king smile? How is one to know? Saint-Simon is never generous in his judgements. Pierre Dubois, who has read through the marshal's entire correspondence, describes a quite different man, not perhaps a great soldier but an astute diplomat, humorous and good-natured, who was able, as soon as he arrived at Toulon, to soothe down the conflicts engendered by the abrasive temperament and inconsiderate orders of the town's commander, Saint-Pater.

In Tessé's defence, it must be said that at the time he reached Briançon there was no clear military strategy for a coherent defence of the Alps: the current practice was simply to move the 'battalions' or the cavalry wherever the enemy threatened. If he moved, we moved: it was a tactic of parallel feints.

A second excuse is that the army at his disposal, reinforced by the soldiers returning from the Milanese (who had been evacuated, with the enemy's consent, after the convention of Turin, agreed with the emperor on 23 March 1707), numbered no more than thirty to forty thousand men. What was more, it was prey to chronic desertion, whereby some regiments were losing up to half their men. De Broglie, one of Tessé's aides, wrote on 2 July 1707 that it had been necessary to make some examples. 'About thirty deserters[235] were put to death. This example, which was timely and ruthless succeeded perfectly; for two weeks I have not heard of any desertions'. That did not prove anything. Desertion was a disease endemic to all armies. There were even organized procedures: deserters made their way to Switzerland, then returned home, and if there were bonuses going, enlisted in the militia, then began all over again. This was an army ill paid, ill fed, ill equipped and short of shoes.

On the other side, the duke of Savoy, Victor-Amadeus II, reinforced by the imperial troops of Prince Eugene, had plenty of soldiers, including 4,000 Frenchmen who had been enlisted, more or less under duress, after the disaster at Turin. He set up three 'camps', the first at Ivrée, on the road to the Val d'Aosta, the little Saint Bernard and the high Tarentaise; the second facing Pignerol and Susa, small forts held by the French at the foot of the Piedmont Alps; the third near Coni, with instructions to watch the roads towards Barcelonnette and the col de Tende leading to Nice and, beyond, to Provence.

So the maréchal de Tessé had to watch several sectors at once: Savoy, Dauphiné, Provence. He knew – all the enemy's preparations said so – that he was going to be attacked. But where? In Provence, his Italian spies were writing to him as early as April. Without believing it himself, he informed the Court. Nonsense, came the reply. Keep your eye on Savoy! And when hostilities had already broken out in the south, and the people in Toulon were begging him to bring down the entire Alpine army to their aid, he was still grumbling: 'Out of the whole of Provence, Languedoc, Dauphiné and Savoy, am I supposed just to save Toulon?' 'I assure you' he added, 'that the King thinks otherwise'.[236] And perhaps he was right. Perhaps Versailles was still anxious about Savoy.

Who would not have been anxious in France in that summer of 1707? The enemy was convinced that French resistance was coming to an end. And Louis XIV's persistent, secret but fruitless negotiations did nothing to shake such views. In reality, France was holding the line quite well. In the North Sea and the Channel, faced with France's chief enemies, the privateers of Dunkerque were inflicting heavy losses on English and Dutch shipping. Marlborough hesitated to attack either Lille or Dunkerque. Here lay the reason for the allied plan to cause a rapid and easy diversion in distant Provence, by striking at the soft underbelly of the French defences: these were assumed to be poorly organized for the protection of Toulon, Marseille, Aix, and beyond them Languedoc, where the enemy was hoping to revive in the Cévennes the Camisard insurrection, which had been crushed only with some difficulty by Villars in 1704 and by Berwick in 1705. Arms sent to the rebels had been intercepted at Beaucaire, and Cavalier, the peasant leader of the Camisards, was known to be following the Savoyard army and dining at the duke's own table.

An entire plan of action had been drawn up then, after lengthy negotiations, traces of which can be found in London, The Hague, Vienna and Turin.[237] And it was the duke of Savoy, backed up by Prince Eugene's troops, who took charge of the campaign on land. The ambitious Victor-Amadeus had everything planned down to the smallest detail, and in great secrecy. But neither the prince nor the duke could conceal troop movements, and if Tessé, perched up in the Alps, could not always observe them exactly, news quickly reached France via San Remo[238] and Genoa. The rumour soon spread of an imminent attack on Provence and Toulon, and since news travelled rapidly from Toulon or Marseille to Versailles (taking no more than a week, or sometimes four days) the Court was finally convinced, by 15 June, that there really was an invasion of Provence on the way.[239] The two naval commanders of Toulon, de Vauvré and the marquis de Langeron – who were both at Versailles – were hastily sent to their posts. They did not arrive in Provence until 23 June.

The first troops of the Savoyard army – several large detachments of 4,000 men, followed by enormous mule-trains, 5,000 strong – finally crossed the col de Tende at the beginning of July and the alert was sounded throughout Provence. At the same time (was this de Tessé's idea? I doubt it), the marquis de Sailly, commander of Nice, abandoned the city on 2 July, and stationed himself with 5 battalions (about 2,000 men) and a few militiamen, across the river Var which was in spate. He did not however prevent the enemy from crossing this little river on the 11th (though not without losing many men, swept away by the torrential floods) nor from building a bridge for their artillery to cross on the 12th.

Meanwhile, Victor-Amadeus, who had entered Nice, lingered there until the 13th. Why the delay? Because the Anglo-Dutch fleet had entered the port of Nice.

> Monsieur de Savoie [writes Saint-Simon in his *Memoirs*] had visited the fleet and requested the money that had been promised him. The English were afraid of running short, and argued about it for a whole day longer than the date fixed for [the fleet's] departure. In the end, seeing that the prince was determined not to budge until he had been paid, they counted out a million[241] for him, which he collected personally. This day's delay was the salvation of Toulon and, we may say, of France: it allowed 21 battalions to reach Toulon in time.

The explanation is plausible but not quite accurate. The invading army had continued to advance after 11 July, with or without its leaders. The forces ranged against them consisted of no more than a thinly-stretched line of troops. But the invaders had a hard time of it, because of the torrid heat, the water shortage and the scarcity of rations; and they were restrained by prudence as well, since it was the duke's intention to handle the Provençal people with care. He wanted to present himself to them as a liberator, ready to deliver them from the French yoke. He came to amicable agreements with the towns, being content to ask Cannes, Saint-Tropez, Fréjus and Grasse only for contributions of rations and fodder. No one refused. Indeed the welcome at Fréjus was friendly and in retrospect amusing. The bishop fell over himself to be hospitable: receiving the duke in the episcopal palace, he 'put on his priestly robes, displayed the holy water and incense at the cathedral door and celebrated a *Te Deum* for the occupation' of the town. What is so amusing about that, you may wonder? Simply that this bishop of Fréjus was the future Cardinal Fleury, later to be tutor to Louis XV, and who by the grace of his pupil, governed France between 1726 and 1740. How did 'this poor man, born to deceive and be deceived',[242] as Saint-Simon put it, manage to wriggle out of this unfortunate 'collaboration'? Apparently without too much trouble.

All this however took up the conquering hero's time.

Monsieur de Savoye [Tessé reported] hands out orders, receives oaths of allegiance, commandeers rations and has that part of Provence he is occupying better organized to his bidding than it would be by one of the king's *intendants* . . . The people have no guns, ammunition or strength; in their hearts they are not disloyal, but they obey and hand over the contents of their granaries to avoid giving money, which Monsieur de Savoye until now has affected not to want.[243]

In the end, it was not until 21 July that the Savoyard detachments, one after another, arrived in Cuers – the last stop, three leagues from Toulon. And this was only the advance guard. A minor sortie by the French marines surprised some of the men asleep in their lodgings.[244] And it was not until 24 July that the Savoyards finally appeared before the walls of the town. They had marched 150 kilometres in 14 days – not exactly record-breaking speed.[245]

Meanwhile Toulon had been receiving Tessé's soldiers in successive detachments: eleven battalions (4,000 men) on 21 July; eight on the 22nd; nine on the 23rd; thirteen or fourteen on the 25th.[246] On the 22nd, the troops of the marquis de Sailly, retreating from the banks of the Var, arrived in turn and encamped under cover of the olive groves outside the town. Finally on 7 August, the comte de Medavy brought six battalions and 42 squadrons of cavalry and dragoons from Savoy;[247] they were lodged at Saint-Maximin from where they would later easily be able to harass the Savoyard troops and interfere with their supplies. So the race against time had been won by the French troops. The maréchal de Tessé, who had been constantly coming and going on horseback ('on my backside' as he put it) between Sisteron, Toulon, Aix, and back to Sisteron, had masterminded the French effort, at some cost to himself.

But even before the relief army arrived, the town of Toulon, which had taken more seriously than Versailles the rumours of an attack on Provence, had itself organized its defence both on land ('La Terre') and on sea ('La Marine'). Soldiers and sailors predictably did not see eye to eye about everything, but the work of fortifying the town was energetically carried out by both corps. They had had three weeks grace, in the course of which feverish activity had transformed the fort. The comte de Grignan played a vital role in this. He was able to win over the townspeople and the villages round about, and everyone, militiamen and volunteers, threw themselves fervently into strengthening the defences. The houses built on the forward ramparts had been demolished, the covered way around the walls had been completed and 200 cannon, brought up from the arsenal, had been installed on the battlements: the cannon were made of cast-iron, it is true, which even with reduced charges could (and did) explode, causing heavier losses among the defenders than enemy bullets. The centrepiece of the defence was the building of an improvised stronghold, a fortified camp equipped with some heavy artillery, on the heights to the north of the town, between the ramparts and the Faron mountain, around the little chapel of Sainte-Anne. As long as this remained in the hands of the defenders, it would keep the besiegers, their artillery and their assault troops away from the town.

Before these defences had been built, 'Toulon was worth nothing'.[248] Or rather its defence had been conceived as a maritime affair entirely, with no effort made on the landward side, as the duke of Savoy had been duly informed. It was therefore to his chagrin and almost immediate discouragement,[249] that he found himself facing a fort full of soldiers, bristling with cannon, plentifully supplied with arms, guns, flints, bayonets and gunpowder and able to count on the enormous reserves of the navy. It was short neither of bread nor wine, salt meat nor (for the officers) fresh meat. Shoes were in short supply, but in Provence in summer after all, shoes were something soldiers could do without. The defenders were well fed[250] at any rate, and since wine was being sold in the town at two sous a jar, they were in good spirits: a drummer boy, exchanging his drum for a pipe, played for them to dance every night.[251] Morale was high too, or became so, among the commanders. Tessé was quite soon confidently saying that the duke of Savoy would be driven back to the Var.

The enemy troops were still arriving in front of the town, and did not occupy the heights around the chapel of Sainte-Catherine until the morning of 2 August.[252] And their heavy artillery was still not in position. In fact the besiegers were lined up facing only the eastern side of the town; they did not surround it, so strictly speaking this was not a siege.

Meanwhile the Anglo-Dutch fleet, which had arrived early, had taken up position on about 10 July off the Hyères islands. It had had to wait for the arrival of the Savoyard troops in order to land rations and artillery for them, and had suffered several days of the *mistral*, which blew so strongly that the ships could not enter Toulon waters.

In the face of this immense threat, the naval command at Toulon had redoubled its precautions. What it most feared was the combination of the enemy's forces on land and sea. How could the ships moored in the harbour be protected if the enemy's *land-based* artillery bombarded them while the enemy fleet prevented them leaving port? And to sail out would in any case have meant arming the ships – a lengthy and *expensive* business. Another problem was how to protect the huge navy stores in the arsenal. The marquis de Langeron, naval commander in chief, took his decisions on (or sometimes against) the advice of the other commanders, cursing and grumbling all the while, complaining about anyone and everyone and generally displaying every sign of a bad character. It is true that when he had arrived on 23 June, he believed it was impossible to defend the town. So his first concern had been to empty it as quickly as possible of some of its rich resources: cast-iron artillery, mortars, tackle, sails, rigging – all of which was hastily dispatched to Arles aboard 72 boats. Some cannon and cables were submerged in the bay: they would be recovered later; the batteries defending the harbours were made shipshape; the ships in harbour were dis-

FIGURE 37
*Plan of Toulon and its surrounding areas at the time of
the 1707 siege*

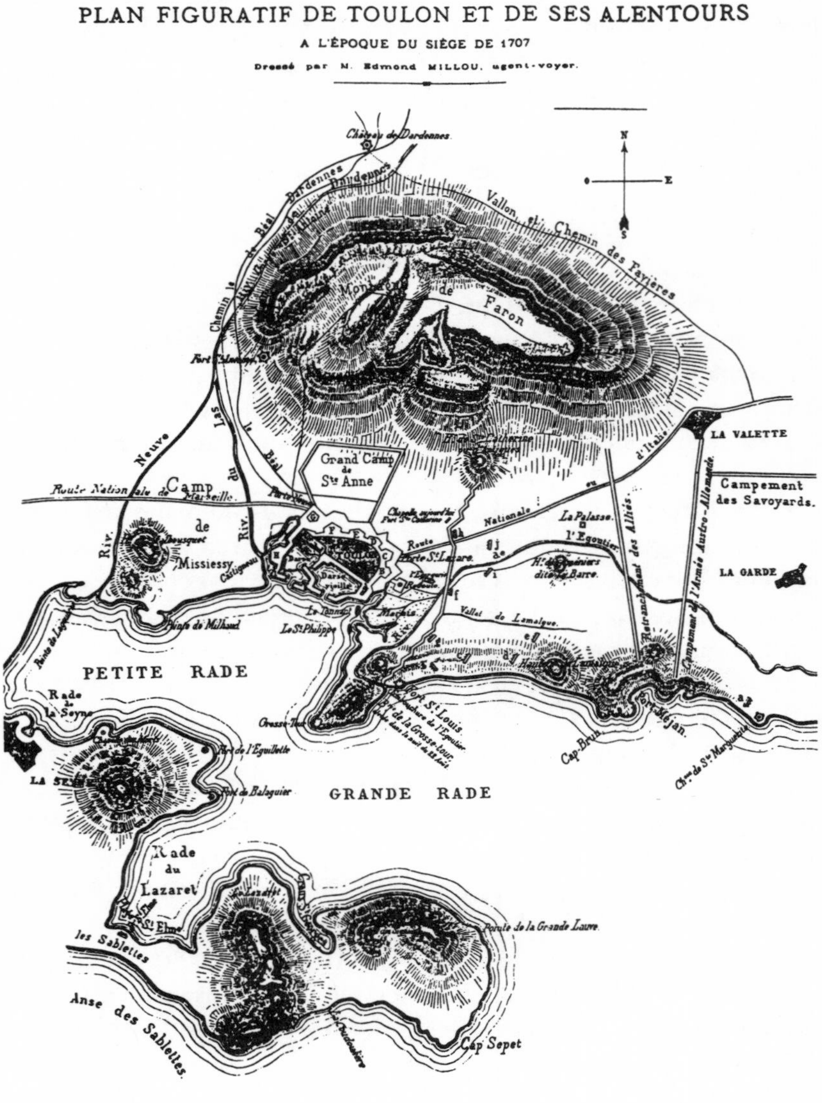

PLAN FIGURATIF DE TOULON ET DE SES ALENTOURS

A L'ÉPOQUE DU SIÉGE DE 1707

Dressé par M. Edmond MILLOU, agent-voyer.

masted and submerged as soon as the enemy approached Toulon, lest they should be set alight by enemy fire or, worse still, fall into enemy hands. In spite of the protests of their commander, the marquis de Roye, seven galleys returning from the Italian coast were packed off to Marseille. In harbour in Toulon, they could have been all too easy targets, though this decision deprived the town of the mobile defence they could have offered, of the firepower of the big guns in their prows, and above all of the labour of the galley-crews, who could have been used for something else. All these measures were arguable, and there were indeed arguments. But, as I shall shortly suggest, they were in fact useful and intelligent. And one of them was a stroke of genius: the use of two ships of the first 'rate',[253] the *Tonnant* and the *Saint-Philippe*, armed with 90 cannon. The *Tonnant*, protected by some old hulks which were deliberately sunk alongside her, and herself anchored on a mudbank facing the Mourillon, interposed her powerful fire between the town and any attacker approaching from the east along the road from Nice. She had been reinforced with hardwood and by hauling on the moorings, it was possible first to discharge the port side guns, then while they were reloading, to swivel round and fire the starboard battery. The *Saint-Philippe*, remaining afloat, was stationed to the west, opposite Castignac and could if necessary move towards the Mourillon – as she did in the course of the siege.

If the reader finds on the map in Figure 37 Toulon's seaward defences, guarding the mouth of the large bay – the artillery emplacements on cape Sepet to the south, and the forts of Sainte-Marguerite and Saint-Louis to the north on cape Brun – he or she will be able to follow the first quite modest operation by the powerful enemy fleet. It contented itself simply with capturing these outer positions. First it took the cape Sepet batteries, only to abandon them, not finding any use for them. Then it turned to Cape Brun. On 16 August, it took the château of Sainte-Marguerite (held by 48 men). Fort Saint-Louis, defended by about a hundred men, stood up to a long bombardment and held out until the 18th, when the garrison was evacuated by sea. These were not great victories: Sainte-Marguerite had yielded because the water ran out.[254] To enter the small inner harbour, the key to the port, the fleet ought to have stormed the Great Tower, an old fortification now restored and provided with artillery, while in the south it should have been putting the Balaguer tower and the fort of l'Eguillette out of action – all of them difficult operations for a fleet which was soon to be discouraged by the patent and premature failure of the Savoyard attack on land.

The Savoyards had taken up position along two parallel lines, between the mountain of la Malgue to the south and the heights of Sainte-Catherine to the north, thereby cutting the road between Toulon and Nice. During the first week of August, operations consisted of no more than some small arms fire, a few cannonades here and there, and the building of exhausting earthworks. Underfed and overworked, the besiegers, although closely watched by a strong police force, were constantly deserting and going over to the French lines. There were in the end thousands of these deserters or 'surrenderers' as they were described, fine soldiers and well clad, but complaining of starvation. They were warmly welcomed and closely questioned, before being sent off to Marseille with an écu in their pockets. Having lost the race against time and thus missed an easy opportunity, the ducal army was falling apart. It was in these conditions that on 15 August, 'at break of day', a sortie by the defenders threw confusion into the enemy's front line, between la Croix Faron and Sainte-Catherine. Over a thousand enemy soldiers were killed, wounded or taken prisoner. French losses were insignificant by comparison: about forty men. The position they had seized was evacuated fourteen hours later. So this was really no more than a warning shot. But the Savoyards took it hard and did not reoccupy the position. The following day, their artillery was wheeled up and sent 'bombs' into the town out of pure vengeance: eight houses were destroyed and 'the lord bishop thought he would be crushed in his bed last night'. In panic, most of the residents fled the town.

In fact this marked the end of hostilities; on the 19th, at the suggestion of the besiegers, there was an exchange of prisoners. The French officers in charge of this delegation were invited to the table of Prince Eugene, and the duke of Savoy afterwards received them 'very civilly' and had them stay to dinner. The talk was of the

FIGURE 38
The siege of Toulon, 1707

operations so far, and of the two 'gerosmes' (as they were called for some reason) the *Tonnant* and the *Saint-Philippe*. The duke offered his guests champagne, with apologies that it was doubtless not as good as that served by M. de Vauvré, the commander of the Toulon garrison, who had the reputation of keeping a very good table.[255] For those in command at least, this was war in kid gloves. Two days later, to make easier the retreat they had now decided upon, the Savoyards transferred their baggage, artillery and wounded to the allied fleet.

The enemy navy was responsible for the parting shot – it can hardly be described as a gallant stand. During the night of the 21st to 22nd, five galliots bombarded Toulon until five o'clock in the morning, before rejoining the fleet which set sail the following evening. This bombardment was much more serious than the bullets and shells of the 'land' attack, since the galliots had sailed right up to the bay under fort Saint-Louis. Two old ships caught fire, and had to be towed into the middle of the harbour to prevent the flames spreading to other vessels, but meantime they provided a splendid flare to guide the enemy fire. Two frigates were damaged and a bomb caused a blaze, fortunately quickly overcome, on the *Diamant*. 'There were also many houses knocked down, although two-thirds of their bombs did not explode, or else they exploded in the air, without which the damage would have been greater'.

Meanwhile the duke of Savoy, having got rid of his artillery and his wounded, was quickly retracing his steps back out of Provence. In the course of this retreat 'in close order', villages were pillaged and burnt, towns ransomed or sacked. The maréchal de Tessé who was pursuing the enemy could not catch up with them, being seven or eight hours behind. He lacked not so much men as horses and vehicles, and the retreating army left nothing behind in the way of rations or fodder. It was the peasantry from all around, commanded by the local nobility, militiamen, and even parish priests, which flung itself upon the looting soldiers,

> so that everywhere there was . . . a chain of ambushes and continual attacks and exchanges of musketry; these did not cease during the whole day and night that the enemies took to

cross the Esterel, where there were six or seven thousand militiamen who killed a lot of them. But this was not without losses on their own side too, and those whom the enemy captured were hanged from trees, which did not however daunt the rest nor slow their pursuit.[256]

The invading army had lost half its men in the Provence expedition. Later it went on to loot the county of Nice, which belonged to the duke, as savagely as it had Provence, and finally disappeared over the col de Tende towards Piedmont. 'A fine mess I've made of it', sighed the duke of Savoy on 26 August.

What does it all prove?

Was the siege of Toulon actually a French victory? That would be going too far. The threat had been averted but a price had visibly been paid. The duke of Savoy had carried off with him, it was said, no more than 200,000 livres, but he had lived off the countryside causing terrible ravages. Provence would of course lick its wounds, as all devastated lands do when peace returns. Life began again, and by the following year the Provençals were displaying their resignation and good will, if not their 'loyalty' as the comte de Grignan, their lord lieutenant put it, when their estates voted the million livres in taxes which the province usually paid the king. The region would in fact be much harder hit in 1709, during the icy winter which – more effectively than the looters and tree-fellers of 1707 – killed off thousands upon thousands of olive trees.

What was more, the losers at Toulon took their revenge. Tessé's army had returned along the Alpine roads to the positions it had left in Dauphiné and Savoy, but it was in no hurry. And this time the enemy moved faster. Prince Eugene, coming from Piedmont, was able to surprise Susa, which the French were occupying in the eastern Alps, on Piedmontese territory. The citadel resisted a little longer, but was taken on 3 October. France thereby lost a convenient gateway into the Piedmont via the Alps (though it is true that Pignerol and Fenestrelle remained). Was it as a result of this loss, or following some denunciation (the army was constantly riven by feuds) that the maréchal de Tessé fell into semi-disgrace and was relieved of his command?

Still, the capture of Susa was a minor matter. More serious and more difficult to estimate were the consequences of the siege of Toulon for the navy. It is commonplace to blame the naval command of Toulon and even to single out as chief culprit the marquis de Langeron. I shall avoid doing so, since it was not at the siege of Toulon that the fate of Louis XIV's navy was decided.

I agree the port of Toulon, once the siege had been lifted, was a sorry sight; 'All those fine ships which were once the pride of the port were now without masts, some lying on their port or starboard side, others stove in at prow or stern, making it doubtful whether they would ever be able to form a fleet again'. When they were raised, they revealed that they had 'suffered terribly; such an unfortunate position had weakened all their seams, introduced leaks that were hard to repair, and hastened the rotting of every part of the vessel'.[257]

Had the marquis de Langeron sacrificed his ships to no purpose? Who, though, could have foreseen that the siege would be such a short, indeed ridiculous affair? Langeron had visualized a proper siege, a long blockade, with the harbour open to enemy fire and the artillery on shore firing freely on ships lined up in the port. In these foreseeable circumstances, he was simply observing rules dictated by experience – just as it was normal practice in towns about to be besieged to take up the cobblestones in case they should be used as missiles (as happened in Toulon). The ships had been rid of their ballast (for the sake of speed, it had simply been emptied out on the spot) and submerged, but not sent to the bottom. As soon as the enemy had beaten the retreat, they were refloated one after another. The marquis de Langeron reported these successive refloatings in his letters as so many victories and, one may imagine, as personal vindications.

So on 30 August 1707, he wrote to Pontchartrain, 'I began this morning to have the water pumped out of the *Foudroyant*, one of the vessels which was reported to you from Marseille to be in such a sorry state; by midday she was afloat'.[258]

On 6 September: malevolent tongues have been 'putting it

about that [he, Langeron] had sunk the King's great vessels to the sea bed'.[259] This is false: 'he had put water into the large vessels only up to the first battery. If he had had to sink a large ship, he would have had it afloat again in four days'.

15 September: 'the *Foudroyant*, the *Soleil Royal*, the *Triomphant* and the *Admirable* have all been emptied and are not taking in a drop of water'. The *Terrible* and the *Intrepid* will soon be afloat again. As for the *Saint-Philippe* and the *Tonnant*, the heroes of the siege, the former had not sunk, and the latter had been raised, 'but the King has no two ships as rotten as these, and they are so far gone that I should not care to answer for them in a summer campaign'.[260] Finally, on 9 October, victory: 'the task is finished'.[261]

That does not mean that Toulon had recovered a magnificent fleet. But was it so magnificent before the siege? This is really the heart of the debate. A note from Arnoul to Pontchartrain written on 11 August, before the siege was lifted, makes one doubt it:[262]

> You are quite right Monseigneur, to say that 30 or 40 vessels would have been more help to Toulon than all the troops one could send there, since the duke of Savoy would indeed not have conceived of attacking the town if he had thought we might have at sea even 20 vessels in a fit state to attack the fleet which was to bring him some of his army's subsistence, along with the artillery and munitions, for such an undertaking. But it is a sad fact, which one cannot deplore too greatly, that the navy was *not* in such a state, and therefore found itself a hair's breadth, so to speak, from total destruction.

Arnoul was the 'inspector' who had reorganized the port of Brest and who, although not a seagoing man, had played the role of supervisor at Toulon – being kept somewhat at arm's length by the defence commanders. He was intelligent and observant, and none too sympathetic. What he says however, points the finger not at the naval commanders at Toulon, but rather at the entire policy of the Versailles government, which had sacrificed the navy to the army, and had since 1692 and La Hougue, staked everything on the guerrilla war of privateering, more or less abandoning full-scale naval engagements as too expensive. Had the king been forced into this choice? Possibly, since privateering was a poor man's option. In the present case, it was not men, whether seamen or shipyard workers, who were in short supply at Toulon, nor was it materials, including the exceptionally long masts which were floated down the Isère and Rhône. What Toulon needed was more money, without which the ships could not be careened or refitted.[263]

After the siege, financial difficulties visibly affected the town. Activity slumped. Vessels which had been kept afloat by tedious pumping carried out by galley-slaves, were allowed to keel over in the mud of the bay. It meant sending them to their graves, and to eventual demolition for firewood. No doubt in every port in Europe, old ships were gently rotting away in the insidious and all too calm waters of the harbour. The hulks in which the English kept French prisoners during the Revolutionary and Napoleonic wars were precisely these – old ships taken out of service. But in Toulon, the arsenal's activities came to a stop and unemployment among the workers was catastrophic. There were still ships and boats leaving the port, to protect French trade in the Levant or the grain ships in North Africa. And Toulon also fitted for privateering the ships lent or hired by the state to private individuals who armed them at their own expense. It was what we would today describe as the privatization of ships from the public sector. Thus in 1712, three ships of the line, three frigates and two galleons left Toulon at the end of March, led by Cassard, one of the most skilled sailors in France, though a disciplinarian hated by the crews. The little squadron went through Gibraltar and on to the Portuguese island of São Tiago in the Cape Verde islands, which it captured and looted. It sailed on to Martinique, surprised and held to ransom the Dutch colonies of Surinam, Essequibo and Berbice, and attacked the English islands of Montserrat and St. Kitts, which were sacked from end to end. Then it came back to Toulon.

But this kind of privateering – occasionally very successful, but by no means always profitable – should not be read as a sign of French naval strength. It was in 1708 that the English took Minorca and Port Mahon from the Spanish. Port Mahon was the safest anchorage in the Mediterranean during the fierce winter storms, and had been threatened by the English since their landing at Barcelona in 1705, but had kept its freedom thanks to supplies brought by the French from . . . Toulon. From now on the English fleet, with a base like this, could winter in the Mediterranean. It was able to loot Sète in 1711. And this success makes sense only in the context of French inactivity.

Evidence that the French had stopped trying comes from a register dated 11 March 1713, that is exactly a month before the signature of the treaty of Utrecht (11 April 1713). It is a list of all the ships present in the port of Toulon: there were 32 large vessels, of the first, second, third and fourth 'rate', carrying between them 2,318 cannon – a huge concentration of fire power. But they were almost all old ships. The most venerable, the *Cheval Marin*, built in 1664, was nearly fifty years old, and would not have been afloat at all had she not been refitted in Brest. Twenty-two of the ships were between 20 and 29 years old; and another eight had seen between 5 and 19 years' service. Only one had been refitted after the siege of Toulon, the *Conquerant* in 1712, and this was a second-rater (74 cannon). Six of the ships had been declared unfit for service, ready for breaking up – and these were among the largest. Their average age was 20 years. But ships in those days deteriorated more quickly the bigger they were. In 1704 for instance the *Royal Louis* had been declared unfit for service[264] – the finest ship in the fleet and equipped with 110 cannon. Built in 1692, she was surveyed out of the service twelve years later.[265]

If I have rightly read the 'situation' outlined in this document from 1713, only seven ships were still seaworthy.[266]

The real problem, which went beyond warships, was the overall health of the French economy of the time. For everything else depended on this. Was it, in these early years of the eighteenth century, as ailing as some historians have suggested? I have found the interior of the country to be more prosperous than it is usually considered, during the last years of the War of the Spanish Succession. Similarly, in the Mediterranean, trade through Marseille and the ports on the Provençal coast continued to prosper: cotton, grain and leather from the Levant, grain and hides from North Africa continued to cross the sea. So was it simply the will that was lacking? Did France under Louis XIV *choose* the unwise course of abandoning the naval effort (for which resources would have been available, if only just), hoping to win through with the land army alone – as was the case, after all, at Toulon?

History and environment:
a few last words

Our excursion to Toulon brings to an end our exercise in retrospective geography. It has enabled us to trace some of the parameters of France's past and to draw attention to the country's diversity (Part I), to the networks linking the different areas within it (Part II), to the elements of unity provided by its geographical context, and lastly to the instructive role of the frontier which, although not insulating the country did surround it, binding its various sectors together (Part III). I have consequently stressed and re-stressed the perennial opposition between singular and plural. The singular in this instance refers to the slowly-constructed unity of a France which revealed its strength, was indeed obliged to display it, along the boundaries of its territory. Did not the provinces acquired on the periphery have to be domesticated, subjugated and brought to heel during a long training period? And did not the long ribbon of the frontiers have to be constantly defended, watched and pushed forward? It called for strenuous effort on both land and sea.

This effort, we should note, was in itself an instrument of unity: in some sense, it penetrated and mobilized the whole country, not merely the frontier regions.

I have laid much emphasis – necessarily so – on the shortcomings of France's naval effort. This was a complicated undertaking which all too often came up against the limits of the possible; all the same, it was a huge and unremitting enterprise. There was not a French river of any size that did not ship or float the timber and masts necessary for the navy; not a cannon foundry or munitions factory that did not work for it; not a naval base that did not build ships; and French vessels had, by Colbert's time, become the equal

373

of the English ships previously the envy of Europe. The supremacy of the Dutch shipyards was at an end. And a navy would have been impossible of course, without the constant, laborious recruitment of sailors, from all the regions bordering the sea: Normandy, Brittany, Languedoc, Provence. In 1632, under Richelieu, the 'press gangs'[267] were set up, but even these were not sufficient. Nor did Holland or England ever succeed in manning their ships from their own population: they had to recruit foreign crews, sometimes with brutality. France was no more successful in assembling adequate crews. Sailors recruited by force slipped away if the vigilance of the guards relaxed for a moment.[268] Under Louis XVI, in desperation, the navy requisitioned river boatmen. And as for the galley-slaves, when they went to Toulon, it was to enter the hell-hole of penal servitude. It was one way of getting rid of criminals, or supposed criminals, but they hardly strengthened the royal navy, even in the Mediterranean, where the galleys for which they were destined had outlived their usefulness.

The question of numbers was not a problem for the army on land. A populous country, France continued to provide soldiers generously. Under the *ancien régime*, there was no province, however remote from the frontier, which did not contribute its share of recruits or its part towards the upkeep of the army – even the Berry and the Limousin, even the Auvergne, the Velay or the Bourbonnais. There was no province that did not resound to the annual tramp of troops on the move, or that was exempt from the burden – there is no other word for it – of billeting infantry and cavalry (and not only during the notorious winter quarters).

These troops had not been assembled to meet an internal threat. They were only rarely used to put down civil disorder. It is true that their mere presence tended to calm a town or province, even if the *intendants* hesitated to use them to the full. It would too often mean taking a hammer to crack a nut, and run the risk of ruining a region, whereas the troublemakers usually removed themselves promptly once the troops arrived. The maintenance and circulation of troops was a precaution. France was doomed to keep a war machine afoot, like the other states and future nations of Europe.

To this end, the country's entire resources and whole population had to be drawn upon. The regiments all bore the names of provinces: the Bresse regiment, the Angoumois regiment, and so on. But fairly soon they lost all real contact with their eponymous provinces, and recruitment to the army mingled Frenchmen of different origins, creating a melting-pot, obliging men who did not speak the same language to live together and sever their provincial ties.[269]

Alongside the crown administration then, the army became the most active instrument in the unification of France. At the beginning of the nineteenth century, it has been calculated fairly reliably that there were 150,000 migrants, general labourers, looking for seasonal work, travelling around France every year and making their contribution to the mingling of the populations. But the French army, between 1709 and 1713 for instance, was responsible for setting between half a million and a million men on the move.[270] So that in the cheerless years at the end of the War of the Spanish Succession, something was happening comparable in scale to the mass levies of Year II of the Revolution. Later, with the national wars of the nineteenth and twentieth centuries, the army's gigantic and gargantuan appetite reached uncontrollable proportions.

In the process of unifying France then, all the combined forces of history were at work: those of society, of the economy, of the state, of culture – the French language, emanating from the Ile-de-France, being the language of power, the administrative tool of this ordering process. All these realities will be discussed in the volumes that follow, as we try to set in context the long slow march towards unity of a France which was many centuries in the making.

Notes

Except for works on local history, the place of publication of all French titles is Paris unless otherwise stated. Where possible, the name of an accessible English translation is provided.

Notes to Introduction

1. Jean-Paul SARTRE, *Question de méthode*, included in *Critique de la raison dialectique*, 1960, p. 29. (Eng. trans. by Hazel Barnes, *The Problem of Method*, London and New York, 1963, cf. p. 29.)

2. Charles PEGUY, *Avertissement* to *Petites garnisons*, *Cahiers de la Quinzaine*, 12, 5, 1904, p. 9, quoted in Eugen WEBER, *Peasants into Frenchmen: the modernization of rural France*, London, 1979, p. 3.

3. Fernand BRAUDEL, *La Méditerranée et le monde méditerranéen à l'époque de Philippe II*, 1949, 1966, 1976; (Eng. trans. by S. Reynolds, *The Mediterranean and the Mediterranean World in the age of Philip II*, London and New York, 1972, 1973); *Civilisation matérielle et capitalisme*, 1967 (Eng. trans. by M. Kochan, London, 1973); *Civilisation matérielle, économie et capitalisme, XVe-XVIIIe siècle*, 1979, 3 vols. (Eng. trans. by S. Reynolds, vol. I, *The Structures of Everyday Life*, 1981; vol. II, *The Wheels of Commerce*, 1982; vol. III, *The Perspective of the World*, 1984, London and New York). All page references hereafter will be to the English editions of these books.

4. Hippolyte TAINE, *Les Origines de la France contemporaine*, 1875, re-edited 1972, p. 6: 'I was in front of my subject as if in front of an insect in metamorphosis'.

5. Alexis de TOCQUEVILLE, *L'Ancien Régime et la Révolution Française*, 1st edition 1856, re-edited in 1952–3, 1960, 1963 (Eng. trans. by S. Gilbert, *The Ancien Régime and the Revolution*, London, 1971.)

6. Jules MICHELET, *Histoire de France*, 1833–1867, 17 vols, re-edited 1893–98, 40 vols.

7. Ernest LAVISSE, *Histoire de France depuis les origines jusqu'à la Révolution*, 18 vols., 1903–11.

8. Ernest LAVISSE, *Louis XIV*, 2 vols., 1978.

9. *Histoire de la France*, series edited by Robert PHILIPPE, 1970–73.

10. Jacques MADAULE, *Histoire de France*, 3 vols., 1943, 1945, 1966.

11. Lucien ROMIER, *L'Ancienne France, des origines à la Révolution*, 1948; *Explication de notre temps*, 1925.

12. Neculai IORGA, *Histoire du peuple français* (trans. from the Rumanian by P. Angelesco) 1945.

13. Ernst Robert CURTIUS, *Die franzözischen Kultur*, Stuttgart, 1930. (Eng. trans. by O. Wyon, *The Civilization of France*, 1932.)

14. Eugène CAVAIGNAC, *Esquisse d'une histoire de France*, 1910.

15. Claude-Frédéric LEVY, letter to the author, 14 September 1981.

16. Jean-Paul SARTRE, *Les Temps modernes*, October 1957, p. 681.

17. Pierre GOUBERT, *Beauvais et le Beauvaisis de 1600 à 1730*, 1960, p. 359.

18. Paul LEUILLIOT, *L'Alsace au début du XIXe siècle*, III, 1960, p. 340.

19. Jean LESTOCQUOY, *Histoire du patriotisme français des origines à nos jours*, 1968, p. 14. On the late emergence of the concept of 'nation', see WEBER, *Peasants into Frenchmen,* op. cit., chapters 7 and 18.

20. Jules MICHELET, *Oeuvres complètes*, 1974 edn, IV, p. 383.

21. Jacques BLOCH-MORHANGE, in *Informations et conjoncture*; cf. what Henri MENDRAS calls 'the elements of the national saga learned in primary school', *La Sagesse et le désordre, France 1980*, 1980, p. 35.

22. Albert MALET and Jules ISAAC, *Cours d'histoire*, many editions, republished under the title *L'Histoire* in 1980, 4 vols.

23. Arnold TOYNBEE, *Civilization on Trial*, New York, 1948, p. 64.

24. Quoted by Roger BASTIDE, *Sociologie et psychanalyse*, 1972, p. 162.

25. Theodore ZELDIN, *France 1848–1945*, 2 vols, Oxford, 1973, 1977, published in France in 5 volumes as *Histoire des passions françaises*, 1978–9.

26. Robert FOSSAERT, *La Société*,

II, *Les Structures économiques*, 1977, p. 447.

27. M. BORDEAUX, 'Voies ouvertes à l'histoire des coutumes par l'hématologie géographique', in *Annales E. S. C.*, November–December 1969, pp. 1275–1286.

28. Marc BLOCH, *Apologie pour l'histoire ou Métier d'historien*, 1949. (Eng. trans. by P. Putnam, *The Historian's Craft*, 1954.)

29. Quoted by Emile CALLOT, *Ambiguités et antinomies de l'histoire et de sa philosophie*, 1962, p. 121.

30. Paul MORAND, *Venises*, 1971, p. 101.

31. Edgar QUINET, *Introduction* to French edition of Johann G. von HERDER, *Idées sur la philosophie de l'histoire de l'humanité*, I, 1827, p. 7.

32. Theodore ZELDIN, 'Français, vous êtes comme ça!', *Paris–Match*, 30 May 1980.

33. D. LANDES and C. FOHLEN, 'Capital formation in the early stages of industrialization', Introduction, in *Second International Economic History Conference*, proceedings, 1962, p. 565.

34. Jean-Paul SARTRE, *Critique de la raison dialectique*, 1960, p. 557, quoted by Georges GURVITCH, *Dialectique et sociologie*, 1962, p. 163.

35. Emile DURKHEIM, 'Sociologie et sciences sociales', in *De la méthode dans les sciences*, 1909, reproduced in Jean-Claude FILLOUX, *La Science sociale et l'action*, 1970, p. 157 note.

36. Robert FOSSAERT, *La Société*, I, *Une théorie générale*, 1977, p. 32.

37. Fernand DUMONT, *Anthropologie*, 1981, p. 17.

38. Raymond RUDORFF, *Le Mythe de la France*, 1971.
39. Miguel de UNAMUNO, *En torno al casticismo* (and other essays), Madrid, 1902, translated into French as *L'Essence de L'Espagne*, 1923.
40. Angel GANIVET GARCIA, *Obras completas*, I, *Granada la Bella, Idearium español*, 1943.
41. José ORTEGA Y GASSET, *España invertebrada*, 1934.
42. Georges GURVITCH, *La Vocation actuelle de la sociologie*, 1963, I, pp. 73 ff.
43. Ferdinand LOT, *La Gaule*, 1947, p. 170.
44. Julien GRACQ, *Lettrines*, 1974, II, p. 71.
45. Jean-Paul SARTRE, in *Les Temps modernes*, September 1957, p. 403, note.
46. I borrowed this expression from Michel LARAN, the remarkable specialist on Russia ancient and modern, whose untimely death robbed us of a generous scholar: but I cannot find a reference for the expression in his published work.
47. Joseph CHAPPEY, *Histoire de la civilisation en Occident, I, La Crise de l'histoire et la mort de l'idée de civilisation*, 1958, p. 38.
48. Peter KRIEDTE, Hans MEDICK, Jürgen SCHLUMBOHM, *Industrialisierung vor der Industrialisierung*, 1977, p. 21.

Notes to Introduction to Part I

1. Marguerite GONON, *Les Institutions et la société en Forez au XIVe siècle d'après les testaments*, 1960; *La Vie familiale en Forez et son vocabulaire d'après les testaments*, 1961.

2. Maurice BERTHE, *Le Comté de Bigorre, un milieu rural au bas Moyen Age*, 1976.
3. Roger BETEILLE, *La Vie quotidienne en Rouergue au XIXe siècle*, 1973.
4. Louis MERLE, *La Métairie et l'évolution agraire de la Gâtine poitevine*, 1958.
5. Michel BELOTTE, *La Région de Bar-sur-Seine à la fin du Moyen Age, du début du XIIIe siècle au milieu du XVIe siècle*, 1973.
6. Lucien FEBVRE, 'Que la France se nomme diversité! A propos de quelques études jurassiennes', in *Annales E.S.C.*, 1946, pp. 271–4.

Notes to Part I

1. René MUSSET, 'La géographie de l'histoire' in *Histoire de France*, ed. Marcel REINHARD, 1954, I, p. 36.
2. Pierre GASCAR, *La France*, 1971, p. 11.
3. Jean-Robert PITTE, *Histoire du paysage français*, 1983, I, p. 14.
4. *Ibid.*, p. 13.
5. Hervé LE BRAS, Emmanuel TODD, *L'Invention de la France*, 1981, p. 7.
6. Archives nationales, Paris (A.N.), F^{10} 1c.
7. A.N., G^7 449, Poitiers, 23 November 1684.
8. Alain CROIX, *La Bretagne aux XVIe et XVIIe siècles*, I, 1981, p. 33.
9. E. BOGROS, *A travers le Morvan*, 1878, p. 108.
10. G. DUHEM, 'Un petit village du Haut-Jura, Lamoura', in *A travers les villes du Jura*, 1963, p. 541.
11. Mgr LUSTIGER in *Paris–Match*, 24 April 1981, p. 9.

12. Lucien FEBVRE, 'Que la France se nomme diversité', op. cit.
13. Eugen WEBER, *Peasants into Frenchmen,* op. cit., *passim,* esp. final chapter.
14. The decree of 21 September 1792 refers to 'the Republic one and indivisible'; exercising a little latitude, we may speak of *France* one and indivisible.
15. The expression is borrowed from Jean FOURASTIE, *Les Trente Glorieuses ou la Révolution invisible de 1946 à 1975,* 1979.
16. LEBRAS and TODD, *L'Invention de la France,* op. cit., p. 7.
17. Yves FLORENNE, *Le Monde,* 9 April 1981.
18. Jean GIONO, *Ennemonde et autres caractères,* 1968, p. 8.
19. Henry DEBRAYE, *Avec Stendhal sur les bords du Rhône,* 1944, p. 86.
20. Pierre AUMOINE and Charles DANGEAU, *La France a cent ans . . . Sommes-nous nés en 1865?,* 1965, p. 297.
21. Henri SPADE, *Et pourquoi pas la patrie?,* 1974, p. 107.
22. Daniel ROCHE, *Le Peuple de Paris,* 1981, p. 6.
23. André MAREZ, teacher at the *lycée* in Perpignan, who died in 1978.
24. Lucien FEBVRE, *Philippe II et la Franche-Comté,* 1970, p. 29.
25. Ernest BENEVENT, 'La vieille économie provençale' in *Revue de géographie alpine,* 1938, p. 533.
26. *Ibid.,* p. 535.
27. Pierre GOUROU, letter to the author, 27 June 1978.
28. J. CHAPELOT and R. FOSSIER, *Le Village et la maison au Moyen Age,* 1980, p. 161; writing about the village of Pélissane (Bouches-du-Rhône).
29. E. BENEVENT, 'La vieille économie provençale', op. cit., p. 542.
30. J. GIONO, *Ennemonde,* op. cit., p. 14.
31. Frédéric GAUSSEN, review of Armand FREMONT, *Paysans de Normandie,* 1981, in *Le Monde,* 4 October 1981.
32. *Ibid.*
33. Hervé FILLIPETTI, *Maisons paysannes de l'ancienne France,* 1979, p. 79.
34. M. BERTHE, *Le Comté de Bigorre,* op. cit., p. 43.
35. Quoted by Pierre FRANCASTEL, *L'Humanisme roman,* 1942, p. 26.
36. Described in detail in Henri VINCENOT, *La Vie quotidienne des paysans bourguignons au temps de Lamartine,* 1976.
37. Roland BARTHES, *Michelet par lui-même,* 1st edn 1954, 2nd edn 1965.
38. H. FILLIPETTI, *Maisons paysannes,* op. cit., p. 10.
39. Julien GRACQ, *Lettrines,* 1974, II, p. 35.
40. Henry de ROUVIERE, *Voyage du tour de la France,* 1713, pp. 11–12.
41. H. FILLIPETTI, *Maisons paysannes,* op. cit., p. 84.
42. E. MEILLET, 1963, p. 157, quoted by Muriel JEAN-BRUNHES DELAMARRE, *Le Berger dans la France des villages,* 1970, p. 213.
43. *Savart, savaret,* names given in the Ardennes and *la Champagne pouilleuse* (lit. flea-bitten Champagne), to high land, uncultivated and almost exclusively used to graze sheep; because of the lack of water, they had little grass. *Hollée;* literally 'shout'. Some sales or annual lettings of uncultivated land were held 'by

earshot', the distance a voice could carry being used as a measurement of land. (Cf. G. CROUVEZIER, *Petit vocabulaire du langage champenois*, 1975).

44. Marcel POETE, *Une première manifestation d'union sacrée. Paris devant la menace étrangère en 1636*, 1916.

45. Jacqueline BONNAMOUR, *Le Morvan, la terre et les hommes. Essai de géographie agricole*, 1966, p. 243.

46. Jacques LEVAINVILLE, *Le Morvan, étude de géographie humaine*, 1909.

47. Ernest RENAN, *Oeuvres complètes*, 1960, IX, p. 1344.

48. J. GIONO, *Ennemonde*, op. cit., p. 127.

49. Jean ANGLADE, *L'Auvergne et le Massif Central d'hier et de demain*, 1981, p. 16.

50. L. GACHON, *La Vie rurale en France*, 3rd edn, 1976, p. 11.

51. Jean ANGLADE, *La Vie quotidienne dans le Massif Central*, 1971, p. 37 (a *sapinière* is a kind of boat used on the Loire and the Allier. Cf. Part II below).

52. A. LEROUX, *Le Massif Central*, I, 1898, p. xv.

53. Pierre DEFFONTAINES and Jean-François GRAVIER, 'La France', in *Géographic universelle Larousse*, ed. P. Deffontaines and M. J.-B. Delamarre, I, 1959, p. 129.

54. Albert DEMANGEON, *La France économique et humaine*, 1946, I, pp. 81–107.

55. Désiré PASQUET, *Histoire politique et sociale du peuple américain*, I, *Des origines à 1825*, 1924, p. 74.

56. At Soyons, on the right bank of the Rhône. Daniel FAUCHER, *L'Homme et le Rhône*, 1969, map, p. 49.

57. Arthur YOUNG, *Travels during the years 1787, 1788 and 1789*, 1792 edn, I, p. 298. (This passage, which comes in Part II, *General Observations*, is not reproduced in most modern editions of Young's *Travels*.) The paliurus is a thorny bush found in the Mediterranean regions, a member of the rhamnaceae family.

58. Jean RACINE, *Lettres d'Uzès*, 1929 edn, p. 57.

59. J.-C. MASANELLI, *Gaujac à l'époque de Louis XIV*, 1981, p. 83.

60. Maximilien SORRE, *Les Fondements biologiques de la géographie humaine*, 1943, I, p. 14.

61. Paul VIDAL DE LA BLACHE, *Tableau de la géographie de la France*, 1913, re-edited 1979, p. 226.

62. *Ibid.*, p. 131.

63. Marie-Hélène JOUAN, 'Les originalités démographiques d'un bourg artisanal normand au XVIIIe siècle: Villedieu-les-Poêles (1711–1790)', in *Annales de la démographie historique*, 1969, pp. 87–124.

64. F. BRAUDEL, *The Wheels of Commerce*, op. cit., p. 320.

65. Abel POITRINEAU, *La Vie rurale en Basse-Auvergne au XVIIIe siècle (1726–1789)*, 1965, re-edited 1979.

66. Henri BAUD, Jean-Yves MARIOTTE, *Histoire des communes savoyardes*, II, *Le Faucigny*, 1980, pp. 392–3.

67. Nicole LEMAITRE 'Ussel ou la difficulté de vivre: familles urbaines et rurales aux XVIIe et XVIIIe siècles', in *Entre faim et loup . . . Les problèmes de la vie et de l'émigration sur les hautes terres françaises au XVIIIe siècle*, 1976, pp. 11 and 16.

68. Nicole LEMAITRE, *Un Horizon bloqué, Ussel et la montagne limousine aux XVIIe et XVIIIe siècles*, 1978, pp. 86 ff.

69. Abel CHATELAIN, *Les Migrants temporaires en France de 1800 à 1914*, 1976, p. 73.

70. Gustave SCHELLE, *Oeuvres de Turgot et documents le concernant*, II, 1914, pp. 4–5.

71. Archives of Dr MORAND, Bonne-sur-Ménoge (Haute Savoie).

72. Alain REYNAUD, Georges CAZES, *Les Mutations récentes de l'économie francaise de la croissance à l'aménagement*, 1973, p. 9.

73. A. DEMANGEON, *La France économique*, op. cit., I, p. 40.

74. Paul ETCHEMENDY, *Les Paysans d'Espelette (Pays Basque) du XIXe siècle à nos jours*, 1981, p. 21.

75. *Le Quotidien de Paris*, 3 February 1982.

76. Georges GURVITCH, *Déterminismes sociaux et liberté humaine. Vers l'étude sociologique des cheminements de la liberté*, 1955, *passim*.

77. Nicolas-Edme RETIF DE LA BRETONNE, *La Vie de mon père*, 1779, re-edited 1963, p. 143.

78. H. TAINE, *Les Origines de la France contemporaine*, op. cit., p. 11.

79. A.N., G⁷ 101; Murat, 26 May 1683.

80. Pierre GOUBERT, *L'Ancien Régime*, 1969, I, p. 110.

81. See Part II below, section on Gondrecourt.

82. A.N., H 1515: Metz, 21 April 1768: list of the number of *laboureurs* (rich peasants) and *manouvriers* (day-labourers) in the various bourgs and villages in the *département* of the three bishoprics:

Sub-délégation	Labour-eurs	Man-ouvriers
Metz	789	3750
Toul	1921	1924
Verdun	1395	2679
Sedan	429	1787
Montmédy	836	1767
Longwy	145	442
Thionville	954	2706
Sarrelouis	452	729
Vic	1192	2707
Sarrebourg	448	1177
Phalsbourg	91	236
	8,652	19,904

83. Paul VIDAL DE LA BLACHE, *La France de l'Est*, 1917, p.18. 'The various statistics attempted in the seventeenth and eighteenth centuries accord in recognizing that [the number of *manouvriers* as opposed to *laboureurs*] is much greater, over half as much again at least, than the number of *laboureurs* with their own land'.

84. H. TAINE, *Les Origines*, op. cit., p. 16.

85. Jules-Marie RICHARD, *La Vie privée dans une province de l'Ouest: Laval aux XVIIe et XVIIIe siècles*, 1922, pp. 355 ff.

86. *Ibid.*, pp. 4–5.

87. A.N., H 2933; *Mémoire sur les péages*, pp. 9–20.

88. A.N., G⁷ 449: 29 May 1683.

89. A.N., G⁷ 347: 6 August 1695.

90. J.-M. RICHARD, *La Vie privée*, op. cit., pp. 3–4.

91. A.N., G⁷ 356.

92. Jacques TENEUR, 'Les commerçants dunkerquois à la fin du XVIIIe siècle et les problèmes économiques de leur temps', in *Revue du Nord*, 1966, pp. 18 ff.

93. Quoted by Marcel MARION, *Dictionnaire des institutions de la*

France aux XVIIe et XVIIIe siècles, 1923, re-ed. 1976, p. 296.

94. Henri FREVILLE, *L'Intendance de Bretagne (1689–1790), essai sur l'histoire d'une intendance en pays d'états au XVIIIe siècle*, 1953, I, p. 95.

95. A.N., G⁷ 382; Metz, 29 August 1708.

96. A.N., F¹⁴ 158. Shipping on the Rhône.

97. A. POITRINEAU, *La Vie rurale*, op cit., p. 38.

98. Jean SIGMANN, 'La Révolution de Maupeou en Bourgogne, 1771–1775,' DES dissertation, Dijon University, 1935, p. 30.

99. A.N., G⁷ 239; Grenoble, 31 July 1679.

100. Pierre DUBOIS, 'Histoire de la campagne de 1707 dans le Sud-Est de la France', unpublished typescript, pp. 28–9.

101. M. MARION, *Dictionnaire*, op. cit., p. 429.

102. On Lyon, see F. BRAUDEL, *The Wheels of Commerce*, op cit., p. 468. On Montpellier, see Guy CHAUSSINAND-NOGARET, *Les Financiers du Languedoc au XVIIIe siècle*, 1970, pp. 235 ff.

103. In all the major phases of history, a contrast can be detected: see J. HURSTFIELD and H. G. KOENIGSBERGER in *The New Cambridge Modern History*, III, *The Counter-Reformation and the Price Revolution 1559–1610*, 1968. pp. 131 and 290.

104. J. RACINE, *Lettres d'Uzès*, op. cit., p. 3; letter to La Fontaine 11 Novembre 1661; *ibid.*, p. 7, letter to M. Vitart, 15 November 1661.

105. *Documents d'histoire du Languedoc*, 1969, p. 239.

106. T. ZELDIN, *France*, op. cit., vol. II, p. 43.

107. Reference to Albert THIBAUDET's book, *Les Princes lorrains*, 1924.

108. Alain KIMMEL, Jacques POUJOL, *Certaines idées de la France*, 1982, p. 67.

109. Ernest RENAN, *La Réforme intellectuelle et morale*, in *Oeuvres complètes*, I, 1947, p. 349.

110. STENDHAL, *Mémoires d'un touriste*, 1838, re-ed. 1927, I, p. 185.

111. H. DEBRAYE, *Avec Stendhal*, op. cit., p. v.

112. Vincent VAN GOGH, *Lettres à son frère Théo*, 1956 edn, pp. 364, 374, 394, 403, 412, 393–4, 368. Eric DARRAGON, 'Van Gogh, Tartarin et la diligence de Tarascon', in *Critique*, January 1982, pp. 42–60.

113. Cf. F. BRAUDEL, *The Mediterranean*, op. cit., I, p. 237.

114. Archivo di Stato, Genoa, *Lettere Consoli*, 28; 20 June–10 July 1673.

115. Philippe MARTEL, 'Les Occitans face à leur histoire: Mary-Lafon, le grand ancêtre', in *Amiras/Répères occitans*, I, January 1982, p. 10.

116. H. DEBRAYE, *Avec Stendhal*, op. cit., pp. 39, 76, 77, 79. Italics in original.

117. Augustin GAZIER, *Lettres à Grégoire sur les patois de la France (1790–1794)* . . ., 1880, p. 292.

118. Michel de CERTEAU, Dominique JULIA, Jacques REVEL, *Une politique de la langue. La Révolution française et les patois: l'enquête de Grégoire*, 1975, p. 162.

119. GAZIER, *Lettres à Grégoire*, op. cit., p. 128.

120. *Ibid.*, p. 107.

121. *Ibid.*, pp. 137–9.

122. *Ibid.*, p. 222.

123. *Ibid.*, pp. 213 and 224.
124. *Ibid.*, pp. 282 and 287.
125. *Encyclopédie*, XII, 1765, p. 174, article 'Patois'.
126. Joachim TROTTE de la CHETARDIE (1613–1714), author of a *Catéchisme de Bourges*, 1708.
127. M. de CERTEAU, D. JULIA, J. REVEL, *Une politique de la langue*, op. cit., p. 163.
128. A. GAZIER, *Lettres à Grégoire*, op. cit., p. 57.
129. *Ibid.*, p. 91.
130. *Ibid.*, p. 90.
131. Abbé Antoine ALBERT, *Histoire géographique, naturelle, ecclésiastique, et civile du diocèse d'Embrun*, 1783, I, p. 93.
132. Louis STOUFF, in *Habiter la ville*, ed. Maurice GARDEN et Yves LEQUIN, 1984, p. 11.
133. *Ibid.*
134. A. GAZIER, *Lettres à Grégoire*, op. cit., p. 137.
135. Pierre BONNAUD, *Terres et langages. Peuples et régions*, I, 1981, p. 44.
136. Robert Louis STEVENSON, *The Cévennes Journal*, ed. G. GOLDING. New York, 1978, pp. 17–18. (This passage from Stevenson's manuscript journal, does not appear in the published version of *Travels with a Donkey in the Cévennes*; it is quoted here since it appears in the notes to the French edition, 1978, p. 205. A line is missing from the Golding edition, hence the square brackets – S.R.)
137. P. BONNAUD, *Terres et langages*, op cit., pp. 2–4, 8, 408 ff.
138. *Ibid.*, p. 63.
139. Robert SPECKLIN, 'Etudes sur les origines', in *Acta Geographica*, 1982.
140. François SIGAUT, 'Formes et évolution des techniques', polycopy, 70 pp. (Report to Economic History Conference, Budapest, 1982, session on 'Large and small landholdings'), p. 63.
141. Jean-Louis FLANDRIN, *Familles, parenté, maison, sexualité dans l'ancienne société*, 1976, p. 7.
142. H. LE BRAS, E. TODD, *L'Invention de la France*, op. cit., pp. 23–8.
143. *Ibid.*, pp. 40–45.
144. *Ibid.*, pp. 53–4.
145. Jean-Pierre GUITTON, *Villages du Lyonnais sous la monarchie, XVIe–XVIIIe siècles*, 1978, p. 9.
146. H. LE BRAS, E. TODD, *L'Invention de la France*, op. cit., pp. 107–8.
147. Micheline BAULANT, 'La famille en miettes; sur un aspect de la démographie du XVIIe siècle', in *Annales E.S.C.*, 1972, pp. 959–968.
148. *Ibid.*, p. 967.
149. Peter LASLETT, *The World We Have Lost*, 2nd edn, 1971, chapter 4.
150. Alan McFARLANE, *The Origins of English Individualism. The Family, Property and Social Transition*, 1978, pp. 138 ff.
151. As is stressed in Hervé LE BRAS's latest book, *Les Trois France*, read in manuscript. The large patriarchal family is here presented as the essential strength of the Midi in resisting the unifying drive of central authority.
152. *Le Monde*, 24 May 1981.
153. *Ibid.*
154. *Mémoires de Jean Maillefer, marchand bourgeois de Reims (1611–1684)*, 1890, p. 15.
155. H. LE BRAS, E. TODD, *L'Invention de la France*, op. cit., p. 76.

156. Paul-Marie DUVAL, 'Archéologie et histoire de la Gaule', in *Annuaire du Collège de France*, 1967, p. 453.

157. Karl BRANDI, *Kaiser Karl V*, 1937, p. 326. (Eng. trans. by C. V. Wedgwood, 1939.)

158. *Ibid.*, pp. 443–4.

159. 18 September 1544.

160. K. BRANDI, *Kaiser Karl V*, op. cit., p. 448.

161. Marquise de LA TOUR DU PIN, *Journal d'une femme de cinquante ans*, II, *1778–1815*, 1923, p. 339.

162. Léo MOUTON, *Le Duc et le Roi: d'Epernon, Henri IV, Louis XIII*, 1924, pp. 133 ff.

163. A.N., G^7 1691, 85.

164. René HERON DE VILLEFOSSE, *Histoire des grandes routes de France*, 1975, p. 185.

165. Marcellin de MARBOT, *Mémoires*, 1891.

166. A.N., F^{10} 226, 23 ventôse, Year II.

167. M. de MARBOT, *Mémoires*, op. cit., I, pp. 45–6.

168. François LEBRUN, *Histoire des pays de la Loire*, Toulouse, 1972, I, p. 163, II, pp. 143–4.

169. Henriette DUSSOURD, *Les Hommes de la Loire*, 1985, p. 89.

170. STENDHAL, *Journal de voyage de Bordeaux à Valence en 1838*, 1927 edn, p. 3.

171. R. HERON DE VILLEFOSSE, *Histoire des grandes routes*, op. cit., p. 230.

172. Pierre de LA GORCE, *Histoire du Second Empire*, I, 1894, p. 223.

173. Francesco FADINI, *Caporetto dalla parte del vincitore*, 1974, p. 449.

174. Roger DION, 'La part de la géographie et celle de l'histoire dans l'explication de l'habitat rural du Bassin parisien', in *Publications de la Société de géographie de Lille*, 1946, p. 32.

175. François MIREUR, *Etats Généraux de 1789. Cahiers des doléances des communautés de la sénéchaussée de Draguignan*, 1889, p. 118.

176. *Assemblée provinciale de l'Ile-de-France*, 1787, p. 212.

177. Abbé A. ALBERT, *Histoire . . . du diocèse d'Embrun*, op cit., pp. 91–2.

178. A. GAZIER, *Lettres à Grégoire*, op cit., p. 287.

179. Jean and Renée NICOLAS, *La Vie quotidienne en Savoie aux XVIIe et XVIIIe siècles*, 1979, pp. 313–15.

180. A. GAZIER, *Lettres à Grégoire*, op. cit., p. 278.

181. A. DEMANGEON, *La France économique*, op cit., p. 398.

182. Robert MUCHEMBLED, *Culture populaire et culture des elites dans la France moderne (XVe–XVIIIe siècles)*, 1978, p. 54.

183. Robert PHILIPPE, ed., *Histoire de la France*, vol. III, exact reference mislaid.

184. R. MUCHEMBLED, *Culture populaire*, op. cit., p. 22.

185. Jacques DUPAQUIER, *La Population rurale du Bassin Parisien à l'époque de Louis XIV*, 1979, p. 204.

186. Nicolas-Edme RETIF DE LA BRETONNE, *Monsieur Nicolas*, 1959 edn, pp. 179–80.

187. Elena FASANO GUARINI, 'Città soggette e contadi nel dominio fiorentino tra Quattro e Cinquecento: il caso pisano', In *Ricerche di storia moderna*, I, 1976, pp. 1–94.

188. Giovanni ZELDIN, reference mislaid.

189. Sanche de GRAMONT, *Les Français, portrait d'un peuple*, 1970, p. 454.

190. Marc FERRO, *La Grande Guerre*

1914–18, 1969, p. 24.
191. Jules MICHELET, reference mislaid.
192. François BOURRICAUD, *Le Bricolage idéologique. Essai sur les intellectuels et les passions démocratiques*, 1980, p. 24.
193. Jean GUEHENNO, *La Mort des autres*, 1968, pp. 178 and 184.
194. I. e. Antoine de Bourbon.
195. François de LA NOUE, *Mémoires*, 1838, pp. 593–4.
196. *Ibid.*, p. 605.
197. Alexandre de TILLY, *Mémoires*, 1965 edn, p. 226.

Notes to Part II

1. Jean-Paul SARTRE, reference mislaid.
2. P. BONNAUD, *Terres et langages*, op. cit., I, p. 24.
3. Jean BUVAT, *Journal de la Régence*, 1865, II, p. 287.
4. A.N., K 1219, n° 62.
5. J. BUVAT, *Journal*, op. cit., II, p. 332.
6. Cf. F. BRAUDEL, *The Wheels of Commerce*, op. cit., p. 120.
7. Paul GAULTIER, *L'Ame française*, 1936, p. 9.
8. André DELEAGE, *La Vie économique et sociale de la Bourgogne dans le Haut Moyen Age*, 1941, I, p. 101.
9. Carl LAMPRECHT, *Etudes sur l'état économique de la France pendant la première partie du Moyen Age*, French edn, 1889.
10. I shall use the term 'farm' (*ferme*) throughout this book to mean an agricultural entity run from a single set of buildings.
11. C. LAMPRECHT, *Etudes*, op. cit., p. 9.
12. *Résultats statistiques du recensement de la population française*, 1891, pp. 64 and 86.
13. Christian ZARKA, 'Evolution de l'habitat champenois', in *Actes du colloque de Châteauroux, Bouges-le-Château, Leroux, 27–29 October 1978*, edited by Olivier BUCHSENSCHUTZ, part 2, *L'Evolution de l'habitat en Berry*, 1981, p. 251.
14. P. BONNAUD, *Terres et langages*, op. cit., II, p. 93.
15. Fernand BENOIT, *La Provence et le Comtat Venaissin*, 1949, p. 41.
16. Marie TAY, *Une commune de l'ancienne France, monographie du village de Rognes*, 1885, p. 5; for statistics on Rognes see *Atlas historique de Provence*, op. cit.
17. L. MERLE, *La Métairie*, op. cit., 1958, pp. 63 ff.
18. Paulette LECLERCQ, *Garéoult: un village de Provence dans la seconde moitié du XVIe siècle*, 1979.
19. André CHAMSON, *Castanet*, 1979, p. 68.
20. A.N., F 1c III; Finistère I.
21. A.N., F20 187; memorandum on statistics of Finistère *département*, 1789 and Year IX.
22. Robert LATOUCHE, 'Un aspect de la vie rurale dans le Maine au XIe et au XIIe Siècle: l'établissement des bourgs', in *Le Moyen Age*, 1937, n° 1–2, p. 21.
23. *Ibid.*, p. 18, note 62.
24. *Ibid.*, p. 17.
25. Roger DION, 'La part de la géographie et celle de l'histoire dans l'habitat rural du Bassin Parisien', in *Publications de la Société de géographie de Lille*, 1946, pp. 49–50.
26. A. CROIX, *La Bretagne*, op. cit., I, p. 23.
27. R. DION, 'La part de la géographie', art. cit., p. 50.
28. A. CROIX, *La Bretagne*, op. cit., I, pp. 147 and 153.
29. Aimé PERPILLOU, *Cartographie*, p. 93.

30. Alain CORBIN, *Archaïsme et modernité en Limousin au XIXe siècle, 1845–1880*, 1975, I, p. 247.

31. *Ibid.*, I, pp. 287–300.

32. Emmanuel LE ROY LADURIE, and André ZYSBERG, 'Géographie des hagiotoponymes en France', in *Annales E.S.C.*, 1983, pp. 1304 ff.

33. Jean GUILAINE, *La France d'avant la France*, 1980, pp. 36–42.

34. Pierre de SAINT-JACOB, 'Etudes sur l'ancienne communauté rurale en Bourgogne. III: La banlieue du village', in *Annales de Bourgogne*, XVIII, Dec. 1946, p. 239, note 2.

35. André PIATIER, *Radioscopie des communes de France. Ruralité et relations villes-campagnes. Une recherche pour l'action*, 1979. p. 55.

36. See the remarkable paper by Noël COULET, 'La survie des communautés d'habitants des villages disparus: l'exemple d'Aix et du pays d'Aix aux XIVe et XVe siècles', in *Villes d'Europe*, conference at Nice 1969, *Annales de la Faculté de Lettres de Nice*, 1969, n° 9–10, pp. 81–91.

37. J. H. von THUNEN, *Der isolierte Staat in Beziehung auf Landwirtschaft und Nationalökonomie*, 1826.

38. R. DION, 'La part de la géographie', art. cit., p. 21.

39. Paul DUFOURNET, *Une communauté agraire secrète et organise son territoire à Bassy (Province de Génevois, Haute-Savoie)*, 1975, p. 422.

40. Albert DEMANGEON, *Géographie économique de la France*, I, p. 192.

41. A.N., H 1514; 1787.

42. Spring wheat and other cereals (barley, oats, millet etc.) sown in March.

43. Ange GOUDAR, *Les Intérêts de la France mal entendus . . .*, I, 1756, p. 90.

44. Lucien GACHON, *La Vie rurale en France*, 1967, p. 58.

45. Michel ROUCHE, *L'Aquitaine des Wisigoths aux Arabes, 418–781, naissance d'une région*, 1979, p. 184.

46. P. DUFOURNET, *Une communauté agraire*, op. cit., p. 72. A *murger* is a scree and a *teppe* land barren either naturally or through neglect.

47. J. CHAPELOT, R. FOSSIER, *Le Village et la maison au Moyen Age*, op cit., p. 33.

48. Archives départementales (A.D.), Meuse, C 1480, I v°; 27 October 1789.

49. There had of course been earlier instances: in 1652 for example, the boundaries were clarified between the parishes of Martigné and Saint-Berthevin in what is today the *département* of Mayenne.

50. Maurice AGULHON, *La Vie sociale en Provence intérieure au lendemain de la Révolution*, 1970, p. 33.

51. A.N., G⁷ 1649, 53.

52. J. BONNAMOUR, *Le Morvan*, op. cit., p. 235.

53. Lucien GACHON, 'France rurale d'aujourd'hui, I. Dans les massifs cristallins d'Auvergne. Le ruine du paysage rural et ses causes', in *Annales E.S.C.*, 1950, p. 452.

54. The Escandorgue is a volcanic plateau in the hills behind Montpellier.

55. Reference mislaid.

56. Abbé Alexandre TOLLEMER, *Journal manuscrit d'un sire de Gouberville et du Mesnil-en-Val, gentilhomme campagnard . . ., Le Journal de Valognes*, 17 February 1870–20 March 1872, p. 384.

57. A.N., MM 928.

58. J. ANGLADE, *L'Auvergne et le Massif Central . . .* op. cit., p. 54.

59. A.N., G⁷ 434.

60. *Mémoires des intendants sur l'état des généralités dressé pour l'instruction du duc de Bourgogne. I. Mémoire de la généralité de Paris*, ed A. M. de BOISLILE, 1881, p. vi, note 5, letters of 29 July 1704, 1 and 22 May 1706, 13 June 1707.

61. Marquis d'ARGENSON, *Journal et Mémoires*, 1864, VI, p. 181.

62. A.N., H. 1462; Versailles, 13 March 1787.

63. F. MIREUR, *Etats générauz de 1789*, op. cit., p. 79.

64. Quoted by Réne DUMONT, *Nouveaux Voyages dans les campagnes françaises*, 1977, p. 385.

65. François DORNIC, *L'Industrie textile dans le Maine et ses débouchés internationaux, (1650–1815)*, 1955, p. 20.

66. Henri VINCENOT, *La Billebaude*, 1978, p. 48.

67. Denis RICHET, 'Une famille de robe: les Séguier avant le chancelier' manuscript thesis, p. 91.

68. On the role of wood in the economy, see F. BRAUDEL, *The Structures of Everyday Life*, op. cit., pp. 362 ff. and notes.

69. P. BONNAUD, *Terres et langages*, op cit., I, p. 51.

70. François JEANNIN, 'L'industrie du verre en Argonne', in *Patrimoine et culture en Lorraine*, ed. Yves LEMOINE, 1980, p. 84.

71. Donatien-Alphonse-François, marquis de SADE, *Justine ou les malheurs de la vertu*, 1791.

72. A.N., G⁷ 237; Châlons, 31 January 1715.

73. A.N., G⁷ 432; 20 November 1704.

74. A.N., G⁷ 501; Rouen, 6 June 1712.

75. A.N., G⁷ 419.

76. A.N., G⁷ 433; July 1706.

77. A.N., MM 928, f° 15; 1698.

78. Marcel REINHARD, André ARMENGAUD, Jacques DUPAQUIER, *Histoire générale de la population mondiale*, 1960, p. 268.

79. R. DION, 'La part de la géographie', art. cit., p. 62.

80. André BURGUIERE, 'Endogamia e comunità contadine sulla pratica matrimoniale a Romainville nel XVIII secolo', in *Quaderni storici*, Sept.– Dec. 1976, pp. 1073–1094.

81. Jean SUTTER and Léon TABAH, 'Les notions d'isolat et de population minimum', in *Population*, n° 3, July–Sept. 1951, pp. 486–9.

82. Michel-Hilaire CLEMENT-JANIN, *Sobriquets des villes et des villages de la Côte d'Or*, 1876, *passim*.

83. P. M. JONES, 'Political commitment and rural society in the southern Massif Central', in *European Studies Review*, 1980, pp. 343–4.

84. A. CROIX, *La Bretagne*, op. cit., I, p. 33.

85. Personal memory, Luméville (Meuse), 1907.

86. Joseph CRESSOT, *Le Pain au lièvre*, 1973, p. 113.

87. *Ibid.*, p. 117.

88. Jacques-Joseph JUGE SAINT-MARTIN, *Changemens survenus dans les moeurs des habitans de*

Limoges depuis une cinquantaine d'années . . ., 1817, p. 14.

89. Yves-Marie BERCE, *Histoire des croquants. Etudes des soulèvements populaires au XVIIe siècle dans le Sud-Ouest de la France*, 1974, p. 297.

90. A. CORBIN, *Archaïsme et modernité en Limousin*, op. cit., I, p. 98.

91. André VAQUIER, *Ermont . . .*, I. *Des origines à la Revolution française*, 1965, pp. 144 ff.

92. Jean PETIT, *Un registre: un village . . . une époque . . . Contribution à l'histoire sociale et économique du monde rural au début du XXe siècle*, 1980.

93. A.N., F¹⁰ 222.

94. F. BRAUDEL, *The Perspective of the World*, op. cit., chapter 4, note 13.

95. Abbé CHALAND, *Mémoires de Saint-Julien-Molin-Molette*, 1852, pp. 5–6.

96. Emile COORNAERT, *Un centre industriel d'autrefois. La draperie-sayetterie d'Hondschoote (XIVe–XVIIIe siècle)*, 1930, p. 249, note 2.

97. A. CORBIN, *Archaïsme et modernité en Limousin*, op. cit., I, p. 298, note 136. On the Pyrenees, see *Hommage à P. Wolff, Annales du Midi*, 1978, pp. 407–8.

98. Richard GASCON, *Grand Commerce et vie urbaine au XVIe siècle. Lyon et ses marchands (environs de 1520–environs de 1580)*, 1971, I, pp. 327–8.

99. Personal testimony of Michel Granjacques of Saint-Nicolas (Haute-Savoie), born in 1896, who was himself a *barlotier*, as his father, Jean-Euchariste, had been before him.

100. A.N., G⁷ 377; Metz, 1 July 1695.

101. A.N., G⁷ 1651; Soissons, 4 June 1709.

102. Jean-Pierre FILIPPINI, 'Les Conséquences économiques de la Guerre de Succession d'Autriche', thesis manuscript, pp. 58–62.

103. Henri RAMEAU, *A l'orée des plateaux de la Haute-Saône, le village d'Andelarre*, 1974, pp. 32–3.

104. Dominique DINET, 'Quatre paroisses du Tonnerrois' in *Annales de démographie historique*, 1969, pp. 62–84.

105. Pierre GAXOTTE, *Mon village et moi*, 1968, p. 129.

106. Séverine BEAUMIER, 'Un homme, un village – les travaux et les jours dans le Haut-Diois au XIXe siècle', in *Le Monde alpin et rhodanien*, 1978, pp. 1–2.

107. Jean PETIT, *Le Chant de mon enfance*, typescript.

108. R. CHAPUIS, 'Une vallée franc-comtoise: la Haute Loue', in *Annales littéraires de l'Université de Besançon*, vol. 23, 1958, pp. 105–6.

109. Henri VINCENOT, *La Vie quotidienne des paysans bourguignons au temps de Lamartine*, 1976, pp. 397–401.

110. Fernand DUPUY, *L'Albine*, 1977, p. 11.

111. S. BEAUMIER, 'Un homme, un village', art. cit., p. 41.

112. Jean-Pierre LAVERRIERE, *Un village entre la Révolution et l'Empire, Viry-en-Savoie (1792–1815)*, 1980, pp. 23–4.

113. *Théâtre d'agriculture et ménage des champs*, 1675, p. 113, quoted by Michel LUTFALLA, *Aux origines de la pensée économique*, 1981, p. 22.

114. *Les Mille visages de la campagne française*, 3rd edn, 1976, p. 242.

115. Bernard BONNIN, 'Les

caractères des migrations dans les régions de montagne du Dauphiné aux XVIIe et XVIIIe siècles', in *Entre faim et loup*, op. cit., 1976, p. 19.

116. Père Pierre-Jean-Baptiste LEGRAND D'AUSSY, *Voyage fait, en 1787 et 1788, dans la ci-devant Haute et Basse Auvergne . . .*, An III, I, pp. 474–483.

117. This example is a reminder; we should not jump to the conclusion that it is an exception. Families were the earliest living cells, the most determined to survive and proliferate. Associations between brothers, *freresches*, peopled vast regions and maintained themselves there. We find records of them only at late dates, but they had been in existence long before. Among notarial contracts in Ginestas (Paul CAYLA, *Essai sur les populations rurales à Ginestas . . . au début du XVIe siècle (1519–1536)*, 1938, pp. 12–13), there are to be found contracts of *effrayramentum* (brotherhood) that is 'the pooling by two families of all their property, legal rights, labour and commitments'. Those who were not united by blood could thus become brothers by legal agreement. And the practice dates, of course, from earlier than the sixteenth century.

118. Emmanuel LE ROY LADURIE, 'Les masses profondes: la paysannerie', in *Histoire économique et sociale de la France*, I, *De 1450 à 1660*, part 2, *Paysannerie et croissance*, ed. F. BRAUDEL and E. LABROUSSE, 1977, p. 669.

119. Georges DUBY, *La Société aux XIe et XIIe siècles dans la région mâconnaise*, 1971, p. 99.

120. Lucien ROMIER, *Explication de notre temps*, 1925, pp. 41–2.

121. Jacques CARORGUY, *Mémoires 1582–1595*, 1880, p. 3.

122. A.N., F^{20} 206.

123. S. BEAUMIER, 'Un homme, un village', art. cit., pp. 121–2.

124. Claude CHEREAU, *Huillé, une paroisse rurale angevine de 1600 à 1836*, n.d., I, p. 2.

125. Marc DROUOT, *Thann à l'époque mazarine (1658–1789), histoire politique et administrative*, 1961, pp. 8–9.

126. A.N., G^7 501; 19 October 1711.

127. See below.

128. A.N., G^7 237.

129. Robert BICHET, *Un village comtois au début du siècle*, 1980, pp. 130–2.

130. See below.

131. Laurence WYLIE, *Village in the Vaucluse*, Cambridge, Mass., 1957, pp. 7–8.

132. A.N., G^7 158.

133. H. LEMOINE, *Département de la Meuse, géographie physique, économique, historique et administrative*, 1909, p. 287.

134. Valentin JAMERAI-DUVAL, *Oeuvres*, I, 1784, p. 58 (autumn 1709).

135. A.N., F^{20} 119.

136. A.D., Meuse, L 343; 1790.

137. According to the register of births, Luméville-en-Ornois, A.D., Meuse.

138. A.N., H 1515. Cf. note 82, Part I, above.

139. The term *varcolier* or *warcollier* – saddler; F. GODEFROY, *Dictionnaire de l'ancienne langue française*, vol. 8, 1895.

140. *Histoire des villes de France*, collection, op. cit.

141. Affaires Etrangères, Archives, M. et D., France, 815.

142. Victor-Eugène ARDOUIN-DUMAZET, *Voyages en France*, 2nd series, 1906, p. 270.
143. Reference mislaid.
144. F. BENOIT DE TOUL, *Pouillé, ecclésiastique du diocèse de Toul*, 1911, II, pp. 265–284.
145. Alfred JOUVIN, *Le Voyageur d'Europe*, 1672, pp. 31–2.
146. A.N., F²⁰ 177, Statistique de la Côte-d'Or. Nuits (Saint-Georges) has a population of 21,700 today.
147. P. CAYLA, *Essai . . . Ginestas*, op. cit., p. 217.
148. Raymond BIERRY, *Rouvray, un relais sur le grand chemin, 448–1976*, 1976, p. 57.
149. See below.
150. Ange GOUDAR, *Les Intérêts de la France*, op. cit., p. 37.
151. A.N., F 1ᶜ III Vaucluse, 9, 173³; 7 pluviôse an IV.
152. Evelyn ACKERMAN, 'The Commune of Bonnières-sur-Seine in the eighteenth century', in *Annales de démographie historique*, 1977.
153. M. AGULHON, *La Vie sociale en Provence intérieure*, op. cit., p. 20.
154. Michel HEBERT, *Tarascon au XIVe siècle*, 1979, pp. 28–32.
155. Emmanuel LE ROY LADURIE, 'La destruction du monde plein', in *Histoire économique et sociale de la France*, ed. F. BRAUDEL and E. LABROUSSE, I, 2, 1977, p. 499.
156. Noël COULET, 'Population et société à Pourrières, 1368–1430. Premier bilan d'une enquête' in *Etudes rurales*, n° 51, 1973, pp. 86–111.
157. Eckart SCHREMMER, *Die Wirtschaft Bayerns*, 1970, p. 26.
158. Rudolf HAPKE, *Brügges Entwicklung zum mittelalterlichen Weltmarkt*, 1908, see F.

BRAUDEL, *The Structures of Everyday Life*, op. cit., p. 504.
159. André LACROIX, *Romans et le Bourg de Péage*, 1897, p. 296.
160. A.N., G⁷ 415–6; Nancy, 9 May 1693.
161. Jean-Marie DUNOYER, '7 milliards d'hommes pour l'an 2000', in *Diagrammes*, 33, November 1959, p. 3.
162. Georges DUBY, *Histoire de la France urbaine*, 1980, II, p. 478.
163. Henri BAUD, in *Dictionnaire des communes savoyardes*, 1981, II, p. 37.
164. Charles-Edmond PERRIN, article in *Annales de la Société d'histoire et d'archéologie de Lorraine*, 37th year, vol. 33, 1924.
165. *Histoire de Besançon*, ed. Claude FOHLEN, 1964, I, p. 145.
166. *Ibid.*, p. 39.
167. P. M. DUVAL, 'Archéologie et histoire de la Gaule', art. cit., p. 453.
168. *Histoire de Besançon*, op. cit., II, p. 10.
169. Loys GOLLUT, *Les Mémoires historiques de la république séquanoise et des princes de la Franche-Comté de Bourgogne*, 1592, Duvernoy edn, 1846, p. 272.
170. Jean BRELOT, in *Histoire de Besançon*, op. cit., II, p. 10.
171. L. GOLLUT, op. cit., quoted in Roland FIETIER, *Recherches sur la banlieue de Besançon*, 1973, p. 39.
172. *Histoire de Besançon*, op. cit., 1964, I, p. 468; quotation from municipal edicts dating from sixteenth century.
173. 300 enclosures and gardens in all, belonging to the church or secular owners. J. BRELOT, in *Histoire de Besançon*, op. cit., I, p. 585.

174. *Histoire de Besançon*, op. cit., I, p. 587.
175. F. BRAUDEL, *The Mediterranean*, op. cit., I, pp. 504 ff.
176. *Histoire de Besançon* op. cit., I, pp. 494–5.
177. *Ibid.*, II, pp. 41–3.
178. Maurice GRESSET, 'Les débuts du régime français en Franche-Comté 1674–1675' in *Provinces et états dans la France de l'Est*, conference at Besançon 3–4 October 1977, published in 1979, pp. 19–37.
179. Maurice GRESSET, *Le Monde judiciaire à Besançon de la conquête par Louis XIV à la Révolution française (1674–1789)*, 1975, p. 1235.
180. *Histoire de Besançon*, op. cit., II, pp. 147–9.
181. A.N., KK 944.
182. *Histoire de Besançon*, op. cit., II, p. 147.
183. Marius POUCHENOT, *Le Budget communal de Besançon au début du XVIIIe siècle*, 1910, p. 3.
184. A.N., D IV bis 47.
185. *Histoire de Besançon*, op. cit., II, p. 337.
186. *Ibid.*, p. 299.
187. *Ibid.*, fig. 113, p. 584.
188. Honoré d'URFE, *Oeuvres complètes*.
189. *Annuaire statistique du département de la Loire*, 1809, p. 187.
190. This happened for instance in 1705 to the étang de Boissy, the property of the duc de Feuillade: the fish were found stranded. A.D., Loire, bailliage ducal de Roanne, B 460.
191. *Annuaire statistique du département de la Loire*, 1809, op. cit., p. 187.
192. *Ibid.*
193. Denis LUYA, *L'Axe ligérien (Loire-Allier) dans les pays hauts, 1682–1858*, thesis, 1980.
194. A.N., H 1510[1]; about 1788. 'Observations sur les deffauts de la culture employée dans la plaine de Forez.'
195. D. LUYA, op. cit., p. 205.
196. Elie BRACKENHOFFER, *Voyage en France 1643–44*, ed. Henry LERR, 1925, pp. 141–2.
197. A.N., G[7] 406; 14 August 1687.
198. A.D., Loire, bailliage ducal de Roanne, B 455, 1704.
199. A.N., F[20] 206; An IX.
200. This was the share-cropping system known as *métayage* or *grangeage aux quatre grains* (four-cereal cropping); wheat, rye, barley and oats.
201. F. TOMAS, 'Problèmes de démographie historique. Le Forez au XVIIIe siècle', in *Cahiers d'histoire*, 1968, p. 395, n° 47.
202. Christophe EXTRAT, *Images et réalités de la vie coopérative agricole dans la Loire de 1945 à 1979*, typescript, 1981, p. 16.
203. F. TOMAS, 'Problèmes de démographie historique', art. cit., and *Annuaire statistique du département de la Loire*, 1809, op. cit.
204. The Villeret dam was inaugurated on 11 September 1982. Cf. Régis GUYOTAT, 'La Loire apaisée' in *Le Monde*, 11 September 1982.
205. Serge DONTENWILL, 'Rapports ville-campagne et espace économique microrégional: Charlieu et son plat pays au XVIIIe siècle' in *Villes et campagnes, XVe–XXe siècle*, 1977, p. 162.
206. Marcel GONIVET, *Histoire de Roanne et de sa région*, III, 1975, p. 131.
207. A *bandolier*, according to Furetière's *Dictionnaire*, was 'a robber in the countryside,

working in groups, and with firearms'.

208. Chanoine REURE, 'Le vin de Garambeau et la question des vins du Roannais au XVIIe siècle', in *Bulletin de la Diana*, 1908, pp. 5–6.

209. *Annuaire statistique du département de la Loire*, 1809, p. 181.

210. *Mémoire de l'intendant de Lyon*, 1762, quoted by Maurice LABOURE, *Roanne et le Roannais. Etudes historiques*, 1957, p. 466.

211. *Annuaire statistique du département de la Loire*, op. cit.

212. D. LUYA, *L'Axe ligérien*, op. cit., p. 91.

213. M. GONIVET, *Histoire de Roanne*, op. cit., I, p. 21.

214. D. LUYA, *L'Axe ligérien*, op. cit., p. 14.

215. Paul BONNAUD, *Essai d'histoire locale. La navigation à Roanne*, 1944, p. 27.

216. Etienne FOURNIAL, *Roanne au Moyen Age, essai d'histoire urbaine*, 1964, pp. 70, 73 and map, p. 72.

217. Albert DEMANGEON, in *Géographie universelle*, ed. P. VIDAL DE LA BLACHE et L. GALLOIS, vol. VI, *La France*, part 2, *France économique et humaine*, 1958, p. 769.

218. E. BRACKENHOFFER, *Voyage*, op cit., pp. 137–8 and 138, note 1.

219. M. LYONNET, *Gens du métier à Nevers à la fin de l'Ancien Régime*, 1941, p. 367, quoted by François BILLACOIS, 'La batellerie de la Loire au XVIIe siècle', in *Revue d'histoire moderne et contemporaine*, July–September 1964, p. 67.

220. D. LUYA, *L'Axe ligérien*, op. cit., p. 75, note 35.

221. *Histoire de la navigation sur l'Allier en Bourbonnais*, 1983,

passim, and pp. 34–5.

222. M. LABOURE, *Roanne*, op. cit., p. 354.

223. R. GASCON, *Grand commerce*, op. cit., I, p. 140.

224. A.N., G⁷ 1646, 373, 7 April 1709.

225. A.N., G⁷ 1647, 335; 11 June 1710.

226. In Paris, the *livre poids de marc* was equal to two *marcs*. The *livre* (pound) was therefore considered as double the *marc* and was divided into 16 ounces.

227. A.N., G⁷ 1647.

228. D. LUYA, *L'Axe ligérien*, op. cit., pp. 280–281.

229. Thomas REGAZZOL, Jacques LEFEBVRE, *La Domestication en mouvement*, 1981, pp. 149 and 152–3.

230. Auguste MAHAUT, *L'Idée de la Loire navigable combattue*, 1909, quoted by Henriette DUSSOURD, *Les Hommes de Loire*, 1985, p. 27.

231. G. BITON, *Bateaux de Loire*, 1972, pp. 2–3.

232. H. DUSSOURD, *Les Hommes de Loire*, op. cit., pp. 36 and 56–7; G. BITON, *Bateaux de Loire*, op. cit., p. 5.

233. A.N., G⁷ 1651, 336; 14 September 1709.

234. H. DUSSOURD, *Les Hommes de Loire*, op. cit., p. 26.

235. J. A. DULAURE, *Description des principaux lieux de France*, 1789, vol. 6, p. 107.

236. A.N., F¹⁴ 1199 A; year 1761.

237. Jeanne et Camille FRAYSSE, *Les Mariniers de la Loire en Anjou – Le Thoureil*, 1978, p. 47, quoted by D. LUYA, op cit., p. 18, note 27.

238. A.D. Loire, bailliage ducal de Roanne.

239. A.N., F¹⁴ 559²; Nevers, 18 May 1813.

240. E. BRACKENHOFFER, *Voyage*, op. cit., p. 140.
241. G. LEFEBVRE, *Etudes orléanaises*, I, 1962, p. 84.
242. René I (the Good), 1409–1480, duc de Bar, duc d'Anjou and comté de Provence, titular king of the kingdom of Naples, which he inherited from his wife, but never conquered.
243. P. CHAUSSARD, *Marine de Loire et mariniers digoinais*, 1970, p. 26.
244. M. GONIVET, *Histoire de Roanne*, op cit., I, pp. 181–2.
245. P. CHAUSSARD, *Marine de Loire*, op. cit., p. 27.
246. *Ibid.*
247. A.N., F[14] 1199A.
248. D. LUYA, *L'Axe ligérien*, op. cit., p. 34.
249. *Ibid.*, p. 223.
250. A.N., F[20] 243.
251. J. A. DULAURE, *Description*, op. cit., pp. 106–7.
252. A.N., G[7] 360, 21; 8 July 1705.
253. A.N., F[14], 1200; Moulins, 11 November 1765.
254. F. BRAUDEL, *The Wheels of Commerce*, op. cit., p. 360.
255. *Ibid.*, p. 372.
256. D. LUYA, *L'Axe ligérien*, op. cit., p. 232.
257. A.N., F[14] 1200.
258. *Histoire générale des techniques*, ed. Maurice DAUMAS, vol. 3: *L'Expansion du machinisme*, 1968, pp. 30 ff, pp. 68–9.
259. D. LUYA, op. cit., p. 237.
260. M. LABOURE, *Roanne*, op cit., pp. 377–8.
261. Serge DONTENWILL, 'Roanne au dernier siècle de l'Ancien Régime. Aspects démographiques et sociaux' in *Etudes foréziennes*, 1971, pp. 49–73.
262. *Ibid.*, p. 72, note 61.
263. Jean-Pierre HOUSSEL, *Le Roannais et le Haut-Beaujolais*, 1978.
264. D. LUYA, op. cit., p. 11.
265. A.N., H 1510[1], about 1788.
266. F. BRAUDEL, *The Structures of Everyday Life*, op. cit.
267. P. VIDAL DE LA BLACHE, *Tableau de la géographie de la France*, op. cit., p. 324.
268. Reference mislaid.
269. A.N., K 1516; 28 December 1788.
270. Unlike Saumur, if the documents are correct; since for contraband salt the Loire was no doubt the major route.
271. A.N., G[7] 521; 1682.
272. A.N., G[7] 521; Mayenne, 19 and 29 November 1693; Saumur, 14 January 1693; Laval, 1 March 1693.
273. A.N., G[7] 521; Laval, 24 May and 3 June 1693.
274. E. LAURAIN, 'Le département de la Mayenne à la fin de l'an VIII', in *Bulletin de la commission historique et archéologique de la Mayenne*, 1938–9, p. 118.
275. A.N., F[10] 242.
276. J. M. RICHARD, *La Vie privée dans une province de l'Ouest. Laval aux XVIIe et XVIIIe siècles*, op. cit., p. 126.
277. A.N., F[10] 242.
278. *Ibid.*
279. René MUSSET, *Le Bas-Maine*, 1917, pp. 320–1.
280. *Ibid.*, p. 323.
281. A.N., F[14] 1207, 234; 20 September 1769.
282. A.N., K 1252.
283. A.N., F[12] 1259 D.
284. *Ibid.*, 27 Brumaire An IX.
285. E. LAURAIN, 'Le département de la Mayenne', art. cit., p. 119.
286. J. SAVARY DES BRULONS, *Dictionnaire du commerce*, V, column 163.
287. *Ibid.*, col. 163, quoting *Journal de commerce*, March 1762, p. 112.

288. F. DORNIC, *L'Industrie textile dans le Maine*, op cit., pp. 1–5.

289. J. M. RICHARD, *La Vie privée dans une province de l'Ouest*, op. cit., pp. 289–90.

290. *Ibid.*, p. 291.

291. *Ibid.*, p. 301.

292. *Ibid.*, pp. 295 ff.

293. *Ibid.*, p. 298.

294. *Ibid.*, pp. 301 ff.

295. *Ibid.*, pp. 344–5 and note 2.

296. *Ibid.*, p. 114.

297. F. DORNIC, *L'Industrie textile*, op. cit., p. 44.

298. J. M. RICHARD, *La Vie privée*, op. cit., p. 289.

299. Jean-Claude PERROT, *Genèse d'une ville moderne, Caen au XVIIIe siècle*, 1975, I, p. 145.

300. *Ibid.*, I, p. 211.

301. A. DEMANGEON, *Géographie universelle*, ed. VIDAL DE LA BLACHE and GALLOIS, vol. VI, *La France*, part 2, *France économique et humaine*, op. cit., p. 591.

302. See note 299 above.

303. For the following analysis, see J. C. PERROT (op. cit. above, note 299), I, pp. 181 ff.

304. *Ibid.*, I, pp. 185 ff.

305. *Ibid.*, I, p. 213.

306. *Ibid.*, I, p. 216.

307. *Ibid.*, I, p. 217.

308. *Ibid.*, pp. 217–8, note 159.

309. *Ibid.*, I, p. 219.

310. *Ibid.*, I, p. 241.

311. M.-H. JOUAN, 'Les originalités . . .', art. cit., pp. 87–124 (see Part I note 63 above).

312. J. C. PERROT, *Genèse . . .*, op. cit., I, p. 358. This wealth undoubtedly prevented Norman agriculture from becoming subservient to industry.

313. *Ibid.*, I, p. 359 note 55.

314. *Ibid.*, I, p. 360 (end of note 55).

315. *Ibid.*, I, pp. 360–66.

316. *Ibid.*, I, p. 8.

317. *Ibid.*, I, pp. 518–9.

318. *Ibid.*, II, p. 948.

319. A.N., D IV bis 47.

320. See below.

321. A.N., G[7] 360; 10 February 1706.

322. Andrea METRA, *Il Mentore perfetto de'negozianti*, 1977.

323. A.N., F[20] 198, 130; Châteauroux.

324. Christian ROMON, *Mendiants et vagabonds à Paris, d'après les archives des Commissaires du Châtelet (1700–1784)*, typescript.

325. Raymonde MONNIER, *Le Faubourg Saint-Antoine, 1783–1815*, 1981.

326. Daniel ROCHE, *Le Peuple de Paris*, op. cit., p. 18.

327. *Ibid.*, p. 31.

328. A.N., G[7] 432; 6 February 1704.

329. *Journal de voyage de deux Hollandais à Paris, en 1656–1658*, ed. A. P. FAUGERE, 1899, p. 29.

330. *Voyages promenades aux environs de Paris avec Caroline Tullié*, no 29, 1790–1792.

331. Guy FOURQUIN, *Les Campagnes de la région parisienne à la fin du Moyen Age*, 1964, p. 220.

332. A. M. de BOISLISLE, *Mémoires des intendants*, I, op. cit., p. 285.

333. My italics.

334. Comte d'HERISSON, *Souvenirs intimes et notes du baron Mounier*, 1896, p. 35.

335. *Mémoires* of the comtesse de BOIGNE, 1971, I, p. 215.

336. C. ACHARD, *La Confession d'un vieil homme du siècle*, 1943, p. 24.

337. A.N., K 1252.

338. André PIATIER, *Radioscopie des communes de France*, 1979, pp. 23–5 and 253 ff.

339. P. BONNAUD, *Terres et langages*, op. cit., *passim*.

340. H. MENDRAS, *La Sagesse et le désordre*, op. cit., p. 37.
341. *Ibid.*, p. 19.
342. Roger BETEILLE, *La France du vide*, 1981; J. GRAVIER, *Paris et le désert français*, 1st edn 1947, 2nd edn 1972.
343. H. MENDRAS, op. cit., pp. 19–20.
344. Michel ROCHEFORT, quoted by A. PIATIER, *Radioscopie*, op. cit., p. 8.
345. A. PIATIER, *Radioscopie*, op. cit., p. 6.
346. *Ibid.*, p. 56.
347. *Ibid.*, p. 6.
348. *Ibid.*

Notes to Part III

1. P. VIDAL DE LA BLACHE, *Tableau de la géographie de la France*, op. cit., p. 7.
2. *Ibid.*, p. 8.
3. Lucien FEBVRE, *La Terre et l'évolution humaine*, 1949, p. 25.
4. Emmanuel de MARTONNE, 'La France physique' in *Géographie universelle*, 1942, p. 1.
5. E. CURTIUS, *Essai sur la France* (French edition of *Die französischen Kultur* op. cit.), pp. 70, 205.
6. Maurice LE LANNOU, 'Les sols et les climats', in *La France et les Français*, ed. Michel FRANÇOIS, 1972, p. 3.
7. Yves RENOUARD, *Etudes d'histoire médiévale*, 1968, II, pp. 721–4.
8. Henri DUBOIS, *Les Foires de Chalon et le commerce dans la vallée de la Saône à la fin du Moyen Age (vers 1280–vers 1430)*, 1976.
9. Thourout is in Belgium, between Ghent and the coast.
10. P. VIDAL DE LA BLACHE, *Tableau*, op. cit., p. 52.
11. M. PARDÉ, quoted by D. FAUCHER, *L'Homme et le Rhône*, 1969, p. 64.
12. Charles LENTHERIC, *Le Rhône, histoire d'un fleuve*, 1892, II, p. 505.
13. A *mouille* is a hollow between the alluvial banks in the bed of a river.
14. Pierre BAYLE, *Histoire de la navigation fluviale de Lyon et le long de sa Majesté 'la Vallée impériale'*, 1980, p. 35.
15. Archives Nationales (A.N.) G^7 359, about 1701.
16. H. de ROUVIERE, *Voyage du Tour de la France*, op. cit., pp. 232–3.
17. D. FAUCHER, *L'Homme et le Rhône*, op. cit., p. 187.
18. General MARBOT, *Mémoires*, op. cit., I, p. 51.
19. Cécile PERROUD, *Le Rhône de nos pères*, 1974, p. 47.
20. *Ibid.*
21. P. BAYLE, *Histoire,* op. cit., p. 17.
22. C. PERROUD, *Le Rhône*, op. cit., pp. 50–51.
23. D. FAUCHER, op. cit., p. 189.
24. *Ibid.*
25. C. PERROUD, op. cit., p. 70.
26. D. FAUCHER, op. cit., p. 193.
27. A.N., exact reference mislaid.
28. D. FAUCHER, op. cit., p. 190.
29. *Ibid.*, p. 199.
30. *Ibid.*, p. 197.
31. C. LENTHERIC, *Le Rhône,* op. cit., p. 512.
32. D. FAUCHER, op. cit., p. 196.
33. C. LENTHERIC, op. cit., p. 512.
34. P. BAYLE, *Histoire,* op. cit., p. 17.
35. A.N., F^{12} 1512 B.
36. The *minot* of salt weighed 100 pounds.
37. Henri FESQUET, *Le Monde*, 5 June 1980.

38. P. BONNAUD, *Terres et langages*, op. cit., I, p. 431.
39. C. PERROUD, op. cit., p. 73.
40. D. FAUCHER, op. cit., p. 90.
41. C. LENTHERIC, *Le Littoral d'Aigues-Mortes au XIIIe et au XIVe siècle*, 1870, pp. 29–30.
42. Pierre GOUROU, letter to the author, April 1980.
43. F. BRAUDEL, *The Perspective of the World*, op. cit., p. 114 and *The Mediterranean*, op. cit., I, pp. 206–7.
44. Renée DOEHAERD, 'Les galères génoises dans la Manche et la mer du Nord à la fin du XIIIe et au début du XIVe siècle', in *Bulletin de l'institut historique belge de Rome*, 1938, pp. 5–76.
45. D. FAUCHER, op. cit., p. 84.
46. A *traille* was a tarred cable which both guided the ferry and protected it against the current.
47. Pierre ESTIENNE, *La France. Les montagnes françaises et l'axe Rhône-Rhin*, 1978, p. 189.
48. Abel CHATELAIN, 'Les fondements de la région historique' in *Revue de géographie de Lyon*, n° 1, 1955, p. 45.
49. Pierre DUBOIS, *Histoire de la campagne de 1707 dans le Sud-Est de la France*, typescript, p. 67.
50. D. FAUCHER, *L'Homme et le Rhône*, op. cit., p. 184.
51. *Ibid.*, p. 178.
52. Letters patent of Charles VI, 1380, quoted in A.N., K 1219, 37, p. 6.
53. D. FAUCHER, op. cit., p. 157.
54. De BASVILLE, *Mémoires pour servir à l'histoire du Languedoc*, 1734, p. 279.
55. André ALLIX, 'Le trafic en Dauphiné à la fin du Moyen Age', in *Revue de géographie alpine*, 1923, pp. 373–408.
56. A.N., K 1219, n° 37.
57. *Ibid.*, p. 27.
58. A.N., G⁷ 300.
59. *Ibid*.
60. *Ibid*. At the time, the Saint-André rock was on the banks of the Rhône.
61. D. FAUCHER, op. cit., takes up the same theme, p. 199.
62. R. GASCON, *Grand Commerce et vie urbaine au XVIe siècle*, op. cit., on the Lyon crisis of 1575–80, which did not coincide either with that in Nantes or that in La Rochelle.
63. P. ESTIENNE, *La France*, op. cit., p. 147.
64. Jean LABASSE, 'Lyon, ville internationale', Report for DATAR, 1982; Yves LERIDON, 'Lyon, la place du second marché', in *Le Point*, 26 November 1984.
65. P. BONNAUD, *Terres et langages*, op. cit., I, pp. 430–1.
66. Jean-François BERGIER, *Les Foires de Genève et l'économie internationale de la Renaissance*, 1963, pp. 369 and 374–87.
67. R. GASCON, *Le Grand Commerce*, op. cit., pp. 287–8.
68. Louis BOURGEOIS, *Quand la Cour de France vivait à Lyon (1491–1551)*, 1980, p. 143.
69. *Ibid.*, p. 155.
70. Maurice GARDEN, *Lyon et les Lyonnais au XVIIIe siècle*, 1975.
71. Carlo PONI, 'Compétition monopoliste, mode et capital: le "marché" international des tissus de soie au XVIIIe siècle', paper given at Bellagio conference.
72. A.N., G⁷ 360, Anisson, député for Lyon, 5 May 1705.
73. J. LABASSE, DATAR report, op. cit., p. 20.
74. François GROSRICHARD, 'Rotterdam dans la bataille des conteneurs – la mer scellée au

fleuve', in *Le Monde*, 23 September 1982.

75. On hydro-electric installations on the Rhône, see 'La polémique sur l'aménagement du Rhône: décision prochaine du gouvernement', in *Le Monde*, 28 August 1982, p. 13. On the Rhône–Rhine link-up project, cf. Claude REGENT, 'Rhône-Alpes. Inquiétude au conseil régional: le canal mer du Nord-Méditerranée à tout petits pas', in *Le Monde*, 15 September 1982.

76. F. GROSRICHARD, art. cit., *Le Monde*, 23 September 1982.

77. P. ESTIENNE, *La France*, op. cit., p. 148.

78. Jules MICHELET, *Journal*, I, p. 76; 28 April 1830.

79. T. ZELDIN, *France 1848–1945*, II, *Intellect, Taste and Anxiety*, 1977, p. 5.

80. Francis HURÉ, *Le Monde*, 23 July 1980.

81. Quoted in Lucien FEBVRE's unpublished work *Michelet et la Renaissance*, forthcoming, p. 131.

82. Florimond papers, A.N., K 1242, 1st bundle, in A. M. de BOISLISLE (ed.) *Mémoire de la généralité de Paris*, 1881, I, p. 284.

83. DAVITY (1625) *Etats de l'Europe*, pp. 64–5 and 81–2, quoted in A. M. de BOISLISLE, *ibid.*, p. 558.

84. R. DION, 'La part du milieu', art. cit., p. 9.

85. Michel ROBLIN, 'L'époque franque', in Michel MOLLAT (ed.), *Histoire de l'Ile-de-France et de Paris*, 1971, p. 56.

86. Edward FOX, *History in a geographical perspective. The Other France*, 1971.

87. Roger DION, 'A propos du traité de Verdun', in *Annales E.S.C.*, 1950, p. 463.

88. E. FOX, op. cit.

89. William H. McNEILL, *Venice, the Hinge of Europe, 1081–1787*, 1974, p. 1.

90. P. BONNAUD, *Terres et langages*, op. cit., II, p. 28.

91. Jean-Robert PITTE, *Histoire du paysage français*, I, pp. 41–2 and 47–8.

92. MICHELET, *Histoire de France*, op. cit., IV, p. 33.

93. Pierre GOUROU, letter to the author, 1980, and *Pour une géographie humaine*, 1973, p. 290.

94. L. MUSSET, 'La géographie de l'histoire', in *Histoire de France*, ed. Marcel REINHARD, I, 1954, p. 32.

95. P. BONNAUD, *Terres et langages*, op. cit., I, p. 438.

96. J. MICHELET, *Journal*, op. cit., I, p. 82.

97. Immanuel WALLERSTEIN, *The Modern World System. Capitalist agriculture and the origins of the European world economy in the sixteenth century*, 1974, p. 32.

98. A. GOUDAR, *Les Intérêts de la France mal entendus*, op. cit., III, p. 34.

99. *Ibid.*, p. 35.

100. 'Regular troops' (*troupes réglées*) as opposed to the militias formed by townspeople, communes, and armed peasants, who only served in certain circumstances. Ange GOUDAR, *ibid.*, III, pp. 72–3.

101. André CORVISIER, *La France de Louis XIV, 1643–1715*, 1979, p. 61.

102. G. PARKER, *The Army of Flanders and the Spanish Road 1567–1659*, 1971, pp. 14–15. Cf. F. BRAUDEL, *The Perspective of the World*, op. cit., fig. 21.

103. Lucien FEBVRE, 'Frontière', in

Bulletin du Centre International de Synthèse, 1928, p. 32.

104. *Ibid.*, pp. 31 ff.

105. A.N., G 337, f° 65, quoted by De ROCHAS, II, p. 89, in Gaston ZELLER, *L'Organisation défensive des frontières du Nord et de L'Est au XVIe siècle*, 1928, p. 60.

106. R. DION, 'A propos du traité de Verdun', art. cit., p. 462.

107. Bernard GUENEE, 'Les limites', in *La France et les Français*, op. cit., 1972, p. 52.

108. Gaston ZELLER, *La France et l'Allemagne depuis dix siècles*, 1932, p. 6.

109. Yves RENOUARD, '1212–1216. Comment les traits durables de l'Europe occidentale se sont définis au début du XIIIe siècle', in *Annales de l'Université de Paris*, 1958, pp. 5–21, reproduced in Yves RENOUARD, *Etudes d'histoire médiévale*, op. cit., I, pp. 77 ff.

110. Walther KIENAST, *Die Anfänge des europäischen Staatensystems im späteren Mittelalter*, 1936, cf. F. BRAUDEL, *The Perspective of the World*, op. cit., p. 56 and note 87.

111. Christians in Spain who kept to their religion under Muslim rule.

112. Henri MARTIN, quoted by Georges LEFEBVRE, *La Naissance de l'historiographie moderne*, 1971, p. 186.

113. F. LOT, *La Gaule*, op. cit., p. 7.

114. On this subject see George HUPPERT, *The Idea of Perfect History, Historical erudition and historical philosophy in Renaissance France*, 1970. When these lines were going to press, I came across Colette BEAUNE's fine book, *Naissance de la nation France*, 1985, and hope to refer to it later.

115. La Popelinière, quoted by G. HUPPERT, *The Idea of Perfect History*, op. cit., p. 171, note 2.

116. *Ibid.*, pp. 73 and 86.

117. *Ordonnances des rois de France*, XIII, p. 408, quoted by Ernst BABELON, *Le Rhin dans l'histoire*, II, 1917, p. 207.

118. G. PARIS, *Histoire poétique de Charlemagne*, p. 62, quoted by E. BABELON, *Le Rhin*, op. cit., II, p. 219.

119. Quoted by E. BABELON, *ibid.*, p. 240.

120. Jean LE BON, *Adages*, 1577, quoted by A. BENOIT, *Notice sur Jean Le Bon*, 1879, p. lxvii.

121. Auguste LONGNON, *La Formation de l'unité française*, 1922, p. 325.

122. B. GUENEE, art. cit., in *La France et les Français*, op. cit.

123. Michel ARIBAUD, *Céret autrefois*, 1932, pp. 119 ff.

124. Bibliothèque de l'Arsenal, Paris, manuscript 4574, f° 205.

125. Abbé GREGOIRE, quoted by Charles ROUSSEAU, *Les Frontières de la France*, 1954, p. 12.

126. Frederick II, quoted by C. ROUSSEAU, *ibid.*, p. 10.

127. Ernst Moritz ARNDT, quoted by C. ROUSSEAU, *ibid.*, p. 13.

128. P. VIDAL DE LA BLACHE, quoted by M. SORRE, *Les Fondements de la géographie humaine*, II, op. cit., p. 461.

129. Charles DARWIN, quoted by M. SORRE, *ibid.*, II, p. 461.

130. Geoffroi de VILLEHARDOUIN, *La Conquête de Constantinople*, 1872 edn, p. 90, quoted by C. de la RONCIERE, *Histoire de la marine française*, 1899, I, pp. 2–3.

131. Noël COLLET, 'Le malheur des temps 1348–1440', in Georges DUBY, *Histoire de France*,

dynasties et révolutions de 1348 à 1852, II, 1971, p. 23.

132. Reference mislaid.

133. Alain GUILLERM, *La Pierre et le Vent. Fortifications et marine en Occident*, 1985, p. 166.

134. *Ibid.*

135. Pierre GOUROU, letter to the author, 4 February 1982.

136. Emile BOURGEOIS, *Manuel de politique etrangère*.

137. Charles de la RONCIERE, *Histoire de la marine française*, op. cit., pp. 14–15; Bibliothèque Nationale, Paris, Fr 17 308, f° 21. On the 30,000 repatriated French sailors, see F. BRAUDEL, *The Perspective of the World*, op. cit., p. 192.

138. Pierre-Victor MALOUET, *Mémoires*, edited by his grandson, 1868, I, p. 173.

139. *Ibid.*, pp. 173–4.

140. A. GOUDAR, *Les Intérets de la France*, op. cit., III, p. 31.

141. A.N., Marine, D² 45. Was this a certain Gagnier? I am not sure.

142. E. PLAN, Eric LEFEVRE, *La Bataille des Alpes 10–25 juin 1940*, 1982.

143. The allied armies withdrew from the left bank of the Rhine on 30 June 1930.

144. Ernest LAVISSE, quoted by C. ROUSSEAU, *Les Frontières*, op. cit., p. 7.

145. Camille VALLAUX, *Le Sol et l'Etat*, 1911, p. 364.

146. Nelly GIRARD D'ALBISSIN, *Genèse de la frontière franco-belge. Les variations des limites septentrionales de la France de 1659 à 1789*, 1970, p. 313.

147. A.N., G⁷ 269; Ypres, 3 November 1682.

148. A.N., G⁷ 256; Lille, 5 December 1689.

149. N. GIRARD D'ALBISSIN, op. cit., p. 26.

150. Colonel ROCOLLE, *2,000 ans de fortification française*, I, 1973, pp. 214 ff.

151. *Ibid.*, II, sketch-map no. 134.

152. E. LAVISSE, *Histoire de France*, op. cit., VIII, i, 1908, p. 131.

153. A.N., G⁷ 377; 28 March 1694.

154. Thionville was ceded to France by Spain in 1659. The famous covered bridge over the Moselle dates from 1673.

155. A.N., G⁷ 381, Metz, 3 May 1707.

156. André BELLARD, *Deux siècles de vie française, Metz 1648–1848*, 1948, p. 5.

157. *Ibid.*, p. 6.

158. Louis TRÉNARD, *Histoire de Lille*, II, 1981, p. 420; Maurice BRAURE, *Lille et la Flandre wallonne au XVIIIe siècle*, 1932, pp. 87 ff.

159. Archives de la Guerre, A 1 15 83, Gauttier d'Aulnot, Metz, 17 December 1701.

160. J. ANCILLON, *Recueil journalier de ce qui s'est passé de plus mémorable dans la cité de Metz, pays Messin et aux environs depuis le mois de juin 1674 jusqu'à 1683 inclusivement*, 1866 edn, II, p. 138.

161. A. BELLARD, *Deux siècles*, op. cit., p. 31.

162. A.N., G⁷ 381; 15 July 1706.

163. A.N., G⁷ 376; May 1693.

164. A.N., G⁷ 375; 7 September 1691.

165. A.N., G⁷ 378; 21 August 1697.

166. A.N., G⁷ 382; 22 November 1709.

167. Archives de la Guerre, A 1 2243, 147; 16 July 1710.

168. *Ibid.*, A 1 2395, 12; 14 January 1712.

169. *Ibid.*, A 1 1583, 116; 16 June 1702.

170. Dubrowski papers, FR 14 4° f° 30 and v°, 1698, Lenin Library, Leningrad.

171. A mountain range in Bavaria.
172. Present-day name, Ebersberg, in Upper Bavaria.
173. Present-day name, Kayserslautern, in the Bavarian Rhineland.
174. Archives de la Guerre, A 1 967, 78; 22 January 1690.
175. *Ibid.*, A 1 469, 188; 13 October 1675.
176. *Ibid.*, A 1 1574, 143 and 146; 25 and 26 August 1702.
177. J. ANCILLON, *Recueil*, op. cit., II, pp. 4, 10.
178. A.N., G^7 382; Metz, 21 June 1710.
179. A.N., G^7 376; 25 February 1693.
180. Archives de la Guerre, A 1 1955, 16; 19 March 1706.
181. *Ibid.*, A 1 1583, 88; 18 May 1702.
182. *Ibid.*, A 1 1583, 141; 1 July 1702.
183. A.N., G^7 379; 20 July 1699.
184. A.N., G^7 378; 31 October 1698.
185. A.N., G^7 378; 9 October 1698.
186. A.N., G^7 377; 13 December 1695.
187. 15,731 *setiers* of grain were transported this way during the siege of Namur, A.N., G^7 376; 27 December 1692.
188. Archives de la Guerre, A 1 1583, 89; 22 May 1702.
189. A.N., G^7 1633, 194; 7 March 1694.
190. A.N., G^7 377; 27 July 1695.
191. Archives de la Guerre, A 1 1559, 104 bis; 11 January 1702; A.N., G^7, 376, 383.
192. A.N., G^7 415–16; 20 March 1692.
193. A.N., G^7 381. Saint-Contest did not agree with this proposal.
194. Archives de la Guerre, A 1 2395, 104; 16 June 1712.
195. A.N., G^7 378; 16 March 1697.

196. The Court Jews who were financiers to the German princes in the eighteenth century.
197. A.N., G^7 378; 16 March 1697.
198. Archives de la Guerre, A 1 1583, 68; 14 April 1702.
199. In 1670, a so-called ritual murder of a Christian child was reported, undoubtedly a false accusation, J. ANCILLON, *Recueil*, op. cit., I, p. 63.
200. *Ibid.*, II, p. 16.
201. The *étape* meant lodgings plus rations allocated to the troops for one day's march.
202. Vitry-le-François (Marne).
203. J. ANCILLON, *Recueil*, op. cit., II, pp. 19–20.
204. A.N., G^7 375; 7 September 1691.
205. A.N., G^7 375; 27 October 1691.
206. A.N., G^7 377; 18 March 1695.
207. A.N., G^7 375; 2 February 1691.
208. A.N., G^7 376; 1693.
209. Archives de la Guerre, A 1 1955, 239; July 1706.
210. R.P.R. stood for 'religion prétendument réformée', 'so-called reformed religion'.
211. A.N., G^7 375; 3 April 1691.
212. A.N., G^7 382; 24 November 1708, 5 July 1709.
213. Marange for instance, A.N., G^7 377; 1691.
214. A.N., G^7 378; 26 October 1697.
215. A.N., G^7 377; 19 November 1696.
216. A.N., G^7 379; 3 January 1699.
217. J. ANCILLON, *Recueil*, op. cit., II, pp. 37–8.
218. A. GUILLERM, *La Pierre et le Vent*, op. cit., p. 152.
219. This book had already been written when I was sent the manuscript of a remarkable and very detailed study by a scholar

of the Var, Pierre DUBOIS, *Histoire de la campagne de 1707 dans le Sud-Est de la France*. I could unfortunately only use it to add or correct a few details in my text.

220. Octave TEISSIER, *Histoire des divers aggrandissements et des fortifications de la ville de Toulon*, 1873, pp. 12–14.

221. *Ibid.*, p. 17.

222. Archives de la Guerre, A 1 2041, 271.

223. *Ibid.*, A 1 2041, 235; 20 July 1707.

224. O. TEISSIER, *Histoire*, op cit., p. 146.

225. An allusion to the scorched earth policy, destroying standing crops before the arrival of an enemy.

226. Archives de la Guerre, A 1 2042, 121.

227. *Ibid.*, A 1 2041, 235; 20 July 1707.

228. *Ibid.*

229. Pierre DUBOIS, typescript, op. cit., p. 53.

230. A.N., G⁷ 469; 1 January 1706.

231. Archives de la Guerre, 15 March 1706.

232. *Ibid.*, 26 March 1706.

233. E. LAVISSE, *Histoire de France*, op. cit., VIII, pp. 103 and 106.

234. *Mémoires et Lettres du Maréchal de Tessé*, II, 1806, p. 235.

235. Arrested in Savoy, some as a result of paid collaboration by the peasants.

236. A.N., Marine B 3 150.

237. Turin Archives, *Materie Militari*, 1707.

238. The Italian port near the French frontier.

239. Maréchal de TESSE, *Mémoires*, op. cit., II, p. 239.

240. Louis de SAINT-SIMON, *Mémoires (1702–1708)*, Pléiade edition, 1969, II, pp. 906–7.

241. *Livres*.

242. SAINT-SIMON, op. cit., II, p. 907.

243. Archives de la Guerre, A 1 2041, 279; Aix, 26 July 1707.

244. *Ibid.*, A 1 2041; A.N., Marine, B 3 150.

245. Archives de la Guerre, A 1 2041, 266.

246. A.N., Marine, B 3 149.

247. Maréchal de TESSE, *Mémoires*, op. cit., II, p. 258.

248. SAINT-SIMON, *Mémoires*, op. cit., II, p. 906.

249. Archives de la Guerre, A 1 2042, 233; 31 July 1707.

250. Archives de la Guerre, A 1 2042, 49; 5 August 1707.

251. *Ibid.*, A 1 2042, 51; 4 August 1707.

252. *Ibid.*, A 1 2042, 14; 2 August 1707.

253. 'Rank' was a former means of classifying ships in the navy according to size and number of guns.

254. Pierre DUBOIS, typescript, op. cit., p. 193.

255. Archives de la Guerre, A 1 2042, 170; 6 August 1707.

256. *Ibid.*, A 1 2042, 366; Grignan, Marseille, 31 August 1707.

257. V. BRUN, *Guerres maritimes de la France: Port de Toulon, ses armements*, I, 1861, pp. 125–6.

258. A.N., Marine, B 3 149; 30 August 1707.

259. Archives de la Guerre, A 1 2042; 6 September 1707.

260. *Ibid.*, 20 October 1707.

261. *Ibid.*, 9 October 1707.

262. *Ibid.*, A 1 2042, 116 bis; 11 August 1707.

263. To maintain for two months, in the year 1707, 6 ships with a total crew of 2,460 men, was estimated to cost 158,566 *livres* (pay 88,200 *livres*; rations 70,366 *livres*); and the costs of

matériel have to be added to that.

264. Not to be confused with the other *Royal Louis*, built in Toulon in 1667, which had been the first ship to carry 120 cannon. Paul MAUREL, *Histoire de Toulon*, 1943, p. 102.

265. V. BRUN, *Guerres maritimes*, op. cit., I, p. 110.

266. *Ibid.*, I, pp. 145–6.

267. 'La presse', the 'press-gang', forcibly enlisted sailors.

268. Moscow, Foreign Affairs Archives, 93/6–497–34 V°; Bordeaux, 27 August 1787.

269. André CORVISIER, *L'Armée française de la fin du XVIIe siècle au ministère de Choiseul*, I, 1964, pp. 241–2.

270. A. CORVISIER, paper at Prato conference, forthcoming.

Glossary

Acknowledgement: In compiling this glossary I was much helped by the glossary provided in Brian Pearce's translation of R. Mousnier's *The Institutions of France under the absolute monarchy*, I, *Society and the State* (Chicago, 1979). S.R.

aides: a form of excise duty on certain goods, especially drink; the principal indirect tax in *ancien régime* France

alleux: freehold land (*allodium*)

allumettes: matches for tinder-boxes

ancien régime: used of the historical period and system of government in France before 1789

argot: slang (used here of underworld slang)

arpent: a land measure, slightly larger than an acre

arrondissement: territorial division within a *département*

bac à traille: cable-ferry

bailliage: the basic administrative and judicial division under the *ancien régime* was the *bailliage* or *sénéchaussée* (usually known as a *bailliage* in northern France, a *sénéchaussée* in the south)

barquette: small passenger ferry on the Rhône

barrières: Paris's city limits

Barrois mouvant: the part of a *seigneurie* that was farmed out was called a *mouvance*. The part of Bar west of the Meuse was within the *mouvance* of the king of France, so the duke of Lorraine had to do homage to him for it.

(bas-) breton: the Breton language, a Celtic tongue unrelated to French

bastide: originally a fortified place; in Provence a manor or country house

bocage: the landscape typically found in north-west France, where fields are divided by many hedges and woods

bourg: settlement, something between a large village and a small town, always the site of a market

bourgeois: can be used of town-dwellers as distinct from peasants, or of wealthier peasants, as well as in its modern sense

Bourse: Stock Exchange

branles: traditional dances

brassier: day-labourer

cabane: passenger ferry on the Loire, with cabins built on deck

cabaret: shop selling drink

cabaretier: proprietor of such a shop

calvados: spirit distilled from apples, much drunk in Normandy

canton: administrative division within an *arrondissement*

chaland: generic word for river-barge (see Figure 25)

chambres de réunion: special assemblies of the local *parlements* on the eastern border of France, to reclaim all territories dependent on the lands annexed in 1648 and 1678

Champagne pouilleuse: the dry part of Champagne (literally 'flea-bitten') as distinct from '*la Champagne humide*', 'wet Champagne'.

chanson de geste: epic poem recounting the deeds of heroes, in this case Charlemagne and the Franks

chaumes: the high mountain pastures in the Vosges

chef-lieu: the administrative centre, literally 'chief place' of a given territorial divison. The *chef-lieu* of a *département* is the *préfecture*

chêne, chenard: type of boat on the Rhône, made of oak

chemin vicinal: road joining two villages

Cinq grosses fermes: under the *ancien régime*, the five main tax farms formed a customs union without internal barriers, covering most of northern France

cluse: a valley in the Jura

commandant: military commander

commune: municipality; the smallest administrative unit in modern France. A *commune* can be a city or a village, but is always headed by a mayor. The 'communal' movement of the Middle Ages refers to the towns' acquisition of autonomy from feudal overlords

contrôleur-général (usually translated in the text as controller-general): minister of finance under the *ancien régime*

corvée: compulsory labour owed to a feudal lord

cour des aides: the court which handled disputes relating to the indirect taxes, the *aides cour des comptes:* the court responsible for supervising tax revenues

coudert: an area where pigs and other animals can run free (local to the Corrèze)

denier: the twelfth part of a *sou*

département: administrative division of France introduced in 1790 and administered by a prefect. Its subdivisions are the *arrondissement* and the *canton.* Used more generally before 1789 of administrative departments

district: originally a judicial division, later used of a group of *communes*

droit de mutation: dues payable to feudal overlord when property changed hands

droit de greffe: feudal due payable on sale of wood

droit de grenette: feudal due payable on sale of grain

écu: unit of currency, of variable value, but worth several *livres* or francs; 'crown'

écu d'or en or: gold crown (currency); (some *écus* were silver)

élection: under the *ancien régime*, the *généralité* (q.v.) was subdivided into *élections*, originally coinciding with dioceses, which were basic units for tax purposes. They were administered by an *élu* (later by a *subdélégué*). This arrangement was confined to provinces without provincial estates (*états*, q.v.); so there were *pays d'élections* and *pays d'états*

étamines: usually muslins, but here fine woollen fabric

états: the three estates (nobility, clergy, commoners) under the *ancien régime*. Their representatives met in the provincial assemblies (*états provinciaux*) in certain provinces, the latest to be joined to the French Crown

faubourg: roughly 'suburb'; outlying area of town

faux-sauniers: salt-smugglers

finage: the total area covered by a village, including agricultural land

franc-salé: privilege enjoyed by certain persons of getting tax-free salt

Fronde: insurrection of 1648–53 against Mazarin and Anne of Austria during Louis XIV's minority

gabarre: flat-bottomed boat or barge on the Loire (cf. Figure 25)

gabelle: tax on salt, which was a state monopoly, under the *ancien régime*

galvacher: migrant carter from the Morvan

garrigue: typical landscape in Mediterranean region: arid limestone, covered with scrub *gâtine:*   infertile land, as in *la Gâtine poitevine*

gavots: name given to mountain dwellers in the Pyrenees who came as seasonal workers to the lowlands

généralité: the 34 areas into which France was divided under the *ancien régime*, roughly equivalent to a province and administered by an *intendant*

grange: a farmstead or country house in Provence

halle(s):   covered market

hectare: land measure: 10,000 m² or 2.47 acres

hectolitre: one hundred litres

(h)erm: local name for grass steppe in south of France

intendant: overseer of a *généralité* or province, representing the Crown, acting as the eyes and ears of the central power, and having certain powers of decision

jachère: fallow land

journalier: day-labourer

laboureur: well-off peasant farmer

liard: a coin worth three *deniers* or a quarter-sou

lieu-dit: locality, usually named after a landmark

livre: unit of account in *ancien régime* France, originally minted in Tours and worth a pound of silver, later devalued; worth 20 *sous*. Also a pound in weight

longue durée, la: literally 'the long term', an expression drawing attention to long-term structures and realities in history, as distinct from medium term factors or trends (*la conjoncture*) and short-term events (*l'évènement*)

mairie: residence or office of mayor of a *commune*. In towns, the town hall (also known as the *hôtel de ville*)

maître des requêtes: judicial official sent on special missions under *ancien régime* (today counsel of *Conseil d'État*)

manouvrier: day-labourer

maquis: scrubby landscape typical of Corsica and southern France. In World War II, used of resisters living rough (*maquisards*)

maréchaussée: rural police force, commanded by *prévôt-maréchal*

mas: farmstead or country house in Provence

ménager: peasant proprietor in certain regions

mistral: northerly wind which blows down the Rhône valley and in Provence

muid: measure of capacity, roughly 268 litres liquid or 1,872 litres dry goods; 'hogshead'

murger: heap of stones (local expression)

noblesse de robe: noble families owing their titles to having held legal or public office

oc, oïl: literally the forms of *oui*=yes in the dialects of southern and northern France respectively. Hence the *langue d'oc* and *langue d'oïl* to denote both language and area

octroi: toll on goods entering town

parigot: popular Parisian speech

parlement: not a parliament in the modern sense but a judicial body under the *ancien régime*, one of the 'sovereign courts'; there was a Paris *parlement* and a number of provincial *parlements* which sat in cities like Grenoble, Bordeaux etc.

patois: local or regional dialect

patrie: 'fatherland', a word with emotional overtones

pays: within France used of districts or regions with their own identity

pays d'élection, pays d'états: provinces associated with the French Crown from early times were administered by the *élection*; those assimilated later maintained their provincial estates (*états*)

penelle: barge used for transporting horses on the Rhône

perche: measure of length, perch

pipe: measure of capacity for wine, variable

poids de marc: a *marc* was 8 ounces of silver, half a pound; used as a standard measure

pluviôse: literally 'rainy', the month in the revolutionary calendar (after 1792) corresponding to February

Ponts et Chaussées: the highways department, the corps of civil engineers

pré carré: literally 'square field', figuratively, 'stamping ground', used here of the area in north-east France fortified by Vauban

préfecture: seat of the prefect, chief town in *département*

président: presiding judge in sovereign courts

409

présidial: appeal court in certain *bailliages*

prévôté: lowest ranking royal court, court of first instance

procureur: attorney or prosecutor on behalf of king

quai: bank, embankment, jetty, in Paris and elsewhere

quartier: urban district, quarter, as in Latin Quarter

quintal: measure of weight, approx. a hundredweight under the *ancien régime* (a metric quintal=100 kg)

Recollets: religious order, branch of the Franciscans

rentes: usually annuities or interest-bearing bonds received in return for loans or capital investment, hence *rentier*, one who lives off a regular unearned income

réserve: the part of a *seigneurie* which the lord owned outright

rue à usoirs: especially in Alsace, a street with broad sidewalks used as farmyards (storage for farm implements, dunghills etc.)

sapin, sapinière: river boat made of deal, usually with a limited life

savarts: name for certain plateaux in Champagne

seigneurie: the feudal domain over which the *seigneur* or lord could claim rights (e.g. *corvée*) even if he did not own the land outright

sénéchaussée: see *bailliage*

sergent de ville: local policeman

setier: grain capacity measure, varying between 150 and 300 litres

sisselan(d)e: river boat built at Seyssel on the upper Rhône

soles: the divisions of land under crop rotation

sou: currency, the twentieth part of a livre

stère: a cubic metre, used to measure timber

subdélégué: administrator of an *élection*, subordinate to an *intendant*

taille: direct tax on commoners, falling chiefly on the peasantry

toise: measure of length or depth; about six feet, or a fathom

tramontane: strong north-west wind which blows in Languedoc and Roussillon

Trois Evêchés: the three bishoprics (Metz, Toul and Verdun) treated as an administrative unit

veillée: gatherings of villagers on winter evenings, to save fuel; people brought work with them and listened to stories round the fire

viguerie: the equivalent of a *prévôté* in certain regions

vin ordinaire: local wine with no pretensions

Index

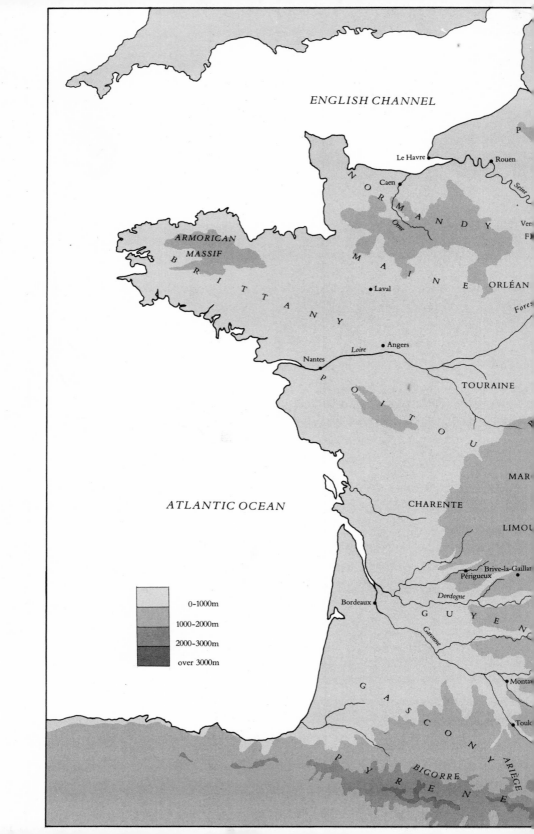

ENGLISH CHANNEL

ATLANTIC OCEAN

P

Le Havre • ● Rouen

Caen ●

Seine

Orne

N
O
R
M
A
N
D
Y

Ver
F

ARMORICAN
MASSIF

B
R
I
T
T
A
N
Y

M
A
I
N
E

ORLÉAN

Fores

● Laval

Loire

Nantes

● Angers

TOURAINE

P
O
I
T
O
U

P

MAR

CHARENTE

LIMOU

Brive-la-Gaillar
Périgueux ●   ●

Dordogne

Bordeaux ●

G U Y E N

Garonne

G

A

S

C

O

N

Y

Montar

Toul

ARIÈGE

P
Y
R
E
N
E

BIGORRE

0-1000m

1000-2000m

2000-3000m

over 3000m